Instructor's Manual

Nutrition
Concepts and Controversies

THIRTEENTH EDITION

Frances Sienkiewicz Sizer

Ellie Whitney

Prepared by

Mary Ellen Clark
Monroe Community College
and St. John Fisher College

Australia • Brazil • Mexico • Singapore • United Kingdom • United States

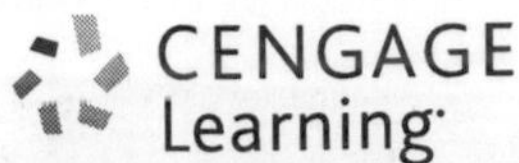

For product information and technology assistance, contact us at **Cengage Learning Customer & Sales Support, 1-800-354-9706**.

For permission to use material from this text or product, submit all requests online at **www.cengage.com/permissions**
Further permissions questions can be emailed to **permissionrequest@cengage.com**.

ISBN-13: 978-1-133-60997-1
ISBN-10: 1-133-60997-X

Cengage Learning
200 First Stamford Place, 4th Floor
Stamford, CT 06902
USA

Cengage Learning is a leading provider of customized learning solutions with office locations around the globe, including Singapore, the United Kingdom, Australia, Mexico, Brazil, and Japan. Locate your local office at: **www.cengage.com/global**.

Cengage Learning products are represented in Canada by Nelson Education, Ltd.

To learn more about Cengage Learning Solutions, visit **www.cengage.com**.

Purchase any of our products at your local college store or at our preferred online store **www.cengagebrain.com**.

Printed in the United States of America
1 2 3 4 5 17 16 15 14 13

Table of Contents

Preface

Resources in the Instructor's Manual

Thank you for choosing *Nutrition: Concepts and Controversies* 13th edition for your course! This instructor's manual (IM) contains the following materials to assist you in preparing for and conducting your course.

- **Quick Lists** – Each chapter begins with a handy list of the materials included in this publication
- *New!* **Chapter Learning Objectives and Key Points** – The text learning objectives and key points, collected together in one place for reference
- **Critical Thinking Questions** – Assignable discussion-type questions to challenge students to recall and think about important chapter concepts; answer keys are included for reference
- **Controversy Discussion Questions** – Similar to the end-of-chapter review questions in the text, these questions (with answer keys) reinforce important information in each chapter's Controversy section
- **Worksheets** – Ready-to-use assignments in a range of formats, including label analysis and intake analysis—allowing students to practice their skills in evaluating food labels and meal plans—as well as self-assessments, exploration activities, and new chapter review crossword puzzles
- **Learning Activities & Project Ideas** – This section includes ideas for in-class or homework activities to reinforce important concepts
- **Chapter Lecture Outlines** – Detailed outlines that summarize each section of the chapter

Acknowledgements

We would like to thank the following instructors who kindly shared their activity/project ideas for the IM:

Lora Beth Brown, Ed.D., R.D., C.D., Brigham Young University

Nancy J. Correa-Matos, Ph.D., R.D., University of North Florida

Peter C. DuBois, M.Ed., Lorain County Community College

Kris Levy, R.D., L.D., Columbus State Community College

Anne O'Donnell, M.S., M.P.H., R.D., of Santa Rosa Junior College

References for Food Label Analysis Worksheets

All the food packages and labels pictured on these worksheets were based on real food or supplement labels. The sources of this information are:

Annie's Homegrown Inc. Organic Shells & Real Aged Cheddar Macaroni & Cheese label. Napa, CA.

ConAgra Foods, Inc. Marie Callender's Fettuccini Alfredo & Garlic Bread frozen entree label. Omaha, NE.

ConAgra Foods, Inc. Marie Callender's Fettuccini with Chicken & Broccoli frozen entree label. Omaha, NE.

Deep Foods, Inc. Tandoor Chef Palak Paneer frozen entree label. Union, NJ.

General Mills Cereals, LLC. Golden Grahams cereal label. Minneapolis, MN.

General Mills Cereals, LLC. Lucky Charms cereal label. Minneapolis, MN.

General Nutrition Centers, Inc. Pro Performance Pro Crunch Peanut Butter Crunch sports bars product information. Accessed 10 September 2007 at: http://www.gnc.com/product/index.jsp?productId=2372973&cp–2167077.2501630.2108317&parentPage=family.

Kellogg Sales Co. Morning Star Farms Tomato & Basil Pizza Burger label. Battle Creek, MI.

Kraft Foods. Capri Sun Splash Cooler juice drink label information. Accessed 14 August 2007 at: http://www.kraftfoods.com/caprisun/main.aspx?s=product&m=product/Product_display&Site=1&Product=8768493700.

Kraft Foods. Planter's Deluxe Mixed Nuts label. Northfield, IL>

Labrada Nutrition. Lean Body Instant Breakfast Shake—Bananas & Cream product information. Accessed 10 September 2007 at: http://www.gnc.com/product/index.jsp?productId=2607072&cp=2167100.2108253&parentPage=family.

Nature's Path Foods, Inc. Acaí Apple Granola with Pomegranate cereal nutrition information. Accessed 14 August 2007 at: http://www.naturespath.com/products/cold_cereals.

Nature's Path Foods, Inc. Flax Plus Pumpkin Raisin Crunch cereal label. Blaine, WA.

Nature's Path Foods, Inc. Optimum Zen Cranberry-Ginger cereal nutrition information. Accessed 14 August 2007 at: http://www.naturespath.com/products/cold_cereals.

Nestle. Good Start Supreme soy DHA & ARA formula nutrition information. Accessed 6 September 2007 at: http://www.verybestbaby.com/GoodStart/NutritionInfo.aspx?ProductId=CD0EA938-4673-4629-9E14-422512C09C4A.

Nestle. NAN H.A.2. hypoallergenic follow-up formula with iron product information. Accessed 6 September 2007 at: http://www.nestle.co.uk/Nutrition/InfantAndChildNutrition/ProductInformation/NAH+H.A.2.htm.

ReNew Life. Organic Triple Fiber supplement label.

Chapter 1 – Food Choices and Human Health

Quick List: IM Resources for Chapter 1

- **Class preparation resources:** learning objectives/key points, suggested activities and projects, lecture outline
- **Assignment materials:** **Related LO**
  - Critical thinking questions (with answer key) 1.4, 1.5, 1.6, 1.7
  - Discussion questions (with answers) for Controversy 1 .... 1.8
  - Worksheet 1-1: Palak Paneer Label Analysis 1.3, 1.4
  - Worksheet 1-2: Intake Analysis—Diet Planning 1.4
  - Worksheet 1-3: Why Do You Eat What You Eat? 1.4
  - Worksheet 1-4: Making Food Choices[1] 1.4
  - Worksheet 1-5: Evaluation of Published Nutrition Information[2] 1.5, 1.8
  - **New!** Worksheet 1-6: Chapter 1 Review Crossword Puzzle
- **Enrichment materials:** Handout 1-1: Can Diet Help Manage Chronic Disease? 1.1

Chapter Learning Objectives and Key Points

1.1 **Discuss how daily food choices can help or harm the body's health over time.**
The nutrients in food support growth, maintenance, and repair of the body. Deficiencies, excesses, and imbalances of energy and nutrients bring on the diseases of malnutrition. Nutrition profoundly affects health. Diet influences long-term health within the range set by genetic inheritance. Nutrition has little influence on some diseases but strongly affects others. Life choices, such as being physically active or using tobacco or alcohol, can improve or damage health.

1.2 **Describe the national *Healthy People* objectives for the nation, and identify some nutrition-related objectives.**
Each decade, the U.S. Department of Health and Human Services sets health and nutrition objectives for the nation.

1.3 **Define the term *nutrient* and be able to list the six major nutrients.**
Foremost among the nutrients in food is water. The energy-yielding nutrients are carbohydrates, fats (lipids), and protein. The regulator nutrients are vitamins and minerals. Food energy is measured in calories; nutrient quantities are often measured in grams. Food conveys emotional satisfaction and hormonal stimuli that contribute to health. Foods also contain phytochemicals.

1.4 **Summarize the five characteristics of a healthy diet and describe cultural or other influences on human food choices.**
Foods that form the basis of a nutritious diet are whole foods, such as ordinary milk and milk products; meats, fish, and poultry; vegetables and dried peas and beans; fruits; and grains. A well-planned diet is adequate, balanced, moderate in energy, and moderate in unwanted constituents, and offers a variety of nutritious foods. Cultural traditions and social values often revolve around foodways. Many factors other than nutrition drive food choices.

1.5 **Describe the major types of research studies and give reasons why national nutrition research is important for the health of the population.**
Scientists ask questions and then design research experiments to test possible answers. Single studies must be replicated before their findings can be considered valid. News media often sensationalize single-study findings, and so may not be trustworthy sources. National nutrition research projects, such as NHANES, provide data on U.S. food consumption and nutrient status.

---

[1] Contributed by Sharon Rady Rolfes

[2] Adapted with permission of: Deborah Fleurant, MOE Thesis, University of New Hampshire, 1989 (Thesis Advisor Sam Smith)

1.6 **List the major steps in behavior change and devise a plan for making successful long-term changes in the diet.**
Behavior change follows a predictable pattern. Setting goals and monitoring progress facilitate behavior change.

1.7 **Define *nutrient density* and explain the advantages of choosing nutrient-dense foods.**

1.8 **Identify misleading nutrition information in infomercials, advertorials, and other sources in the popular media.**

Critical Thinking Questions

1. *Why is it important to develop an eating plan that incorporates adequacy, balance, calorie control, moderation, and variety in order to prevent or delay the development of a nutrition-related chronic condition?*

   If someone has high blood pressure, for example, he would want an **adequate** diet that provides all of the essential vitamins, minerals, fiber, carbohydrates, proteins, and lipids to support the health of the body's cells. There are studies that suggest that certain minerals such as calcium and potassium may help reduce blood pressure.

   This person would want to eat a **balanced** diet including foods from all of the major food groups. This way, he is likely to get all of the nutrients he needs without getting an excessive amount of any one nutrient. For example, a person who eats a lot of meat but little grains, vegetables, or fruits will likely be getting too much saturated fat but not enough fiber, minerals, vitamins, or carbohydrates. He can use the MyPlate online tools to help him assess his dietary balance.

   This person would want to practice **calorie control** to balance energy intakes with expenditures and thus maintain his weight. Excess weight is associated with many chronic conditions (including high blood pressure).

   This person would want to eat the recommended portions of each food group to avoid taking in too many calories or too much of any one nutrient or harmful food component. Most eating plans that are successful in terms of weight management and adequacy incorporate this concept of **moderation** as well.

   Dietary **variety** prevents monotony and sometimes over-consumption of unhealthful contaminants that may be present in a particular food source. If a person wishes to exercise variety in his eating plan, he will include several different vegetables or grains from different sources. This will increase the adequacy of the diet as well.

2. *Imagine someone in this situation: a single mother who is working two jobs to support herself and her two young children. What factors will likely influence her choices of foods for herself and for her family?*

   She is likely on a budget, so she will choose foods that are inexpensive. She may not have much free time and will look for foods that are easy to prepare. She may not have time to read food labels and may choose foods that are filling but may not have all of the essential nutrients. She may also choose foods that are familiar to her since she doesn't have time to investigate new foods. This could lead to her choosing fast foods or processed foods, which are inexpensive and easy to prepare but often lack essential ingredients.

   It is possible for a person who has limited time and finances to eat well if she/he has received nutrition education. For example, this person could select staple foods, such as brown rice, as a base for quick meals. Brown rice has more nutrients than many fast foods and is inexpensive. She could also buy whole foods like apples that could be stored at room temperature and can be taken along with her to work or with her children.

3. *Nutrition researchers want to study the link between a high-fiber diet and the reduced risk of colon cancer. Describe how they could carry out each of the following types of studies:*

   a. *Interventional study*

   The researchers could have 2 groups of people who eat a preplanned diet. The control group eats a typical diet that has 10-15 grams of fiber per day. The experimental group eats a diet that has more high-fiber foods, and they consume 25-30 grams per day for a given amount of time. The researchers could have the subjects fill out questionnaires or even have them go in for colonoscopies to see the effects of high fiber intakes on the walls of their colons. The two groups would be compared to see the effects of fiber on the health of their colon.

b. *Epidemiologic study*

The researchers would observe a group of people who tend to eat a higher-fiber diet versus a group of people who tend to eat a lower-fiber diet. The researchers could have the groups of people fill out health assessment surveys to determine whether their diet can be correlated with a higher or lower risk of colon cancer.

c. *Laboratory study*

The researchers would work with animals such as rats or mice in the lab and would manipulate their diets. One group of animals would receive a high-fiber diet and the other group would receive a low-fiber diet. After a given amount of time, the researchers could examine the colons of each group of animals to determine whether there is any increase in the rate of cancer. By manipulating the animals' diets, the researchers could determine whether the increase of cancer is due to the level of fiber in the diet.

4. *You decide that you want to increase your intake of fruits and vegetables up to 3 cups a day for both. Describe how you would work towards this goal using the 6 steps to behavior change listed in Chapter 1.*

First of all, you may not realize that you have a problem with this but you see reports on TV or in the newspaper about the importance of eating enough fruits and vegetables. At this point, you are in the **pre-contemplation** stage.

You then think about whether you want to start eating more fruits and vegetables (produce). You consider the pluses such as eating more nutrients with fewer calories. You also consider the minuses such as the fact that fruits and vegetables cost more and don't last as long as other foods. You decide whether or not you want to start this eating plan. You decide to do it and pick a date to start. You are in the **contemplation** stage.

Next, you decide which fruits and vegetables you like are easy to prepare. You also consider how you can eat more of these while you are at work. You are in the **preparation** stage and are making plans to change your eating behaviors.

You then start to add ½ to 1 cup of the fruits and vegetables to your daily meals. You are actively involved in your new behavior; this is the **action** stage. You note how you feel as you add more produce to your diet.

You continue with your new behavior but you sometimes don't make your goal. You keep track of your produce intake and you also note what obstacles interfere with your progress. You are in the **maintenance** stage of your behavior change. You may have setbacks, but you keep acting on your behavior change.

You have been eating more produce without even thinking about having setbacks. This is a normal part of your eating behavior. You now wish to increase your whole grain intake. So you have moved on to new goals and are in the **adoption** stage as far as eating more fruits and vegetables each day is concerned.

5. *How can the concept of nutrient density of foods help you to develop a healthier eating pattern?*

Nutrient density describes the essential nutrient contents of a food relative to its calorie content. A food that is more nutrient dense will have more nutrients such as fiber, vitamins, or minerals but fewer calories. For example, instead of having fried chicken with a lot of calories, you can have baked chicken, which has fewer calories with the same key nutrients, such as protein and vitamin B_{12}. You can compare the nutrient density of foods at the grocery store by reading the labels and selecting the food that has more fiber, minerals, and vitamins and less saturated and *trans* fat and sugar. Eating nutrient-dense foods will help you achieve adequacy with calorie control in your eating plan.

6. *What strategy could you develop to overcome each of the excuses for not eating well that are listed in Table 1-6?*

No time to cook: You could try cooking a few meals on the weekend and then freezing them into smaller portions for easy reheating during the week. There are also many healthy options for meals that serve one person. Just check the labels to make sure that the meal does not supply too many calories, sugar, salt, or fat.

Not a high priority: You could ask any healthcare provider what chronic diseases could be caused by a poor diet. You could also talk with people who have these conditions to see how their quality of life has been impacted.

Crave fast food and sweets: It may work well to allow yourself a small serving of fast food or sweets each day. If you eliminate these foods all together, you will crave them. You can also make small, simple substitutions of a piece of fruit for sweets or pretzels or some other lower-fat food for potato chips.

Too little money: You should go to the grocery store and compare the price of produce (fruits and vegetables) with processed or snack foods. You may only want to buy a couple of pieces of fruit at a time so that you will eat them before they spoil. You could also try growing fruits or vegetables in your own garden or as part of a community garden.

Take vitamins instead: You could try eating a piece of fruit or a vegetable daily and see how you feel over time as compared with taking a supplement with coffee or some other beverage. Your body will absorb nutrients much more efficiently from foods than from supplements.

Controversy Discussion Questions

1. *Your good friend asks you if there is any particular type of diet that you can recommend for her sister who has multiple sclerosis. You have taken a consumer nutrition course at your local community college. What can you tell her to do to get reliable nutrition information?*

   You could suggest that she check out the website of the Academy of Nutrition and Dietetics (www.eatright.org) or the American Society for Clinical Nutrition for information. If she does not want to use the Internet, she could look in her phone book for registered dietitians in her area. If she cannot find this information on her own, she could ask her doctor for a referral to a registered dietitian. She may also be able to find reliable information online from the National Multiple Sclerosis Society.

2. *Discuss how anecdotal evidence for the effectiveness of a weight-loss supplement differs from scientific evidence of the effectiveness of a weight-loss supplement. Which source of evidence would you trust more and why?*

   Anecdotal evidence comes in the form of patient testimonies as to how well the product works. There may only be testimonies from a few people who make the product sound wonderful. There is often a disclaimer that says that the results are not typical in small print. There is usually no cited study from a credible research center. This type of anecdotal evidence would be seen on TV or would be published in a popular magazine as a story.

   Scientific evidence would actually describe a study that is done at an accredited research or clinical center. There would be results from a large number of people and the study would employ the suitable controls such as a group of patients who get the weight-loss supplement versus patients who get a placebo. The results of this study would be reviewed by and then published in a journal that is read by experts in the fields of nutrition and medicine.

   Most people would trust information from a well-designed and published scientific study, since large numbers of people have participated in the study and the results are more easily repeatable by other researchers.

3. *Your community leaders decide to have a speaker come to discuss the management of diabetes using lifestyle approaches. They have a choice between inviting a physician who specializes in internal medicine or a certified diabetes educator. Which of these individuals is more apt to have reliable nutrition information related to diabetes and why?*

   A certified diabetes educator is a health professional who has obtained additional training in nutrition and other lifestyle factors related to the management of diabetes and earned a certification on diabetes education through work experience and successful completion of an examination. Many certified diabetes educators are also either registered dietitians or registered nurses. The National Certification Board for Diabetes Educators has a website (www.ncbde.org) with information about the certification requirements.

   A physician does receive extensive schooling (4 years beyond college for the medical doctor degree) and completes a 2- to 4-year residency. Most medical school programs only devote a small amount of time to the study of nutrition—often, they spend less time on this topic than students who take nutrition at the undergraduate level! In fact, very few medical schools teach 25 hours of instruction in the field of nutrition. There are some physicians who are trained in clinical nutrition and are highly qualified to give nutritional advice on diabetes management and other health issues. Unless a physician specializes in clinical nutrition, she or he will have spent much LESS time learning about nutrition than a certified diabetes educator.

4. *Discuss any 3 websites with reliable sources of nutrition information and explain why you chose them.*

   The Academy of Nutrition and Dietetics website or the American Society for Clinical Nutrition website are the first choices for reliable nutrition information. If you are looking for nutrition information related to cardiovascular disease, the American Heart Association has a website. The American Diabetes Association, the Arthritis Foundation, and the American Cancer Society all have websites that will contain reliable nutrition information.

Worksheet Answer Key

Worksheet 1-1: Palak Paneer Label Analysis

1. Cheery Chef Foods, Inc.
2. a. 5 ounces (142 grams)
   b. *Open question (answers will vary)*
3. 2
4. a. 14
   b. 126 kilocalories
5. 2,000 kilocalories
6. There are microwave or conventional cooking directions
7. a. Spinach
   b. It is reassuring to know that a product with the word *spinach* in the name (*palak* = spinach) has spinach as the main ingredient instead of another artificial ingredient.
8. a. Citric acid
   b. Preservative
9. 35% of the DV of vitamin A is provided by this product

Worksheet 1-2: Intake Analysis—Diet Planning

1. Fruits, vegetables, and whole grains
2. Beer and 1 enchilada instead of 2
3. a. Milk, whole-wheat bread, cereal, and meat
   b. It has a lot of grains and dairy products
   c No fruit, few vegetables, and too much beer
4. a. Lots of fruits, vegetables, and whole grains
   b. A bit light on complex carbohydrates

Worksheet 1-6: Chapter 1 Review Crossword Puzzle

1. essential
2. staple foods
3. nutrient dense
4. Healthy People 2020
5. intervention
6. organic
7. fortified
8. control group
9. gram
10. balance
11. epidemiologic
12. calories
13. nitrogen
14. maintenance
15. hypothesis
16. adequacy

Learning Activities & Project Ideas

Activity 1-1: Brief Research Report on Milk[3] LO 1.5

Most students don't understand that there are harmful effects of everyday foods, along with "tainted" marketing. This project helps students to discover the truth in marketing foods for themselves. Explain: "I'd like to see some current research on how good milk really is for you. Certainly you should include the different types of milk (whole milk vs. 2% vs. skim) along with the organic varieties. Be sure to include the good and the bad. Your citations should be from either this year or last year."

[3] Contributed by Peter C. DuBois, M.Ed., Lorain County Community College

Activity 1-2: Students' Burning Questions[4]
The first day of class, give each student three "Post-It" notes. On each note, students are to write down a "burning" question they have about nutrition. While they are doing this, tape fifteen large pieces of construction paper around the room, each with a title that roughly corresponds to chapters of the text.

When they finish writing their questions, have them categorize their Post-It notes according to the fifteen chapters by placing their Post-It on the piece of construction paper that relates to their question. When they finish, ask them to take turns reading the questions that they have generated. Before the next class, check the categorization of their questions and rearrange the Post-It notes so that they are placed with the appropriate chapter sheet if necessary. As you begin a new chapter, bring the corresponding piece of construction paper to class, and read the questions aloud.

This activity helps reassure students, early on, that you will (or won't) be covering some of their "burning" questions. It also helps show students the relevance of the information you're covering in class, and helps show instructors the interests of the students.

Activity 1-3: Scheduled Interruption—Think/Pair/Share[5]
Examination of student attention levels throughout class indicate that students' attention levels are the highest during the first five minutes of class, then levels slowly decline throughout a lecture. To enhance students' attentiveness, teaching authorities suggest scheduled interruptions. One planned interruption is think, pair, and share. The purpose of this activity is to encourage the participation of all students, especially those who are quiet. Pose a statement, problem, or situation. Instruct students to quietly write their comments including their thoughts and feelings regarding this topic. Next, pair students with a partner and instruct them to share their comments. Circulate while students are talking. After they have shared with their partner, ask for comments to be shared with the entire class.

Activity 1-4: Controversies Presentations Project[6] LO 1.8
For controversies, divide the students into 2 teams per chapter to present the controversies. Instruct the students to look for peer-reviewed journal articles that include points in favor and points against. Students should also interview 15 people outside of their nutrition class to get the general public opinion. Afterwards, the 2 teams will present the two sides of the issue and the rest of the class will discuss and then vote. The leader of each team will receive extra points.

Chapter Lecture Outline

I. Introduction – The science of how food nourishes the body
   A. What is this chapter about??
   B. Why care about nutrition?
   C. What are the nutrients in foods and what roles do they play in the body?
   D. What constitutes a nutritious diet?
   E. How do we know what we know about nutrition?
   F. How do people go about making changes to their diets?

II. A Lifetime of Nourishment
   A. Introduction
      1. The nutrients in food support growth, maintenance, and repair of the body.
      2. Deficiencies, excesses, and imbalances of nutrients can lead to malnutrition that can negatively impact health over time.
   B. The Diet and Health Connection
      1. Nutrition profoundly affects health.
      2. Chronic diseases have a connection to a poor diet.
         a. Which of these diseases are chronic? Chronic diseases include: Heart disease, chronic lung disease, diabetes, some cancers, dental disease, adult bone loss

---

[4] Contributed by Caroline Roberts, R.D., M.P.H., Nutrition Education Specialist for California Department of Education and Instructor at Sierra College
[5] Contributed by Lori W. Turner, Ph.D., R.D., University of Alabama
[6] Contributed by Nancy J. Correa-Matos, Ph.D., R.D., University of North Florida

b. Cannot be prevented by a good diet alone
c. To some extent determined by genetics, activities, and lifestyle

C. Genetics and Individuality
1. Inherited disease – condition that is passed from a parent to a child, e.g., hemophilia, sickle cell anemia, Down syndrome, cystic fibrosis, and many others
2. Acquired disease – condition that is associated with infections, lifestyle behaviors or diet, e.g., heart attack, diabetes, stroke, mineral or vitamin deficiencies
3. Choice of diet influences long-term health within the range set by genetic inheritance.
4. Nutrition has little influence on some diseases but strongly affects others.
5. Nutrition may play a role in how the genes in human DNA are expressed as well.

D. Think Fitness: Why Be Physically Active?
1. Regular physical activity should be integrated into everyone's daily lives.
2. There are many short- and long-term health benefits of physical activity.

E. Other Lifestyle Choices
1. Only two common lifestyle habits have a stronger influence on long-term health than dietary choices. Can you guess which?
a. Smoking & other tobacco use
b. Excessive alcohol consumption
2. Tobacco use and alcohol and other substances can destroy health.
3. Staying active, getting enough sleep, and stress can all affect health.

III. *Healthy People*: Nutrition Objectives for the Nation
A. U.S. Department of Health and Human Services sets nutrition objectives for the nation each decade
B. In 2010, the nation's health report shows some negative and positive trends.
1. Most people lacked enough fruits, vegetables, and whole grains in their diets as well as physical activity each day.
2. Blood cholesterol levels have come down and the number of foodborne illnesses has also dropped.
3. The number of people with diabetes and obesity has increased.

IV. The Human Body and Its Food
A. Meet the Nutrients
1. Classes of nutrients – 6 different families of molecules of food required for the body's functioning
2. Roles: Provide energy, building material, maintenance and repair, support growth
3. Which are organic? – carbohydrates, fats, proteins, vitamins
4. Gram – a unit of weight. For instance, one teaspoon of sugar weighs roughly 5 grams.
5. The Energy-Yielding Nutrients – Which nutrients provide energy? – carbohydrates (4 cal/g), fats (9 cal/g), proteins (4 cal/g)
6. Vitamins and Minerals – Which regulate body processes and provide no calories? – vitamins, minerals
7. The Concept of Essential Nutrients – must be obtained in the diet because the body does not make them; found in all 6 classes of nutrients
8. Calorie Values
a. Calorie is a unit of heat energy
b. Scientists have determined the amount of calories and nutrients people need based on their gender, age, and activity level.

B. Can I Live on Just Supplements?
1. Elemental diets – diets with a precise chemical composition
a. Lifesaving for people who cannot eat ordinary food
b. Not appropriate over long periods for healthy people as "meal replacers" or "insurance" against malnutrition
2. Food is better than supplements.
a. The digestive system can break down and absorb nutrients most efficiently from whole foods.
b. People in the hospital improve more quickly after eating food than when receiving their nutrients through IVs.
c. Eating provides physical, psychological, and social comfort for people as well.
d. Food provides phytochemicals and other bioactive compounds that interact with the body's metabolism.

V. The Challenge of Choosing Foods
   A. The Abundance of Foods to Choose From
      1. Foods come in a bewildering variety in the marketplace, but the foods that form the basis of a nutritious diet are basic foods.
      2. The original foods were whole foods that underwent little if any processing.
      3. There are fast foods, processed foods, functional foods, and staple foods that people need to consider in their daily food choices.
   B. How, Exactly, Can I Recognize a Nutritious Diet? – Elements of a healthy diet = ABCMV
      1. Adequacy – get enough of essential nutrients as well as fiber and energy.
      2. Balance – contains a good proportion of nutrients. No overemphasis of a food group.
      3. Calorie Control – choose foods to maintain ideal body weight.
      4. Moderation – eat any food in reasonable-size portions.
      5. Variety – eat different types of food to prevent boredom and to ensure dietary adequacy.
   C. Why People Choose Foods
      1. Eating is an intentional act. People choose: What to eat, where to eat, whom to eat with, how to prepare it
      2. People often have a variety of excuses for not eating well such as no time to cook, not making nutrition a health priority, craving fast foods or sweets, and taking supplements instead.
      3. Cultural and Social Meanings Attached to Food
         a. Food ways – the sum of a culture's habits, customs, beliefs, and preferences concerning food
         b. Omnivore – a person who eats food of both plant and animal origin, including animal flesh
         c. Vegetarian – avoid animals out of respect for them or for health benefits
            1. Lacto-ovo – animal products but no flesh
            2. Vegan – neither animal products nor flesh
      4. Factors That Drive Food Choices
         a. Advertising
         b. Availability
         c. Cost
         d. Emotional comfort
         e. Habit
         f. Personal preference
         g. Positive or negative associations
         h. Region of the country
         i. Social pressure
         j. Values or beliefs
         k. Weight
         l. Nutrition and health benefits

VI. The Science of Nutrition
   A. Introduction
      1. Nutrition is a science so scientists and dieticians work together to develop studies that are well designed, controlled, and reviewed by other experts.
      2. Many studies take a long time to complete so information may not be available as quickly as most people would like it to be.
   B. The Scientific Approach
      1. The scientific method is used to advance the knowledge within nutrition in a consistent way.
      2. The findings of such studies are published in journals that are reviewed and read by other scientists.
   C. Scientific Challenge
      1. Once a finding is published, it is still only preliminary.
      2. One experiment does not "prove" or "disprove" anything.
      3. Must be duplicated, supported, and challenged by other scientists
      4. A finding that has stood up to repeated, rigorous testing may become a theory.
      5. A theory is still subject to challenge by other studies and is not "set in stone."
      6. Research designs
         a. Include case studies, epidemiologic studies, controlled clinical studies, and lab studies

   b. Controlled clinical studies should have large number of experimental as well as control subjects so that the effects of a variable (such as a nutrient) can be studied more thoroughly.
7. When many of these types of studies together confirm a relationship between the intake of a nutrient and a health outcome, one can confidently state that the relationship is supported.

D. Can I Trust the Media to Deliver Nutrition News?
   1. Read nutrition information with an educated eye.
   2. Consider the source of the information: Is it from a reputable journal? A magazine? An Internet chat room? A talk show? Your mother???
   3. Scientists watch trends and evaluate nutritional studies to see if they are properly carried out before the scientist endorses the data from the study.
   4. Popular media may release information about preliminary findings without describing details of the studies being done – An example is the cholesterol lowering effects of oats in the diet

E. A Consumer's Guide to Reading Nutrition News
   1. Tricks and Traps
      a. Nutrition headlines are constantly changing, which leads to consumer frustration.
      b. Reporters use phrases like "now we know or truth is" to get the reader's attention.
      c. Scientists use more tentative language when describing their research findings.
   2. Markers of Authentic Reporting
      a. Only peer-reviewed journals contain reliable information from clearly described studies.
      b. The subjects in the studies should be clearly described as well and the harms and benefits of a studied treatment should be clearly stated.
      c. Review articles written by nutrition experts will reference reliable studies.
      d. Scientific journals contain credible sources of nutrition information.
   3. Moving Ahead – All consumers should read nutrition news with a critical eye and with the scientific method in mind.

F. National Nutrition Research – National Health and Nutrition Examination Surveys (NHANES)
   1. Includes *What We Eat in America* survey
   2. Asks about 50,000 people what they have eaten
   3. Records measures of their health status

VII. A Changing Behaviors

A. Introduction
   1. Nutrition knowledge is useful if it helps people improve their diets.
   2. People need to change behaviors.

B. The Process of Change – Psychologists describe 6 stages of behavior change: precomtemplation, comtemplation, preparation, action, maintenance, and adoption or moving on.

C. Taking Stock and Setting Goals
   1. Track food intake over several days and compare to standards.
   2. Set small, achievable goals in areas that need changing.

D. Start Now
   1. As you read this book, little reminders entitled "Start Now" appear in each chapter.
   2. They invite you to go to the website to take inventory of your current behaviors and set goals for needed changes.

VIII. Food Feature: How Can I Get Enough Nutrients without Consuming Too Many Calories?

A. Nutrient density – a measure of nutrients per calorie

B. Whole foods like vegetables have high nutrient density.

C. People are pressed for time and tend to choose convenience foods like frozen pizzas or ramen noodles which are not the most nutrient-dense choices.

IX. Controversy: Sorting the Impostors from the Real Nutrition Experts

A. More Than Money at Stake – Costs include worsened health & wasted money

B. Information Sources
   1. Misinformation is spread through television, magazines, urban legends
   2. Table C1-1 shows quackery and Internet terms to look out for.

C. Nutrition on the Net
   1. PubMed is a reliable website with links to scientific and medical journals.
   2. Tables C1-2 and C1-3 show credible sources of nutrition information.

D. Who Are the True Nutrition Experts?
   1. The Academy of Nutrition and Dietetics is the professional organization of dietitians and provides nutrition recommendations for other healthcare providers as well as directly to clients.
   2. The Academy of Nutrition Dietetics Proposal – nutrition education should be included in the curriculum for health-care professionals
   2. Registered Dietitians: The Nutrition Specialists – Table C1-4 describes terms associated with nutrition advice.

E. Detecting Fake Credentials – essential to avoid getting inaccurate information
   1. Educational Background
      a. Look out for diploma mills.
      b. See Table C1-6 for terms related to nutritional education.
   2. Accreditation and Licensure
   3. A Failed Attempt to Fail
   4. Would You Trust a Nutritionist Who Eats Dog Food?
   5. Staying Ahead of the Scammers

Worksheet 1-1: Palak Paneer Label Analysis

Instructions: Use the label for frozen palak paneer to answer the questions that follow on a separate sheet of paper.

DIRECTIONS: (Do not thaw)
Microwave Oven:

1. Remove tray from carton and puncture film 3-4 times.
2. Heat on high setting for 3 minutes.
3. Remove film completely.
4. Gently stir contents, turn dish and heat for additional 2 minutes.
5. Gently stir before serving.

Conventional Oven: See side panel.

INGREDIENTS: Spinach, paneer (milk, part skim milk, vinegar, salt), tomatoes (tomatoes, tomato juice, salt, calcium chloride, citric acid), cream, onions, tomato puree (water, tomato paste, citric acid), milk, canola oil (expeller pressed), water, spices, sea salt, garlic, green peppers, tumeric, bay leaves, citric acid.
Allergens: Milk
Made in a facility that processes peanuts, tree nuts, soy, milk and wheat.

Cheery Chef Foods, Inc.
Belmont, CA 94002

Nutrition Facts
Serving Size 5 oz. (142g)
Servings Per Container 2

Amount Per Serving	
Calories 170	Calories from Fat 130
	% Daily Value*
Total Fat 14g	**22%**
Saturated Fat 6g	**31%**
Trans Fat 0g	
Cholesterol 35mg	**12%**
Sodium 600mg	**25%**
Total Carbohydrate 6g	**2%**
Dietary Fiber 2g	**9%**
Sugars 1g	
Protein 6g	
Vitamin A 35% •	Vitamin C 30%
Calcium 8% •	Iron 10%

* Percent Daily Values are based on a 2,000 calorie diet. Your Daily Values may be higher or lower depending on your calorie needs.

1. Who is the manufacturer of your product?
2. a. What is the serving size of your product?
   b. Does this serving size seem reasonable to you based on your perception of portion sizes?
3. How many servings are in each container of your product?
4. a. How many grams of total fat are in your product?
   b. How many calories does this amount of fat represent?
5. What total calorie per day diet is the label information based on?
6. How can this product be prepared?
7. a. Which ingredient is present in the highest amount?
   b. Why might this information be important to know?
8. a. What ingredient is present in the least amount?
   b. What is this ingredient?
9. What percentage of the Daily Value for vitamin A is contained in this product?

Worksheet 1-2: Intake Analysis—Diet Planning

Eating Plan A (1 Day's Intake)	Eating Plan E (1 Day's Intake)
1 cup of Corn Flakes cereal	¾ cup Nature's Path flax cereal
1 cup of 1% fat milk	½ cup soy milk
2 cups of coffee	½ cup acai juice + seltzer water
2 slices of whole-wheat bread	1 medium banana
2 ounces thinly sliced baked ham	12 ounces coffee
2 ounces cheddar jalapeño cheese	6 ounces 6-grain yogurt
8 ounces chocolate milk	½ cup blueberries
3 12-ounce beers	¾ cup raspberries
2 beef and cheese enchiladas	2 Mushroom Lover's Veggie Burgers
	1 cup roasted carrot soup
	½ cup sweet green peppers
	6 carrot sticks
	2 whole-wheat wasa crackers
	8 ounces Vruit juice
	8 ounces soy milk
	1 peanut butter Fiber One Bar
	6 ounces grilled salmon
	10 cooked asparagus spears
	6 ounces white wine
	½ cup olives
	½ cup sun-dried tomatoes
	½ cup whole-wheat angel hair pasta
	¼ cup mixed nuts

Look at Eating Plans A and E:

1. What types of foods could you add to Eating Plan A to increase its adequacy?

2. What foods could you reduce in Eating Plan A to help ensure moderation?

3. a. What are the strengths of Eating Plan A in terms of nutritional adequacy?

   b. What are the strengths of Eating Plan A in terms of representation of the major food groups?

   c. What are its weaknesses based on your findings in 3 a. and 3 b. above?

4. a. What are the strengths of Eating Plan E?

   b. What are its weaknesses?

Worksheet 1-3: Why Do You Eat What You Eat?

Instructions: Record what you eat and drink for 1 day in the spaces provided below. Note what helped you decide to pick a particular food. Some examples could be convenience, taste, familiarity, cost, or other reasons.

	Food	Preparation Level	Amount	Reason
Breakfast:				
Snack:				
Lunch:				
Snack:				
Dinner:				
Snack:				

Table 1-5 in the textbook shows a glossary of food types. Compare your food types recorded with the food types described.

1. Do you see any patterns in the food types that you choose?

2. Do you eat any one type of food type more than others and, if so, what factors may influence you to select this type of food more often?

3. How could you adjust your food choices such that you can included more whole foods or fortified foods?

Worksheet 1-4: Making Food Choices

We decide what to eat, when to eat, and even whether to eat for a variety of reasons. Examine the factors that influence your food choices by keeping a food diary for 24 hours. Record the times and places of meals and snacks, the types and amounts of foods eaten, and a description of your thoughts and feelings when eating. Now examine your food record and consider your choices.

1. Which, if any, of your food choices were influenced by emotions (happiness, boredom, or disappointment, for example)?

2. Was any particular social pressure a factor in any food decisions that you made on this day?

3. Which if any, of your food choices were influenced by marketing strategies or food advertisements?

4. How large a role do food availability, convenience, and economy play in your food choices?

5. How might your age, ethnicity, or health concerns influence your food choices?

6. At what times did you eat because you were truly hungry? How often did you think of health and nutrition when making food choices?

7. Were these food choices based on your level of hunger or on your appetite?

8. If you were to record your intakes for 3-5 days instead of one day, do you think that there would be a time of day that you would consistently eat more based on your appetite?

Compare the choices you made in your 24-hour food diary to the USDA Food Patterns recommendation for your age, gender, and activity level (see Table 2-2 on page 45).

Food Groups	Suggested Quantity	Quantity Consumed
Fruits		
Vegetables		
Grains		
Protein foods		
Milk		
Oils		
Solid fats and added sugars	Limit intakes	

9. Do you eat appropriate amounts of food from each of the five major groups daily?

10. Do you try to vary your choices within each food group from day to day? If not, suggest some foods that you would be willing to eat regularly to increase the variety.

11. a. What dietary changes could you make to improve your chances of enjoying good health?

    b. What choices can you make within each food group to improve your chances of enjoying good health?

Worksheet 1-5: Evaluation of Published Nutrition Information

Assignment for discussion: Carefully read a nutrition article and answer the following questions on a separate sheet of paper:

1. a. What type of information source did you use to find this article?

   b. Summarize the basic idea of the article in a short paragraph.

2. a. What are the credentials of the author(s)? What do the initials, signifying degrees, after the name(s) mean? Do they enhance the authors' credibility? Explain.

   b. Is the author(s) affiliated with an organization or institution? Does the affiliation with the organization or institution enhance the authors' credibility? Briefly explain.

   c. Does the periodical have an editorial board? Do the editors' credentials enhance the article's credibility? Where does one look in a periodical for the editorial board?

   d. Does the website that you used (if applicable) have a .gov, .edu., or .org URL? These types of websites often use information that has been published and scrutinized by experts.

3. a. Is scientific research being presented or discussed? Is the research current (from within the last 3-5 years)?

   b. If so, what specific kinds of research or data are presented or cited to support the ideas?

   c. Were references listed to allow readers to investigate the information's original source? Were full citations provided?

4. a. What is the underlying hypothesis (if/then, cause/effect, etc.)?

   b. What are the article's conclusions/recommendations?

   c. Are the conclusions or recommendations supported by the research discussion? Explain briefly why or why not.

5. a. Develop and describe potential additional research that could more decisively test the hypothesis identified. Describe any control measures that you would use in your study.

   b. Indicate what variables will be measured.

   c. State the type of experimental design and type of experiment that is being described in your article.

6. Identify the statements in the article that you believe and those that you do not believe, and discuss why or why not for each.

7. What sources other than those listed in the periodical would you refer to if you were to research the article's topic further?

Source: Adapted with permission of: Deborah Fleurant, MOE Thesis, University of New Hampshire, 1989 (Thesis Advisor Sam Smith)

Worksheet 1-6: Chapter 1 Review Crossword Puzzle

1 2 3 4 5 6 7 8 9 10 11 12 13 14 15 16

(clues on following page)

Across	Down
1. A nutrient that must be taken in through the diet 4. Most current objectives of nutrition for the nation 5. Studies in which an experimental variable is manipulated by the researchers 8. The subject group that does not receive a treatment is called a _____. 11. Studies that examine correlations between dietary intakes and disease in populations 14. The act of making a new behavior part of everyday life 15. A tentative explanation of a relationship between 2 variables 16. Facet of a nutritious diet that ensures all nutrients are present in the necessary amounts	2. Foods that make up a large part of a diet such as rice or pasta 3. Foods that provide a lot of nutrients and not a lot of calories 6. Carbon containing and made by living things 7. Foods that have nutrients added to them 9. Metric unit of weight 10. A dietary facet that emphasizes foods from all of the different food groups 12. Units used to measure energy from foods 13. Unique element found in protein

Handout 1-1: Can Diet Help Manage Chronic Disease?

A chronic disease cannot be cured, can progress, and can be due to genetic factors or lifestyle choices (or a combination of the two). Why do some people with chronic diseases seem more active or more able to function than others with a similar chronic disease? Could it be due to their genetic make-up? Could their food choices affect their ability to cope with their condition? Can a person's diet help him to manage his condition by allowing him to function more fully or be able to use a lower dose of medicine or fewer medicines?

You can look up information about any condition that you are interested in learning more about. You can consult the following web sites to get reliable information about a variety of chronic conditions:

- www.mayoclinic.com
- www.diabetes.org
- www.cancer.org
- www.heart.org
- www.eatright.org
- www.nih.gov
- www.ama-assn.org

There are other web sites that you can get to by using a general search engine such as Google or Yahoo and typing a key word to access your site of interest. Be sure to look for a .gov, .edu, or .org website as these sites use reliable sources of information.

After you select a condition of interest, you can research whether a certain food may help you cope with a particular condition. For example, people with rheumatoid arthritis are encouraged to eat fish in order to get essential fatty acids. These polyunsaturated acids may play a role in reducing inflammation and pain. You can also find out if a certain food is an accepted part of a treatment plan for a chronic condition by consulting more than one website that has reliable information about that particular condition. If any particular food is recommended by more than one reliable website, it is relatively likely to be considered by several experts to be an acceptable part of a treatment plan for a chronic condition.

Chapter 2 – Nutrition Tools—Standards and Guidelines

Quick List: IM Resources for Chapter 2

- **Class preparation resources:** learning objectives/key points, suggested activities and projects, lecture outline
- **Assignment materials:** **Related LO**
  - Critical thinking questions (with answer key)........2.1, 2.3, 2.4
  - Discussion questions (with answers) for Controversy 2........2.7
  - Worksheet 2-1: Breakfast Cereal Label Analysis........2.5
  - Worksheet 2-2: Intake Analysis—More Diet Planning........2.4
  - Worksheet 2-3: Dietary Reference Intakes and Food Composition Tables[1]........2.1
  - Worksheet 2-4: Estimating Amounts[2]........2.3, 2.4
  - Worksheet 2-5: Guessing Portion Sizes—How Well Can You Do It?........2.3, 2.4
  - Worksheet 2-6: Compare Your Food Intake to Recommended Daily Amounts from Each Group......2.3, 2.4
  - Worksheet 2-7: Homemade or On-the-Go?........2.6
  - **New!** Worksheet 2-8: Chapter 2 Review Crossword Puzzle
- **Enrichment materials:** Handout 2-1: Most Frequently Eaten Raw Fruits, Vegetables, and Fish/Shellfish......2.3

Chapter Learning Objectives and Key Points

2.1 **Identify the full names and explain the functions of the RDA, AI, UL, EAR, and AMDR and discuss how the Daily Values differ in nature and use from other sets of nutrient standards.**
The Dietary Reference Intakes are U.S. and Canadian nutrient intake standards. The Daily Values are U.S. standards used on food labels. The DRI set nutrient intake goals for individuals, standards for researchers and public policy makers, and tolerable upper limits. RDA, AI, UL, and EAR lists are DRI standards, along with AMDR ranges for energy-yielding nutrients. The DRI are up-to-date, optimal, and safe nutrient intakes for healthy people in the United States and Canada. The DRI are based on scientific data and generously cover the needs of virtually all healthy people in the United States and Canada. Estimated Energy Requirements are predicted to maintain body weight and to discourage unhealthy weight gain. The Daily Values are standards used solely on food labels to enable consumers to compare the nutrient values of foods.

2.2 **List the four major topic areas of the *Dietary Guidelines for Americans* and explain their importance to the population.**
The *Dietary Guidelines for Americans* address problems of undernutrition and overnutrition. They recommend following a healthful eating pattern and being physically active.

2.3 **Describe how and why foods are grouped in the USDA Food Patterns, including subgroups.**
The USDA Food Patterns divide foods into food groups based on key nutrient contents. People who consume the specified amounts of foods from each group and subgroup achieve dietary adequacy, balance, and variety. Following the USDA Food Patterns requires choosing nutrient-dense foods most often. Solid fats, added sugars, and alcohol should be limited.

2.4 **Outline the basic steps of diet planning with the USDA Food Patterns, and address limits for solid fats and added sugars.**
The USDA Food Patterns for various calorie levels can guide food choices in diet planning. The concepts of the USDA Food Patterns are demonstrated in the MyPlate online educational tools. The USDA Food Patterns can be used with flexibility by people with different eating styles. Exchange lists group foods that are similar in carbohydrate, fat, and protein to facilitate control of their consumption.

2.5 **Evaluate a food label, delineating the different uses of information found on the Nutrition Facts panel, on the ingredients list, and in any health claims or other claims made for the product.**

---

[1] Contributed by Kris Levy, R.D., L.D., Columbus State Community College

[2] Contributed by Lora Beth Brown, Ed.D., R.D., C.D., Brigham Young University

2.6 **State specific nutritional advantages of a carefully planned nutrient-dense diet over a diet chosen without regard for nutrition principles.**

2.7 **Discuss the positive and negative findings for dietary phytochemicals with regard to health, and make a case for food sources over supplements to provide them.**

Critical Thinking Questions

1. *The RDA values for essential nutrients are intended to meet the needs of 97-98% of the healthy population. The EER values, in contrast, are much less generous. Why is there such a difference in the proportion of the population whose needs are met by the RDA versus the EER?*

   If the RDA values were adequate for only 50% of healthy adults, then only 50% or fewer of all people adhering to these recommendations would get enough of these micronutrients for their bodies' needs. The remainder of the people would be deficient in them. Instead, RDA values are generous enough to be adequate for almost all healthy people and thus prevent deficiencies.

   The EER values are set mid-way along the population curve because most people obtain too much energy for their bodies' needs. This results in unnecessary weight gains with risk to health. The DRI committee has purposefully set the EER value at a less generous level so that most people adhering to them do not exceed their energy needs for the day.

2. *You wish to increase your intake of whole grains without taking in excessive amounts of calories. How would you utilize the USDA ChooseMyPlate.gov website to find out about whole-grain foods and the correct portion sizes and amounts to incorporate into your eating plan?*

   You would visit the www.choosemyplate.gov website and click on Daily Food Plans under SuperTracker & Other Tools, then click on the Daily Food Plan link. You would enter your age, sex, weight, height, and physical activity level and submit this information, and receive a Daily Food Plan listing how many ounces or cups recommended from each food group per day. In the Grains section of the customized plan, you would then click on tips for a list of suggestions for eating more whole grains. From this page, you could navigate to other grains group information, including "What Counts as an Ounce?" to learn how to achieve the desired portion sizes. You could develop a one-day eating plan with some of the whole-grain choices given the portion amounts that are recommended for you.

3. *Which of the following people does the RDA for vitamin D not apply to and why? (a) A middle-aged active woman; (b) a growing child; (c) an elderly man; or (d) an adolescent male with cystic fibrosis.*

   The correct choice is d. The RDA values are designed to meet the nutritional needs of most healthy people at various life stages. The RDAs may not apply to people with chronic diseases due to their condition or the impact of their condition on absorption or use of a given nutrient. People with cystic fibrosis secrete abnormally thick mucus that may reduce pancreatic function and interfere with nutrient digestion and absorption.

4. *The Acceptable Macronutrient Distribution Ranges (AMDR) for the energy-yielding nutrients are generous. Describe the group of people who would benefit from the lower limits of each range—for carbohydrates, lipids, and proteins. Which groups of people would benefit from the higher limits of each range—for carbohydrates, fats, and proteins?*

   The AMDR for carbohydrates is 45-65% of total calories. A person who is very physically active will need a lot of carbohydrates to supply their muscles with glucose for ATP (energy). They may easily need 65% of all calories in the form of carbohydrates. An inactive person may only need 45% of all calories from carbohydrates since their muscles don't need as much glucose for movement.

   The AMDR for fat is 20-35% of total calories. Again, a physically active person can likely eat up to 35% of their calories from fat. A person who must watch their fat intake, such as someone with high blood triglycerides or a disease that causes fat malabsorption, may want to take in only 20% of their calories from fat.

   The AMDR for protein is 10-35% of total calories. Someone who engages in physically demanding activity may need more protein to maintain her muscles. She can easily keep her muscles strong by getting 35% of her total calories in the form of protein. A person with kidney disease may need to watch his protein intake and may only want to take in 10% of all calories in the form of protein.

5. *Describe any two reasons why it is important to have broad-reaching guidelines for each of the major nutrient groups when considering meal planning each day.*

   People have different food preferences and may not eat a given food group. Vegetarians may not eat meats but will eat beans and nuts, which are part of the protein foods group. Some vegetarians may not eat dairy products or eggs and will need to get calcium from other sources Many people cannot tolerate wheat gluten and need to find gluten-free alternatives. Many people may be allergic to dairy products as well. People also eat different types of foods based on their native cultures.

   Some people are more active than others and may need more carbohydrates or proteins than others. One key point is that these guidelines are designed for healthy people. People with health conditions should work with their healthcare team, which hopefully will include a registered dietitian.

6. *How can a nutrient-dense food be changed into an empty-calorie food?*

   See Figure 2-6 in the textbook. For example, a potato that provides 117 calories when baked provides 258 calories plus added solid fats when fried in fat. One could look up a whole food that is nutrient dense using Appendix A in the textbook or the MyPlate website and then compare that food's calorie, vitamin, and mineral contents to a similar food that is prepared with added fat or sugar.

Controversy Discussion Questions

1. *Describe what the term "oxidative stress" means in terms of the body tissues. Give any 3 examples of how oxidative stress can cause disease in the body.*

   Oxidative stress refers to the buildup of free radicals, which are oxygen-like molecules that are charged and react with the body's proteins, fats, and tissues. Free radicals are a natural by-product of cellular respiration, which is the production of energy (ATP), in the presence of oxygen. Too many of these molecules can cause inflammation in the tissues as well as changes in blood lipids and cell DNA, which can lead to harmful changes in the body.

   Examples of how oxidative stress can lead to disease are:
   - Oxidation of low-density lipoprotein in the blood can cause inflammation of the blood vessels in the body. This could be a serious problem for blood vessels supplying the heart and the brain tissue and could lead to heart attack or stroke.
   - Oxidative stress can cause changes in the brain tissue that can lead to memory loss or loss of brain function as we age.
   - Free radicals can attack DNA molecules, which store genetic information and control cell development. This could lead to changes in the cells that cause them to start to grow uncontrollably and lead to cancer.

2. a. *What is a phytoestrogen?*

   A phytoestrogen is a chemical compound found in plants that is similar in structure to estrogen made in the body. The phytoestrogens may act in similar ways to the actual hormone in the body.

   b. *List any 2 foods that are a major source of compounds that can become phytoestrogens.*

   Soy beans can have a lot of phytoestrogens in them or they may contain substances that can be converted into phytoestrogens by intestinal bacteria.

   Flaxseeds contain lignans that can be converted into phytoestrogens by the intestinal bacteria.

   c. *Why should people NOT take phytoestrogens in the form of supplements?*

   Supplements may contain phytoestrogens in much higher concentrations than are found in foods. There is a lot of research examining the effects of phytoestrogens in the body. Some studies suggest that high levels of phytoestrogens may actually increase the risk of development of certain types of cancer, whereas other studies suggest the opposite effects. Pregnant women should never take phytoestrogen supplements either.

3. *Why would people want to ingest probiotics or foods with prebiotics when their colons already contain bacteria?*

Probiotics are bacteria that are found in yogurt cultures such as *Acidophilus* or *Lactobacillus*. These organisms do not harm the body and may actually help the digestive system in the long run. Everyone's colon contains many bacteria that actually help the body obtain nutrients such as vitamin K. Bacteria in the digestive system can digest nutrients in food and release molecules that may reduce the inflammation in the lining of the digestive tract.

Such normal flora can be destroyed when antimicrobial medications are used. This can cause the overgrowth of other more harmful bacteria, which can lead to diarrhea and other illnesses. Probiotics can be taken to repopulate the digestive system with more beneficial bacteria that will help control the growth of more harmful bacteria.

Prebiotics are nutrients found in foods that feed the probiotic bacteria such that they continue to grow and help aid in the digestive process.

People with depressed immune systems should not take in large amounts of prebiotic- or probiotic-containing foods.

4. a. *Give any one example of a functional food.*

Cranberries or garlic would be an example of a natural functional food. Margarines that contain phytosterols are an example of a manufactured functional food. This type of margarine is consumed with the intention of lowering blood cholesterol values such as low-density lipoprotein (LDL) levels.

b. *Should this food be considered a drug? Why or why not?*

If the functional food is consumed in large quantities with the intent to treat a condition in the body, it could be considered a drug. This would certainly hold true if the functional food were used in place of more conventional medicine to treat a condition.

If the functional food is consumed in moderation along with other foods and combined with other lifestyle changes, in addition to medical treatment, it would not be considered a drug.

Worksheet Answer Key

Worksheet 2-1: Breakfast Cereal Label Analysis

1. Marshmallow Magician lists that it contains 12 vitamins and minerals and 110 kilocalories per serving of cereal, and is a good source of calcium and whole grain. Zen-Tastic lists high fiber, low fat, low sodium, whole grain, vegetarian, and contains no *trans* fats.

2. a. Zen-Tastic does with 9 grams of fiber.
   b. The sources of fiber in this cereal include brown rice flour, rolled oats, wheat bran, and dried cranberries.

3. a. Marshmallow Magician does, with 10% for both vitamins.
   b. Yes—Marshmallow Magician would usually be considered a high-sugar cereal.
   c. Marshmallow Magician could provide some extra vitamins and minerals for a person who eats a lot of fast food or processed food, which may not have a lot of vitamins or minerals.

4. a. Added to the cereal as pyroxidine hydrochloride
   b. Added to the cereal
   c. Vitamin B_6 is listed further down on the ingredients list.

5. a. *Open answer (answers will vary)* [it's a marketing term with no legal definition]
   b. Perhaps this cereal promotes regularity and energy that may help a person feel better overall.

6. a. Skim milk
   b. *Open answer*

Worksheet 2-2: Intake Analysis—More Diet Planning

1. Biscuits, sweetened iced tea, vanilla ice cream
2. They do not contribute a lot of nutrients such as vitamins or minerals but they do contribute calories.
3. Vitamin C, vitamin A; lots of fruits and vegetables, including deep orange ones
4. To reduce vitamin C, less strawberries or replace the orange with a whole-grain snack. To reduce vitamin A, reduce the amount of apricots or replace them with another snack item.
5. Very strict vegan diet of fruits and vegetables
6. Nuts and whole grains could be added to increase protein and minerals.

Worksheet 2-3: Dietary Reference Intakes and Food Composition Tables

1. RDA – the recommended average daily nutrient intake level that meets the needs of nearly all of healthy people in a particular life stage and gender group. RDA values are used whenever available to assess the nutrient needs of healthy individuals. These values will be used to evaluate a person's food intake or they may be used to plan meals for large groups of people.

2. AI – the recommended average daily nutrient intake level based on intakes of healthy people in a particular life stage and gender group and assumed to be adequate. AI values are used for assessing nutrient needs of healthy individuals when scientific data are insufficient to allow establishment of an RDA value.

3. EAR – the average daily nutrient intake estimated to meet the requirement of half of the healthy individuals in a particular life stage and gender group. EAR values are used in nutrition research and for making public policies, and as the basis of the RDA values.

4. UL – the highest average daily nutrient intake level that is likely to pose no risk of toxicity to almost all healthy individuals of a particular life stage and gender group. The UL values are used to determine when an individual's intake of a nutrient is too high and could result in a toxicity. These values can be used to evaluate vitamin and mineral supplements.

5. 1300 mg

6. 1000 mg

7. 1200 mg

8. Calcium needs are greater during youth, while the body is growing and bone mass is increasing. Adults need less calcium than teens since the adolescent growth spurt has been completed. Calcium is still important to maintain adult bone health. During the older adult or senior years, calcium needs are increased again as a way to further protect bones. [Note: This is an excellent opportunity to briefly introduce students to the concept of osteoporosis and the possible resulting bone fractures.]

9. 45%-65%

10. 20%-35%

11. 10%-35%

12.

	Calories	**Iron (mg)**	**Vitamin A (RAE ug)**
1 cup 2% milk (with nonfat milk solids)	*125*	*0.12*	*137*
3 oz. ground beef extra lean, broiled well (plain hamburger without bun)	*214*	*2.21*	*0*
8 raw baby carrots	*28*	*0.71*	*552*
Totals	*367*	*3.04*	*689*

[Note: When reviewing this calculation, another topic that could be briefly discussed by an instructor would be milk anemia. Discuss the iron content of meat versus milk. Since carrots are a source of vitamin A, it could be reinforced that vitamin A (in the form of beta-carotene) is found in deep orange-colored fruits and vegetables.]

13. 18 mg iron and 700 µg RAE vitamin A

14. Although there is no UL for thiamin, this supplement contains nearly 3 times Molly's RDA, and is therefore unnecessarily high in thiamin (excess thiamin is merely excreted in urine, and so is a waste of money). The

vitamin C supplement is dangerously high in vitamin C. The UL for vitamin C is 2000 mg, which equals 2 grams. Molly is taking 5 grams of vitamin C which is 2.5 times the UL. She may experience vitamin C toxicity symptoms.

Worksheet 2-8: Chapter 2 Review Crossword Puzzle

1. sodium
2. flavonoids
3. A: probiotics, D: protein
4. Macronutrient
5. UL
6. MyPlate
7. lycopene
8. discretionary
9. Exchange
10. Adequate
11. serving

Learning Activities & Project Ideas

Activity 2-1: Do It Yourself—Crafting Consumer Tips Project[3] LO 2.2

Imagine that you are to create a marketing campaign selling the *Dietary Guidelines* (Table 2-1) to consumers. Develop a list of specific tips to guide and motivate your audience into complying with each of the recommendations. Create your own tips customized to the needs, likes, and dislikes of your particular audience. The more focused and individualized your messages are, the more likely consumers will act on them.

Boost the effectiveness of your tips by using these guidelines:

- Keep tips positive, short and simple.
- Be specific; describe an action (where appropriate). As a supporting tip for the message, "Increase physical activity and reduce time spent in sedentary behaviors," you might write, "Walk the dog; don't just watch the dog walk."
- Don't assume consumers always know the payoff or benefit of incorporating changes from the *Dietary Guidelines*. Consider continuing the tip with, "You'll feel good and have more energy, too" or "You could reduce your risk of heart disease," which people can easily relate to.
- Make it manageable. For instance, the tip, "Try one new fruit or vegetable each month" was well received by consumers as part of the "Eat a variety of foods" part of the *Guidelines*.
- Don't over promise results; show realistic outcomes that can result when people make small changes in their daily eating plan.
- Include examples of foods and activities that reflect the lifestyle, preferences, and culture of your audience.
- Use humor when possible and appropriate.
- Incorporate time-saving tips whenever possible, since consumers cite "lack of time" as one of the biggest barriers to good health. For instance, consumers could be encouraged to break up physical activity into several short sessions to accommodate busy schedules.

Activity 2-2: Estimating Amounts[4] LO 2.3, 2.4

As an assignment, have students walk past a display and estimate the portion size of various foods and complete Worksheet 2-4. They should write down their estimates before the lecture about portions; you can post the answers near the display for self-checking, and also review answers later in class. This activity is not graded. The display can be made available all day, in a wide hallway outside the classroom.

Prior to the assignment, you will need to set up the display, which will include the following food items: McDonald's Big Mac, large order of McDonald's French fries, a potato, a Taco Bell bean burrito, a pouch of fruit drink, an apple, green beans, ice cream, single-serving milk bottle, Teriyaki Stix rice bowl, peanut butter, bread, fat-free salad dressing, and regular salad dressing.

The ice cream is a NASCO food model. On the milk and fruit drink containers, the amount is covered with masking tape. The burger, fries, burrito, and rice bowl are all freshly purchased. You can also use 2 apples and 2 potatoes—a small and a large of each. To make the "key," measure the volume of the apples and potatoes by displacement. (Volume is used with the MyPlate recommendations.) Students are usually surprised at how large the "normal" apple and potato actually are.

---

[3] Source: Dietary Guidelines Alliance, Chicago, IL.

[4] Contributed by Lora Beth Brown, Ed.D., R.D., C.D., Brigham Young University

Activity 2-3: Estimating Amounts (with Instructor-Chosen Foods) LO 2.3, 2.4

Before class, make copies of Worksheet 2-5 for students, and set up the classroom for the activity by staging pre-measured amounts of foods of your choice. Each food should be displayed with a card listing the name and unit of measure students should use to estimate the portion sizes. When students arrive, have them complete items 1-4 at the top of the worksheet; then, debrief students by revealing the actual quantities and calorie contributions of the food samples. An excellent resource for a class discussion of portion sizes is the www.choosemyplate.gov website. If you have computer projection equipment and Internet access available, you can show pictures of portion sizes from the "Food Gallery" (URLs where you can link to the gallery are listed below). You can have students complete the questions at the bottom of the worksheet as a homework assignment if desired.

Grains Food Gallery:	http://www.choosemyplate.gov/food-groups/food_library/grains/brownrice.html
Vegetables Food Gallery:	http://www.choosemyplate.gov/food-groups/food_library/vegetables/spinach.html
Fruits Food Gallery:	http://www.choosemyplate.gov/food-groups/food_library/fruit/bananas.html
Dairy Food Gallery:	http://www.choosemyplate.gov/food-groups/food_library/dairy/skim.html
Protein Foods Gallery:	http://www.choosemyplate.gov/food-groups/food_library/proteinfoods/lean_beef.html

Activity 2-4: Perceived vs. Standard Grain Portion Sizes[5] LO 2.3, 2.4

Just before class on the day you plan to teach portions, invite several students (males and females) to pour out some dry cereal into a bowl (a wide variety of sizes are available) or spoon out some pasta (freeze dried so it looks more like what they would eat) onto a plate. Don't identify who served what. Measure out how much they have served for the whole class to see. The range is often quite broad—from ½ to 1 ¼ cups of grape nuts (¼ c = 1 oz. grain for "dense" cereals), from about 1 ½ cups to 3 cups of corn flakes (~1 c = 1 oz. grain for flaky, puffy cereals), and from 1 to 4 cups of macaroni (½ c cooked = 1 oz. grain). Remind students that a portion size of cereal, on a food label, can also vary in amount.

Activity 2-5: Beverage Portion Sizes[5] LO 2.3, 2.4

While discussing milk or other beverage portions, show several glasses and tell how much each holds (from 1 cup—which looks extremely small—to 20 ounces—which looks "normal" to many students). In one of the large glasses we have poured wax to show how miniscule 1 cup looks in a large glass. Since it is hard to find 1-cup glasses for sale, most students probably have 12- to 20-oz. glasses in their apartments. Using large glasses might easily lead to consuming more than one expects, because most people fill up a glass when they pour a beverage.

Activity 2-6: Models of MyPlate Portion Sizes[5] LO 2.3, 2.4

As you discuss the MyPlate groups, pass around NASCO food models so students can see close up what specific portions look like—they can compare them with their hand, finger, thumb, or whatever as a frame of reference. (Research by an MS student several years ago established that handling the food models resulted in the greater accuracy in estimating portions, compared to using 2-D representations.)

Activity 2-7: Compare Your Food Intake to the USDA Food Patterns LO 2.3, 2.4

Provide students with a copy of Worksheet 2-6 (Compare Your Food Intake to Recommended Daily Amounts from Each Group). Instruct them to record everything they ate on the previous day, including beverages and snacks. Assist them with estimating food portions and translating their food selections into food groups. Have them complete their total food group intakes for the entire day and compare this to the recommended food patterns. Students could be instructed to enter both their profile information and their daily intake information into the Super Tracker tool at www.supertracker.usda.gov as a means of assessment. They will be able to see how their daily intake compared with the recommended amounts of servings or nutrients based on their profile at the Super Tracker website. Discuss ways that they can improve their dietary habits.

Activity 2-8: Voluntary Food Labeling of Fresh Foods LO 2.5

Take a quick poll by asking students what their favorite raw fruit, raw vegetable, or fish species is (choose the food category you would like to emphasize). Mark responses on the board or overhead projection and take a quick tally to see what the favorites are in the class. Explain that the FDA has a voluntary nutrition labeling program for the 20 most frequently consumed raw fruits, vegetables, and fish, in addition to the required labeling for processed foods,

[5] Contributed by Lora Beth Brown, Ed.D., R.D., C.D., Brigham Young University

in order to help consumers choose healthful fresh and whole foods. You can also discuss the students' choices of fresh foods in terms of nutrient density and their places in the USDA Food Patterns/MyPlate. If desired, distribute Handout 2-1, which lists the FDA's lists used for the voluntary labeling program.

Activity 2-9: Review—USDA Food Patterns Jeopardy![6] LO 2.3
Create a jeopardy game board with six category columns. Each column should have a category name (i.e. fruits, vegetables, etc.). Under each category name have 5 game cards, each with a different question that is relevant to the particular category of interest. Have the game cards increase in "point" value. Each game card should contain an answer. The students are required to state their answer in the form of a question. If this process is too involved for your class, you can write the questions on the cards and allow the students to provide the simple answer. This activity can be conducted in large classes in which teams compete or in small groups. This activity can also be adapted for other nutrition, wellness, and activity topics. Try this game with the *Physical Activity Guidelines for Americans* and food groups combined. It creates an atmosphere for application and fun!

Activity 2-10: Phytochemical Commercials Project[7] LO 2.7
Assign the students to research a specific phytochemical (organosulfur compounds in onions, lycopene in tomatoes, etc.) and find the benefits of this compound to health. The students will then do a short presentation as if they are doing a TV commercial, trying to sell a product (food) that contains the phytochemical and to convince the audience to consume it. They can also bring samples of foods rich in the phytochemical to class, and students will taste them. This is a way to expose students to healthy foods.

Chapter Lecture Outline

I. Introduction
   A. Eating well is easy in theory:
      1. Just choose a selection of foods that supplies appropriate amounts of the essential nutrients, fiber, phytochemicals, and energy, without excess intakes of unhealthy fats, sugar, and salt.
      2. Be sure to get enough exercise to balance the foods you eat!!
   B. In practice, eating well proves harder than it appears.
      1. Many people are overweight, or undernourished, or suffer from nutrient excesses or deficiencies that impair their health.
      2. They are malnourished.

II. Nutrient Recommendations
   A. Dietary Reference Intakes
      1. The Dietary Reference Intakes are nutrient intake standards set for people living in the United States and Canada.
      2. The Daily Values are U.S. standards used on food labels that allow consumers to compare the nutrient content of 2 foods.
      3. The DRI committee has set values for: Vitamins, minerals, carbohydrates, fiber, lipids, protein, water, energy
   B. The DRI Lists and Purposes
      1. RDA and AI—Recommended Nutrient Intakes
         a. Both are nutrient goals
         b. RDA – Recommended Dietary Allowances are based on solid experimental evidence.
         c. AI – Adequate Intake values are set up if there is not enough information about a nutrient to establish an RDA value for that nutrient.
      2. EAR—Nutrition Research and Policy – The EAR values form the scientific basis from which the RDA values are derived.
      3. UL—Safety
         a. UL – Tolerable Upper Intake Levels
         b. To identify potentially hazardous levels of nutrient intakes

[6] Contributed by: Don Simpson, University of Arkansas, Fayetteville

[7] Contributed by Nancy J. Correa-Matos, Ph.D., R.D., University of North Florida

c. Beneficial to those who take supplements or who consume foods with added vitamins or minerals
d. Not all nutrients have an established UL value

4. AMDR—Calorie Percentage Ranges
   a. A diet consisting of the macronutrients in these proportions will help ensure nutritional adequacy with a reduced risk of developing chronic diseases.
   b. 45 to 65 percent from carbohydrates
   c. 20 to 35 percent from fat
   d. 10 to 35 percent from protein

C. Understanding the DRI Recommended Intakes
1. DRI for Population Groups
   a. Separate recommendations for men, women, pregnant, lactating, infants, and children
   b. Specific age ranges
   c. Recommendations for healthy people
2. Other Characteristics of the DRI
   a. The values are based on available scientific research and updated periodically in light of new knowledge.
   b. The values are based on the concepts of probability and risk.
   c. The values are recommendations for optimal intakes, not minimum requirements. They include a generous margin of safety.
   d. The values are set in reference to specific indicators of nutrient adequacy such as blood nutrient concentrations or reduction of particular chronic conditions, rather than prevention of deficiency symptoms alone.
   e. The values reflect daily intakes to be achieved, on average, over time. The values are set high enough to ensure that body stores will meet nutrient needs during periods of inadequate intakes.
3. The DRI Apply to Healthy People Only – A person who is ill may require a higher intake of certain nutrients or may not be able to tolerate the DRI recommendations.

D. How the Committee Establishes DRI Values—An RDA Example
1. Determining Individual Requirements – How does the DRI committee set values?
   a. For determining RDA, a balance study is performed.
   b. Determines a person's requirement to achieve balance for nutrient X
2. Accounting for the Needs of the Population – The EAR value of a nutrient would be set at the mean for the entire population.
3. The Decision – The RDA value is set such that 97-98% of the population receives enough nutrient X for optimal functioning.

E. Setting Energy Requirements
1. In contrast to the RDA for nutrients, the value set for energy, the Estimated Energy Requirement (EER), is not generous.
2. It is set at an average value so as to maintain body weight and to discourage unhealthy weight gain.
3. The AMDR values help achieve a healthy balance of nutrients in the diet as well as reduce the risk of chronic diseases.

F. Why Are Daily Values Used on Labels?
1. One set of values that applies to everyone found only on food labels
2. Reflect the needs of an "average" person – someone eating 2,000 to 2,500 calories a day
3. Enable consumers to compare the nutrient values among foods
4. The Daily Values do not serve as nutrient intake goals for individuals.

III. *Dietary Guidelines for Americans*

A. The *Guidelines* Promote Health – offer science-based advice for people ages 2 and up – Table 2-1

B. Four Major Topic Areas
1. Balance calories to manage a healthy body weight. – Overweight or obese people should consume fewer calories from food and beverages.
2. Reduce intakes of certain foods and food components.
   a. Reduce intake of foods high in sodium to lower risk of kidney disease or high blood pressure.
   b. Limit saturated fats to less than 10% of daily calories as well as consuming less than 300 mg/day of cholesterol.
   c. Limit *trans* fat, solid fat, added sugar, and refined grain intakes.

d. Consume alcohol in moderation.
3. Increase intakes of certain nutrient-dense foods.
   a. Eat a larger quantity and variety of fruits and vegetables.
   b. Consume at least half of grain intake as whole grains.
   c. Increase intake of fat-free or low-fat dairy products
   d. Choose a variety of lean protein sources, especially seafoods, legumes, nuts, or soy products.
   e. Avoid solid fats in protein and fat/oil choices.
   f. Choose foods with more potassium, fiber, calcium, and vitamin D.
4. Build a healthy eating pattern.
   a. Select an eating plant that meets nutrient needs at an appropriate calorie level.
   b. Follow food safety guidelines to minimize risk of food-borne illness.

C. How Does the U.S. Diet Compare to the Guidelines?
   1. Based on the NHANES surveys 2001-2004 or 2005-2006) – comparison of recommendations to actual intakes
   2. Figure 2-4 shows that we eat too few of the food groups that supply key nutrients as well as fiber, potassium, vitamin D, and calcium and we consume too many calories, sugars, and solid fats.

D. Our Two Cents' Worth – Enjoy eating healthfully but eat less.

IV. Diet Planning with the USDA Food Patterns

A. Introduction
   1. A major recommendation of the *Dietary Guidelines for Americans* is to choose a diet based on the food group plan concept.
   2. If you design your diet around the USDA Food Patterns, you will achieve adequacy, balance, and variety.

B. The Food Groups and Subgroups
   1. Vegetables Subgroups and Protein Foods Subgroups
      a. Not every vegetable supplies nutrients found in all of the foods of the vegetables group – Example: vegetables are divided into red and orange, dark green, starchy, legumes based on their content of various nutrients
      b. The fat content of protein foods can vary widely.
      c. Meats tend to have higher saturated fat content while seafood, nuts, seeds, and soy foods have less saturated fats and enough essential fatty acids.
   2. Grains Subgroups and other Foods
      a. The nutrient contest of foods in the grains group vary widely.
      b. Refined grains usually lack fiber and other beneficial nutrients but supply energy.
      c. Whole grains should be included in each day's intakes.
      d. Spices, herbs, and coffee provide few nutrients but may contain beneficial phytochemicals.
   3. Variety Among and Within Food Groups – Select a variety of foods between food groups and within each food group to ensure nutritional adequacy.

C. Choosing Nutrient-Dense Foods
   1. Solid Fats, Added Sugars, and Alcohol Reduce Nutrient Density
      a. Choose the most nutrient-dense foods from each group to prevent overweight or obesity.
      b. Solid fats, added sugars, and alcohol reduce nutrient density of foods
   2. The Concept of Discretionary Calories
      a. Difference between cal needed for nutrient-dense foods to provide dietary adequacy and total cal requirement
      b. The discretionary calorie allowance can help people who want to limit calorie intake to avoid weight gain.
      c. Nutrient-dense foods are the best choices for "spending" the allowance.

V. Diet Planning Application

A. Plan a day's meals to follow the USDA Food Patterns within a given caloric budget.
   1. Use Table 2-2 to determine the daily calorie budget for a given group of people as well as to determine the number of servings of foods from each major food group.
   2. See Table 2-3 to determine the amount of vegetable and protein food subgroups needed for the week.

3. Table 2-4 demonstrates a sample diet plan that shows how the food groups are broken up between the day's meals.

B. MyPlate Educational Tool
   1. The concepts of the USDA Food Patterns are conveyed to the consumer through the MyPlate educational tool.
   2. More information at www.choosemyplate.gov

C. Flexibility of the USDA Food Patterns
   1. Allows for substitutions according to personal preferences, national and cultural food choices as shown in Figure 2-9
   2. Vegetarians can use the USDA Food Patterns for meal planning as well. They can choose among the plant protein foods and count legumes (in the vegetables group) as protein foods.

D. A Note about Exchange Systems
   1. Exchange lists facilitate calorie control by providing an understanding of how much carbohydrate, fat, and protein are in standardized portions of foods from each group.
   2. Appendix D describes the foods within the exchange groups as well as their associated macronutrient contents.

E. The Last Word on Diet Planning
   1. Small changes each day can add up to substantial changes over time.
   2. These changes may help reduce the risk of developing chronic diseases.

F. A Consumer's Guide to Controlling Portion Sizes at Home and Away – to control calories, must pay attention to portion sizes
   1. How Big Is Your Bagel? – Be aware of large portion sizes
   2. Practice with Weights and Measures – Be able to recognize actual portion sizes as recommended by the USDA Food Patterns and relate them to common objects.
   3. Colossal Cuisine in Restaurants – The percentage of total calories from foods eaten away from home has doubled over the last 30 years (see Figure 2-10).
   4. Moving Ahead – Make portion control a habit to avoid overeating.

VI. Checking Out Food Labels

A. What Food Labels Must Include
   1. Introduction
      a. The Nutrition Education and Labeling Act of 1990
      b. Every packaged food must state:
         1. The common name of the product.
         2. The name and address of the manufacturer, packer, or distributor.
         3. The net contents in terms of weight, measure, or count.
         4. The nutrient contents of the product (Nutrition Facts panel).
         5. The ingredients, in descending order of predominance by weight.
         6. Essential warnings, such as alerts about ingredients that often cause allergic reactions or other problems.
      c. Small items like candy may only have a telephone number on the label.
      d. Tuna fish will have a small label with abbreviated information.
   2. The Nutrition Facts Panel
      a. The following are found on all labels:
         1. Serving size, servings per container, calories/calories from fat
         2. Nutrient amounts and percentages of Daily Values for: Total fat, cholesterol, sodium, total carbohydrate/sugars/dietary fiber, protein
      b. In addition, the label must state the contents of these nutrients expressed as percentages of the Daily Values: Vitamin A, vitamin C, calcium, iron
      c. The labels also have a calories per gram reminder as a handy reference.
   3. Ingredients List – may seem straightforward but sugar can have many other names
      a. Ingredients are listed in descending order by weight
      b. This can help consumers spot ingredients that they are allergic to, drinks that are made of juice versus water and sugar, and whole-grain foods versus refined grains.

4. More About Percentages of Daily Values
    a. The calculations used to determine the "% Daily Value" figures for nutrient contributions from a serving of food are based on a 2,000-calorie diet.
    b. Example: If a food contributes 13 milligrams of vitamin C per serving, and the DV is 60 milligrams, then a serving of that food provides about 22 percent of the DV for vitamin C.
    c. Labels also have calorie/gram reminders that can help consumers plan meals.

B. What Food Labels *May* Include
1. Introduction: So far, we have looked at the accurate and reliable facts on nutrition labels. Let's look at more reliable claims but also unreliable but legal claims that can be made on food labels.
2. Nutrient Claims: Reliable Information
    a. If a food meets specific criteria, the label may display certain approved nutrient claims, as shown in Table 2-6.
    b. The term "good source" means that the product will contain 10-19% of the Daily Value per serving.
3. Health Claims: Reliable and Not So Reliable
    a. The FDA allows health claims that are supported by weak evidence as well as those with a high degree of scientific evidence to appear on labels.
    b. "Qualified" claims must contain statements that describe the extent to which studies back up a given claim.
    c. Table 2-7 shows examples of reliable health claims on labels.
4. Structure-Function Claims: Best Ignored
    a. No prior approval is needed from the FDA.
    b. Structure-function claims can appear on a food or supplement.
    c. For claims on a supplement, the manufacturer must notify the FDA after marketing, and the label has to have a disclaimer stating that the FDA has not evaluated the claim.
5. Label Short Cuts
    a. Label short cuts are icons on food packages that may be endorsements from professional or academic groups.
    b. The FDA is developing a standardized set of symbols for all products that meet the criteria of the *Dietary Guidelines for Americans 2010.*

VII. Food Feature: Getting A Feel For the Nutrients in Foods

A. Comparing the Nutrients – Figures 2-14 & 2-15 show two very different intakes for 2 days.

B. Monday's Meals in Detail – Monday's meals are clearly more nutrient dense than Tuesday's meals.

C. Tuesday's Meals in Detail – No fruit or whole grains, little vegetables or dairy, too much energy and unhealthful food components

D. Use a Computer—Or Not? – People use the computer with diet analysis programs or track their meals on paper to assess their food options and make more informed choices.

VIII. Controversy: Are Some Foods Superfoods for Health?

A. A Scientist's View of Phytochemicals – Blueberries, chocolate, flaxseed, garlic, soybeans and soy products, tomatoes; tea, whole grain, and wine; yogurt
1. Phytochemicals, such as flavonoids, may reduce inflammation in the body and serve as antioxidants
    a. See Table C2-2 for potential health effects and food sources of phytochemicals
    b. See Figure C2-1 for antioxidant capacity of selected foods
2. Blueberries and the Brain – Blueberries provide flavonoids that may reduce oxidative damage in brain tissue.
3. Chocolate, Heart, and Mood – Chocolate contains flavonoids that may protect heart tissue from oxidative damage.
4. Flaxseeds provide lignans, which are converted into phytoestrogens that may lower the risk of intestinal cancer, breast cancer, prostate cancer, and heart disease.
5. Garlic contains organosulfur compounds that may reduce the risks of some cancers, heart disease, and some infections.
6. Soybeans and Soy Products – Soy products contain phytoestrogens that may reduce the risks of some cancers, reduce hot flashes, and help reduce blood cholesterol.
7. Soy's Potential Downsides – ACS recommends moderation for those with a history of breast cancer

8. Tomatoes contain lycopene, which may help reduce the risk of some cancers.
9. Tea – source of flavonoids; green tea consumption may reduce blood lipids
10. Grapes and Wine – Wine contains resveratrol, a compound that may exhibit anticancer properties and extend the lifespan of some cells.
11. Yogurt contains beneficial bacteria called probiotics that may help regulate digestion and help reduce allergies in some people.

B. Phytochemical Supplements
   1. Foods deliver 1000s of phytochemicals in addition to nutrients.
   2. Supporters of Phytochemical Supplements – say:
      a. Evidence is good enough to recommend supplements.
      b. People have been eating them forever and so they must be safe to consume as supplements.
   3. Detractors of Phytochemical Supplements – say:
      a. The body is not used to handling them in large concentrations, especially flaxseed, which can interfere with vitamin and mineral absorption.
      b. They alter body functions in ways not yet understood fully.
      c. Evidence for the safety of isolated phytochemicals in humans is lacking.
      d. No regulatory body oversees their safety. No studies are required to prove they are safe or effective before they are marketed.
      e. The manufacturers of phytochemical supplements make structure-function claims that are unproven or untested by the FDA.

C. The Concept of Functional Foods
   1. Manufactured functional foods consist of processed foods that are fortified with nutrients or enhanced with phytochemicals or herbs.
   2. What are better choices: snack foods sprinkled with phytochemicals or whole foods?
   3. Are smoothies that contain medicinal herbs safe for everyone to consume?

D. The Final Word
   1. ...is that moderation of intake of any one superfood is very important.
   2. It is important to consume a variety of grains, beans, fruits, and vegetables.

Worksheet 2-1: Breakfast Cereal Label Analysis

Instructions: Compare the "Zen-Tastic" and "Marshmallow Magician" cereals and answer the questions that follow.

What's so great about Zen-Tastic organic cereal?

High fiber
Low fat
Low sodium
Whole grain
Vegetarian
No *trans* fats

INGREDIENTS:
Organic brown rice flour, organic evaporated cane juice, organic rolled oats, organic wheat bran, organic sweetened dried cranberries (organic cranberries, organic evaporated cane juice), organic whole wheat meal, organic soy flour, organic whole oat flour, organic oat bran, inulin, organic soy oil, organic soy fiber, organic molasses, organic barley malt extract, organic yellow corn flour, organic whole millet, organic oat syrup solids, sea salt, organic quinoa, organic ginger, organic buckwheat flour, organic barley flour, organic rice bran extract, organic cinnamon, tocopherols (natural vitamin E), organic cloves, organic nutmeg.

Produced in a facility that contains peanuts, tree nuts & soy.

Nutrition Facts

Serving Size $^3/_4$ cup (55g)
Servings Per Container about 6

Amount Per Serving	Cereal	Cereal + 125 ml fortified skim milk
Calories	190	230
Calories from Fat	25	25
	% Daily Value**	
Total Fat 2.5g*	**4%**	**4%**
Saturated Fat 0g	**0%**	**0%**
Trans Fat 0g		
Cholesterol 0mg	**0%**	**0%**
Sodium 95mg	**4%**	**7%**
Total Carbohydrate 41g	**14%**	**16%**
Dietary Fiber 9g	**36%**	**36%**
Sugars 13g		
Protein 5g		
Vitamin A	0%	6%
Vitamin C	0%	0%
Calcium	2%	15%
Iron	10%	10%

* Amount in cereal. One half cup skim milk contributes an additional 40 calories, 65mg sodium, 6g total carbohydrate (6g sugars), and 4g protein.
**Percent Daily Values are based on a 2,000 calorie diet. Your Daily Values may be higher or lower depending on your calorie needs.

	Calories	2,000	2,500
Total Fat	Less than	65g	80g
Sat Fat	Less than	20g	25g
Cholesterol	Less than	300mg	300mg
Sodium	Less than	2400mg	2400mg
Total Carbohydrate		300g	375g
Dietary Fiber		25g	30g

Nutrition Facts

Serving Size $^3/_4$ cup (27g)
Servings Per Container about 12

Amount Per Serving	Cereal	with $^1/_2$ cup skim milk
Calories	110	150
Calories from Fat	10	10
	% Daily Value**	
Total Fat 1g*	**1%**	**1%**
Saturated Fat 0g	**0%**	**0%**
Trans Fat 0g		
Polyunsaturated Fat 0g		
Monounsaturated Fat 0g		
Cholesterol 0mg	**0%**	**1%**
Sodium 190mg	**8%**	**10%**
Total Carbohydrate 22g	**7%**	**9%**
Dietary Fiber 1g	**5%**	**5%**
Sugars 11g		
Other Carbohydrate 9g		
Protein 2g		
Vitamin A	10%	15%
Vitamin C	10%	10%
Calcium	10%	25%
Iron	25%	25%
Vitamin D	10%	25%
Thiamin	25%	30%
Riboflavin	25%	35%
Niacin	25%	25%
Vitamin B_6	25%	35%
Folic Acid	50%	50%
Vitamin B_{12}	25%	35%
Phosphorus	4%	15%
Magnesium	2%	6%
Zinc	25%	30%

* Amount in cereal. A serving of cereal plus skim milk provides 1g total fat, less than 5mg cholesterol, 250mg sodium, 250mg potassium, 28g total carbohydrate (16g sugars) and 6g protein.

**Percent Daily Values are based on a 2,000 calorie diet. Your Daily Values may be higher or lower depending on your calorie needs.

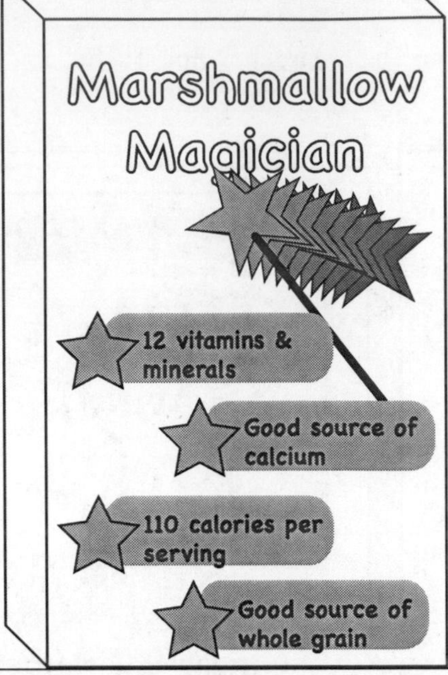

INGREDIENTS: WHOLE GRAIN OATS, MARSHMALLOWS (SUGAR, MODIFIED CORN STARCH, CORN SYRUP, DEXTROSE, GELATIN, CALCIUM CARBONATE, YELLOW 5&6, BLUE 1, RED 40, ARTIFICIAL FLAVOR), SUGAR, OAT FLOUR, CORN SYRUP, CORN STARCH, SALT, CALCIUM CARBONATE, TRISODIUM PHOSPHATE, COLOR ADDED, ZINC AND IRON (MINTERAL NUTRIENTS), VITAMIN C (SODIUM ASCORBATE), A B VITAMIN (NIACINAMIDE), ARTIFICIAL FLAVOR, VITAMIN B_6 (PYRIDOXINE HYDROCHLORIDE), VITAMIN B_2 (RIBOFLAVIN), VITAMIN B_1 (THIAMIN MONONITRATE), VITAMIN A (PALMITATE), A B VITAMIN (FOLIC ACID), VITAMIN B_{12}, VITAMIN D, VITAMIN E (MIXED TOCOPHEROLS) ADDED TO PRESERVE FRESHNESS.

1. What are the nutritional claims of each cereal?

2. a. Which cereal has a higher level of fiber?

   b. What is the source of fiber in this cereal?

3. a. Which cereal has a higher % Daily Value of vitamins A and C?

   b. Does this surprise you? Why or why not?

   c. When can the addition of this cereal to a morning meal help add to the overall nutrition for a person during the course of a day?

4. a. What is the source of vitamin B_6 in the Marshmallow Magician cereal?

   b. Is it a naturally occurring ingredient?

   c. How can you tell?

5. a. What is “inner harmony” (from the Zen-Tastic package)?

   b. How does this cereal contribute to inner harmony?

6. a. What type of milk is listed in the right side of the Nutrition Facts panel of the Marshmallow Magician cereal?

b. Does this seem like a reasonable choice for this cereal?

Worksheet 2-2: Intake Analysis—More Diet Planning

Eating Plan G (1 Day's Intake)	Eating Plan H (1 Meal)
1 cup honey dew melon	1 cup New England clam chowder
1 cup fresh strawberries	1 2-ounce cheesy biscuit
1 large apple	4 ounces broiled lobster tail
½ avocado	4 ounces broiled scallops
½ cup sweet green peppers	3 Tbsp. drawn, melted butter
½ cup sweet red peppers	1 cup rice pilaf
¼ cup black olives	1 cup boiled carrot and green beans
1 medium orange	12 ounces sweetened ice tea
1 medium banana	1 cup vanilla ice cream
1 cup boiled green beans	
10 cooked asparagus spears	
1 cup sautéed mushrooms	
1 cup kidney beans	
¼ cup dried apricots	
¼ cup dried Craisins	
5 dried, pitted dates	

Look at Eating Plan H:

1. Name the foods that would contribute discretionary calories to the daily intakes of the person eating this meal.

2. Why are these foods not counted towards the principal diet in terms of nutritional adequacy?

Look at Eating Plan G:

3. Which key nutrients are present in very large amounts, and how would you know this?

4. What food choice substitutions would you suggest to reduce these nutrients?

5. What type of diet is represented here?

6. What types of foods could be added to ensure enough minerals and protein?

Worksheet 2-3: Dietary Reference Intakes and Food Composition Tables

The **Dietary Reference Intakes** are a collection of 4 nutrient values used for different purposes. Provide the definitions for the abbreviations in your own words. When or why would these values be used?

1. RDA –

2. AI –

3. EAR –

4. UL –

Find the DRI tables in your textbook.

5. How much calcium would a 15-year-old girl need each day? ________

6. How much calcium would a 35-year-old man need? ________

7. How much calcium would a 60-year-old woman need? ________

8. Why do you think these individuals require different amounts of calcium? Think about the body and bone health throughout the lifecycle.

The Dietary Reference Intakes also provide a percentage of carbohydrate, protein, and fat necessary for a balanced diet. These are called the AMDR or Acceptable Macronutrient Distribution Ranges. Fill in the numbers for the ranges.

9. Carbohydrate ________________

10. Fat ________________

11. Protein ________________

Food Composition Tables: Appendix A of the textbook has a food composition table. This will provide detailed information about the nutrient content of foods and beverages. In the next section, you will look up the values for three food items. At the top of each right-hand page in Appendix A there is a key to locate the various types of foods. Within each section, the foods are listed in alphabetical order. The caloric value is listed as "Ener (cal)." This process could be very tedious and time consuming! Today, we have computer programs that will perform these calculations of an individual's food intake.

12. Case Study: Molly ate the following meal. Total the amount of calories, iron, and vitamin A in her meal. *Hint: Use the food composition table at the end of your textbook.*

	Calories	Iron (mg)	Vitamin A (RAE µg)
1 cup 2% milk (with nonfat milk solids)			
3 oz. ground beef extra lean, broiled well (plain hamburger without bun)			
8 raw baby carrots			
Totals			

13. Molly is a 22-year-old female. How much iron and vitamin A are recommended for her? Look in the DRI tables.

14. Molly takes a thiamin supplement that provides 3 mg of thiamin per day. She also takes a vitamin C supplement that contains 5 grams of vitamin C per day. What do you think about this?

    (Hint #1: Look up the UL values for these nutrients. Some nutrients do not have a UL value. It may be that sufficient research has not been completed to set a UL value. So then compare the supplement to the value listed in the main DRI table.)

    (Hint #2: Be careful with the measuring units for vitamin C. She is taking 5 GRAMS. The UL for vitamin C is listed in milligrams.)

Worksheet 2-4: Estimating Amounts

Instructions: Visually estimate the amounts and USDA Food Patterns cup/ounce equivalents. Also estimate calories and nutrient density of each food. Guessing is OK!

Food	Estimate		Nutrient Density (circle)
McDonald's Big Mac	Ounces of cooked meat: Equivalent ounces of grains: Calories for the Big Mac: Cup(s) of vegetables:	________ ________ ________ ________	High or Low
McDonald's French fries (large)	Cup(s) of vegetables: Calories:	________ ________	High or Low
Potato	Approximate volume: Calories if baked:	________ cup(s) ________	High or Low
Taco Bell Bean Burrito	Cup(s) of beans (legumes): Equivalent to ________ ounce(s) protein foods or ________ cup(s) vegetables Equivalent ounces of grains: Calories for the burrito:	________ ________ ________	High or Low
Fruit drink	Cup(s):	________	High or Low
Apple	Approximate volume:	________ cup(s)	High or Low
Green beans	Cup(s):	________	High or Low
Ice cream	Cup(s): Equivalent cup(s) of milk:	________ ________	High or Low
Single-serving milk bottle	Cup(s): Equivalent cup(s) of milk:	________ ________	High or Low
Teriyaki Stix Rice Bowl	Cup(s): Equivalent ounces of grain:	________ ________	High or Low
Peanut butter	Tbsp. peanut butter: Equivalent to ________ ounces of meat	________	High or Low
Wheat bread	Ounces of grain: The bread is (circle): whole grain or refined grain	________	High or Low
Fat-free salad dressing	Calories in packet: tsp.:	________ ________	High or Low
Regular salad dressing	Calories in packet: tsp.:	________ ________	High or Low

After you have estimated portions, check your responses with the answer key. Think about what you learned by trying to estimate amounts. Write down your new insights:

Worksheet 2-5: Guessing Portion Sizes—How Well Can You Do It?

1. Your instructor will set up food at stations around the classroom. You will be told what the food is but you will not be provided with the size or calories of the food shown.
2. You will be asked to estimate the size of the portions of food that you see at each station. There will be a card at each station that will specify the unit of measurement such as ounces (oz.) as fluid or weight, tablespoons, or cups.
3. Estimate the portion on your own to the best of your abilities. Fill in the Estimated Size column of the table.
4. Take a guess at the number of calories for the food at each station as well. Record this in the Estimated Calories column of the table.

Food Item	Estimated Size	Actual Size	Estimated Calories	Actual Calories

5. Your instructor can supply the actual size and calories for you to copy onto your table. Or, given the actual size, you can use an online food composition database, a diet analysis program, or Appendix A in your textbook to find the calorie value of each food.
6. Answer the following questions based on your individual findings. Your answers do not need to be lengthy. Attach your answers to your filled-in table. You may be asked to hand in your answers in written form or your instructor may have you discuss your findings as a group.

Questions to Consider:

1. How did you decide on a portion size?
2. What type of visual aids in your everyday life may help you to estimate the portion size?
3. Did you overestimate or underestimate the portion sizes more often?
4. Which types of food did you overestimate? Which ones did you underestimate?
5. Did you have more difficulty measuring liquid or solid volumes?
6. Give an example of how your ability to estimate food portions affects your present diet.
7. What type of foods do you have difficulty estimating in your own diet? Why?

Worksheet 2-6: Compare Your Food Intake to Recommended Daily Amounts from Each Group

List food item and amount.	Indicate amount consumed from each food group, using the appropriate unit of measurement (in parentheses).						Estimate values.
Food Item	**Fruits (cups)**	**Vegetables (cups)**	**Grains (oz.)**	**Protein foods (oz.)**	**Milk (cups)**	**Oils (tsp.)**	**Discretionary kcalories**
Breakfast:							
Snack:							
Lunch:							
Snack:							
Dinner:							
Snack:							
Total consumed							
Recommended based on EER							

Record your eating and drinking intakes for one day. Use the website: www.supertracker.usda.gov to enter your intakes. You can see how your diet compares to the latest guidelines.

Worksheet 2-7: Homemade or On-the-Go?

Do you have any idea how many calories are in a homemade hamburger versus a hamburger from McDonald's or Wendy's? You can find out! Fast-food restaurants have websites that describe the nutritional content of their popular meals or sides. The following table contains the list for common fast-food establishments and their websites. You can generally click on the "Food," "Menu," or "Nutrition" tab or link within the website to find the nutritional content of all of their items.

Name	Website URL
Arby's	http://www.arbys.com
Burger King	http://www.bk.com
McDonald's	http://www.mcdonalds.com
Pizza Hut	http://www.pizzahut.com/nutrition.html
Subway	http://www.subway.com
Taco Bell	http://www.tacobell.com/nutrition
Wendy's	http://www.wendys.com/food
KFC	http://www.kfc.com

You can also use Appendix A of your textbook to find the nutritional content of many foods that you can prepare at home. The appendix also lists many brands of frozen, prepared foods that can be warmed at home. If you want to closely examine the nutritional content of your food, you can also consult the USDA database at http://ndb.nal.usda.gov/ndb/search/list.

Food	Source of Food	Total Calories	Total Fat (g)	Total Carbohydrate (g)

You can fill out the table to compare foods to each other for calorie, fat, or carbohydrate content. You can also compare the protein, vitamin, or mineral content of foods as well.

Worksheet 2-8: Chapter 2 Review Crossword Puzzle

Across	Down
3. Bacteria found in yogurt that can aid digestive health 4. Healthy ranges for intakes of proteins, carbohydrates, and fats are known as Acceptable _____ Distribution Ranges. 8. The difference in calories needed for the body's energy needs and those needed to ensure adequacy is called the _____ calorie allowance. 10. The intake value set for a nutrient that does not have sufficient data to establish an RDA is called the _____ Intake. 11. The information on the Nutrition Facts panel of a food label is based on a specified _____ size.	1. The Dietary Guidelines for Americans state that _____ should be consumed in quantities less than 2300 mg per day and less than 1500 mg per day for those 51 years and older. 2. Antioxidants that help protect the brain and enhance its function 3. The AMDR for _____ is set between 10% and 35% of total calories. 5. The nutrition guideline that is useful for those who take supplements safely 6. The USDA's interactive meal planning/diet analysis tool 7. Substance found in tomatoes with anti-cancer properties 9. A diet planning tool used by diabetics or those who want to control calories is called the _____ System.

Handout 2-1: Most Frequently Eaten Raw Fruits, Vegetables, and Fish/Shellfish[8]

Fruits	Vegetables	Fish
Banana	Potato	Shrimp
Apple	Iceberg lettuce	Cod
Watermelon	Tomato	Pollock
Orange	Onion	Catfish
Cantaloupe	Carrot	Scallops
Grape	Celery	Salmon (Atlantic/coho/Chinook/ sockeye, chum/pink)
Grapefruit	Sweet corn	Flounder/sole
Strawberry	Broccoli	Oysters
Peach	Green cabbage	Orange roughy
Pear	Cucumber	Ocean perch
Nectarine	Bell pepper	Rockfish
Honeydew melon	Cauliflower	Clam
Plum	Leaf lettuce	Haddock
Avocado	Sweet potato	Blue crab
Lemon	Mushroom	Rainbow trout
Pineapple	Green onion	Halibut
Tangerine	Green (snap) bean	Lobster
Sweet cherry	Radish	Swordfish
Kiwifruit	Summer squash	Tilapia
Lime	Asparagus	Tuna

[8] Source: FDA, http://www.accessdata.fda.gov/scripts/cdrh/cfdocs/cfcfr/CFRSearch.cfm?fr=101.44 (accessed 2-21-2013)

Chapter 3 – The Remarkable Body

Quick List: IM Resources for Chapter 3

- **Class preparation resources:** learning objectives/key points, suggested activities and projects, lecture outline
- **Assignment materials:** **Related LO**
  - Critical thinking questions (with answer key) 3.2, 3.3, 3.4, 3.5, 3.8
  - Discussion questions (with answers) for Controversy 3 .... 3.9
  - Worksheet 3-1: Fiber Supplement Label Analysis 3.6
  - Worksheet 3-2: Intake Analysis—Digestive Health 3.6
  - Worksheet 3-3: Food Habits and Digestive Problems[1] 3.6
  - **New!** Worksheet 3-4: Chapter 3 Review Crossword Puzzle
- **Enrichment materials:**
  - Handout 3-1: Where the Foods Are Broken Down 3.5
  - Handout 3-2: Transport of Nutrients in Blood and Lymph 3.2, 3.5
  - Handout 3-3: Alcohol's Effects on Nutrients in the Body 3.9

Chapter Learning Objectives and Key Points

3.1 **Describe the levels of organization in the body, and identify some basic ways in which nutrition supports them.**
The body's cells need energy, oxygen, and nutrients, including water, to remain healthy and do their work. Genes direct the making of each cell's protein machinery, including enzymes. Specialized cells are grouped together to form tissues and organs; organs work together in body systems.

3.2 **Describe the relationships between the body's fluids and the cardiovascular system and their importance to the nourishment and maintenance of body tissues.**
Blood and lymph deliver needed materials to all the body's cells and carry waste materials away from them. The cardiovascular system ensures that these fluids circulate properly among all tissues.

3.3 **Summarize the interactions between the nervous and hormonal systems and nutrition.**
Glands secrete hormones that act as messengers to help regulate body processes. The nervous system and hormonal system regulate body processes, respond to the need for food, govern the act of eating, regulate digestion, and call for the stress response when needed.

3.4 **State how nutrition and immunity are interrelated, and describe the importance of inflammation to the body's health.**
A properly functioning immune system enables the body to resist diseases. Inflammation is the normal, healthy response of the immune system to cell injury. Chronic inflammation is associated with disease development and being overweight.

3.5 **Compare the terms *mechanical digestion* and *chemical digestion*, and point out where these processes occur along the digestive tract with regard to carbohydrate, fat, and protein.**
The preference for sweet, salty, and fatty tastes is inborn and can lead to overconsumption of foods that offer them. The digestive tract is a flexible, muscular tube that digests food and absorbs its nutrients and some nonnutrients. Ancillary digestive organs, such as the pancreas and gallbladder, aid digestion. The mechanical digestive actions include chewing, mixing by the stomach, adding fluid, and moving the tract's contents by peristalsis. After digestion and absorption, wastes are excreted. Chemical digestion begins in the mouth, where food is mixed with an enzyme in saliva that acts on carbohydrates. Digestion continues in the stomach, where stomach enzymes and acid break down protein. Digestion progresses in the small intestine where the liver and gallbladder contribute bile that emulsifies fat, and the pancreas and small intestine donate enzymes that break down food to nutrients. Bacteria in the colon break down certain fibers. The healthy digestive system can adjust to almost any diet and handle any combination of foods with ease. The mechanical and chemical actions of the digestive tract efficiently break down foods to nutrients, and large nutrients to their smaller building blocks. The

[1] Contributed by Mary Ellen Clark and Sharon Rady Rolfes

digestive system feeds the rest of the body and is itself sensitive to malnutrition. The folds and villi of the small intestine enlarge its surface area to facilitate nutrient absorption through countless cells to the blood and lymph, which deliver nutrients to all the body's cells.

3.6 **Name some common digestive problems and offer suggestions for dietary alterations that may improve them.**
Maintenance of a healthy digestive tract requires preventing or responding to symptoms with a carefully chosen diet and sound medical care when problems arise.

3.7 **Identify the excretory functions of the lungs, liver, kidneys, and bladder, and state why they are important to maintain normal body functioning.**
The kidneys adjust the blood's composition in response to the body's needs, disposing of everyday wastes and helping remove toxins.

3.8 **Identify glycogen and fat as the two forms of nutrients stored in the body, and identify the liver, muscles, and adipose tissue as the body tissues that store them.**
The body stores limited amounts of carbohydrate as glycogen in muscle and liver cells. The body stores large quantities of fat in fat cells. To nourish a body's systems, nutrients from outside must be supplied through a human being's conscious food choices.

3.9 **Define the term *moderate alcohol consumption*, and discuss the potential health effects, both negative and positive, associated with this level of drinking.**

Critical Thinking Questions

1. *You go to your grandmother's house and when you walk inside, you smell freshly baked apple pie. Your mouth begins to water and your stomach begins to rumble. You are hungry but you didn't really pay attention to your hunger until you got inside of your grandmother's house. Describe how your senses have stimulated your digestive system to notice the hunger.*

   The senses of sight and smell can send a signal to the hypothalamus in the brain. This portion of the brain also monitors the body for available water and nutrients in the blood. If the blood glucose or amino acid levels are low, the hypothalamus will send signals to the digestive system. This will cause the stomach to release its digestive juices and it will start churning. This produces hunger pangs that will encourage you to eat.

2. *Why are malnourished people often more susceptible to colds or other infectious diseases?*

   The immune system needs to be healthy in order to protect people from infectious disease. The blood contains white blood cells that specifically attack bacteria and viruses. There are other white blood cells that engulf and destroy foreign particles such as bacteria in the body. These cells need to be replenished on a regular basis, so the diet must supply enough protein and vitamins to allow for the development of functional white blood cells. People who lack either protein or vitamins may not produce enough white blood cells to protect their body from infection.

3. *Describe how a piece of steak in your mouth can become an amino acid in your blood that your cells can use to build muscle tissue, insulin, or other hormones.*

   The piece of steak is moistened and ripped up into smaller pieces as it is chewed in the mouth. Protein digestion does not begin until the food reaches the stomach, where proteins in the steak are scrambled (denatured) by hydrochloric acid. This opens up the steak proteins such that the stomach's pepsin enzyme can start to break the amino acid chains of the protein apart. The steak protein is the consistency of water when it leaves the stomach. The smaller peptide fragments are then broken down further in the small intestine by the action of proteases that originate from the pancreas. The individual amino acids are absorbed through the cells of the small intestine into the blood. The cells of the pancreas can use amino acids from the blood to make insulin to control the blood glucose. The muscle cells can incorporate new amino acids into muscle fibers. This is possible because the cell's ribosomes can build new proteins from pools of amino acids in the cell cytoplasm.

4. *Describe how the body may make use of or store energy-yielding nutrients in the following two situations:*

   a. *A person has eaten a high-carbohydrate meal and is now running a marathon.*

   The body will store as much glucose as it can in the form of glycogen. This stored form of glucose is found in the muscles and liver. As this person starts to run, her liver cells will break down glycogen into glucose, which will be converted into ATP (energy) for the muscles. The body can also break down fat from fat cells located under the skin and within the muscle tissue. The resulting fatty acids can be broken down to release ATP (energy) that will supply the muscles as well.

   b. *A person has eaten a high-carbohydrate meal and is now playing video games for several days.*

   The glucose will initially be used immediately for energy or stored in the form of glycogen. (An abundance of blood glucose will allow fats in the meal to be stored in fat cells while the other cells utilize the glucose.) Once the cells' energy needs are met and the glycogen storage capacity of the liver and muscle tissues has been exceeded, any remaining glucose will then be converted to fatty acids and will be stored in the form of fat.

5. a. *Describe how the body's major organ systems work together to get glucose from the digestive system to the muscle cells of the leg.*

   The digestive system must break down carbohydrate to glucose. This glucose is absorbed into the blood. The cardiovascular system must move the glucose from the digestive system to the rest of the body, including the muscle tissue. The insulin from the pancreas stimulates the muscle cells to take up glucose for use.

   b. *What other body systems are necessary for the muscle cell to make use of the glucose by producing energy such that it does not tire?*

   The muscle cells can break down glucose completely in the presence of oxygen to produce energy. The respiratory system (lungs) must deliver oxygen to the red blood cells and the cardiovascular system must deliver the red blood cells with their oxygen to the muscle tissue. The respiratory, cardiovascular, and urinary systems must remove waste products from the cells to be released from the body

6. *How does malnutrition affect the function of the digestive system and why does malnutrition result in a vicious cycle?*

   The microvilli of the small intestine break down and are not easily repaired if the diet lacks carbohydrates, vitamins, minerals, or protein. The absorptive area of the small intestine shrinks to a tenth of its original size. This can lead to further malnutrition because, even when more nourishing food becomes available, the digestive system may not be able to absorb the needed nutrients.

Controversy Discussion Questions

1. *Describe any 2 harmful, short-term and 2 harmful, long-term effects of chronic, excessive alcohol use. How do these effects impact the health of the person overall?*

   Short-term effects of excessive alcohol use include increased risks of being in accidents, being involved in violent activity, or engaging in risky behaviors that can damage health in the long run. Alcohol can severely dehydrate body tissues, which can lead to the unpleasant symptoms of a hangover.

   Long-term effects of excessive alcohol use include damage to almost every major organ system, and especially to the liver. A heavy drinker may develop fatty liver, which can progress to fibrosis and cirrhosis, which is irreversible damage. Alcohol can also prevent a person from consuming enough vitamins and minerals. The brain and heart can be affected as well. Heavy drinkers are more likely to develop dementia and have high blood pressure that can lead to enlargement of the heart.

2. *Why is moderate drinking considered 1 drink/day for women but 2 drinks/day for men? Give any 2 reasons.*

   Men have more alcohol dehydrogenase (ADH) enzyme in their stomach than women. ADH breaks down alcohol into acetaldehyde, which does not have the same effect on the brain or body as alcohol.

Men have more lean muscle tissue than women. Lean tissue helps to dilute alcohol within the body more effectively than fat tissue.

3. *Describe any 3 effects that alcohol can have on the liver. Which of these are long-term and which are short-term effects?*

   Excess alcohol can lead to liver tissue inflammation due to the activity of the alcohol-metabolizing enzymes.

   Excess alcohol can cause fats to accumulate in the liver, leading to **fatty liver**. This condition can interfere with the liver's ability to metabolize lipids and other nutrients in the blood.

   Long-standing inflammation of liver tissue along with the toxic effects of alcohol can lead to the formation of scar tissue in the liver. If this **fibrosis** is recognized early on and alcohol consumption is stopped, then liver tissue can regenerate and recover. If liver fibrosis continues, the healthy liver tissue is replaced with scar tissue, and the liver cannot recover. This condition is known as **cirrhosis** of the liver and is not reversible!

4. a. *Why is alcohol considered fattening?*

   The body will use alcohol as a source of energy before all other nutrients such as carbohydrates or fats because the body will want to rid itself of the toxic alcohol first. If alcohol is consumed with excess fats or sugars, the body will use the alcohol for energy and store the excess fats and carbohydrates in the form of fat in the abdominal area.

   b. *If someone has a beer belly and drinks quite a bit, why are they likely deficient in B vitamins and in vitamin A?*

   Long-term alcohol use can damage the liver tissue, decreasing its ability to convert beta-carotene to active vitamin A. Liver cells have a reduced capacity to process vitamin A to active forms that the body can use. Alcohol contains few nutrients but provides many empty calories. Many alcoholics do not eat enough food to provide them with the vitamins and minerals that their bodies need. A form of thiamin deficiency known as Wernicke-Korsakoff syndrome common in alcoholics resolves if the person stops drinking and ingests more thiamin. Excess alcohol can cause a release of folate from the liver into the blood. The kidneys excrete the folate from the body and so the body's cells and tissues are further damaged by the folate deficiency.

Worksheet Answer Key

Worksheet 3-1: Fiber Supplement Label Analysis

1. This product is used to promote regularity or prevent constipation.
2. a. Insoluble fiber does not dissolve in water.
   b. Skins of fruits such as apples, corn, or celery.
   c. Insoluble fiber helps to bulk up the waste products so that they pass more easily through the colon.
3. a. Gluten is a protein found in wheat products that can irritate the small intestine in some individuals.
   b. People who are sensitive to gluten can use this product without worrying about the effects of gluten in their digestive system.
   c. Celiac disease
4. a. Flaxseed
   b. A good source of omega-3 and essential fatty acids that the body cannot produce on its own.
5. There is a choking hazard associated with this product if it is not prepared with enough water. It is also important to drink water with a fiber supplement to avoid dehydration, since fiber draws water into the gut.

Worksheet 3-2: Intake Analysis—Digestive Health

1. a. For A: too low in fiber, omega-3 and -6 essential fatty acids, and vitamin C
   For F: too low in fiber, thiamin, folate, vitamin C, magnesium, and potassium

   b. Fiber: whole-grain cereals, whole-grain pastas, fruits such as apples, or others
   Essential fatty acids: fatty fish like salmon or sardines, nuts, or vegetable oils
   Vitamin C: oranges, strawberries, or sweet peppers (also contribute fiber)

Folate: green vegetables, red peppers, fruits
Thiamin: nuts, fish, berries
Potassium: green leafy vegetables, fruits, other vegetables, fish, eggs
Magnesium: green leafy vegetables, fruits, other vegetables, fish, eggs

c. For A: Include more fruits, vegetables, and nuts
For F: Include more fruits, vegetables, nuts, and whole grains as breads or cereals

2. Diverticulosis, constipation, colon polyps, or hemorrhoids

Worksheet 3-4: Chapter 3 Review Crossword Puzzle

1. gallbladder
2. elimination
3. salivary
4. accessory
5. cirrhosis
6. inflammation
7. glycogen
8. phagocytes
9. ethanol
10. A: hypothalamus, D: heartburn
11. pancreas
12. bicarbonate
13. pyloric valve

Learning Activities & Project Ideas

Activity 3-1: Demonstration of the Digestive System[2] LO 3.5

Coil a 26-foot rope, hose, or tube in a small bag. Pull the rope out of the bag and instruct the students to guess how long the entire alimentary canal is. Have the students pass the rope down the rows of the classroom until the full rope is exposed. The rope could have unique markings in sections that correspond to the length of the esophagus, small intestine, and large intestine.

Activity 3-2: Evaluation of Products for Digestive Problems[2] LO 3.6

Have students bring over-the-counter products designed to treat common digestive problems (heartburn, constipation, diarrhea, hemorrhoids). Ask the students when they would use each of these medicines. Discuss the appropriate and inappropriate uses of these medications and adverse health implications associated with misuse and overuse of certain medications. For example, overuse of medications for heartburn may foster a basic environment in the stomach and therefore hinder iron absorption. Present alternative dietary or lifestyle solutions to these common digestive problems as presented in Chapter 3.

Activity 3-3: "Who Wants to Be a Millionaire?" as a Tool for Review (and Fun)[3]

Purpose: To review material, motivate students to study, and have fun.
Tools: Microsoft Power Point with animation and sound effects.

Setup: A computer projection system is used for the questions and an overhead projector for the point scale. The room is set up with a chair facing a table, which faces the projection screen. The student selected to play sits in the chair and has the three lifelines taped to the edge of the table. Once a student uses that lifeline, it is flipped over.

How To Play: Selection of the student to play begins with the "fast finger" round. Every student receives an index card. The question may relate specifically to the subject matter or may be something like university trivia. The question is shown on the screen and the students have approximately 10-20 seconds to write down their answer (see sample). The correct answer is shown and every student who answers correctly puts the index card in a hat or jar. One name is then randomly selected to play. The play then follows the format of the television game (see sample questions). The lifelines are Ask The Audience (take a class vote on the possible answers), 50/50 (take away two of the wrong answers), and Phone a Friend (ask anyone in the classroom). The point scale (see sample) shows the levels of bonus points to be added to the upcoming exam. If a student becomes a millionaire, he or she receives 100 points (the value of the test).

Student Reaction: Student comments have been very positive. It helps them review material and they have really enjoyed the game and the effort put into its construction. There is a lot of encouragement from the class for the student player. A few students in different semesters became "Millionaires" and the class cheered for them!

---

[2] Contributed by Lori W. Turner, Ph.D., R.D., University of Alabama

[3] Contributed by Dr. Inza Fort and Dr. Ro Di Brezzo, University of Arkansas

Comments: Although the initial construction was quite time consuming, once a set is done with the animation and sound effects, the file can be copied and new questions substituted.

Point Scale:

$1,000,000	= 100 pts.	$32,000	= 10 pts.	$1,000	= 5 pts.
$500,000	= 25 pts.	$16,000	= 9 pts.	$500	= 4 pts.
$250,000	= 20 pts.	$8,000	= 8 pts.	$300	= 3 pts.
$125,000	= 15 pts.	$4,000	= 7 pts.	$200	= 2 pts.
$64,000	= 12 pts.	$2,000	= 6 pts.	$100	= 1 pt.

Chapter Lecture Outline

I. Introduction
   A. Your genes, in the form of DNA, direct your body's development and basic functions.
   B. Many of your genes are ancient in origin and have not changed for thousands of centuries.
   C. There is no guarantee that a diet haphazardly chosen from today's foods will meet the needs of your "ancient" body.
   D. You need to learn how your body works, what it needs, and how to select foods to meet its needs.

II. The Body's Cells
   A. The human body is made of trillions of cells.
      1. Cells work in cooperation to support the whole body.
      2. Cells need: Energy, oxygen, nutrients (essential), water
      3. All cells have different life spans and replenish themselves at different rates.
   B. Genes Control Functions
      1. Gene – a blueprint that directs the production of a piece of protein machinery
      2. Different genes are active in different cells.
         a. In a small intestinal cell, genes that encode digestive enzymes are active while the genes for keratin (a protein that makes up skin and nails) are silent.
         b. In fat cells, genes that encode enzymes for fat metabolism are active while the genes for digestive enzymes are silent.
      3. A gene variation (mutation) can cause disease: e.g., phenylketonuria – an inborn error of metabolism that requires a special diet low in the amino acid phenylalanine
      4. Genes and nutrients interact in ways that affect health.
      5. Certain vitamins and minerals influence genes to make a protein.
   C. Cells, Tissues, Organs, Systems
      1. Cells are organized into tissues that perform specialized tasks.
      2. Tissues are grouped into organs.
      3. Organs work together to form body systems.

III. The Body Fluids and the Cardiovascular System
   A. Blood and lymph deliver nutrients to all the body's cells and carry waste materials away from them.
   B. Blood also delivers oxygen to cells.
   C. The cardiovascular system ensures that these fluids circulate properly among all organs.
   D. One needs adequate fluid intake to ensure efficient circulation to and from the body's cells.
   E. The blood cells, including red blood cells that carry oxygen to the body's cells, need to be replenished and require adequate nutrition.

IV. The Hormonal And Nervous Systems
   A. Introduction
      1. Blood carries chemical messengers, hormones, from one system of cells to another.
      2. Hormones communicate changing conditions that demand responses from the body organs.
   B. What Do Hormones Have To Do With Nutrition?
      1. Glands secrete hormones.
      2. Hormones affect nutrition by:
         a. Regulating hunger and affecting appetite

   b. Carrying messages to digestive system
   c. Regulating blood glucose levels – pancreas (a gland) secretes insulin & glucagon (hormones)
   d. Hormones affect women's menstrual cycles and the associated fluctuations in their appetites.
   e. Overly thin women experience hormone changes that can cause their bones to lose minerals and become weak.

C. How Does the Nervous System Interact with Nutrition?
   1. Nervous system's role is coordinated by the brain
      a. Cortex – senses hunger and appetite
      b. Hypothalamus – monitors many body conditions, including nutrients and water availability
   2. Fight-or-flight reaction or stress response – When danger is sensed, nerves release epinephrine and norepinephrine.
      a. Metabolisms speeds up
      b. Pupils of eyes widen
      c. Breathing quickens
      d. Muscles tense
      e. Blood glucose increases
      f. Digestive system shuts down

V. The Immune System
   A. A properly functioning immune system enables the body to resist infectious disease caused by unwanted microbes
   B. Immune Defenses – White blood cells
      1. Phagocytes engulf pathogens and foreign particles and leave a chemical trail that helps other immune cells to destroy the source of the infection.
      2. Lymphocytes are white blood cells that specifically destroy pathogens.
         a. T cell - killer T cells destroy pathogens and helper T cells coordinate the function of both T and B cells
         b. B cells secrete protein antibodies that react specifically with pathogen and assist other white blood cells in eliminating the pathogens
   C. Inflammation – A typical inflammatory response helps the body's defense system contain pathogens and is a normal response to cellular injury.
      1. Causes redness, pain, swelling, and loss of function as its signs and symptoms
      2. Low-level chronic inflammation has been discovered to be associated with heart disease, diabetes, and severe arthritis.
         a. May be promoted or inhibited by lipids or phytochemicals
         b. Often associated with an overweight condition

VI. The Digestive System
   A. Taste buds guide you in judging whether foods are acceptable: Sweet, sour, bitter, salty, savory or *umami*
   B. Why Do People Like Sugar, Salt, and Fat?
      1. Sweet, salty, and fatty foods are universally and instinctively desired and often lead to overeating
      2. Bitter and sour are often disliked
   C. The Digestive Tract
      1. A flexible, muscular tube that digests food and absorbs its nutrients and some nonnutrients
      2. 26 feet long!!
   D. The Mechanical Aspect of Digestion
      1. Begins in the mouth with chewing
      2. Saliva moistens food for easier swallowing.
      3. Peristalsis – wavelike muscular squeezing of the digestive tract that pushes their contents along
      4. Stomach and intestines liquefy foods by mashing and squeezing.
      5. The stomach's pyloric valve at its lower end controls the exit of the chyme.
      6. Chyme is squirted into small intestine after a few hours in the stomach
      7. Small intestine contracts to move contents to large intestine (colon)
      8. Colon's main roles: Reabsorb water, absorb minerals
      9. Rectum – stores feces until excretion
      10. Feces – fiber, undigested material, sloughed intestinal cells, bacteria

E. The Chemical Aspect of Digestion
1. Introduction
a. Several organs of the digestive system secrete juices that contain enzymes.
b. Salivary glands, stomach, pancreas, liver, small intestine
2. In the Mouth
a. Digestion begins in the mouth.
b. Saliva contains an enzyme that begins starch digestion, and another enzyme that initiates a little digestion of fat.
3. In the Stomach
a. Protein digestion begins in the stomach.
b. Gastric juice contains water, enzymes, and hydrochloric acid.
c. Question?? Why aren't the stomach lining cells digested along with food? (protected by mucus)
4. In the Intestine
a. Small intestine – the organ of digestion and absorption
1. Gallbladder sends bile, an emulsifier, into the intestine
2. Pancreas sends bicarbonate to neutralize stomach acid that entered small intestine
3. Pancreas sends the largest number and variety of digestive enzymes to act on chemical bonds that hold the large nutrients together
4. Intestinal cell walls also have digestive enzymes on their surfaces.
5. Absorption of carbohydrate, fat, protein, vitamins and most minerals occurs.
6. Water, fiber, and minerals remain in the tract.
b. In large intestine (colon)
1. Some fiber is broken down by resident bacteria
2. Small fat fragments released from the fiber provide a tiny bit of energy

F. Are Some Food Combinations More Easily Digested Than Others?
1. The digestive system adjusts to whatever mixture of foods is presented to it.
2. All foods, regardless of identity, are broken down by enzymes into the basic molecules that make them up.
3. The pancreas can adjust its output of digestive enzymes based on the nutrient content of the food leaving the stomach.
4. A higher-carbohydrate chyme will receive more starch- and sugar-digesting enzymes from the pancreas.

G. If "I Am What I Eat," Then How Does A Peanut Butter Sandwich Become "Me"?
1. Introduction
a. Digestion and absorption are remarkably efficient.
b. Within about 24 to 48 hours of eating, a healthy body digests and absorbs about 90 percent of the energy nutrients in a meal.
c. Let's follow a peanut butter and banana sandwich on whole-wheat, sesame bread through the tract.
2. In the Mouth – for less than a minute
a. Teeth/tongue crush and mash food
b. Digestion of starch to sugar in bread, banana, and peanut butter begins
3. In the Stomach – about 1-2 hours
a. Food is collected in upper storage area
b. Starch digestion stops in presence of gastric juices
c. Food enters digesting area of stomach
d. Proteins in bread, PB, and seeds are unwound
e. Enzymes clip proteins
f. Chyme
4. In the Small Intestine – about 7-8 hours
a. Sugars from banana cross lining of small intestine
b. Bile from liver arrives to blend with fat from PB and seeds
c. Pancreas and intestinal cells send digestive enzymes
d. Small units from energy nutrients absorbed
e. Vitamins and minerals absorbed
5. In the Large Intestine (Colon) – about 12-14 hours
a. Fiber fragments, fluid, and some minerals are absorbed

   b. Fiber in seeds, bread, PB, and banana is partly digested by bacteria
   c. Most fiber excreted as feces

H. Absorption and Transport of Nutrients
   1. The body cells await the delivery of the absorbed nutrients.
   2. Cells of the intestinal tract absorb nutrients and deposit them in the blood and lymph.
   3. The Intestine's Absorbing Surface – Villi and microvilli increase the absorbing surface of the small intestine.
   4. Nutrient Transport in the Blood and Lymph Vessels
      a. Lymphatic vessels initially transport most of the products of fat digestion and a few vitamins, later delivering them to the bloodstream.
      b. The blood vessels carry the products of carbohydrate and protein digestion, most vitamins, and the minerals from the digestive tract to the liver.
   5. Nourishment of the Digestive Tract
      a. If there is a long-term lack of fiber, protein, or carbohydrates in the food that reaches the small intestine, the absorptive surface of the small intestine will decrease dramatically.
      b. This will worsen a condition of malnutrition.

I. A Letter From Your Digestive Tract
   1. Why do we occasionally belch, have gas, and the hiccups? <u>Answer</u>: eat or drink too fast, chew gum, drink carbonated sodas
   2. What is a heartburn? <u>Answer</u>: acidic stomach juices back up into the esophagus
   3. What should you do to avoid heartburn or GERD? Lie down after eating, overeat, smoke, or lose weight? <u>Answer</u>: lose weight
   4. What effect do these have on the body?
      a. Antacids – Antacids temporarily neutralize stomach acid.
      b. Acid reducers – Acid reducers restrict ability of stomach to produce acid.
      c. Laxatives – Laxatives promote a bowel movement.
   5. What is irritable bowel syndrome? <u>Answer</u>: Intermittent disturbance of bowel function, especially diarrhea alternating with constipation
   6. What happens when you choke? <u>Answer</u>: Food gets lodged in the windpipe, blocking flow of air into/out of the lungs
   7. What do you do to help a choking person? <u>Answer</u>: The Heimlich maneuver

VII. The Excretory System

A. Cells generate a number of wastes that need to be eliminated
   1. Carbon dioxide leaves via the lungs
   2. Other wastes are processed by the liver and leave the body with feces or sent to the kidneys for disposal in the urine

B. Kidneys
   1. Remove waste and water
   2. Adjust blood's composition
   3. Nutrients, including water, and exercise help keep the kidneys healthy

VIII. Storage Systems

A. Introduction
   1. Humans are designed to eat at intervals of about 4 to 6 hours
   2. Cells need nutrients 24 hours a day
   3. Body's major storage sites for nutrients are: Liver, muscles, fat cells

B. When I Eat More Than My Body Needs, What Happens to the Extra Nutrients?
   1. Nutrients from the digestive system arrive at the liver
   2. Liver processes nutrients
   3. Excess nutrients are converted to: Glycogen (a carbohydrate) or fat
      a. Liver glycogen can sustain cell activities when the time between meals is long.
      b. Muscle cells make and store glycogen for their own use.
      c. Fat made in the liver is shipped to body cells for energy and excess is stored in adipose tissue.

C. Variations in Nutrient Stores
   1. Some nutrients are stored in the body in much larger quantities than others.
   2. Some vitamins are stored without limit, even in toxic quantities, in the liver and fat.
   3. Bones store reserves of calcium and other minerals.
   4. Fat tissue has virtually infinite storage capacity.

IX. Conclusion
   A. In addition to the systems just described, the body has many more: Bones, muscles, reproductive, etc.
   B. All body systems have to be supplied nutrients from the outside through a human's conscious food choices.

X. Controversy: Alcohol and Nutrition: Do the Benefits Outweigh the Risks?
   A. U.S. Alcohol Consumption
      1. On average, people in the United States consume from 6 to 10 percent of their total daily energy intake as alcohol
      2. People follow several possible drinking pattenrs:
         a. Some don't drink at all
         b. Social drinkers – choose alcohol over other beverages in social settings
         c. Heavy drinking or binge drinking
            1. Seen in college-age people
            2. One in 6 adults is a binge drinking
         d. Moderate drinking is defined as:
            1. No more than 1 drink a day for the average woman
            2. No more than 2 drinks a day for the average male
   B. Does Moderate Alcohol Use Benefit Health?
      1. Introduction
         a. Alcohol in moderation may reduce risk of: Heart attacks, strokes, dementia, diabetes, osteoporosis
         b. May also be associated with increased mental acuity
      2. The influence of age
         a. Benefits of alcohol intakes are seen in middle age people who may be developing cardiovascular problems
         b. Alcohol use in younger people is associated with increased risk of death by accidents or homicides with little benefits to cardiovascular health
      3. The Influence of Drinking Patterns:
         a. Light moderate drinkers in France may have a lower risk of heart disease
         b. Heavy episodic drinkers may be increasing their risk of heart disease even if their alcohol intake is similar in amount to that of light moderate drinkers.
      4. Is Wine a Special Case?
         a. Wine, in moderation, may contain high potassium and phytochemicals that may help maintain normal blood pressure
         b. Large amounts of wine intake may cause inflammation and elevation of blood pressure
         c. Large amounts of alcohol may lead to digestive tract cancers
   C. What Is Alcohol?
      1. Class of chemicals whose names end in *-ol*
      2. Alcohols easily penetrate the cells' outer lipid membrane
      3. Denature proteins and kill cells once inside them – Useful disinfectants and antiseptics
      4. The alcohol of alcoholic beverages is ethanol
      5. Alcohol in the brain produces euphoria
      6. Who should never drink alcohol? – those at risk for problem drinking
         a. People who cannot moderate their drinking
         b. People younger than the legal drinking age
         c. Women who are pregnant or may become pregnant
         d. People taking medicines that could interact with alcohol
         e. People with medical conditions like liver disease or high blood cholesterol
         f. People who need to drive or operate machinery

D. What Is a "Drink"?
  1. The relative amount of alcohol is a low percentage of the beverage's volume
  2. The percentage of alcohol is stated as proof.
    a. Proof equals twice the percentage of alcohol.
    b. For example, 100 proof liquor is 50 percent alcohol.
  3. Amount of beverage containing ½ oz. ethanol
    a. Figure C3-1 shows what a one drink serving looks like
    b. The alcohol of alcoholic beverages is ethanol

E. Drinking Patterns
  1. Defining Moderation
    a. Tolerance differs among individuals
    b. Women have lower tolerance than men
    c. Asians and Native Americans have lower tolerance than average
    d. No more than 2 drinks a day for the average male
    e. No more than 1 drink a day for the average woman
  2. Problem Drinkers and Alcoholism
    a. People should be on the look out for symptoms in others
    b. See Table C3-3
  3. Heavy Epidsodic Drinking
    a. Defined as 4 drinks in a row for women and five for men
    b. Also defined as 14.5 drinks a week on average and not spaced out.
    c. Binge drinking accounts for 90% of all alcohol consumed by young people.
  4. Harms from Heavy Episodic Drinking – Results in more accidents and risky behaviors

F. Immediate Effects of Alcohol
  1. Alcohol Enters the Body
    a. Alcohol needs no digestion and diffuses through the stomach walls and reaches the brain within a minute.
    b. Too high a dose triggers the body's response against poisons – vomiting.
    c. If it is drunk slowly enough, vomiting will not occur.
    d. To drink socially and avoid intoxication:
      1. Drink slowly
      2. Eat food
      3. Add ice to drinks or water to dilute them
      4. Alternate alcoholic with nonalcoholic beverages
  2. Alcohol Dehydrates the Tissues
    a. Alcohol increases urine output (by depressing the brain's production of antidiuretic hormone)
    b. Water and minerals such as magnesium, potassium, calcium, and zinc are lost

G. Alcohol Arrives in the Brain (Figure C3-2)
  1. If a person drinks slowly enough, the alcohol, after absorption, will be collected by the liver and processed without much effect on the rest of the body.
  2. A Lethal Dose of Alcohol – If a person drinks more rapidly, alcohol bypasses the liver and flows to the brain. See Figure C3-3 that shows blood alcohol levels
  3. Alcohol Toxicity, Oxidative Stress, and the Brain
    a. Excess, long-term alcohol use can cause oxidative damage to the brain tissue
    b. This can cause inflammation of the brain tissue resulting in the shrinkage of functional brain tissue
  4. Alcohol and Accidents – Alcohol is a key contributor to many types of accidents as well as violent behavior
    a. 20% of boating deaths
    b. 23% of suicides
    c. 39% of traffic deaths (Figure C3-4)
    d. 40% of home fire deaths
    e. 47% of homicides
    f. 65% of domestic violence incidents

H. Alcohol Arrives in the Body
   1. Introduction
      a. The liver cells make the largest share of the body's alcohol-processing machinery
      b. Liver detoxifies alcohol
   2. A Liver Enzyme for Alcohol Breakdown –Alcohol dehydrogenase (ADH)
      a. Removes hydrogens.
      b. Handles about 80 percent of alcohol.
      c. Converts ethanol to acetaldehyde
   3. Alcohol Breakdown in the Stomach – stomach enzyme ADH (men make more than women) breaks down some alcohol before it reaches the bloodstream
   4. Excretion in Breath and Urine – Breath and urine excrete the remaining 10 percent.
   5. Rate of Alcohol Clearance
      a. Body takes about 1.5 hours to metabolize one drink. Depends on:
         1. Person's size
         2. Drinking history
         3. State of health
         4. Male or female (males have more ADH in the stomach walls)
      b. Only the liver can dispose of significant amounts of alcohol.
         1. Walking and fresh air have no effect as muscles do not detoxify alcohol.
         2. Drinking coffee will not affect the rate.

I. Alcohol Affects the Liver
   1. Fatty Liver
      a. Upon exposure to alcohol, the liver speeds up its synthesis of fatty acids.
      b. Alcohol detoxification in the liver can produce free radicals, which can cause inflammation and damage to the liver tissue
      c. Causes fatty liver
   2. Liver Fibrosis – can lead to cirrhosis
      a. Fibrosis is build up of fibrous scar tissue in the liver but is reversible with abstinence from alcohol and good nutrition
      b. Cirrhosis is the hardening and death of liver cells which is not reversible

J. The Hangover – Caused by:
   1. Congeners and Dehydration
   2. Formaldehyde and Methanol – formaldehyde arises from methanol which forms when too much alcohol overruns the body's detoxification enzymes
   3. The Sure Cure for Hangover = time; best cure is to prevent it (drink less alcohol the next time)

K. Alcohol's Long-Term Effects on the Body
   1. Effects in Pregnancy – Devastating to a fetus
   2. Effects on Heart and Brain – Brain disease such as dementia; heart disease
   3. Cancer – Increased risk of several types of cancers, including breast cancer in women
   4. Long-Term Effects of Alcohol Abuse
      a. Bladder, kidney, pancreas, and prostate damage
      b. Bone deterioration and osteoporosis
      c. Brain disease, CNS damage, strokes
      d. Deterioration of testicles and adrenal glands
      e. Diabetes (type 2)
      f. Disease of heart muscles
      g. Feminization and sexual impotence in men
      h. Impaired immune response
      i. Impaired memory and balance
      j. Increased risk of death from all causes
      k. Malnutrition
      l. Nonviral hepatitis
      m. Skin rashes and sores
      n. Ulcers and inflammation of the stomach and intestines

L. Alcohol's Effect on Nutrition
   1. Alcohol and Appetite – Moderate amounts of alcohol may improve appetite for those who have trouble eating enough
   2. Alcohol and Body Weight
      a 7 calories per gram
      b. Alcohol promotes fat storage in the abdominal area – the "beer belly"
      c. See Table C3-6 for Calories in Alcoholic Beverages and Mixers
   3. Alcohol's Effects on Vitamins
      a. Not likely a person will eat enough food if they drink a lot
      b. Triggers the release of histamines and excess stomach acid, which can promote tissue inflammation
      c. Liver damage can cause the reduced activation of vitamin D and vitamin A
      d. The kidneys release too many needed minerals such as magnesium, calcium, potassium, and zinc
      e Reduces the absorption of folate, thiamin, and vitamin B_{12}, among others
         1. Reduced folate in the blood causes a build-up of a compound associated with increased risk of cardiovascular disease
         2. Wernicke-Korsakoff syndrome – a thiamin deficiency
         3. Pellagra, beriberi, scurvy, protein-energy malnutrition

M. The Final Word – Some benefits of moderate alcohol consumption for middle-aged adults

Worksheet 3-1: Fiber Supplement Label Analysis

Instructions: Use the label to answer questions 1-5 on a separate sheet of paper.

Supplement Facts

Serving Size 1 scoop (approx. 11g)
Servings Per Container 30

Amount Per Serving	
Calories 40	Calories from Fat 9
	% Daily Value*
Total Fat 1g	**2%**
Total Carbohydrate 5g	**2%**
Dietary Fiber 4g	**16%**
Soluble Fiber 1g	
Insoluble Fiber 3g	
Protein 3g	**6%**
Proprietary Blend 11.3g	
Organic Flaxseed	**
Organic Oat Bran	**
Organic Acacia Gum	**
Vitamin A 4% •	Vitamin C 2%
Calcium 16% •	Iron 4%

* Percent Daily Values are based on a 2,000 calorie diet. Your Daily Values may be higher or lower depending on your calorie needs.
**Daily Value not established.

Directions: Take one scoop in 8 ounces of water in the morning. May be repeated at midday and in the evening, if necessary. Drink plenty of water while using this product.

Note: This organic fiber blend should be consumed with a full glass of water or juice. Consuming this fiber supplement without enough liquid could cause choking. Do not consume this fiber supplement if you have difficulty swallowing.

1. What is the intended use of this product?
2. a. What is meant by the term "insoluble fiber"?
   b. What is a natural source of insoluble fiber?
   c. How does insoluble fiber help the body?
3. a. What is gluten?
   b. Why is the claim "gluten free" advertised on this product?
   c. What condition can be made worse by gluten?
4. a. What is the source of fat in this product?
   b. What are the health benefits of this fat source?
5. What is the concern with taking this product without enough water?

Worksheet 3-2: Intake Analysis—Digestive Health

Eating Plan A (1 Day's Intake)	Eating Plan F (1 Day's Intake)
1 cup of Corn Flakes cereal 1 cup of 1% fat milk 2 cups of coffee 2 slices of whole-wheat bread 2 ounces thinly sliced baked ham 2 ounces cheddar jalapeño cheese 8 ounces chocolate milk 3 12-ounce beers 2 beef and cheese enchiladas	2 scrambled eggs 1 cup whole milk 2 slices bacon 2 1-ounce Slim Jims 6 ounces lean ground beef 2 ounces provolone cheese ¼ cup blue cheese dressing 12 ounces water 2 ounces cheddar cheese cubes 6 ounces grilled chicken breasts 1 scrambled egg 1 cup lettuce ½ cup blue cheese dressing 2 ounces pork rinds 12 ounces water

Look at Eating Plans A and F:

1. a. What nutrients required for digestive health are lacking in Eating Plans A and F?

   b. What are some sources of these missing nutrients?

   c. Provide an alternative eating plan that would increase the levels of these needed nutrients.

2. What digestive conditions could be triggered by over-indulgence in diets that lack the missing nutrients?

Worksheet 3-3: Food Habits and Digestive Problems

Digestion transforms the foods we eat into nutrients and absorption moves nutrients from the GI tract into the blood. Optimal digestion and absorption depend on the good health of the digestive tract, which is affected by such lifestyle factors as sleep, physical activity, state of mind, and the meals you eat.

One common digestive tract complaint is heartburn. Consider the following information, and then answer the questions that follow.

Heartburn: How to Deal With It?![4]

Other names:.. Acid reflux, gastroesophageal reflux disease (GERD)

What is it? .... Splashing of acidic stomach contents back into the esophagus, which can irritate the delicate lining of the esophagus and cause a burning pain between the throat and chest. It can cause a cough, a sore throat, difficulty swallowing, or bad breath in some people.

What causes it? .... The sphincter between the stomach and esophagus can loosen and allow stomach contents to leak upward into the esophagus.

Some peoples' stomachs produce too much acid, which can also splash up into the esophagus. Triggers like stress, caffeine, smoking, alcohol, chocolate, greasy foods, or spicy foods can cause symptoms in some people but not the same triggers bother everyone.

What happens if it is left untreated?... The cells of the esophagus can undergo some changes due to the chronic irritation of long-term, untreated GERD. In a small percentage of people, these abnormal cells may become cancerous.

Lifestyle Options for Heartburn:

- Sit up after eating so that the stomach contents cannot leak back into the esophagus.
- Lose excess weight, which may be associated with a looser esophageal sphincter.
- Find out what foods trigger pain. Eliminate one food at a time and note if symptoms become less frequent or severe.
- Eat smaller meals, which may not expand the stomach as much.
- Wear looser clothing that will not squeeze the stomach.
- Quit smoking. Smoking may trigger the stomach to secrete more acid or weaken the esophageal sphincter.

---

[4] References: Dr. Andrew Weil's Self Healing, June 2004, pages 4-5.
Nutrition Action Health Letter, Gut Check, Volume 30 (3), April 2003, pages 3-4.

1. Identify which of these foods and food habits promote or impede healthy digestion and absorption.

Foods and Food Habits	Promote	Impede
a. Take small bites of food.	☐	☐
b. Chew thoroughly before swallowing.	☐	☐
c. Exercise immediately after eating to prevent weight gain.	☐	☐
d. Eat a low-fiber diet.	☐	☐
e. Drink plenty of fluids.	☐	☐
f. Eat a few large meals instead of several smaller ones.	☐	☐
g. Eat quickly and then lie down to rest.	☐	☐
h. Create a meal using citrus fruits and meat.	☐	☐
i. Tackle family problems at the dinner table.	☐	☐

2. Do you experience digestive distress regularly?

3. What changes can you make in your eating habits to promote digestive health?

Worksheet 3-4: Chapter 3 Review Crossword Puzzle

(clues on following page)

Across	Down
1. Organ that stores bile until it is needed for fat digestion	2. The functions of the digestive system are breakdown, absorption, and _____.
5. Permanent scarring of liver tissue is known as _____.	3. The _____ glands produce a starch-digesting enzyme known as amylase.
7. Excess glucose can be stored as _____ in the body.	4. The _____ organs of digestion never contact the food directly but assist the functions of the organs along the digestive tract.
9. Alcohol (the kind in beverages) is also referred to as _____.	6. Condition of increased heat, redness, and swelling of tissue that is seen but can be hidden too
10. Structure deep in the brain that monitors the body's needs for nutrients or water	8. White blood cells that engulf invaders (like disease-causing bacteria) and eliminate them
12. Substance released by the pancreas to neutralize acidic contents (chyme) released from the stomach	10. Occasional backflow of stomach acid into the esophagus that can be painful
13. The circular muscle of the lower stomach that regulates the flow of partly digested food into the small intestine	11. Organ that helps regulate blood glucose levels and produces enzymes for digestion of food

Handout 3-1: Where the Foods Are Broken Down

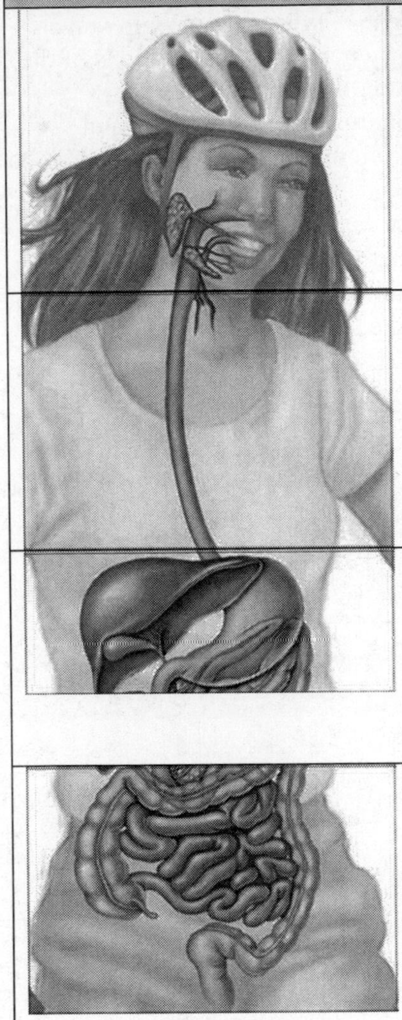

Location & Molecules	Cracker (Carbohydrates)	Peanuts (Proteins)	A Pat of Butter (Lipids)
Mouth (Salivary amylase & lingual lipase are produced in infants)	Starches are broken down into oligosaccharides	Not broken down	Triglycerides and a few saturated fatty acids
Esophagus	Just passes through	Just passes through	Just passes through
Stomach (Hydrochloric acid, pepsin, and gastric lipase)	Just sloshes along since salivary amylase is denatured by stomach acid	Proteins get scrambled (denatured) by acid; smaller polypeptides are formed due to pepsin	Still triglycerides and a few saturated fatty acids
Small Intestine (lipases, sucrase, maltase, lactase, proteases, and trypsin, many of which are produced by the pancreas)	Starches are broken down into disaccharides and then into monosaccharides	Smaller polypeptides are broken down into di- and tripeptides and then into single amino acids	Triglycerides are broken down into saturated fatty acids and glycerol
Large Intestine	Water and some minerals are absorbed into the bloodstream and the rest is eliminated	Water is absorbed into the bloodstream and the rest is eliminated	Any remaining foodstuffs are eliminated

Handout 3-2: Transport of Nutrients in Blood and Lymph

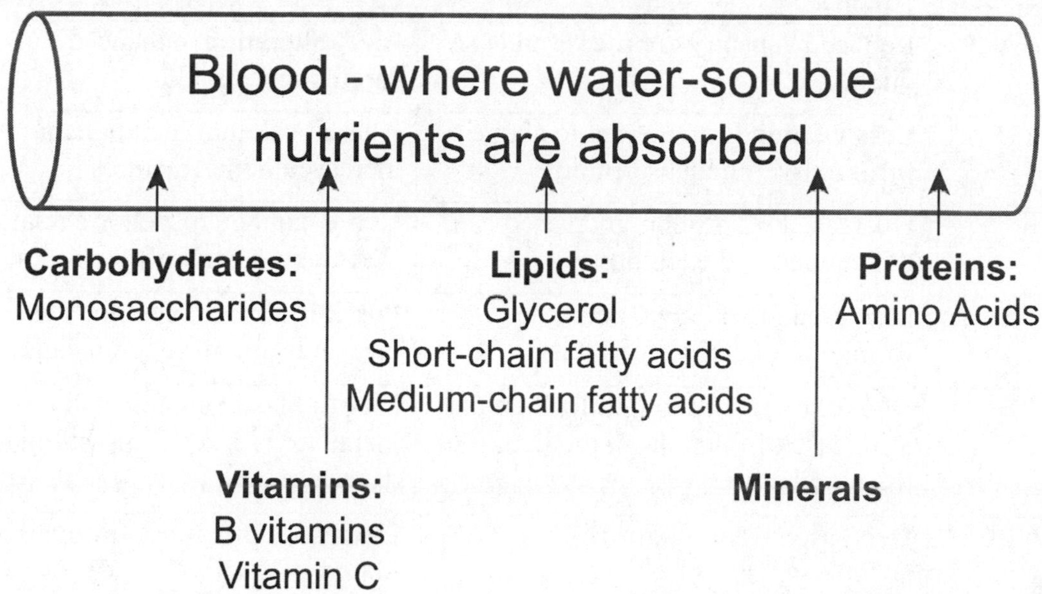

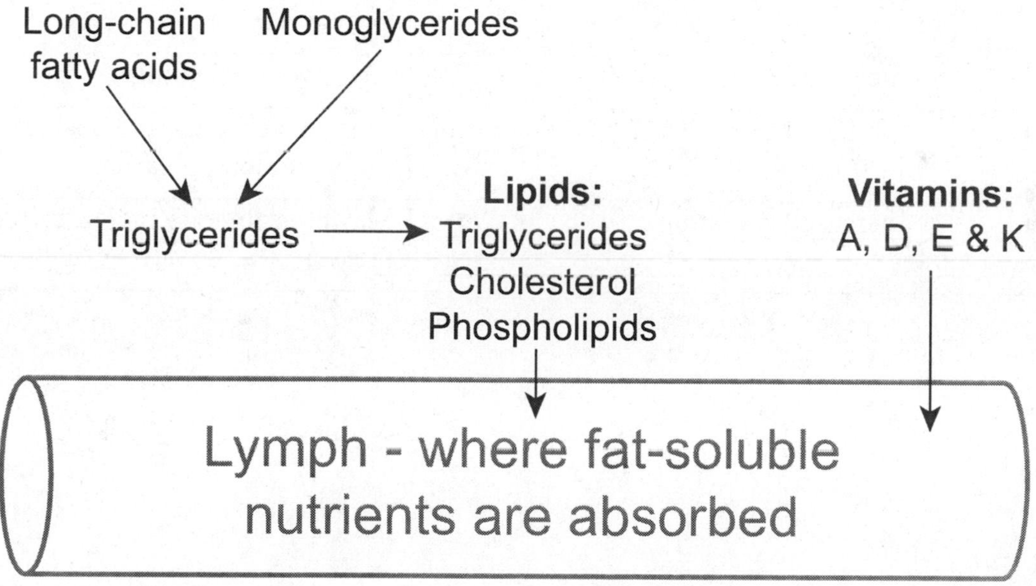

Handout 3-3: Alcohol's Effects on Nutrients in the Body[5]

Nutrient	Effect	Possible Consequence
Vitamin A	Reduced capacity to process and use vitamin A	Liver alteration, enhanced carcinogenesis
Vitamin D	Less vitamin D converted to active form in liver, malabsorption	Altered calcium metabolism, increased bone fractures
Thiamin	Decreased absorption, increased destruction and excretion	Nerve damage, psychosis related to Wernicke-Korsakoff syndrome
Pyridoxine	Increased breakdown, decreased formation of active cofactor	Possible abnormal amino acid measures and nitrogen balance
Folate	Decreased absorption, utilization due to release of folate from the liver into the blood	Megaloblastic anemia and possible increased risk of cardiovascular disease
Vitamin C	Decreased absorption	Decreased protection from ethanol toxicity
Iron	Possible overload, possible increased absorption	Buildup of iron causes damage to liver
Magnesium	Increased excretion	Electrocardiogram changes, delirium tremens (DTs)
Zinc	Increased excretion	Slow wound healing
Potassium	Increased excretion	Muscle weakness and possible elevated blood pressure
Calcium	Increased excretion	May contribute to increased blood pressure

[5] Source: Adapted from M. S. Meskin, Alcohol-Nutrient Interactions, *Nutrition and the MD*, December 1992, p. 4.

Chapter 4 – The Carbohydrates: Sugar, Starch, Glycogen, and Fiber

Quick List: IM Resources for Chapter 4

- **Class preparation resources:** learning objectives/key points, suggested activities and projects, lecture outline
- **Assignment materials:** **Related LO**
  - Critical thinking questions (with answer key) 4.2, 4.5, 4.6, 4.8
  - Discussion questions (with answers) for Controversy 4 .... 4.9
  - Worksheet 4-1: Label Analysis Carbohydrates 4.8
  - Worksheet 4-2: Intake Analysis—Carbohydrates 4.2, 4.6, 4.8
  - Worksheet 4-3: Choosing Carbohydrates with Fiber in Mind[1] 4.2, 4.8
  - Worksheet 4-4: Where Is the Sugar? 4.8
  - **New!** Worksheet 4-5: Chapter 4 Review Crossword Puzzle
- **Enrichment materials:**
  - Handout 4-1: Characteristics of Fiber[2] 4.2
  - Handout 4-2: How to Use the Exchange System to Estimate Carbohydrate[1] 4.8
  - Handout 4-3: Where Sugar Can Hide Out! 4.8

Chapter Learning Objectives and Key Points

4.1 **Compare and contrast the major types of carbohydrates in foods and in the body.**
Through photosynthesis, plants combine carbon dioxide, water, and the sun's energy to form glucose. Carbohydrates are made of carbon, hydrogen, and oxygen held together by energy-containing bonds: carbo means "carbon"; hydrate means "water." Glucose is the most important monosaccharide in the human body. Monosaccharides can be converted by the liver to other needed molecules. Starch is the storage form of glucose in plants and is also nutritive for human beings. Glycogen is the storage form of glucose in animals and human beings. Human digestive enzymes cannot break the chemical bonds of fiber. Some fiber is susceptible to fermentation by bacteria in the colon.

4.2 **Explain the important roles of carbohydrates and fiber in the body, and describe the characteristics of whole-grain foods.**
The body tissues use carbohydrates for energy and other functions. The brain and nerve tissues prefer carbohydrate as fuel, and red blood cells can use nothing else. Intakes of refined carbohydrates should be limited. Soluble fibers dissolve in water, form viscous gels, and are easily fermented by colonic bacteria. Insoluble fibers do not dissolve in water, form structural parts of plants, and are less readily fermented by colonic bacteria. Foods rich in viscous soluble fibers help control blood cholesterol. Foods rich in viscous fibers help to modulate blood glucose concentrations. Both kinds of fiber are associated with digestive tract health. Fibers in foods help to maintain digestive tract health. Eating patterns that are adequate in fiber assist the eater in maintaining a healthy body weight. Few consume sufficient fiber. The best fiber sources are whole foods, and fluid intake should increase along with fiber. Very-high-fiber vegetarian diets can pose nutritional risks for some people. Whole-grain flours retain all edible parts of grain kernels. Refined grain products are less nutritious than whole grains. A diet rich in whole grains is associated with reduced risks of overweight and certain chronic diseases.

4.3 **Explain how complex carbohydrates are broken down in the digestive tract and absorbed into the body.**
The main task of the various body systems is to convert starch and sugars to glucose to fuel the cells' work. Fermentable fibers may release gas as they are broken down by bacteria in the large intestine. In lactose intolerance, the body fails to produce sufficient amounts of the enzyme needed to digest the sugar of milk, leading to uncomfortable symptoms. People with lactose intolerance or milk allergy need alternatives that provide the nutrients of milk.

---

[1] Contributed by Sharon Rady Rolfes

[2] Contributed by Lori W. Turner, Ph.D., R.D., University of Alabama

4.4 **Describe how hormones control blood glucose concentrations during fasting and feasting, and explain the response of these hormones to various carbohydrates in the diet.**
Without glucose, the body is forced to alter its uses of protein and fats. To help supply the brain with glucose, the body breaks down its protein to make glucose and converts its fats into ketone bodies, incurring ketosis. The muscles and liver store glucose as glycogen; the liver can release glucose from its glycogen into the bloodstream. The hormones insulin and glucagon regulate blood glucose concentrations. The liver has the ability to convert glucose into fat, but under normal conditions, most excess glucose is stored as glycogen or used to meet the body's immediate needs for fuel. The glycemic index reflects the degree to which a food raises blood glucose. The concept of good and bad foods based solely on the glycemic response is an oversimplification.

4.5 **Describe the scope of the U.S. diabetes problem, and educate someone about the long- and short-term effects of untreated diabetes and prediabetes.**
Diabetes is a major threat to health and life, and its prevalence is increasing. Diabetes involves the body's abnormal handling of glucose and the toxic effects of excess glucose. Prediabetes silently threatens the health of tens of millions of people in the United States. Medical tests can reveal elevated plasma glucose. Type 1 diabetes is an autoimmune disease that attacks the pancreas and necessitates an external source of insulin for its management. Inadequate insulin leaves blood glucose too high, while cells remain undersupplied with glucose energy. Type 2 diabetes risk factors make the disease likely to develop, but prevention is possible.

4.6 **Identify components of a lifestyle plan to effectively control blood glucose, and describe the characteristics of an eating plan that can help manage type 2 diabetes.**
Diet plays a central role in controlling diabetes and the illnesses that accompany it. Regular physical activity, in addition to diet and medication, helps to control blood glucose in diabetes.

4.7 **Describe the symptoms of hypoglycemia, and name some conditions that may cause it.**
In hypoglycemia, blood glucose falls too low; it arises mainly in people with diabetes or other conditions or by medications and is rare among healthy people.

4.8 **Identify the main contributors of various forms of carbohydrates in foods.**

4.9 **Discuss current research regarding the relationships among added sugars, obesity, diabetes, and other ills.**

Critical Thinking Questions

1. *Give any 3 reasons why people who wish to lose body weight are encouraged to eat a high-carbohydrate diet as opposed to a low-carbohydrate diet.*

   Carbohydrates are the body's preferred source of fuel for producing ATP (energy). With ample blood glucose for the cells to break down for energy, the person will feel more energetic, which will allow him to move around more and expend more calories. Carbohydrates supply 4 calories per gram whereas fat supplies 9 calories per gram. Carbohydrate-containing foods such as fruits, vegetables, and whole grains are often high in fiber, which helps people feel fuller. These foods are low in calories and supply many essential vitamins and minerals that the body needs to produce energy.

   A diet with enough carbohydrates will allow the body to use dietary protein for maintaining muscle and tissue health. This is called the protein-sparing action of carbohydrates. If the body does not have enough carbohydrates, it may use proteins from the lean tissue as a source of energy. The body needs lean tissue to help it expend calories as well.

2. *The glycemic index of foods describes the extent to which individual foods can elevate blood glucose levels. Why are many diabetics NOT encouraged to choose foods based on their glycemic index values?*

   Many studies have shown that a foods do not raise blood glucose in all persons to the same extent; people have different glucose tolerances. Also, foods in combination may raise blood glucose levels differently than foods eaten in isolation. While white bread alone may raise blood glucose levels quickly, when eaten with peanut butter it may not, since the fat and protein digestion occurring along with the starch digestion may slow down the absorption of glucose into the blood.

Diabetics should be encouraged to eat whole foods that will provide natural sugars together with fiber, which may raise blood glucose levels more slowly.

3. *Give any 2 reasons why many people may not know that they are at risk for pre-diabetes or diabetes.*

   Pre-diabetes and diabetes may not have obvious symptoms that alert a person. A person may feel tired, gain weight, get infections more often, or want to eat more, but they may just attribute such changes to a stressful lifestyle. They need to have a blood test to determine if the levels of glucose are in a healthy range.

   Many people assume that diabetes, especially type 2 (90-95% of cases), only runs in families. There are many new cases of type 2 diabetes that cannot be accounted for by heredity alone. The condition is far more common than people realize.

4. *Suggest any 3 reasons why a person with type 2 diabetes might have trouble with following the recommendations for diet and exercise to effectively manage her diabetes.*

   These individuals may feel very tired and may not want to exercise. Studies have shown that regular exercise can help stabilize blood glucose levels since the muscle cells may become more sensitive to the effects of insulin.

   Many diabetics may not want to prick their fingers several times a day to measure their blood glucose levels. There are meters that will take small blood samples from the forearm but some individuals don't like to take any blood samples.

   Many diabetics don't feel any symptoms even if their blood glucose levels are higher than they should be. These individuals often don't realize that chronically high blood glucose levels can lead to complications later even if they don't feel any effects in the present.

5. *Suggest 3 ways that you could reduce your intake of refined sugars each day and replace these with more fiber in your daily eating plan.*

   The first step might be to become familiar with the other names for sugar such as honey, molasses, dextrose, etc. One can read the labels of foods eaten to see if they contain large amounts of sugar. If sugar is listed toward the beginning of the ingredients list, it is a large contributor to the weight of the food. To replace white bread with whole-grain bread to increase fiber, one can read the food label to confirm that fiber-containing grains are listed at the beginning of the ingredients list.

   The second step might be to replace one sweet treat such as a donut with a piece of fruit. The fruit still contains sugar and is sweet but it also will provide more fiber and vitamins. Small daily changes in eating will be easier to maintain and build upon.

   One can also eat more beans with meals, because beans provide a lot of fiber and will be filling. This will reduce the urge to eat foods that are sweet and have less fiber.

6. *Why is there such a strong connection between obesity and type 2 diabetes?*

   Obese individuals experience chronic, low levels of inflammation in their tissues. Though asymptomatic, inflammation can cause the cells of the muscles and liver to resist the action of insulin. When cells don't respond to insulin, they do not take up glucose and it stays in the blood. Studies also suggest that the body's appetite control system may be influenced by insulin resistance, causing the person to overeat. The body can still digest and absorb excess fat, which can be stored. Fat tissue may also release hormones that trigger inflammation and insulin resistance, which can lead to type 2 diabetes.

Controversy Discussion Questions

1. *Discuss why the statement "carbohydrates make us fat" is not accurate considering peoples' diets in other parts of the world.*

   People in China, parts of Africa, and Japan ingest a lot of carbohydrates in the form of rice and noodles and yet have a much lower rate of obesity than people who consume a Western, meat-centered diet. Analysis of their intakes suggests that they eat more complex carbohydrates and less simple sugars. They may also eat less animal fat from meats. When these people move and adopt a more Western-type diet, their rate of obesity increases to the level seen in the West.

2. *How are carbohydrates and diabetes related to each other?*

   They are associated with each other only when the overall diet provides more calories than are needed by the body. This pattern will result in weight gain. People who consume a lot of simple sugars as part of a diet providing excess energy relative to their bodies' energy needs may have an increased risk of developing diabetes. Also, these people may eat or drink foods rich in simple sugars that displace more nutrient-dense whole foods. People who consume a lot of simple sugars but within a diet that does not supply excess energy may not be at increased risk of developing diabetes.

3. *Why are people who consume many of their carbohydrates in the form of high-fructose corn syrup (HFCS) more apt to overeat than people who consume carbohydrates in the form of starches or sucrose (table sugar)?*

   Most foods that contain table sugar or starches are filling since they take up space in the stomach and may be combined with protein or fats, which can also reduce the appetite. Most sodas now contain HFCS, and if people drink a lot of soda in addition to other foods, they are likely to be taking in excess calories, which can lead to weight gain. People do not perceive soda as being filling since it is a liquid and not a solid.

4. *Why is it difficult to attribute the increase in obesity and related illnesses to added sugars alone?*

   Regardless of diet composition, it is a calorie intake in excess of needs that causes weight gain. Many people who eat processed foods that contain added sugars may be obese because these same foods contain an abundance of high-calorie saturated and *trans* fats as well. Ultimately, foods with added sugars are eaten in addition to foods that supply the diet with essential nutrients (or in some cases replace such foods!) and this leads to an overconsumption of calories, which results in the development of obesity and its associated illnesses.

Worksheet Answer Key

Worksheet 4-1: Label Analysis—Carbohydrates

1. a. 11 grams of fiber – Significant amount of fiber coming from one product.
   b. 11 grams/30 grams (average) × 100 = 37% of the Daily Value
   c. 2500 cal × 14 grams/1000 cal = 35 grams; 11 grams/35 grams × 100 = 31% of the DRI
2. Not really because there are a lot of calories for the nutrients provided.
3. 23%
4. There are no calories that come from fiber since the body cannot break down fiber for energy.
5. a. 19 grams come from complex carbohydrates.
   b. Sources are rice flour, oats, wheat bran, wheat meal, soy flour, barley, and corn flour.
6. The sources of simple sugars are cane juice, cranberries, molasses, malt extract, and oat syrup solids.
7. a. Yes
   b. Look at where the simple sugars appear in the ingredients list. If they are near the top of the list, they are present in large amounts relative to the other ingredients.

Worksheet 4-2: Intake Analysis—Carbohydrates

1. a. Low-carbohydrate diet like the Atkin's Diet
   b. Weight loss (rapid), reduction of sweet cravings, or possibly reduction of insulin release
   c. Carbohydrates, fiber, thiamin, folate, vitamin C, and minerals such as magnesium and potassium
   d. The body needs carbohydrates for energy so that protein is used to build lean tissue, enzymes, hormones, or other functional proteins. The body needs fiber for digestive and overall health as well as vitamins to help the body make use of the energy-yielding nutrients. This diet is not balanced in that it does not have foods from each group.

2. a. Broccoli, spinach pie, and granola bar
   b. Raspberries, asparagus, and tomatoes
   c. Vanilla yogurt, grapefruit juice, raspberries, cantaloupe, granola bar, asparagus, blueberry juice, tomatoes, and vanilla ice cream
   d. Vanilla yogurt and vanilla ice cream

3. a. Yes
   b. If there are several small meals throughout the day with a mixture of whole foods from all of the food groups, this will cause the blood sugar to stay within a constant range without a lot of dips (fasting) or spikes (refined sugars).

Worksheet 4-5: Chapter 4 Review Crossword Puzzle

1. lactose
2. Soluble
3. diverticula
4. endosperm
5. glycemic
6. hypoglycemia
7. polysaccharide
8. cholesterol
9. fructose
10. fibers
11. cellulose
12. constipation
13. ketosis
14. glucagon

Learning Activities & Project Ideas

Activity 4-1: Breakfast—Energy Scores[3] LO 4.4

Have the students close their eyes, relax, and get in touch with their feelings. Ask them to score themselves from 1 to 10 for "energy level," and write this score on a piece of paper (no name). Then ask them to record what they ate for breakfast, and at what time. Collect the papers, eliminate those who ate more than 5 or fewer than 2 hours earlier, sort the remaining ones into high-protein, low-protein, no-protein, and no-breakfast piles, and average the energy scores. Show the students the breakfast nutrient categories as well as the average energy scores for each category.

In over two dozen demonstrations, the results have been in the expected direction: those who ate high-protein breakfasts feel the most energetic; those with no-protein, least. (This only works for morning classes, of course.) If it doesn't "work," explain what you would expect to see, and why. Criticize the demonstration as unscientific (it's not blind, there may be bias); but point out that it at least illustrates that a balanced breakfast can influence a morning's performance, while the many deviations from the average show that a multitude of other factors are working, too.

This exercise may help students remember that dietary protein influences blood glucose regulation—a first stone in the foundation for understanding metabolism.

Activity 4-2: Cookie Comparison LO 4.8

This activity gives students an opportunity to practice reading labels, identifying added sugars in foods, and comparing similar products for nutrient content. Make copies of Handout 4-3 and of the labels from 2 brands of cookies for your students (you can cut these off of the packages, or print them out from the manufacturers' web sites). Have them use the instructions on the handout to compare the percentage of calories from sugar for the 2 types of cookies, and identify any added sugar ingredients in each product. Also, have the students note where in the ingredients list the sugar appears. Ingredients listed at the beginning constitute a higher amount per weight of the cookie than those ingredients listed further down in the label.

Activity 4-3: Sugar in Soda[4] LO 4.8

Bring a teaspoon, sugar, and a glass to class. Ask students how much sugar they put in coffee or tea. Start putting sugar in the glass and have students tell you when they would stop adding sugar to their beverages. Keep adding sugar to the glass until you have put in 8-10 teaspoons. Hold the glass up, and ask if they would drink something poured into the glass with that much sugar. Explain that this is the amount of sugar in one-12 ounce can of soda. This activity will get their attention. Discuss the implications, especially considering that many people drink more than 12 ounces of soda in a typical serving.

---

[3] Contributed by Lori W. Turner, Ph.D., R.D.

[4] Contributed by Lori W. Turner, Ph.D., R.D.

Chapter Lecture Outline

I. Introduction
  A. Ideal nutrients to meet your body's energy needs, feed your nervous system, keep your digestive system healthy, and keep you lean
  B. Complex carbohydrates – starch, fiber, glycogen
  C. Simple carbohydrates – sugars

II. A Close Look at Carbohydrates
  A.. Photosynthesis is a process by which plants get energy from the sun and produce glucose and starch.
    1. The glucose is used for energy by the plant itself, or
    2. Stored in a fruit or vegetable or seed and consumed by animals
  B. Sugars
    1. 6 sugar molecules are important in nutrition
      a. Monosaccharides – single sugars
      b. Disaccharides – double sugars
    2. Monosaccharides – Where are they found in foods?
      a. Glucose – not abundant as glucose in foods
      b. Fructose – in fruits, honey, and HFCS (high-fructose corn syrup)
      c. Galactose – rarely free in foods; often tied up in lactose (milk sugar)
    3. Disaccharides – Where are they found?
      a. Sucrose – table sugar
      b. Maltose – germinating seeds and whenever starch is being digested
      c. Lactose – dairy products
      d. Disaccharides are split into monosaccharides by enzymes in the small intestinal cells.
      1. The monosaccharides are absorbed into the bloodstream and are all converted to glucose by the liver.
  C. Starch – Polysaccharides
    1. Starch is a plant's storage form of glucose
    2. Found in seeds in granules
    3. Nutritive for humans as a source of energy
  D. Glycogen
    1. Storage form of glucose in animals and human beings
    2. Glycogen is made up of highly branched chains of glucose molecules.
    3. Undetectable in meats because glycogen breaks down rapidly when the animal is processed for its meat
  E. Fibers
    1. Structural form of glucose in plant leaves, stems, and seeds
    2. Other fibers play other roles, for example, to retain water and protect the seeds from drying out.
    3. Human digestive enzymes cannot break the chemical bonds holding the sugar units together, i.e., indigestible in human beings
    4. Bacteria in the large intestine can break down fiber by fermentation, which produces fat fragments, which are absorbed by the large intestine.

III. The Need for Carbohydrates
  A. Glucose is a critical energy source for the nervous system, including the brain.
    1. Fat is not normally used by the nervous system and brain as a source of energy.
    2. Protein-rich foods are usually more difficult for the body to use for energy and offer no advantage over carbohydrates in terms of energy yield.
    3. Sugars attached to proteins may affect the function of those proteins such that they function more effectively.
    4. Sugars also serve as cell signal communication aids on the surface of the cell membrane.
  B. If I Want to Lose Weight and Stay Healthy, Should I Avoid Carbohydrates?
    1. Lower in Calories – Are carbohydrates "fattening"? – NO!! They have 4 calories per gram.
    2. An Exception: Refined Sugars
      a. Avoid excessive intake of refined sugars, which often don't supply other nutrients

   b. A person that eats 400 calories of sugar only gets the calories but a person who eats 400 calories of whole grains also gets fiber and other nutrients.
3. Guidelines (see Table 4-1)
   a. People who wish to lose fat, maintain lean tissue, and stay healthy should get enough carbohydrates to maintain their energy levels and to use protein for tissue maintenance.
   b. Pay attention to portion size.
   c. Control total calories as opposed to the source of the calories.
   d. Design a diet around whole foods that supply carbohydrates in balance with other nutrients.

C. Why Do Nutrition Experts Recommend Fiber-Rich Foods?
1. Fiber benefits the body (see Figure 4-4) by:
   a. Helping to normalize blood cholesterol levels
   b. Helping to normalize blood glucose levels
   c. Maintaining healthy bowel functions
   d. Possibly maintaining a healthy body weight
2. Soluble Fibers – Are water soluble and form viscous gels
   a. These fibers can be fermented by intestinal bacteria.
   b. Found in oats, barley, legumes, and citrus fruits
   c. May help lower blood cholesterol and control blood glucose levels
3. Insoluble Fibers – Do not dissolve in water and are not easily fermented by bacteria
   a. Found on outer layers of whole grains, in strings of celery, or skins of corn kernels
   b. Help the colon eliminate wastes
4. Lower Cholesterol and Heart Disease Risk
   a. Diets higher in fiber tend to emphasize foods that are low in saturated fats and cholesterol and high in phytochemicals.
   b. Fiber may bind to bile in the digestive tract and help pull excess bile out of the body.
   c. This may lead to a reduction of cholesterol in the blood (see Figure 4-6).
5. Blood Glucose Control
   a. High-fiber foods—especially whole grains—play a key role in reducing the risk of type 2 diabetes.
   b. How can they do this? – Soluble fibers delay glucose absorption and may prevent spikes in blood glucose levels.
6. Maintenance of Digestive Tract Health – How does fiber play a role in maintaining proper colon function?
   a. Fiber feeds the intestinal bacteria that contribute to colon health.
   b. Cellulose enlarges and softens the stools and speeds up transit.
   c. Prevents constipation
   d. Lower risk of hemorrhoids
   e. Lower risk of appendicitis
   f. Lower risk of diverticula
7. Digestive Tract Cancers
   a. Meta-analysis of several studies of the rectum suggests that people who ate 24 grams fiber/day reduced their risk of colon cancer by almost 30%
   b. Fiber attracts water, so may dilute potential cancer-causing agents and speed their removal from the colon
   c. Fiber-rich foods supply folate, which may be protective.
   d. Resident bacteria multiply rapidly in fiber-rich intestinal contents and produce small fat molecules that lower the pH of the colon contents.
   e. A colon well supplied with butyrate from a diet high in soluble fibers may resist chemical injury that could otherwise lead to cancer formation.
8. Healthy Weight Management – How can fiber help maintain a healthy weight?
   a. Whole foods rich in complex carbohydrates tend to be low in fats and added sugars and therefore promote weight loss by delivering less energy per bite.
   b. Fiber provides a feeling of fullness.
   c. Fiber delays hunger because fibers swell as they absorb water.

D. Fiber Intakes and Excesses
1. Do you get enough fiber?
   a. Most adults need between 25 grams (women) & 38 grams (men) of total fiber daily.

b. People can replace some of their animal-based protein with plant-based proteins.
c. This will increase fiber and lower fat intakes.

2. Can My Diet Have Too Much Fiber?
   a. Too much fiber and too little liquids can overwhelm the digestive system.
   b. Too much fiber may displace nutrients and energy from the diet
3. The Binders in Fiber
   a. Binders in some fibers act as chelating agents.
   b. Fiber can bind important minerals and carry them out of the body.
   c. Fiber can carry water out of the body.
   d. Consume extra beverages.

E. Whole-Grains

1. Flour Types
   a. Are described as refined, enriched, fortified, or whole grains
   b. Parts of wheat kernel: bran, germ, endosperm, husk (see Figure 4-8)
   c. Table 4-4 describes grain foods
   d. Whole-grain flour uses the whole grain
2. Enrichment of Refined Grains – The U.S. Enrichment Act of 1942 was passed by Congress to prevent deficiencies that developed when people turned to refined breads.
   a. Required iron, niacin, thiamin, and riboflavin be added to all refined grain products
   b. Amended in 1996 to include the vitamin folate (folic acid on food labels)
3. Health Effects of Whole grains
   a. People who eat more whole grains tend to be leaner and feel full longer than those who eat more refined grains.
   b. People who eat more whole grains also may have lower risks of heart disease, type 2 diabetes, and some types of cancers.
4. A Consumer's Guide to Finding Whole-Grain Foods
   a. Not Every Choice Must Be 100 Percent Whole Grain – whole/enriched blends, white durum wheat products with milder flavors available
   b. High Fiber Does Not Equal Whole Grain – wheat bran or purified cellulose may be added to refined grain products to make them high in fiber
   c. Brown Color Does Not Equal Whole Grain – look for whole grains as the first ingredient
   d. Label Subtleties – look for the words "whole grain" (not "natural," "multi-grain," etc.)
   e. After the Salt – ingredients listed after salt = < a teaspoonful per loaf of bread
   f. A Word about Cereals – check ingredients for added sugars, sodium, & saturated fat
   g. Moving Ahead – include whole grains at every meal to make half of grain choices whole

IV. From Carbohydrates to Glucose

A. Introduction

1. Body must have glucose available for its cells at a steady rate all day
2. Body cannot use polysaccharides or disaccharides or even fructose or galactose

B. Digestion and Absorption of Carbohydrate

1. Starch
   a. Starch digestion begins in the mouth.
   b. The starch in refined white flour breaks down quickly into glucose.
   c. The starches in beans are digested more slowly and release glucose later in digestion.
   d. Resistant starch may be digested but slowly and is often considered a type of fiber.
2. Sugars
   a. Disaccharides are split to monosacharides on the surface of the small intestinal cells.
   b. Monosaccharides are absorbed into the blood.
   c. Galactose, fructose, and glucose travel to liver, which converts galactose and fructose to glucose or related products.
   d. Circulatory system transports glucose to cells
   e. Liver may store some glucose as glycogen
   f. All body cells can split glucose to produce ATP (energy).

3. Fiber
    a. Fiber is not digested by human digestive enzymes.
    b. Fiber is digested (fermented) by colon bacteria, producing odorous gases.

C. Why Do Some People Have Trouble Digesting Milk?
1. Introduction
    a. As people age, upward of 75% of the world's people lose the ability to produce the enzyme lactase, which digests lactose.
    b. About 12% of the U.S. population develops lactose intolerance but up to 80% of people of African, Asian, Hispanic, Indian, or Native American descent may develop lactose intolerance.
    c. Almost all mammals lose some of their ability to produce lactase as they age.
2. Symptoms of Lactose Intolerance – Symptoms of lactose intolerance after consuming lactose-containing products:
    a. Nausea, pain, diarrhea, excessive gas
    b. Milk allergy is due to the immune system's reaction to milk protein.
3. Consequences to Nutrition – can include loss of a key source of calcium, which can lead to weakened bones
4. Milk Tolerance and Strategies
    a. Many people can tolerate as much as a cup or two of milk a day.
    b. Often people overestimate the severity of their lactose intolerance.
    c. Alternatives (see Table 4-7) include:
        1. Cheese, yogurt, lactose-free milk
        2. Over-the-counter lactase pills and drops
        3. Calcium-fortified juices, soymilk, canned sardines or salmon with the bones

V. The Body's Use of Glucose – Glucose is the basic carbohydrate that each cell of the body uses for energy.

A. Splitting Glucose for Energy – When a cell splits glucose for energy, it performs a series of chemical reactions.
1. The Point of No Return – occurs when glucose is broken down into small molecules that cannot be reassembled into glucose
2. Below a Healthy Minimum – When there is inadequate carbohydrate in the diet, the body has two problems:
    a. Having no glucose, the body turns to protein and fat to make some glucose.
        1. Called the protein-sparing action of carbohydrate
        2. Fat cannot regenerate enough glucose to feed the brain and prevent ketosis
    b. Without carbohydrate in the diet, fat cannot be used correctly for energy, and the body converts its fats into ketone bodies.
3. Ketosis
    a. Ketosis results when an undesirably high concentration of ketone bodies accumulates in the blood, which can severely threaten health.
    b. A therapeutic ketogenic diet and medication may lower the number of seizures in people with hard to treat cases of epilepsy.
4. The DRI Minimum Recommendation for Carbohydrate – The amount of digestible carbohydrate set by the DRI committee to adequately feed the brain and reduce ketosis = 130 grams a day for an average-sized person

B. How Is Glucose Regulated in the Body?
1. Regulating blood sugar depends on two pancreatic hormones (see Figure 4-13):
    a. Insulin – removes excess glucose from blood to become glycogen or fat
    b. Glucagon – triggers the breakdown of liver glycogen to free glucose
2. Insulin
    a. After a meal, as blood glucose rises, the pancreas releases insulin, which signals the body's tissues to take up the surplus glucose.
    b. Muscle and liver cells can convert the glucose to glycogen.
3. Tissue Glycogen Stores
    a. 2/3 stored in muscles for physical activity
    b. Brain stores a little glycogen in case of emergency
    c. Remainder stored in liver for release into blood

4. The Release of Glucose from Glycogen
    a. When blood glucose concentrations drop, a pancreatic hormone, glucagon, is released.
    b. Glucagon stimulates the breakdown of glycogen into glucose, which is released into the blood.
5. Be Prepared: Eat Carbohydrate – Epinephrine also breaks down liver glycogen during emergencies ("fight or flight" reaction).

C. Excess Glucose and Body Fatness
1. Carbohydrate Stored as Fat
    a. Once immediate energy needs are met and glycogen stores are full, the liver breaks extra glucose into molecules it can reassemble as fat.
    b. Glycogen storage is limited (~2000 cal in the liver) but fat storage is nearly unlimited at over 70,000 calories.
2. Carbohydrate and Weight Maintenance – 45-65% cal from unrefined carbohydrates

D. The Glycemic Index of Food
1. Introduction
    a. Some carbohydrate-rich foods raise blood glucose and insulin concentrations higher relative to others.
    b. Foods can be ranked on a scale known as the glycemic index (see Figure 4-14).
    c. Foods that contain mixtures of macronutrients may have a lower glycemic index than foods that are made up of starch or sugars alone.
2. Diabetes and the Glycemic Index
    a. The glycemic load takes the glycemic index of a food into account along with the amount of that food that is eaten.
    b. Many diet books use the glycemic index, but evidence on effects of low-GI diets on weight loss is mixed.
    c. Soluble fiber in low-GI diet may be responsible for some of its effects
    d. Choosing low-GI foods may provide modest benefits but is not a primary concern in diabetes.
3. Nutrition Concerns
    a. An oversimplification of a complicated situation since the glycemic response to the same food can differ for each person, based on individual metabolism, meal timing, ripeness of produce, combination of foods, etc.
    b. Often the healthiest foods are already low on the glycemic index

VI. Diabetes – Abnormal use of carbohydrates

A. Introduction
1. Almost 26 million people in the U.S. have diabetes.
2. About 7 million of those people are unaware that they have the condition.
3. About 79 million people have pre-diabetes.

B. The Dangers of Diabetes
1. Overview
    a. Diabetes ranks seventh among killers in U.S.
    b. Doubles the risk of heart disease and stroke
    c. Leading cause of permanent blindness and fatal kidney failure
    d. Diabetes costs around $174 billion dollars in health care services, disabilities, and lost work
2. Toxicity of Excess Blood Glucose
    a. Chronically elevated blood glucose alters metabolism in every cell in the body.
    b. Inflammation – chronic inflammation may contribute to uncontrolled diabetes
    c. Blindness, kidney disease, heart disease, nerve damage, increased infections, amputations of limbs
3. Circulation Problems
    a. May lead to loss of blood flow to the kidneys, which can cause permanent damage
    b. Poor circulation increases risk of infections and amputation of limbs.

C. Prediabetes and the Importance of Testing
1. Fasting blood glucose (milligrams per deciliter)
    a. Normal: 100 mg/dL
    b. Prediabetes: 100-125 mg/dL
    c. Diabetes: 125 mg/dL
2. Warning signs of diabetes are shown in Table 4-9

D. Type 1 Diabetes
   1. Type 1 causes 5 to 10% of diabetes
   2. Autoimmune disorder where person's immune system attacks insulin-producing pancreas cells
   3. External sources of insulin needed to assist cells to take up glucose
      a. Insulin cannot be ingested since it is a protein that would be destroyed by digestion.
      b. Insulin needs to be injected by a syringe or pump.
      c. Long- and short-acting insulins help control blood glucose levels.

E. Type 2 Diabetes
   1. Overview
      a. Type 2 causes 90 to 95% of diabetes
      b. Muscle, adipose, and liver cells lose their sensitivity to insulin, i.e., insulin resistance
   2. Type 2 Diabetes and Obesity (see Figure 4-16)
      a. Obesity-related in young and older people
      b. Genetic factors also involved
   3. Preventing Type 2 Diabetes
      a. Maintain healthy body weight
      b. Choose a diet high in vegetables, fruits, poultry, fish, and whole grains
      c. Exercise regularly
      d. Moderate alcohol intake
      e. Abstain from smoking

VII. Management of Diabetes

A. Introduction
   1. Goal is to keep blood glucose levels within the normal range
   2. Use a daily routine of diet, exercise, blood glucose monitoring, and medication
   3. Long-term blood glucose control will reduce risk of diabetes-associated complications

B. Nutrition Therapy
   1. How Much Carbohydrate Is Best?
      a. Varies with glucose tolerance, but >130 g/day
      b. Timing of carbohydrate intake is important to avoid low blood glucose levels (hypoglycemia) as well.
   2. Sugar Alcohols and Nonnutritive Sweeteners – Products like cookies and candies sweetened with sugar alcohols should be consumed in moderation.
   3. Diet Recommendations in Summary
      a. Controlled in total carbohydrate & moderate in added sugars
      b. Low in saturated & *trans* fat
      c. Adequate nutrients from foods
      d. Adequate in fiber
      e. Limited in added sugars
      f. Not too much protein in case the kidneys have suffered damage

C. Physical Activity
   1. Physical activity heightens the cells' sensitivity to insulin, which may delay the onset of type 2 diabetes.
   2. People with type 1 diabetes need to work with their healthcare provider to reduce the risk of developing hypoglycemia.

VIII. If I Feel Dizzy between Meals, Do I Have Hypoglycemia?

A. Hypoglycemia is abnormally low blood glucose; requires a blood test to diagnose

B. People need to replace refined sugars with complex carbohydrates and protein at each meal.

C. Hypoglycemia can be caused by certain medications, pancreatic tumors, overuse of insulin, too much alcohol, uncontrolled diabetes, or other illnesses.

IX. Food Feature: Finding the Carbohydrates in Foods

A. For a 2,000-calorie diet
   1. Carbohydrates should provide 45% to 65% of calories

2. 225 to 325 grams each day
3. See Figure 4-17 for average fiber contributions of each food group

B. Fruits
1. Fruits contain sugars and fiber.
2. Most fruits supply about 15 grams of carbohydrate per ½ cup.

C. Vegetables
1. Vegetables contain starches and fiber.
2. Starchy vegetables can contribute about 15 grams of carbohydrate per ½ cup.

D. Grains
1. Breads, grains, cereals, rice, and pasta are a good source of carbohydrates.
2. Most contribute about 15 grams of carbohydrate per ounce equivalent.

E. Protein Foods – Meat, poultry, fish, dry beans, eggs, and nuts
1. Dry beans and nuts contain fiber and about 15 grams of carbohydrates per ½ cup.
2. Meats contain little if any carbohydrates.

F. Milk & Milk Products – Milk, cheese, and yogurt may contain carbohydrates
1. May contain about 12 grams of carbohydrates per cup
2. Soy products may contain up to 14 grams of carbohydrates per cup.

G. Oils, Solid Fats, and Added Sugars – added sugars = almost pure simple carbohydrates

H. The Nature of Sugar
1. It can be found as molasses, honey, high-fructose corn syrup, and many others – See Table 4-10 for terms that describe sugar
2. Watch out for empty calories from added sugars – See Table 4-11 for tips for reducing the intakes of added sugars

X. Controversy: Are Added Sugars "Bad" for You?

A. Do Added Sugars Cause Obesity?
1. We are actually taking in more calories.
   a. Americans have gained weight in the last 20-30 years (see Figure C4-1).
   b. Average cal intakes have increased by 300 cal/day, as shown in Figure C4-2.
   c. Increase from average of 42% of all calories as carbohydrates in the 1970s to 49% today
2. Intakes of Added Sugars
   a. On average, an American takes in 31 teaspoons of added sugar each day.
   b. Figure C4-3 shows food sources of sugar.
3. Carbohydrates or Calories? – People in other cultures eat diets higher in carbohydrates but lower in protein and are not overweight to the same extent.

B. Do Added Sugars Cause Diabetes?
1. Increased rates of diabetes are more strongly associated with increased rates of obesity.
2. Refined Carbohydrates and Diabetes – in some (particularly Native Americans), consumption of refined CHO & sugar in place of whole grains is associated with diabetes development.
3. People who eat more whole foods may have a lower risk of developing diabetes but they may also be more active and engage in other healthy behaviors.

C. Do Liquid Calories Pose Special Risks?
1. Researchers tested whether the sugar in beverages fools the appetite control mechanisms.
   a. Gave subjects jelly beans or soda before a meal
   b. Subjects who ate jelly beans ate less food
   c. Subjects who drank sugary beverages ate the entire meal
   d. People may not perceive the drink as being filling even though it is high in calories.
2. A 16-ounce soft drink can add 200 calories to a person's intake, and many people drink several.

D. Hints of Metabolic Mayhem
1. Is it the Insulin?
   a. Insulin interacts with many body tissues to regulate metabolism and promote the storage of body fat.
   b. Insulin works in balance with other hormones and mechanisms in normal-weight individuals who consume a reasonable diet.

2. Is it the Fructose?
   a. Fructose makes up about 50% of all sweet sugars (see Figure C4-4).
   b. Young people may consume 140 grams of fructose per day from added sugar sources.
   c. Fructose is found in many foods, as shown in Table C4-1.
   d. Fructose does not stimulate the release of insulin to the extent that glucose does.
   e. Insulin tends to suppress the appetite.
3. Fructose and Body Fatness – Studies suggest that fructose does not seem to cause weight gain if total calorie intake doesn't exceed the energy needs of the body.
4. Fructose and Blood Lipids
   a. If people ingest a very large amount of fructose relative to other nutrients, unhealthy blood lipids may accumulate.
   b. People who consume as little as 1-2 soft drinks a day may have increases in blood lipids that could increase the risk of cardiovascular disease.
5. Fructose and Fatty Liver
   a. High levels of fructose intake may result in nonalcoholic fatty liver disease to varying degrees.
   b. Most people can take in moderate amounts of fructose safely.
   c. More research is needed.

E. High-Fructose Corn Syrup (HFCS)
   1. HFCS is a cheaper sweetener for food and beverage manufacturers to use than sucrose.
   2. Studies that compare intakes of HFCS versus sucrose do not clearly demonstrate that HCFS increases risks of cardiovascular disease any more than excess intake of sucrose.

F. Conclusion
   1. Research is ongoing, but it appears that eliminating added sugars would not cure obesity.
   2. The source of sugar matters in terms of disease risks.
      a. Fruits contain fructose but they also contain fiber, vitamins, minerals, and phytochemicals.
      b. Sweets should be enjoyed in moderation.

Worksheet 4-1: Label Analysis—Carbohydrates

Instructions: Use the label for the fettuccini Alfredo and garlic bread meal to answer questions 1-3 on a separate sheet of paper.

Uncle Pasquale's Frozen Delights

Fettuccini Alfredo & Garlic Bread

INGREDIENTS: COOKED FETTUCCINI PASTA (WATER, SEMOLINA [DURUM WHEAT, NIACIN, IRON, FERROUS SULFATE, THIAMINE MONONITRATE, RIBOFLAVIN, FOLIC ACID], EGG WHITES), GARLIC BREAD (BLEACHED ENRICHED FLOUR [MALTED BARLEY FLOUR, NIACIN, REDUCED IRON, THIAMINE MONONITRATE, RIBOFLAVIN, FOLATE], WATER, VEGETABLE OIL [SOYBEAN AND/OR COTTONSEED OIL], YEAST, SALT, HIGH FRUCTOSE CORN SYRUP, ENRICHED WHEAT FLOUR [FLOUR, NIACIN, REDUCED IRON, THIAMINE MONONITRATE, RIBOFLAVIN, FOLIC ACID], DATEM, VEGETABLE SHORTENING [PARTIALLY HYDROGENATED SOYBEAN OIL, TBHQ ADDED TO PRESERVE FRESHNESS], CONTAINS LESS THAN 2% OF THE FOLLOWING: ASCORBIC ACID, L-CYSTEINE HYDROCHLORIDE, AZODICAR-BONAMIDE, ENZYMES, CALCIUM PEROXIDE, CALCIUM PROPIONATE, ENZYME, TOPPINGS [LIQUID AND PARTIALLY HYDROGENATED SOYBEAN OIL, WATER, SALT, LECITHIN, MONOGLYCERIDES, SODIUM BENZOATE {PRESERVATIVE}, CITRIC ACID, NATURAL FLAVOR, ARTIFICIAL FLAVOR, BETA CAROTENE, VITAMIN A PALMITATE, CALCIUM DISODIUM EDTA {TO PROTECT FLAVOR}, PARSLEY FLAKES]), WATER, CARROTS, BROCCOLI, HEAVY WHIPPING CREAM, SOYBEAN OIL, CREAM CHEESE (PASTEURIZED MILK AND CREAM, CHEESE CULTURES, SALT, CAROB BEAN GUM), ROMANO (FROM COW'S MILK) AND PARMESAN CHEESE (PART-SKIM MILK, CHEESE CULTURES, SALT, ENZYMES, CELLULOSE POWDER [PREVENTS CAKING]), HALF AND HALF (MILK, CREAM), CONTAINS 2% OR LESS OF: GARLIC SHERRY WINE, STABILIZER (MODIFIED FOOD STARCH, SODIUM PHOSPHATE, MONO- AND DIGLYCERIDES, DEHYDRATED GARLIC, XANTHAN AND GUAR GUMS, SALT, PAPRIKA), SUGAR, SALT, BUTTER (CREAM, SALT), FLAVORINGS, BUTTER FLAVOR (PARTIALLY HYDROGENATED SOYBEAN OIL, FLAVOR [BUTTER OIL, ENZYME MODIFIED BUTTERFAT, WHEY POWDER, NONFAT DRY MILK POWDER, SOY LECITHIN {EMULSIFIER}]), POLYGLYCEROL ESTERS OF FATTY ACIDS, SPICE, PAPRIKA, BETA CAROTENE.

Nutrition Facts

Serving Size 1 Meal (397g)

Amount Per Serving	
Calories 770	Calories from Fat 420
	% Daily Value*
Total Fat 46g	**?%**
Saturated Fat 16g	**?%**
Trans Fat 0.5g	
Cholesterol 30mg	**?%**
Sodium 129mg	**?%**
Total Carbohydrate 69g	**?%**
Dietary Fiber 11g	**?%**
Sugars 9g	
Protein 19g	

Vitamin A 80%	•	Vitamin C 0%
Calcium 35%	•	Iron 6%

* Percent Daily Values are based on a 2,000 calorie diet. Your Daily Values may be higher or lower depending on your calorie needs.

	Calories	2,000	2,500
Total Fat	Less than	65g	80g
Sat Fat	Less than	20g	25g
Cholesterol	Less than	300mg	300mg
Sodium	Less than	2400mg	2400mg
Total Carbohydrate		300g	375g
Dietary Fiber		25g	30g

1. a. Is this product a good source of fiber?
   b. Calculate the percentage of the Daily Value for fiber for a 2,500-calorie diet that is contributed by this product.
   c. Calculate the percentage of the DRI for a 2,500-calorie diet that is contributed by this product.
2. Is this a nutrient-dense product? Why or why not?
3. What percentage of the Daily Value for total carbohydrate (for 2,000 cal) comes from this product?

Instructions: Use the label for Zen-Tastic cereal to answer questions 4-7 on a separate sheet of paper.

What's so great about Zen-Tastic organic cereal?

High fiber
Low fat
Low sodium
Whole grain
Vegetarian
No *trans* fats

INGREDIENTS:
Organic brown rice flour, organic evaporated cane juice, organic rolled oats, organic wheat bran, organic sweetened dried cranberries (organic cranberries, organic evaporated cane juice), organic whole wheat meal, organic soy flour, organic whole oat flour, organic oat bran, inulin, organic soy oil, organic soy fiber, organic molasses, organic barley malt extract, organic yellow corn flour, organic whole millet, organic oat syrup solids, sea salt, organic quinoa, organic ginger, organic buckwheat flour, organic barley flour, organic rice bran extract, organic cinnamon, tocopherols (natural vitamin E), organic cloves, organic nutmeg.

Produced in a facility that contains peanuts, tree nuts & soy.

Nutrition Facts

Serving Size $^3/_4$ cup (55g)
Servings Per Container about 6

Amount Per Serving	Cereal	Cereal + 125 ml fortified skim milk
Calories	190	230
Calories from Fat	25	25
	% Daily Value**	
Total Fat 2.5g*	**4%**	**4%**
Saturated Fat 0g	**0%**	**0%**
Trans Fat 0g		
Cholesterol 0mg	**0%**	**0%**
Sodium 95mg	**4%**	**7%**
Total Carbohydrate 41g	**14%**	**16%**
Dietary Fiber 9g	**36%**	**36%**
Sugars 13g		
Protein 5g		
Vitamin A	0%	6%
Vitamin C	0%	0%
Calcium	2%	15%
Iron	10%	10%

* Amount in cereal. One half cup skim milk contributes an additional 40 calories, 65mg sodium, 6g total carbohydrate (6g sugars), and 4g protein.
**Percent Daily Values are based on a 2,000 calorie diet. Your Daily Values may be higher or lower depending on your calorie needs.

	Calories	2,000	2,500
Total Fat	Less than	65g	80g
Sat Fat	Less than	20g	25g
Cholesterol	Less than	300mg	300mg
Sodium	Less than	2400mg	2400mg
Total Carbohydrate		300g	375g
Dietary Fiber		25g	30g

4. What percentage of calories comes from fiber in this product?
5. a. What is the major type of carbohydrate contributed to the diet by this cereal?
   b. What are the major sources of this type of carbohydrate listed in the ingredients section?
6. What are the sources of simple sugars in this cereal?
7. a. Do they make up a significant portion of the ingredients?
   b. How can you tell?

Worksheet 4-2: Intake Analysis—Carbohydrates

Eating Plan B (1 Day's Intake)	Eating Plan F (1 Day's Intake)
6 ounces grapefruit juice	2 scrambled eggs
2 scrambled eggs	1 cup whole milk
1 ounce cheddar cheese	2 slices bacon
20 ounces coffee	2 1-ounce Slim Jims
2 ounces soy milk	6 ounces lean ground beef
1 cup fresh raspberries	2 ounces provolone cheese
1 cup cantaloupe	¼ cup blue cheese dressing
1 honey oat granola bar	12 ounces water
1 cup vanilla yogurt	2 ounces cheddar cheese cubes
6 ounces grilled salmon	6 ounces grilled chicken breasts
10 cooked asparagus spears	1 scrambled egg
1 cup broccoli	1 cup lettuce
4 ounces white wine	½ cup blue cheese dressing
4 ounces blueberry juice + seltzer water	2 ounces pork rinds
20 barbecue flavor soy crisps	12 ounces water
1 cup wasabi peas	
1 3" x 3" spanakopita	
1 cup spinach	
⅓ cup feta cheese	
¼ cup black olives	
5 grape tomatoes	
3 Tbsp. oil & vinegar dressing	
6 ounces white wine	
¼ cup mixed nuts	
1 cup vanilla ice cream	

Look at Eating Plan F:

1. a. What type of diet does this represent?

   b. What are the suggested health benefits of this sort of diet?

   c. What types of nutrients are lacking from this diet?

   d. Why is this lack of nutrients a concern for overall health?

Look at Eating Plan B:

2. Point out:

   a. the sources of starch.

   b. the sources of fiber.

   c. the sources of simple sugars.

   d. the sources of refined sugars.

3. a. Would this eating plan help stabilize blood sugar?

   b. Why or why not?

Worksheet 4-3: Choosing Carbohydrates With Fiber in Mind

Most of the energy we receive from foods comes from carbohydrates. Healthy choices rich in water-soluble vitamins and dietary fiber provide complex carbohydrates or naturally occurring simple carbohydrates. A diet that is consistently low in dietary fiber and high in added sugar can lead to health problems. Look at these examples of related foods and identify which are most similar to your food choices.

1. Look across each row in the table and circle the food choice in each row that best matches your daily intakes.

High in fiber/ low in added sugar	Intermediate	Low in fiber/ high in added sugar
Apple with peel	Applesauce, sweetened	Fruit drink, 10% apple juice
Brown rice	Cream of rice cereal	Puffed rice/marshmallow treat
Pumpernickel bread	Bagel, plain	Danish pastry
Baked sweet potato	Candied sweet potato casserole	Sweet potato pie
Corn on the cob	Creamed corn	Frosted corn flakes
Oatmeal	Granola	Granola breakfast bar

2. Do you consistently choose foods that are good sources of any one of the categories of fiber?

3. Do you select whole-grain products and fresh fruits and vegetables? If so, name some examples of these foods that you regularly eat.

3. Do you choose foods that increase your intake of fiber and limit your intake of sugars?

4. If you don't typically choose fiber-containing foods, what types of foods could you add (that you already enjoy) to your diet to increase your fiber intake?

Worksheet 4-4: Where Is the Sugar?

- Do you know how much sugar is in your favorite snack food?
- Do you know where to look on the food label to find out?
- If the term "sugar" is not listed, could there still be sugar in your snack food?

Check It Out:

1. Select 3 of your favorite snack foods; or, your instructor can provide you with a list of snack foods. Your foods could be 3 similar types of a snack food that you would like to compare.

2. Read the ingredients list on the food label. This is found below the Daily Values table on the label.
   a. Do you see the word "sugar" listed anywhere?

Sugar's other names: brown sugar, corn sweetener, corn syrup, dextrose, fructose, fruit juice concentrates, glucose, high-fructose corn syrup, honey, invert sugar, lactose, maltose, molasses, raw sugar, and syrup.

   b. Do you see any of these names listed?

3. The ingredients are listed in order from the ingredient with the highest percentage of the total weight of the product (listed first) to the ingredient with the lowest percentage of the product's weight.

   Does your product have one of sugar's "other names" listed near the beginning of the ingredient list? If so, this product has a lot of sugar in it.

4. You can also check the number of grams of sugar in the product. This is found right below the serving size information on the food label.

   It is recommended that you keep the total number of calories from sugar to less than 10% of your total calories.

   You can multiply the number of grams of sugar by 4 to get the number of calories from sugar.

5. You can compare your snack food to another brand or a similar snack food that may claim to be healthier or contain less added sugar. You now know where to look.
   a. You can compare any type of food for sugar content. This can help you to reduce the amount of added sugar in your diet.
   b. A check of labels can be done using the www.choosemyplate.gov website. This website will give suggestions of foods with more fiber and complex carbohydrates as opposed to foods with sugars.

Reference: *Tuft's University Health & Nutrition Letter*. Volume 22 (4) June 2004, page 3.

Worksheet 4-5: Chapter 4 Review Crossword Puzzle

1 2 3 4 5 6 7 8 9 10 11 12 13 14

Across	Down
1. A disaccharide composed of glucose and galactose; commonly known as milk sugar	2. _____ fibers can form a viscous gel when mixed with water.
5. The measure of a food's ability to raise blood glucose levels is known as its _____ index.	3. Outward pouches that form in the colon wall as a result of weakened muscle layers
7. Starch is made up of many linked glucose sugars and is also known as a _____.	4. The part of the wheat kernel that contains starch and protein for nourishment of the seed and is used in white flour
10. Indigestible plant components; mostly non-starch polysaccharides	6. Low levels of blood glucose that can affect the function of the brain
11. An insoluble fiber that is found in plants	8. Adequate fiber intake may help reduce blood _____ that may also help reduce the risk of heart disease or stroke
12. A diet that contains adequate fiber and water can prevent _____.	9. A simple sugar that when consumed in excess is associated with obesity, particularly abdominal fatness
13. Condition resulting from lack of glucose in the cells for energy production; can lead to serious consequences	
14. Hormone produced by the pancreas that releases glucose from glycogen during fasting/sleeping	

Handout 4-1: Characteristics of Fiber

Dietary fibers are classified according to a number of characteristics, including their solubility in water and whether they are a polysaccharide. These differences influence their physiological effect on the body.

	Water Soluble	Water Insoluble
Polysaccharides	• Gums • Hemicellulose [a] • Mucilages • Pectins • Psyllium	• Cellulose • Hemicellulose [a]
Nonpolysaccharides		• Lignins
Food Sources	• Fruits • Oats • Barley • Legumes	• Vegetables • Wheat • Grains
Health Effects	• Lower blood cholesterol • Lower rate of glucose absorption • Increased satiety, which helps with appetite control	• Softened stools • Acceleration of intestinal transit • Reduced risk of diverticulosis, hemorrhoids, appendicitis, and colon cancer
Food Examples	• Fruits such as apple flesh (not skin) or peaches • Legumes such as chickpeas or kidney beans	• Vegetables such as corn or celery • Skin of apples • Seeds

[a] Some hemicelluloses are water soluble and others are water insoluble.

Handout 4-2: How to Use the Exchange System to Estimate Carbohydrate

The exchange system described in Chapter 2 provides a convenient way to estimate carbohydrate intake because the foods on each list have a similar carbohydrate content. To use the system, you need to know the carbohydrate value for each exchange list (see the table below) and the foods on that list with their portion sizes.

One Exchange	Carbohydrate (g)
Starch	15
Fruits	15
Other carbohydrates	15
Milks	12
Nonstarchy vegetables	5
Meats (animal origin)	---
Plant-based proteins	varies
Fats	---
Sugars (1 tsp.) [a]	5

[a] The exchange system has no sugar list, but sugars do contribute to carbohydrates and energy intake.

Familiarity with portion sizes makes estimations easier. For example, it helps to recognize that the bowl of cereal you prepare for your breakfast contains 1 cup shredded wheat with 1 cup of milk and ½ banana. Then you can translate these portions into exchanges: 2 starches, 1 milk, and ½ fruit. Finally, you can calculate 15 grams of carbohydrate for each starch, 12 grams for the milk, and 8 grams for the ½ fruit. (Consult the food gallery at www.choosemyplate.gov for pictures of specific portion sizes.)

Using the exchange system to estimate, this breakfast provides about 50 grams of carbohydrate. A computer diet analysis program came to a slightly higher conclusion (59 grams), as would a diet analysis using the values in Appendix A of your text. Small variations between values arrived at differently may seem disconcerting, but remember that all are only estimates. Estimates save time; often only a ballpark figure is needed anyway.

Breakfast		Exchange	Carbohydrate (g)	
			Estimate	Actual
1 cup shredded wheat	=	2 starches	30	34
1 cup milk	=	1 milk	12	12
½ banana	=	½ fruit	8	13
			50	59

Most estimates of the nutrient contents of foods are rough but serviceable approximations. A "90-kcalorie potato" actually means a "90-kcalorie potato plus or minus about 20 percent potato," which makes it not significantly different from a 100-kcalorie potato. For most purposes, a variation of about 20 percent is considered reasonable, which is the difference between the values in this example.

Fiber appears in only the starches, vegetables, and fruits lists. To estimate fiber, remember that most items on these lists provide at least 2 grams of fiber per serving; some provide 3 or more. Knowing this a reasonable fiber estimate for this breakfast (with 2 starches and ½ fruit) would be 5 to 7 grams—and a diet analysis report of 5 grams would agree.

Just a few calculations of this kind will give you a feel for the carbohydrate content of a diet. Once you are aware of the major carbohydrate-contributing foods you eat, you can return to thinking simply in terms of foods, developing a sense of how much of each is enough.

Handout 4-3: Where Sugar Can Hide Out!

You've made a point to swear off added fat or salt in your diet, so you try low-salt or low-fat alternatives to your traditional favorites. You hope to also be able to reduce the number of calories that you take in. Have you ever compared the calorie totals between a low-fat food and that of its full-fat counterpart and not noticed much of a difference in the number of calories? Why is that? You may want to check the amount of sugar in the product. Sometimes, extra sugar may be added to give the product flavor or a different texture.

Have you ever noticed that low-salt soups can taste sweet? The food manufacturers often add sugar to help flavor the soup so that it is not bland tasting without the salt. You should check out the amount of sugar in the low-salt soup as compared with that of its salted counterpart.

What types of products should you check out?

- Low-fat cookies
- Low-fat sweet snacks
- Low-salt juices
- Low-salt soups
- All of the full-fat or -salt versions these foods

One way to appreciate the contribution of the sugar calories (amount) to the total calories of a product is to calculate the percentage of calories from a given macronutrient. You can use these percentages of total calories from sugar to directly compare the products.

Example:	Cookie A:	120 calories per serving 15 grams of sugar per serving
	Cookie B:	150 calories per serving 14 grams of sugar per serving

Cookie A: 15 grams sugar × 4 calories/gram = 60 calories (sugar)
60 calories (sugar) ÷ 120 calories × 100 = 50% of total calories come from sugar

Cookie B: 14 grams of sugar × 4 calories/gram = 56 calories (sugar)
56 calories (sugar) ÷ 150 calories = 37% of total calories come from sugar

If you wish to find a low-salt or low-fat product with less sugar, you may need to look around for other similar products that may have less sugar. You could also consider reducing the serving size of the low-fat or -salt food. You could also try reducing your portion size for the traditional favorite if you want to watch your sugar intake as well.

Chapter 5 – The Lipids: Fats, Oils, Phospholipids, and Sterols

Quick List: IM Resources for Chapter 5

- **Class preparation resources:** learning objectives/key points, suggested activities and projects, lecture outline
- **Assignment materials:** **Related LO**
  - Critical thinking questions (with answer key) 5.1, 5.5, 5.6, 5.8
  - Discussion questions (with answers) for Controversy 5 .... 5.10
  - Worksheet 5-1: Label Analysis—Lipids 5.8, 5.9
  - Worksheet 5-2: Intake Analysis—Lipids 5.6, 5.8, 5.9
  - Worksheet 5-3: Choosing Lower-Fat Foods[1] 5.8
  - **New!** Worksheet 5-4: Chapter 5 Review Crossword Puzzle
- **Enrichment materials:**
  - Handout 5-1: Why All Cholesterol Is Not Created Equally! 5.5
  - Handout 5-2: Why Omega-3 Fats are Considered Good Fats 5.6
  - Handout 5-3: How to Use the Exchange System to Estimate Fat[2] 5.8
  - Handout 5-4: How to Modify a Recipe 5.9

Chapter Learning Objectives and Key Points

5.1 **Identify the roles of lipids in both the body and food, and explain why some amount of fat is necessary in the diet.**
Lipids provide and store energy, cushion vital organs, insulate against temperature extremes, form cell membranes, transport fat-soluble substances, and serve as raw materials. Lipids provide abundant food energy in a small package, enhance aromas and flavors of foods, and contribute to satiety.

5.2 **Compare and contrast the chemical makeup and physical properties of saturated fats, polyunsaturated fats, monounsaturated fats, and phospholipids.**
The body combines three fatty acids with one glycerol to make a triglyceride, its storage form of fat. Fatty acids in food influence the composition of fats in the body. Fatty acids are energy-rich carbon chains that can be saturated (filled with hydrogens) or monounsaturated (with one point of unsaturation) or polyunsaturated (with more than one point of unsaturation). The degree of saturation of the fatty acids in a fat determines the fat's softness or hardness. Phospholipids play key roles in cell membranes. Sterols play roles as part of bile, vitamin D, the sex hormones, and other important compounds. Plant sterols in foods inhibit cholesterol absorption.

5.3 **Summarize how and where dietary lipids are broken down and absorbed during digestion and how they are transported throughout the body.**
In the stomach, fats separate from other food components. In the small intestine, bile emulsifies the fats, enzymes digest them, and the intestinal cells absorb them. Glycerol and short-chain fatty acids travel in the bloodstream unassisted. Other lipids need special transport vehicles—the lipoproteins—to carry them in watery body fluids.

5.4 **Describe the body's mechanisms for fat storage and use of body fat, including the role of carbohydrate in fat metabolism.**
The body draws on its stored fat for energy. Carbohydrate is necessary for the complete breakdown of fat.

5.5 **Summarize the relationships between lipoproteins and disease risks, and explain how various fats and cholesterol in food affect cholesterol in the blood.**
A small amount of raw oil is recommended each day. Energy from fat should provide 20 to 35 percent of the total energy in the diet. The chief lipoproteins are chylomicrons, VLDL, LDL, and HDL. High blood LDL and low HDL are major heart disease risk factors. Saturated fat and *trans* fat intakes raise blood cholesterol. Dietary cholesterol raises blood cholesterol to a lesser degree. To lower LDL in the blood, follow a healthy

---

[1] Contributed by Sharon Rady Rolfes; modified by Mary Ellen Clark

[2] Contributed by Sharon Rady Rolfes

eating pattern that replaces dietary saturated fat and *trans* fat with polyunsaturated and monounsaturated oils. To raise HDL and lower heart disease risks, be physically active.

5.6 **Compare the roles of omega-3 and omega-6 fatty acids in the body, and name important food sources of each.**
Deficiencies of the essential fatty acids are virtually unknown in the United States and Canada. Linoleic acid and linolenic acid are converted into eicosanoids, which influence diverse body functions. The omega-6 family of polyunsaturated fatty acids includes linoleic acid and arachidonic acid. The omega-3 family includes linolenic acid, EPA, and DHA. EPA and DHA may play roles in brain communication, disease prevention, and human development. The *Dietary Guidelines* recommend increasing seafood consumption. Supplements of omega-3 fatty acids are not recommended.

5.7 **Describe the hydrogenation of fat and the formation and structure of a *trans*-fatty acid.**
Vegetable oils become more saturated when they are hydrogenated. Hydrogenated vegetable oils are useful, but they lose the health benefits of unsaturated oils. The process of hydrogenation creates *trans*-fatty acids. *Trans* fats act like saturated fats in the body.

5.8 **Outline a diet plan that provides enough of the right kinds of fats within calorie limits.**
Meats account for a large proportion of the hidden solid fat in many people's diets. Milk products bear names that identify their fat contents. Cheeses are major contributors of saturated fat in the U.S. diet. Solid fat in grain foods can be well hidden.

5.9 **Identify at least 10 ways to reduce solid fats in an average diet.**

5.10 **Discuss evidence for the benefits and drawbacks of specific dietary fats in terms of their effects on human health.**

Critical Thinking Questions

1. *Your friend believes that all fats must be bad for one's health, so he is trying to restrict his dietary fat intake to a minimum. Give him 3 reasons why he should never restrict his fats to a very low level.*

   This person needs to obtain omega-3 and omega-6 fatty acids to maintain his body tissues. The essential fatty acids (linolenic and linoleic) are not made by the body. Adequate levels of omega-3 fatty acids may also reduce inflammation in the body as well as support the health of the nervous and cardiovascular systems.

   This individual may not be getting enough fat-soluble vitamins such as vitamins A, D, and E from his diet. If the fat restriction is temporary, the body can draw on stored vitamins, but if the fat restriction is long term, the person may become deficient in any one or all of these vitamins.

   He needs fat for energy so that his body is not using protein for energy. If he is taking in enough carbohydrates, he may be getting enough energy, but he still needs fats to supply some of the body's energy needs. The body also needs fat stores for cushioning of organs as well as for insulation.

2. *All lipoproteins are made up of proteins, triglycerides, and cholesterol. Why are low-density lipoproteins (LDL) considered unhealthy, and people encouraged to lower LDL, while high-density lipoproteins are considered healthy and people are encouraged to increase HDL?*

   While LDL and HDL contain proteins, triglycerides, and cholesterol, they do not contain these molecules in the same proportions. LDL contains more lipids while HDL contains an equal proportion of lipids to protein. These composition differences affect the function of these lipoproteins.

   LDL molecules carry triglycerides and cholesterol to the body's tissues. LDL can build up in the lining of the blood vessels and are more susceptible to reactions with oxygen (oxidation), which can cause them to induce inflammation in the walls of the blood vessels. It is thought that having a lower level of these LDL molecules will reduce the risk of cardiovascular disease.

   HDL contains a higher proportion of protein relative to triglycerides and cholesterol. HDL functions to remove cholesterol and other lipids from the blood and tissues and return it to the liver for use in the digestive system. Having more of these HDL molecules will reduce the lipids and cholesterol in the blood, which may protect the cardiovascular system.

3. *Your family does not like to eat fish but you are concerned that they are not getting enough omega-3 fatty acids. Your mother suggests that you all take fish oil supplements but you disagree. Give her any 2 reasons why she should not take fish oil supplements and suggest any 2 foods that could supply omega-3 fatty acids in place of fish.*

   Fish oil supplements may provide omega-3 fatty acids at levels that are unsafe. Most fish have a lot of omega-3 fatty acids, but not at such a concentrated level as found in supplements. High levels of omega-3 fatty acids can impair blood clotting, which can lead to dangerous hemorrhages.

   Fish oil supplements are produced from the fat under the skin of most fish. This tissue can accumulate high levels of toxic heavy metals such as methylmercury. Most supplements do not undergo rigorous testing since they are not subject to FDA approval. These fish oil supplements could thus contain toxic levels of heavy metals.

   She could try flaxseed oil or crushed flaxseed with her food. Flaxseed contains omega-3 fatty acids at safe levels. She can also try eggs that contain omega-3 fatty acids or foods fortified with omega-3s.

4. *Many people like to buy frozen entrees such as pasta or lasagna but they also want to watch their fat intake. Describe how they should examine food labels for any two similar items to compare the fat content and to make an informed decision.*

   They should first examine the Daily Values section of the label to confirm that the percentage of calories from fat is under 25% and the percentage from saturated fat is under 5%. They should also look at the ingredients list to check that cheese or creams (sources of saturated fats) are listed further down in the ingredients list. This would suggest that the product is high in pasta or vegetables as opposed to saturated fat sources.

5. *List a one-day eating plan that is typical for the American diet. Develop a meal plan that has similar meals but is substantially lower in saturated and* trans *fat. Any type of ingredient substitution or food substitution can be considered.*

   This is wide open. If someone eats fast food, she can substitute food prepared at home or some lower-fat, frozen food items such as steamed vegetables or frozen baked or broiled fish. If she is describing a casserole or lasagna dish, she can reduce the amount of butter or full-fat cheese in the recipe. She can also substitute lower-fat items for the full-fat items such as cheeses or creams. She can also replace butter with olive oil or corn oil.

6. *If a person needs 2500 calories a day, what is the range of grams of all fats that he should consume to stay within the* Dietary Guidelines*? What maximum amount of saturated fat should he consume based on the same guideline?*

   Step 1: Figure out how many calories should come from fat based on the AMDRs:
   $2500 \times 0.2 = 500$ calories (20%) $2500 \times 0.35 = 875$ calories (35%)

   Step 2: Divide the number of calories by 9 calories per gram:
   500 calories ÷ 9 calories/gram = 55.6 grams (20%) 875 calories ÷ 9 calories/gram = 97.2 grams (35%)

   For saturated fat: 2500 calories × 0.1 = 250 calories (10% maximum) ÷ 9 kilocalories/gram = 27.8 grams

Controversy Discussion Questions

1. *Describe any 2 ways that the Mediterranean diet may be more healthful than a typical American diet.*

   The Mediterranean diet incorporates more nuts, fruits, and whole grains than a typical American diet. These foods contribute more fiber, vitamins, and minerals without a lot of calories or saturated fats.

   The Mediterranean diet also incorporates far less red meats and more fish (with healthy omega-3 fatty acids) than the typical American diet. This also reduces the amount of saturated fats consumed each day.

2. *Your father knows that you are taking a consumer nutrition course at the community college. He asks you if he should use butter or margarine on his food. What advice would you give to him?*

   Tell your father that moderation is the key here! Butter contains more saturated fats and cholesterol since it is made from animal products. Hard margarines, from plant sources, can contain significant amounts of hydrogenated fats, which can pose the same risks as saturated fats. Softer margarines contain much less hydrogenated fats and may be a healthier choice.

   You may want to suggest alternatives to butter or margarine as well. Perhaps your father could cook his eggs with olive oil instead of butter. He could use yogurt or salsa on his baked potato instead of margarine or butter.

3. a. *Discuss any 3 nutritional benefits of eating nuts.*

   Nuts are an excellent source of fiber. They also contain vitamin E, which is a valuable antioxidant. They contain vegetable oils, which may help protect the heart and reduce the levels of LDL in the blood.

   b. *What is one obvious nutritional drawback to eating nuts?*

   Nuts do derive much of their calories from fat. They can be high in calories, so portion control when eating nuts is essential to obtaining the maximum nutritional benefits.

4. *Your aunt wants to lower her LDL cholesterol by changing her diet before having to resort to taking medication. Give her any 3 suggestions for reducing her intake of dietary saturated and* trans *fats.*

   You can suggest that your aunt reduce her consumption of red meat. While preparing meat, she can cut away all visible signs of fat. She can also pick the leanest cut of meat. This way, she will reduce her intake of saturated fats, which may cause an increase in her LDL levels.

   You can suggest that she replace animal products such as butter in recipes with vegetable oils such as olive oil or corn oil. This way, she can still get the flavor and texture from fats but she will be getting more unsaturated fats in place of saturated fats in her diet. This may also help her to decrease her blood LDL levels.

   You can also suggest that your aunt increase her intake of dietary fiber. Fiber may, in itself, reduce the level of LDL in her blood, but if she chooses more whole grains, fruits, and vegetables to increase her fiber intake while controlling calories, she will automatically reduce her intake of meats and other sources of saturated fats.

Worksheet Answer Key

Worksheet 5-1: Label Analysis—Lipids

1. 43 grams × 9 kcal/gram ÷ 670 total kcal × 100 = 57.8 %

2. a. 17 grams × 9 kcal/gram ÷ 670 total kcal × 100 = 22.8%
   b. Most people should limit the levels of saturated fat in their diets to lower blood cholesterol or control heart disease.

3. a. The cream cheese, Romano and Parmesan cheeses, and the half and half cream contribute the most saturated fats.
   b. *Open answer (answers will vary)*
   c. The amount of the high-fat ingredients could be reduced.

4. 1 meal; no

5. a. 43 g ÷ 65 g × 100 = 66%
   b. 17 g ÷ 20 g × 100 = 85%

Worksheet 5-2: Intake Analysis—Lipids

1. a. Butter, cheese biscuit, and ice cream
   b. Quarter Pounder with cheese and French fries

2. a. H: 22.6 grams × 9 kcal/gram ÷ 1119.2 kcal × 100 = 18.2% (This one!)
   J: 15.73 grams × 9 kcal/gram ÷ 1306 kcal × 100 = 10.8%

b. H: 2.94 × 9 kcal/gram ÷ 1119.2 kcal × 100 = 2.4% (This one!)
J: 2.31 × 9 kcal/gram ÷ 1306 kcal × 100 = 1.6%

3. Replace the French fries with mashed potatoes

4. Food-borne contamination from shellfish or seafood

5. a. Butter
b. Vegetable oil with seasonings or less butter

Worksheet 5-3: Choosing Lower-Fat Foods

1. Pretzels
2. Turkey sandwich
3. low-fat milk
4. baked chicken
5. tuna packed in water
6. Spaghetti with marinara sauce
7. Bagels
8. mushroom pizza
9. trout
10. Beef bacon
11. sugar cookie

Worksheet 5-4: Chapter 5 Review Crossword Puzzle

1. satiety
2. salmon
3. cholesterol
4. hydrogenation
5. emulsifier
6. monounsaturated
7. adipose
8. essential
9. Olestra
10. avocado
11. protein
12. linolenic acid
13. insulation

Learning Activities & Project Ideas

Activity 5-1: Saturated Fat Demonstration[3] LO 5.5, 5.8

To show the students how much saturated fat goes into the arteries, melt the skin of a chicken, or cook a burger, a strip of bacon, etc., and then set it aside. By the end of the class, have students look at the white, solid portion that is created (saturated fat). Then place it on a piece of a hose, and try to add water to the clogged hose. The students then have a visual experience on the amount of fat we are consuming. Inform students that, at home, they can also cook many types of soups, let them cool, and then skim off the fat from the top. This will show how much hidden fat is found in other types of food.

Activity 5-2: Compare Energy Values of Food Prepared by Different Techniques[4] LO 5.8

Instruct students to calculate and compare the percent of kcalories from fat in a baked, broiled, or steamed food versus the same food after frying. Use the table of nutrient composition of foods and fast foods in Appendix A of the textbook, an online database (e.g., https://www.supertracker.usda.gov/foodapedia.aspx), or a diet analysis program to find the kilocalorie and gram amounts of fat for each food.

Activity 5-3: Recipe Modification[5] LO 5.9

Recipes can be modified to retain flavor and texture while the fat content is reduced during food preparation. Provide students with a copy of Handout 5-4 ("How to Modify a Recipe"). Discuss the items substituted for fat. Instruct students to bring in their own traditional recipes and practice modifying them according to these suggestions. You can even designate a day for students to bring in food items they prepared from a modified recipe.

Activity 5-4: Discussion of Guidelines for Fat Intake[6] LO 5.8, 5.10

At the beginning of this chapter, ask students to write on a sheet of paper their beliefs about fat intake recommendations. Instruct them to be as specific as possible. Give them 5-10 minutes to complete this exercise. Then ask each student to share what they believe and compile a list. You can tell them that we will explore these

---

[3] Contributed by Nancy J. Correa-Matos, Ph.D., R.D., University of North Florida
[4] Contributed by Lori W. Turner, Ph.D., R.D., University of Alabama
[5] Contributed by Sandra Woodruff, M.S., R.D.
[6] Contributed by Lori W. Turner, Ph.D., R.D., University of Alabama

statements in this chapter and compare them to the actual guidelines, and can talk about the challenge of presenting nutrition information to the public.

Chapter Lecture Outline

I. Introducing the Lipids
   A. Lipids in foods and the human body fall into three classes: triglycerides, phospholipids, sterols
   B. How are Fats Useful to the Body? – When we say "fat," we generally mean triglycerides
      1. Fuel Stores – Provide energy for muscles, reserves for illness/starvation (Figure 5-1 = fat cell)
      2. Efficiency of Fat Stores – Glycogen holds a lot of water and is bulky whereas fats provide more than twice as many calories per gram.
      3. Cushions, Climate, and Cell Membranes
         a. Serve as cushioning and insulation
         b. Part of cell membranes
      4. Transport and Raw Material – transported around the body and can be made into a variety of substances
   C. How Are Fats Useful in Food?
      1. Concentration Calorie Source – important for people who expend a lot of calories (see Figure 5-2)
      2. Fat-Soluble Nutrients and Their Absorption
         a. Helps body absorb fat-soluble vitamins such as A, D, E, and K
         b. Provides essential fatty acids
      3. Sensory Qualities – fats give foods enticing aromas and flavors
      4. A Role in Satiety – fats give people a feeling of fullness after a meal

II. A Close Look at Lipids
   A. Triglycerides: Fatty Acids and Glycerol
      1. Most dietary fat and stored fat in the body
      2. Triglyceride is made up of 1 glycerol + 3 fatty acids
   B. Saturated vs. Unsaturated Fatty Acids
      1. Saturation of Fatty Acids (see Figure 5-4)
         a. Saturated fatty acid – filled to capacity with hydrogen atoms
         b. Unsaturated fatty acid – missing hydrogen
            1. Monounsaturated – one point of unsaturation
            2. Polyunsaturated – two or more points of unsaturation (PUFA)
      2. Melting Point and Fat Hardness – Fats melt at different temperatures:
         a. Saturated fats – solid at room temperature
         b. Unsaturated fats – liquids at room temperature
         c. Homogenized fats are actually saturated fats that stay in liquid form due to processing.
      3. Where the Fatty Acids Are Found (Figure 5-5)
         a. Saturated fats – Found in most animal products and in coconut oil
         b. Unsaturated fats – Found in most plant products
   C. Phospholipids and Sterols
      1. Phospholipids
         a. Glycerol + two fatty acids + phosphorus combined with oxygen
         b. Phosphorus part makes it soluble in water
         c. Fatty acids make it soluble in fat
         d. Therefore, can serve as an emulsifier
         e. Key role is in stabilizing cell membranes
         f. Some phospholipids help generate signals inside of cells in response to hormones such as insulin.
      2. Sterols
         a. Large molecules consisting of interconnected rings of carbon atoms with side chains of carbon, hydrogen, and oxygen attached
         b. Cholesterol
            1. Is found in all animal cell membranes
            2. Is nonessential
            3. Forms plaques that cause atherosclerosis

c. Cholesterol serves as the raw material for:
   1. Bile
   2. Vitamin D
   3. Steroid hormones including the sex hormones

III. Lipids in the Body
   A. Introduction
      1. Lipids affect the body's functioning and condition.
      2. Lipids demand special handling because they are insoluble in water and body fluids consist largely of water.
   B. How Are Fats Digested and Absorbed?
      1. Fat In the Stomach – fat floats on the watery fluids and is not digested
      2. Fat In the Small Intestine
         a. Bile is produced by the liver and emulsifies fats so that they can be broken down.
         b. Emulsified fat is then digested by enzymes supplied by the pancreas.
         c. The enzymes cleave triglycerides into free fatty acids, glycerol, and monoglycerides.
         d. People who do not have a gallbladder have bile released from the liver directly into the small intestine.
      3. Fat Absorption (Figure 5-7)
         a. Digestive tract absorbs triglycerides from a meal with up to 98% efficiency
         b. The bile may be reabsorbed by the small intestinal cells and reused by the body or it may be eliminated with the feces.
   C. Transport of Fats
      1. At the intestinal lining, shorter-chain fatty acids and glycerol are absorbed directly into the bloodstream.
      2. The cells of the intestinal lining convert large lipid fragments back into triglycerides and combine them with protein, forming chylomicrons that travel in the lymph.
      3. Lipoprotein – how fat is transported in the body; a mixture of fat and protein

IV. Storing and Using the Body's Fat
   A. The Body's Fat Stores
      1. When low on fuel, the body draws on its stored fat for energy.
      2. The fats can be stored under the skin or in the fat pads of the abdomen, the breasts, or other tissues.
      3. The body can also store excess carbohydrate as fat (see Figure 5-8).
   B. What Happens When the Tissues Need Energy?
      1. Fat cells respond to the call for energy by dismantling stored fat molecules and releasing fat components into the bloodstream.
      2. Upon receiving these components, cells break them down further into fragments. Each fragment is combined with a fragment derived from glucose, and the energy-releasing process continues, liberating energy, carbon dioxide, and water.
   C. Carbohydrate in Fat Breakdown – Without glucose present, fat is incompletely broken down to ketones.

V. Dietary Fat, Cholesterol, and Health
   A. Overview – Cardiovascular diseases (CVD) is the leading cause of death of adults in the U.S. and Canada.
      1. Heart & Artery Disease
         a. A diet too high in saturated or *trans* fats can increase the risk of heart and artery disease.
         b. Replacing saturated fats with olive oil, nuts, seafood, soy products, or whole grains may have a beneficial effect on blood lipids.
         c. Replacing saturated fats with refined carbohydrates may not lower CVD risk.
      2. Obesity
         a. More likely with fat overconsumption in the diet since fat has 9 calories per gram
         b. A larger waist may increase blood triglycerides, which may increase the risk of heart disease.
   B. Recommendations For Lipid Intakes – Table 5-2 = lipid intake recommendations for healthy people
      1. A Healthy Range of Fat Intakes
         a. 20-35% total energy, enough essential fatty acids
         b. Less than 10% of daily calories should come from saturated fats

2. U.S. Fat Intakes – 34% total energy from fat, 11% from saturated fat
3. Too Little Lipid
    a. Athletes or people with eating disorders may take in less than 20% of calories from lipids.
    b. Risk inadequate energy intake as well as deficiencies of fat-soluble vitamins

C. Lipoproteins and Heart Disease Risk
1. Overview
    a. The just-eaten fat travels in the bloodstream as chylomicrons.
    b. Body tissues can extract whatever fat they need from chylomicrons.
    c. The remnants are then picked up by the liver, which dismantles them and reuses their parts.
2. Major Lipoproteins: Chylomicrons, VLDL, LDL, HDL – In addition to the chylomicron, the body uses three other types of lipoproteins (Figure 5-10) to carry fats:
    a. Very-low-density lipoproteins (VLDL), which carry triglycerides and other lipids made in the liver to the body cells for their use
    b. Low-density lipoproteins (LDL) transport cholesterol and other lipids to the tissues. LDL are made from VLDL after they have donated many of their triglycerides to body cells.
    c. High-density lipoproteins (HDL), which are critical in the process of carrying cholesterol away from body cells to the liver for disposal
    d. HDL and LDL play major roles with regard to heart health and are the focus of most recommendations made for reducing the risk of heart disease.
3. The LDL and HDL Difference
    a. Both LDL and HDL carry lipids in the blood but LDL are larger, lighter, and contain more cholesterol; HDL are smaller, denser, and contain more protein.
    b. LDL – Delivers cholesterol and triglycerides from the liver to the tissues; HDL scavenge excess cholesterol and phospholipids from the tissues for disposal
    c. Higher levels of LDL can cause buildup in the linings of the arteries and can trigger inflammation, leading to increased risk of heart disease.
    d. High LDL levels may suggest increased risk of heart attack.
    e. Low HDL levels may be associated with a higher risk of heart attack.
4. The Importance of Cholesterol Testing – high LDL & low HDL = 2 major CVD risk factors

D. What Does *Food* Cholesterol Have to Do With *Blood* Cholesterol?
1. Does cholesterol matter? – Saturated food fats (and *trans* fat) raise blood cholesterol more than food cholesterol does.
2. Dietary Cholesterol Guidelines and Sources
    a. Dietary cholesterol makes a smaller but still significant contribution to elevated blood cholesterol.
    b. The *Dietary Guidelines* suggest that most people keep their cholesterol intakes under 300 milligrams per day.
    c. On average, women consume about 240 mg of cholesterol each day; men, about 350 mg
3. Genetic Influence – A small percentage of people respond to a high cholesterol intake with greatly increased blood cholesterol.

E. Recommendations Applied
1. Trimming Saturated Fat to Lower LDL
    a. To lower LDL cholesterol, eat less fat, especially the saturated fat and *trans* fat, from foods.
    1. Figure 5-11 shows that when fat is removed from food, the saturated fat and calories decline.
2. Raising HDL—Recent Revelations
    a. Regular physical activity may raise HDL levels
    b. People who have taken medication to raise HDL levels very high do not seem to enjoy any extra reduction in the risk of heart disease.

VI. Essential Polyunsaturated Fatty Acids – Linoleic acid and linolenic acid

A. Why Do I Need Essential Fatty Acids?
1. Linoleic and linolenic acid must be supplied by the diet & have important functions (see Table 5-4)
2. Deficiencies of Essential Fatty Acids – Have many effects in the body
    a. When the diet is deficient in all of the polyunsaturated fatty acids, symptoms include:
        1. Reproductive failure
        2. Skin abnormalities
        3. Kidney and liver disorders

4. Growth and vision impairment in infants
b. The body stores essential fatty acids, so extreme deficiencies are rare.
3. Meet the Eicosanoids – Essential fatty acids can be converted to eicosanoids, which are hormone-like substances that regulate smooth muscle function, immune system function, inflammatory responses, and blood lipid levels.

B. Omega-6 And Omega-3 Fatty Acid Families
1. Linoleic acid is the "parent" member of the omega-6 fatty acid family.
   a. Abundant in vegetable oils
   b. Linoleic acid can be converted to other members of this family, for example, arachidonic acid
2. Linolenic acid is the "parent" member of the omega-3 fatty acid family – Linolenic acid can be converted to other members of this family, for example, EPA and DHA
3. In Heart Health – EPA and DHA:
   a. Are made in limited amounts in the body
   b. Abundant in fish oils
   c. Lower blood pressure
   d. Prevent blood clot formation
   e. Protect against irregular heartbeats
   f. May reduce inflammation
4. In Cancer Prevention
   a. Omega-3 fatty acids may suppress inflammation, which can promote some cancers.
   b. Surprisingly, men with more DHA in the blood were MORE likely to have an aggressive prostate cancer than men with less blood DHA.
5. In Cell Membranes – EPA and DHA may collect in cell membranes (see Figure 5-4) and help enhance the health of the cells.
6. Brain Function and Vision – EPA and DHA may collect in the cell membranes
   a. May reduce inflammation and age related brain diseases
   b. Essential for normal infant growth and development, and DHA is found in human breast milk

C. Where are the Omega-3 Fatty Acids in Foods?
1. Overview
   a. The *Dietary Guidelines* recommend eating 8-12 ounces of seafood each week.
   b. Each serving should provide about 250 milligrams of EPA and DHA.
2. Special Populations
   a. Children and pregnant women need EPA and DHA but they need to be watchful of mercury contamination in fish.
   b. Young children need about 3-6 ounces of seafood each week.
   c. Pregnant women need 8-12 ounces of seafood each week.
3. What About Fish Oil Supplements? – Fish oil supplements are not recommended because:
   a. They may raise LDL
   b. High intakes may increase bleeding times
   c. High intakes may interfere with wound healing
   d. High intakes may suppress immune function
4. Omega-3 Enriched Foods
   a. Egg producers fortify certain brands of eggs by adding fish/algal oil to chicken food.
   b. The chickens lay DHA-enriched eggs.
   c. Flaxseed is a source of linolenic acid, which is converted to EPA & DHA in the body to a limited extent.

D. A Consumer's Guide to Weighing Seafood's Risks and Benefits
1. Finding the EPA and DHA – Cod is often used in fast-food places and does not contain much EPA or DHA.
2. Concerns about Toxins
   a. Some fish is contaminated with methylmercury (due to associated bacteria) and is not safe to eat.
   b. Mercury can accumulate in the liver, immune system tissue, and brain over time.
   c. Pregnant or lactating women should avoid consuming fish with suspected mercury contamination.
   d. The benefits of consuming fish outweigh the risks.
3. Cooked versus Raw
   a. Many people like sushi but risk contracting serious bacterial or viral infections.

   b. Cooking the fish will kill microbes that cause illness.
4. Fresh from the Farm – Farmed fish may have lower levels of methylmercury than their wild counterparts but many farm fish cages may still be exposed to contamination from the water.
5. Moving Ahead – This consumer guide can point you to your best seafood choices:
   a. Substitute fish and shellfish for red meat.
   b. Use the dietary principles of adequacy, moderation, and variety to obtain the benefits of seafood while minimizing the risks.
   c. Avoid eating raw seafood.
   d. Learn what seafoods are high in EPA and DHA.

VII. The Effects of Processing on Unsaturated Fats – Vegetable oils make up most of the added fat in the U.S. diet. Why??

A. What Is "Hydrogenated Vegetable Oil," and What's It Doing in My Chocolate Chip Cookies?
   1. Hydrogenation of Oils
      a. Hydrogenation forces hydrogen into the liquid oil, making the oil more saturated as it accepts the hydrogens.
      b. Hydrogenated fats:
         1. Resist rancidity; more resistant to oxidation
         2. Are firmer textured; more spreadable
         3. Have a higher smoking point than unsaturated oils
   2. Nutrient Losses
      a. Hydrogenation may affect essential fatty acids, vitamin K
      b. Alternatives to hydrogenation: antioxidant additives, refrigeration

B. What Are *Trans*-Fatty Acids, and Are They Harmful? – *Trans* fatty acids are a health risk.
   1. Formation of *Trans*-Fatty Acids – Occurs during hydrogenation (see Figure 5-13)
   2. Health Effects of *Trans*-Fatty Acids – Consuming *trans* fat poses a risk to heart and arteries by:
      a. Raising blood LDL cholesterol
      b. Lowering blood HDL cholesterol
      c. Increasing tissue inflammation, a key player in heart disease
      d. Replacing heart-healthy oils
      e. *Trans*-fatty acids occur in small amounts in nature, mostly in dairy products, but these *trans* fats have little effect on blood lipids.
   3. Swapping *Trans* Fats for Saturated Fats?
      a. Largest contributor of *trans* fat to the U.S. diet has been commercially fried foods.
      b. Newly formulated commercial oils and fats can now perform the same job as the old hydrogenated fats, but with fewer *trans* fatty acids.
      c. Many new fats merely substitute saturated fat for *trans* fat.
      d. Take-home message: Just because a food lacks *trans* fat, this does not mean it is good for you.

VIII. Fat in the Diet

A. Get to Know the Fats in Foods
   1. Essential Fats
      a. Everyone needs the essential fatty acids and vitamin E provided by fish, nuts, and vegetable oils.
      b. A few teaspoons of oil each day and two serving of seafood per week are adequate
      c. Most people get more than enough.
   2. Replace, Don't Add
      a. All fats bring abundant calories to the diet and excess fats lead to more stored body fat.
      b. These amounts provide about 5 grams of pure fat, providing 45 calories:
         1. 1 tsp oil or shortening
         2. 1 ½ tsp mayonnaise, butter, or margarine
         3. 1 T regular salad dressing, cream cheese, or heavy cream
         4 1 ½ T sour cream
   3. Visible vs. Invisible Fats – "invisible" fats (e.g., marbling in meat, fat in avocados, cheese, etc.) are big contributors to dietary fat in the U.S.

B. Fats in Protein Foods
   1. People can select meats based on their labels.

2. Meat: Mostly Protein or Fat? (Figure 5-14 = fat/calorie data for ground meats)
   a. Most fat in meats is invisible.
   b. A 4-ounce hamburger can contain 23 g of protein and 23 g of fat, over 8 g of that fat is saturated
3. Clues to Lower-Fat Meats – choose "loin" or "round"; avoid processed or ground

C. Milk & Milk Products (Figure 5-15)
   1. Choose nonfat varieties
   2. Cream and butter are not listed in the milk and milk products group because they do not contain a lot of protein or calcium.

D. Grains (Figure 5-16)
   1. Choose natural whole grains; avoid processed grains & high-fat sauces
   2. Grain-based desserts such as cookies, pastries, and cakes are the leading single contributor of solid fats to the U.S. diet.

E. Food Feature: Defensive Dining
   1. How can we meet the guidelines?
      a. Select the most nutrient-dense foods from all food groups.
      b. Consume fewer and smaller portions of foods and beverages that contain solid fats.
      c. Replace solid fats with liquid oils when possible.
      d. Check food labels and select foods with little saturated fats and no *trans* fats.
      e. Use Table 5-7 to identify solid fat ingredients in foods.
   2. In the Grocery Store
      a. Use food labels to compare foods' saturated fat and *trans* fat contents.
      b. Eat lower-fat foods more often and reserve the higher-saturated fat foods for occasional treats.
      c. Vegetables without added butter or sauces can be used as a staple food as opposed to a treat.
      d. Choosing among Margarines
         1. Soft or liquid margarines are made from unsaturated oils
         2. Many margarines contain olive oil or omega-3 fats, making them a heart-healthy option.
         3. May contain plant sterols, which may accumulate in the tissues of the arteries and brain
         4. It is important to read labels and select margarines with no *trans* fats.
      e. Choosing Unsaturated Oils
         1. It is good to try different unsaturated oils since they each have unique benefits.
         2. Peanut and safflower oils have vitamin E.
         3. Olive oil also has antioxidant phytochemicals.
         4. Canola oil has a lot of unsaturated and essential fatty acids.
         5. High cooking temperatures can destroy omega-3 fatty acids.
      f. Fat-Free Products and Artificial Fats
         1. Fat replacers are made up of carbohydrates and proteins that provide flavors like fats but with fewer calories.
         2. Olestra is an artificial fat.
         3. Consume these foods in moderation.
   3. Revamp Recipes
      a. Modify high-fat recipes to reduce the amount of saturated or *trans* fat.
      b. Grill, roast, bake, microwave, stir-fry, or poach foods.
      c. Reduce or eliminate food "add-ons" like high fat sauces or dressings.
      d. Cut recipe amounts of meat in half; use only lean meats.
      e. Sift off solidified fat from a gravy and use the defatted broth as seasoning for other meals.
      f. Make prepared mixes, such as rice, without the fats called for on the label.
      g. See Table 5-8 for practical ways to cut down on solid fats.
   4. Feasting on Fast Foods (see Figure 5-17)
      a. Eat salads but watch out for toppings that have fat in them.
      b. Eat a small hamburger, broiled chicken, or veggie burger.
      c. Chili, without the sour cream and cheese, over a baked potato can be filling.
      d. Top tacos, beans, or burritos with salsa instead of cheese.
      e. Eat broiled fish or chicken sandwiches instead of fried.
      f. Limit the number of chicken wings since the skins are high in saturated fat.
   5. Change Your Habits – one small change at a time

IX. Controversy: Good Fats, Bad Fats—U.S. Guidelines and the Mediterranean Diet
   A. Introduction
      1. To consumers, advice about dietary fats appears to change almost daily.
      2. To researchers, the evolution of advice reflects decades of following leads and testing theories about the effects of dietary fats on health.
   B. The Objections to "Low-Fat" Guidelines
      1 For years, consumers were urged to cut fat in all of their food choices.
         a. Now the advice emphasizes reducing saturated and *trans* fats and calorie control.
         b. Many people found it difficult to adhere to a low-fat diet.
      2. Are Low-Fat Diets Helpful—or Not?
         a. Low-fat diets that are low in fiber and high in carbohydrates may raise blood triglycerides.
         b. Low-fat diets may exclude healthy foods such as fatty fish, nuts, seeds, and vegetable oils that provide essential fatty acids, plus phytochemicals.
      3. Research on High-Fat Diets
         a. People obtaining >40% of all calories from fat were not more likely to have CVD.
         b. On closer examination, people from Crete had the lowest rate of heart disease and consumed 10% of all calories from saturated fats.
            1. Known as the Mediterranean diet
            2. Many young people there are eating a more western diet and are no longer as healthy.
      4. Recent Revelations – suggest that higher saturated fat intake may not increase the risk of heart disease on its own but rather the combinations of food eaten together may be responsible
      5. The Current Guidelines
         a. DRI committee now recommends a diet containing fat up to 35% of total calories but reduced in saturated and *trans* fat and controlled in calories to lower risk of heart disease, cancer, diabetes, and obesity.
         b. For healthy people, researchers recommend a "wise-fat" approach.
         c. Replace the "bad" saturated and *trans* fats with "good" unsaturated fats within calorie limits.
   C. High-Fat Foods of the Mediterranean Diet
      1. Olive Oil: The Mediterranean Connection – A Mediterranean diet rich in olives and olive oil:
         a. Provides phytochemicals that act as antioxidants
         b. Reduces blood-clotting factors
         c. Interferes with the inflammatory response that leads to disease progression
         d. Olive oil should not be used as a magic potion against heart disease.
         e. Olive oil also provides 9 calories per gram like any other fat.
      2. The Mediterranean Diet beyond Olive Oil – Olive oil cannot take all the credit for lower rates of heart disease seen with the Mediterranean diet.
         a. Lower intakes of red meats
         b. Higher intakes of nuts, vegetables, and fruits, which increase fiber and phytochemicals
         c. Higher intake of fish and seafood
         d. Other important factors are increased intake of monounsaturated and polyunsaturated fats
         e. Low or absent *trans* fat intakes
         f. Rich in carbohydrates and fiber from whole foods
         g. Rich in vitamins, minerals, and phytochemicals
      3. Fatty Fish: A Key Mediterranean Food – Increased levels of omega-3 fatty acids associated with fish intake may reduce the risk of cardiovascular disease.
         a. Omega-3 fatty acids also come from unusual foods such as wild plants and snails.
         b. Meat and dairy products are higher in omega-3 fatty acids since the animals graze in fields.
      4. Nuts: More than a High-Calorie Snack Food
         a. Nuts and Body weight
            1. Nuts provide up to 80 percent of their calories from fat and one ounce has over 200 calories.
            2. Many people who eat nuts tend to be leaner and have smaller waistlines and lower disease risks.
            3. Nuts should replace not be added to other foods and fats in the diet.
         b. Nuts for the Heart – Nuts may lower heart disease because they are:
            1. Low in saturated fats
            2. High in fiber, vegetable protein, and vitamin E

3. Contain plant sterols that can block cholesterol absorption
4. High in phytochemicals that act as antioxidants
5. Moderation in nut consumption is essential to gain benefits without excessive calories.

c. Potential Mechanisms

1. Nuts supply anti-inflammatory phytochemicals and the antioxidant vitamin E, which may reduce inflammation that can lead to heart disease.
2. Increased nut intake may reduce the inflammation markers in the blood but more research is needed.

D. Fats to Avoid: Saturated Fats and *Trans* Fats

1. Saturated fat is the number one dietary determinant of LDL cholesterol levels.
2. *Trans* fat intake also increases LDL cholesterol.
3. Foods have a blend of fatty acid types so it is impossible to totally eliminate saturated and *trans* fats.
4. Eating more vegetables, fruits, legumes, nuts, soy products, and whole grains will reduce saturated fat intakes.

E. Conclusion

1. The Synergy of a Whole Foods Diet Pattern and Lifestyle – Adding foods of the Mediterranean diet to a Western diet may not improve health.
2. Application

a. Note sources of saturated fat in the diet and try to replace them with unsaturated fats or choices more in line with a Mediterranean diet (see Table C5-1 for Food Sources of Fatty Acids).

b. See Figure C5-2 to see how using the principles of a Mediterranean diet reduces the level of saturated and unsaturated fats in the sample meal plan.

c. Be physically active as well.

Worksheet 5-1: Label Analysis—Lipids

Instructions: Use the label for a frozen meal below to answer the questions that follow on a separate sheet of paper.

INGREDIENTS: COOKED FETTUCCINI PASTA (WATER, SEMOLINA [DURUM WHEAT, NIACIN, FERROUS SULFATE, THAMINE MONONITRATE, RIBOFLAVIN, FOLIC ACID], EGG WHITE), COOKED CHICKEN BREAST CHUNKS (CHICKEN BREAST CHUNKS, WATER, MODIFIED FOOD STARCH, SALT, SODIUM TRIPOLYPHOSPHATE), BROCCOLI, HEAVY WHIPPING CREAM, WATER, CREAM CHEESE (PASTEURIZED MILK AND CREAM CHEESE CULTURES, SALT, CAROB BEAN GUM), SOYBEAN OIL, ROMANO (FROM COW'S MILK) AND PARMESAN CHEESE (PART-SKIM MILK, CHEESE CULTURES, SALT, ENZYMES, CELLULOSE POWDER [PREVENTS CAKING]), HALF AND HALF (CREAM, MILK), CONTAINS 2% OR LESS OF: GARLIC, SHERRY WINE (CONTAINS SULFUR DIOXIDE), STABILIZER (MODIFIED FOOD STARCH, SODIUM PHOSPHATE, MONO- AND DIGLYCERIDES, DEHYDRATED GARLIC, XANTHAN AND GUAR GUMS, SALT, PAPRIKA), SALT, MODIFIED CORN STARCH, BUTTER (CREAM, SALT), FLAVORINGS, BUTTER FLAVOR (PARTIALLY HYDROGENATED SOYBEAN OIL, FLAVOR [BUTTER OIL, ENZYME MODIFIED BUTTERFAT, WHEY POWDER, NONFAT DRY MILK POWDER], SOY LECITHIN [EMULSIFIER]), SPICES, PAPRIKA.
CONTAINS: WHEAT, EGG, MILK, SOY.

Nutrition Facts

Serving Size 1 Meal
Servings Per Container 2

Amount Per Serving	
Calories 670	Calories from Fat ?
	% Daily Value*
Total Fat 43g	**?%**
Saturated Fat 17g	**?%**
Trans Fat 1g	
Cholesterol 65mg	**?%**
Sodium 1180mg	**?%**
Total Carbohydrate 39g	**?%**
Dietary Fiber 6g	**?%**
Sugars 1g	
Protein 32g	

Vitamin A 15%	•	Vitamin C 30%
Calcium 25%	•	Iron 10%

* Percent Daily Values are based on a 2,000 calorie diet. Your Daily Values may be higher or lower depending on your calorie needs.

	Calories	2,000	2,500
Total Fat	Less than	65g	80g
Sat Fat	Less than	20g	25g
Cholesterol	Less than	300mg	300mg
Sodium	Less than	2400mg	2400mg
Total Carbohydrate		300g	375g
Dietary Fiber		25g	30g

1. What percentage of the total calories comes from fat?
2. a. What percentage of the total calories comes from saturated fat?
   b. Why might the information about saturated fat be important information for most people?
3. a. What ingredients likely contribute the largest amount of saturated fat?
   b. How could you substitute these ingredients to reduce the total amount of saturated fat in this product?
   c. What could you do to reduce the total amount of fat?
4. What is the serving size? Would this be considered a standard serving size based on what you know about serving sizes?
5. a. What percentage of the Daily Value for total fat is contributed by this particular product?
   b. What percentage of the Daily Value for saturated fat is contributed by this particular product?

Worksheet 5-2: Intake Analysis—Lipids

Eating Plan H (1 Meal)	**Eating Plan J (1 Meal)**
1 cup New England clam chowder 1 2-ounce cheesy biscuit 4 ounces broiled lobster tail 4 ounces broiled scallops 3 Tbsp. drawn, melted butter 1 cup rice pilaf 1 cup boiled carrot and green beans 12 ounces sweetened ice tea 1 cup vanilla ice cream	1 medium French fries 1 Quarter Pounder with cheese 20 ounces root beer

Look at Eating Plans H and J:

1. a. What are the sources of saturated fat in Eating Plan H?

   b. In Eating Plan J?

2. a. Which of these diets has a higher percentage of calories coming from saturated fat?

   b. From essential fatty acids?

3. Suggest ways to reduce the *trans* fats in Eating Plan J.

4. What food safety concerns might you have about Eating Plan H?

5. a. What are the sources of added fats in Eating Plan H?

   b. Suggest lower-fat alternatives to these added fats.

Worksheet 5-3: Choosing Lower-Fat Foods

Fats give foods their flavor, texture, and palatability. Unfortunately, these same characteristics entice people to eat too much from time to time. Do you know how to select low-fat foods that will help you meet dietary fat recommendations? Look at these examples of foods and consider how often you select the item that is lower in fat.

Which food in each of the following pairs is lower in fat? (Circle the lower-fat food in each pair.)

1. Pretzels or peanuts?
2. Turkey sandwich or hot dog?
3. Whole milk or low-fat milk?
4. Fried chicken or baked chicken?
5. Tuna packed in oil or tuna packed in water?
6. Spaghetti with marinara sauce or with Alfredo sauce?
7. Bagels or croissants?
8. Sausage pizza or mushroom pizza?
9. Salmon or trout?
10. Beef bacon or pork bacon?
11. Oatmeal cookie or sugar cookie?

You can find out the fat content of each item by checking the food tables found in Appendix A of your textbook, by using a diet analysis program, or by consulting an online database like the one at https://www.supertracker.usda.gov/foodapedia.aspx. Making such fat-free or low-fat food choices regularly can help you meet dietary fat recommendations. In addition, eating plenty of whole-grain products, fresh vegetables, legumes, and fruits daily will help to keep your fat intake under control.

Worksheet 5-4: Chapter 5 Review Crossword Puzzle

Across	Down
3. Only 300 milligrams or less of this lipid should be consumed each day 6. Fatty acid in which one carbon-carbon pair is bonded with fewer than 2 hydrogen atoms apiece 9. An artificial fat that was used in potato chips 11. High-density lipoprotein (HDL) is made up mostly of _____, which gives it a higher density than other lipoproteins. 12. Another name for the essential omega-3 fatty acid that helps maintain the health of the central nervous and vision systems	1. Feeling of fullness after a meal that contains an adequate amount of fat 2. This fish contributes high levels of EPA and DHA without excessive mercury 4. Addition of hydrogen to fatty acids to preserve them longer 5. Bile can help keep fats dispersed in water and serves as an _____. 7. Fat tissue is called _____ tissue. 8. Fatty acids that must be supplied by the diet 10. This fruit contains a very high level of monounsaturated fatty acids 13. Body fat serves as _____ to help the body maintain a stable temperature.

Handout 5-1: Why All Cholesterol Is Not Created Equally!

What Is Cholesterol?

- Cholesterol is a wax-like substance that is made up of sterol lipids. It is needed for cell membrane stability and for nerve cell membrane function.
- Cholesterol can be converted into bile, which aids in fat digestion and can be converted into hormones such as estrogen and testosterone.
- Vitamin D is also a sterol molecule.

Where Is Cholesterol Produced?

- Cholesterol is transported in the blood as a lipoprotein since the blood is water based. Cholesterol is produced in the liver and allows lipids to travel through the lymphatic system into the blood stream.

What Types of Cholesterol Are There?

- Very-low-density lipoproteins (VLDL) are made in the liver and converted into low-density lipoproteins (LDL). LDL have a higher proportion of lipids and cholesterol to protein.
- High-density lipoproteins (HDL) have a higher proportion of protein to lipid and cholesterol.

What Do LDL and HDL Do in the Body?

- LDL carries lipids and cholesterol from the liver to the body's cells. LDL molecules can get deposited on the walls of the blood vessels. Oxidation of LDL molecules can trigger inflammation in the blood vessels that can lead to clot formation. Oxidized LDL molecules can also attract white blood cells called macrophages that try to remove the LDL. This can lead to clots being released from the blood vessel walls.
- HDL carries cholesterol from the blood to the liver, where cholesterol is converted into bile. Higher levels of HDL are associated with lower incidence of cardiovascular disease.

What Can Be Done to Lower LDL and Raise HDL Levels?

- Reduce saturated fats in the diet to lower LDL levels. Studies suggest that high amounts of dietary saturated fatty acids may reduce the ability of the liver to remove excess LDL from the blood.
- Reduced body weight and moderate alcohol consumption may decrease the levels of VLDL molecules that are converted into LDL molecules in the liver.
- Increasing dietary plant sterols may interfere with the absorption of cholesterol from food. This could reduce the amount of LDL getting into the bloodstream.
- Increased physical activity has been associated with increased levels of HDL.

References:

How Safe Are Statins?: *Dr. Weil's Self-Healing Letter*. October 2003, page 1.
Cholesterol Busters: *University of California, Berkeley Wellness Letter*. Volume 20 (5), February 2004, page 4.
Controlling Elevated Cholesterol & Triglycerides: *Dr. Weil's Self-Healing Letter*. December 2002, pages 4-5.
Merck Manual, 16th Edition. 1992: Rahway, N.J. pages 373-383.

Handout 5-2: Why Omega-3 Fatty Acids Are Considered Good Fats

What Is the Main Omega-3 Fatty Acid?	• An essential fatty acid called linolenic acid found in plant oils that has many points of unsaturation (polyunsaturated) along the carbon-hydrogen backbone
What Happens to Linolenic Acid in the Body?	• The body converts some linolenic acid into EPA (eicosapentaenoic acid) and DHA (docosahexanenoic acid)
What Are Other Sources of EPA and DHA?	• Cold-water fish such as salmon or mackerel contain EPA and DHA
	• Vegetable sources of the precursor linolenic acid include flaxseed, walnuts, pecans, tofu, and green leafy vegetables
Why Are EPA and DHA So Good?	• They encourage the production of prostaglandin G1 series that are cyclic fatty acids that decrease platelet stickiness and overall inflammation in the blood vessels and other tissues
	• People with higher levels of EPA and DHA in their blood may have a lower level of inflammation in their tissues as shown by lower CRP levels
	• C-reactive protein (CRP) is a marker of inflammation that may predict who is at risk of cardiovascular disease and other types of chronic inflammation
	• EPA may be released from cell membranes, especially in the heart muscle where higher EPA levels may protect against deadly arrhythmias
	• Research inks higher blood levels of EPA and DHA in the blood with fewer heart attacks and less severe heart failure.
How to Get Enough Linolenic Acid?	• People should get 3 grams a day from a variety of sources such as cold-water fish, ground flaxseeds (flaxseed oil), pecans, walnuts, tofu, green leafy vegetables (see Table 5-6)

References:

Tuft's University Health & Nutrition Letter, Volume 21 (12), February 2004.
Special Supplement: *Tuft's University Health & Nutrition Letter*. Volume 20 (3) May 2002
Face the Fats: *Nutrition Action Health Letter*. Volume 29 (6) July/Aug 2002, pages 3-7
Merck Manual. 16th Edition. 1992: Rahway, N.J., pages 2659-2666.

Handout 5-3: How to Use the Exchange System to Estimate Fat

The exchange system is especially informative about the fats in foods. To use the exchange system, you need to know the fat value for each list (see the table below) and the foods on that list with their portion sizes. Two of the lists—non-starchy vegetables and fruits—contain no fat. A third list—starch—provides only a little. (Starch foods prepared with fat are counted as one starch exchange *plus* a fat exchange.) So you only need to learn the fat values for three lists: milks, meats/meat substitutes, and fats.

One Exchange	Fat (g)
Milks	
Nonfat (and low-fat)	0-3
Reduced-fat	5
Whole	8
Meats/meat substitutes	
Lean	0-3
Medium-fat	4-7
High-fat	8+
Plant-based proteins	varies
Fats	5
Starch	0-1
Vegetables (nonstarchy)	---
Fruits	---
Other carbohydrates	varies

The milk list offers three fat values for nonfat, reduced-fat, and whole milk. Think of nonfat milk as milk and of reduced-fat and whole milk as milk with added fat.

The meat list offers fat values for lean, medium-fat, and high-fat products; fat contents of plant-based proteins vary. People are often surprised to learn how much fat comes from meats and cheeses. An ounce of lean meat or low-fat cheese supplies about half of its energy from fat (28 protein kcalories and 27 fat kcalories). An ounce of high-fat meat or most cheese supplies 72 percent of its energy from fat (28 protein kcalories and 72 fat kcalories). As for the meat alternate, peanut butter, 2 tablespoons supply 76 percent of their energy from fat (32 protein kcalories and 144 fat kcalories). Note that one meat exchange is a single ounce; to use the exchange system, learn to recognize the number of ounces in a serving.

The fat list includes butter, margarine, and oil, of course, but it also includes bacon, olives, avocados, and many kinds of nuts. These foods are grouped together because a portion of any of them contains as much fat as a pat of butter and, like butter, offers negligible protein and carbohydrate. Fortunately, the fat list is sorted into saturated, monounsaturated, and polyunsaturated groups, which helps people make heart-wise selections when choosing fat.

Suppose you ate some spaghetti, corn on the cob, green beans, a spinach and carrot salad topped with garbanzo beans, sunflower seeds, and ranch dressing, angel food cake, and milk for dinner. (You seasoned the green beans and corn with butter.) To estimate the fat in this meal, you first need to recognize that a spaghetti dinner is really 1 cup of pasta, with 1 cup of tomato sauce and 3 ounces of lean ground beef. Then you need to translate these portions into exchanges: 2 starches, 1 vegetable, and 3 lean meats, respectively. Ignore the vegetables in the salad, but count the ½ cup of garbanzo beans as 1 starch + 1 lean meat, and the sunflower seeds and ranch dressing as 1 fat each.

Using the exchange system to estimate, this dinner provides about 39 grams of fat. A computer diet analysis program came to a similar conclusion (35 grams), as would a diet analysis using the values in a food composition table. To keep from underestimating fat intake, count "0-1" as "1 gram of fat" and count "0-3" as 3 grams of fat.

Diet Analysis of Entire Dinner:

Dinner		Exchange	Fat (g) Estimate	Fat (g) Actual
Salad:				
1 cup raw spinach, carrots, mushrooms	=	free	0	0
½ cup garbanzo beans	=	1 starch and 1 lean meat	4	2
1 tbs. sunflower seeds	=	1 fat	5	4
1 tbs. ranch salad dressing	=	1 fat	5	6
Entrée: spaghetti with meat sauce				
1 cup pasta (cooked)	=	2 starches	2	} 12
1 cup tomato sauce	=	1 vegetable (nonstarchy)	---	
3 oz. ground meat	=	3 lean meats	9	
½ cup green beans	=	1 vegetable (nonstarchy)	---	0
1 medium corn on the cob	=	1 starch	1	0
2 tsp. butter	=	2 fats	10	8
Dessert: $^{1}/_{12}$ angel food cake	=	1 other carbohydrate	---	0
Beverage: 1 cup 1% low-fat milk	=	1 nonfat milk	3	3
			39	35

Handout 5-4: How to Modify a Recipe

Example #1: Lasagna[7]

Original	Modified
1/3 c olive oil (to sauté vegetables)	[omit oil]
1 ½ c diced onions	1 ½ c onion, 1 green pepper, ½ lb mushrooms
2 cloves garlic	2 cloves garlic
1 ½ lb ground chuck	¾ lb ground round
2 t salt	[omit salt]
2 lb tomato sauce	use no-added-salt type tomato sauce
28 oz canned tomatoes	use no-added-salt type canned tomatoes
6 oz canned tomato paste	use no-added-salt type tomato paste
1 tbsp oregano	2 t oregano, 2 t basil, ¼ c fresh parsley
2 tsp onion salt	[omit salt]
1 lb lasagna noodles	1 lb whole wheat lasagna noodles
2 tbsp olive oil (to cook noodles)	[omit oil]
16 oz ricotta	16 oz low-fat cottage cheese, pureed
8 oz mozzarella	8 oz part skim mozzarella
10 oz parmesan	4 oz parmesan
oil to grease pan	spray to grease pan

Yield: 16 servings (2 9" x 12" pans)

Analysis	Original	Modified
Energy (kcal)	513	281
Protein (g)	35	21
Fat (g)	29 (6 t)	7 (1.4 t)
Sodium (mg)	1121	380
Cholesterol (mg)	73	32
% of calories from fat	51%	24%

Example #2: Spanakopita (Spinach Pie)[8]

Original	Modified
2.5 cups of boiled and drained spinach	2.5 cups of boiled and drained spinach
0.5 pounds 4.5% fat cottage cheese	
0.5 pounds feta cheese	0.75 pounds of reduced-fat feta cheese
4 Eggland's Best whole eggs	4 Eggland's Best whole eggs
0.5 pounds of phyllo dough	0.5 pounds of phyllo dough
1 teaspoon table salt	1 teaspoon table salt
1 teaspoon chopped parsley	3 tablespoons chopped parsley
0.75 cups of chopped white onions	0.75 cups of chopped white onions
0.75 pounds of unsalted butter	0.4 pounds of unsalted butter

---

[7] Source: Culinary Hearts Kitchen Course, Tallahassee, Florida, as taught by Sandra Woodruff, M.S., R.D., with permission.

[8] Contributed by Mary Ellen Clark of Monroe Community College

Example #2: Spanakopita (Spinach Pie, continued)

Analysis	Original (Serving)	Modified (Serving)
Energy (kcal)	4376.60 (365)	3121.9 (260.2)
Protein (g)	118.86 (9.9)	128.12 (10.7)
Fat (g)	364.71 (30.4)	225.1 (18.8)
Saturated fat (g)	223.06 (18.6)	130.9 (10.9)
Sodium (mg)	7447.5 (620.6)	8828.9 (735.7)
Cholesterol (mg)	1684.6 (140.4)	1227.4 (102.3)
% of calories from fat	75%	65%
% of calories from saturated fat	46%	38%

Chapter 6 – The Proteins and Amino Acids

Quick List: IM Resources for Chapter 6

- **Class preparation resources:** learning objectives/key points, suggested activities and projects, lecture outline
- **Assignment materials:** **Related LO**
  - Critical thinking questions (with answer key) 6.1, 6.3, 6.4, 6.5
  - Discussion questions (with answers) for Controversy 6 .... 6.7
  - Worksheet 6-1: Label Analysis—Protein 6.4, 6.6
  - Worksheet 6-2: Intake Analysis—Protein 6.4, 6.6, 6.7
  - Worksheet 6-3: Do You Get Enough or Too Much Protein Each Day? 6.4
  - Worksheet 6-4: Where Are the Proteins? Meats versus Vegetables as Sources 6.6
  - Worksheet 6-5: Plant Proteins in Human Nutrition—Myths and Realities[1] 6.4, 6.6
  - **New!** Worksheet 6-6: Chapter 6 Review Crossword Puzzle
- **Enrichment materials:** Handout 6-1: Using the Exchange System to Estimate Protein[2] 6.6

Chapter Learning Objectives and Key Points

6.1 **State why some amino acids are essential, nonessential, or conditionally essential to the human body, and outline how the body builds a protein molecule.**
Proteins are unique among the energy nutrients in that they possess nitrogen-containing amine groups and are composed of 20 different amino acid units. Of the 20 amino acids, some are essential and some are essential only in special circumstances. Amino acids link into long strands that make a wide variety of different proteins. Each type of protein has a distinctive sequence of amino acids and so has great specificity. Often, cells specialize in synthesizing particular types of proteins in addition to the proteins necessary to all cells. Nutrients can greatly affect genetic expression. Proteins can be denatured by heat, acids, bases, alcohol, or the salts of heavy metals. Denaturation begins the process of digesting food protein and can also destroy body proteins.

6.2 **Describe the digestion of protein and the absorption and transport of amino acids in the body.**
Digestion of protein involves denaturation by stomach acid and enzymatic digestion in the stomach and small intestine to amino acids, dipeptides, and tripeptides. The cells of the small intestine complete digestion, absorb amino acids and some larger peptides, and release them into the bloodstream for use by the body's cells.

6.3 **List the roles that various proteins and amino acids can play in the body, and describe the influence of carbohydrate on amino acid metabolism.**
The body needs dietary amino acids to grow new cells and to replace worn-out ones. Proteins provide structure and movement; serve as enzymes, hormones, and antibodies; provide molecular transport; help regulate fluid and electrolyte balance; buffer the blood; contribute to blood clotting; and help regulate gene expression. Amino acids can be used as fuel or converted to glucose or fat. No storage form of protein exists in the body. Amino acids can be metabolized to protein, nitrogen plus energy, glucose, or fat. They will be metabolized to protein only if sufficient energy is present from other sources. When energy is lacking, the nitrogen part is removed from each amino acid, and the resulting fragment is oxidized for energy.

6.4 **Compute the daily protein need for a given individual, and discuss the concepts of nitrogen balance and protein quality.**
The protein intake recommendation depends on size and stage of growth. The DRI recommended intake for adults is 0.8 gram of protein per kilogram of body weight. Factors concerning both the body and food sources modify an individual's protein need. Protein recommendations are based on nitrogen balance studies, which compare nitrogen excreted from the body with nitrogen ingested in food. Digestibility of protein varies from food to food, and cooking can improve or impair it. A protein's amino acid assortment greatly influences its usefulness to the body. Proteins lacking essential amino acids can be used only if those amino acids are present from other sources.

---

1 Contributed by Lori W. Turner, Ph.D., R.D., University of Alabama

2 Contributed by Sharon Rady Rolfes

6.5 **Discuss potential physical problems from an eating plan that is too low or too high in protein.**
Most U.S. protein intakes fall within the DRI recommended protein intake range of 10 to 35 percent of calories. No Tolerable Upper Intake Level exists for protein, but health risks may follow the overconsumption of protein-rich foods. Gluten-free diets often relieve symptoms of celiac disease or gluten allergy, but no evidence supports claims that they cure other ills.

6.6 **Identify protein-rich foods, and list some extra advantages associated with legumes.**

6.7 **Summarize the health advantages and nutrition red flags of vegetarian diets, and develop a lacto-ovo vegetarian eating pattern that meets all nutrient requirements for a given individual.**

Critical Thinking Questions

1. a. *What may happen inside of the cells of an individual who does not obtain all of the essential amino acids?*

   The body does not store amino acids, so the construction of a protein that is being made will be stopped where the missing amino acid cannot be added. This protein will be broken down by cellular enzymes and the amino acids can be used in other proteins, broken down to release energy, or made into glucose or storage fat.

   b. *What may eventually happen to the body's tissues if the diet does not contain essential amino acids?*

   If a particular amino acid is chronically missing, the body will break down tissues such as muscles to get the missing amino acid that is needed to make new proteins. This will result in muscle wasting. It may also affect cells of the immune system, which will lead to increased susceptibility to infection. The body will resort to breaking down proteins in critical organs such as the heart if no amino acids become available.

2. *Consider the key functions of proteins in the body and explain how the symptoms of severe protein deficiency relate to these functions.*

   Children with severe malnutrition develop swelling of the belly and ankles. Their diet does not allow them to make albumin, a protein that helps keep fluid within the blood. When albumin is lacking in the blood plasma, fluid can leak out of the blood vessels and into the tissues.

   The swollen belly may also be due to fatty liver. The liver needs protein to produce lipoproteins, which transport triglycerides and cholesterol in the blood. Without sufficient transport proteins, the fats in the blood get stored in the liver as fatty deposits. Over time, this can lead to damage to the liver tissue.

   These children may be more susceptible to infection due to lack of protein to maintain the cells of their immune systems. The antibody proteins, produced by B lymphocytes, also protect the body against infection.

3. *Why is it important for the diet to have enough carbohydrates in order for the body to be able to make optimal use of dietary protein?*

   If the body has enough carbohydrates, it will break them down to produce energy. The dietary protein can be broken down into amino acids that can be used for maintenance of body tissues, for antibody production, or for hormone production. The body does not need to use amino acids to make glucose or provide energy since there is an ample amount of glucose already present.

4. a. *What can happen to an amino acid if the body has more than enough dietary protein in a given day?*

   The amino acid will not be used to make proteins and will be "wasted." The amino acid loses its nitrogen-containing group (amino group) and its carbon skeleton can be metabolized for energy, used (in some cases) to produce glucose if needed, or converted into fatty acids.

   b. *How does chronic, excess dietary protein affect the body?*

   If the excess protein occurs with excess calorie intake, the amino acids are "wasted," as described above, and can be converted to and stored as fat in the body.

   Excess protein causes the excess amino groups to be converted to urea, which puts a strain on the liver and kidneys in individuals with diseases affecting these organs.

5. a. *Which foods contain incomplete proteins?*

   Many vegetables, grains, and fruits do not have all 9 essential amino acids.

   b. *Can someone just eat these foods and get all of the essential amino acids? Why or why not?*

   Yes, this person can eat these foods in combinations within a day such that they receive all 9 essential amino acids from the foods. This is called protein complementation. The essential amino acids from one food will combine with different amino acids from another food. Together, these amino acids can be used to make new proteins.

6. *Why might a high-protein diet not be the healthiest option for weight loss and weight loss maintenance?*

   High-protein diets may include a lot of meats, dairy products, and added fats in place of vegetables, fruits, and whole grains. This will increase the intake of saturated fat, which could increase blood LDL levels. High-fat diets are low in fiber, which may affect the health of the digestive system as well as blood LDL levels. The body needs an ample amount of carbohydrates to spare proteins and prevent amino acid wasting. Also, intakes of the many vitamins and minerals abundant in fruits, vegetables, and whole grains would be inadequate.

   A vegetarian may try a high-protein diet including nuts, nut butters, and dairy products (if desired or tolerated). Again, fiber, vitamins, and minerals may be lacking if this individual does not eat adequate amounts of fruits, vegetables, or whole grains.

Controversy Discussion Questions

1. *Discuss any 3 reasons why strict vegans are more likely to maintain a healthy body weight and have a reduced risk of cardiovascular disease as compared to their meat-eating peers.*

   Vegans avoid all animal products such as meats, milk, and dairy products, which can contribute high levels of saturated fats and calories to their diet. They will likely consume fewer excess calories, which will result in less weight gain. A lower saturated fat intake may decrease the levels of LDL in the blood, which reduces the risk of cardiovascular disease.

   Vegans eat more whole grains, nuts, fruits, and vegetables to obtain all of the essential amino acids. These foods leave them feeling fuller after eating, making them less likely to over-consume calories and gain weight. These foods also contain fiber, which may reduce the levels of cholesterol in the blood.

   Vegans tend to live more active lifestyles, so they are likely to expend more calories each day. This will result in less weight gain as well.

2. *Give any 2 reasons (in terms of nutrition) why a pregnant woman may want to consider eating a meat-containing diet.*

   It is difficult to obtain sufficient amounts of vitamin B_{12}, vitamin D, zinc, and iron if a woman is a vegan. If she is a lacto-ovo vegetarian, she can get most of the nutrients. She may need to supplement her iron intake.

   Meat and animal products contain all of the essential amino acids. A vegan woman who is allergic to soy products may have a harder time getting all of her essential amino acids from only plant-based foods.

3. *Describe any 3 challenges that a vegan faces when developing an eating plan that ensures nutritional adequacy.*

   She will need to get enough vitamin B_{12}, vitamin D, and zinc from her foods or from supplements since these nutrients are more abundant in animal-based foods.

   She will need to obtain enough non-heme iron from plant sources to ensure adequate iron intake. Meats contain heme iron, which is more absorbable than non-heme. She will want to consume more vitamin C to help her absorb the non-heme iron more efficiently.

   She will need to get enough omega-3 fatty acids, since they come primarily from fish. She can find these fatty acids in flaxseeds and walnuts, but she will want to make sure that she does not take in large portions with excessive calories.

She will need to make sure that she receives enough calcium from a variety of plant sources since she does not eat dairy products.

4. *List a one-day eating plan that ensures adequate nutrition for a strict vegetarian.*

   Wide open: Eating Plan E from Worksheet 6-2 in the Instructor's Manual lists a vegan eating plan that is adequate. Overall, a variety of fruits, vegetables, whole grains, vegetable oils, and nuts should supply all of the essential nutrients that this person needs. They should look for foods that are fortified with vitamin B_{12} or they may wish to take a supplement containing this vitamin.

5. *Your friend is a meat eater who would like to develop a healthier, less meat-centered diet. Provide any 3 suggestions as to how your friend can achieve this goal.*

   You could suggest that he cut down from eating meat 5-6 times a week to 3-4 times a week at first. He can slowly reduce his meat consumption further as he finds other foods to replace the meat at the center of the diet.

   He could replace meat with fish to maintain his protein intake but reduce his saturated fat intake at the same time. This would also ensure that he is getting enough omega-3 fatty acids.

   He could start eating more pasta dishes to reduce his meat intake but still enjoy a filling, nutritious meal.

   He could try some of the vegetarian products such as veggie burgers or soy-based products to still obtain complete proteins but reduce his overall calorie and saturated fat intakes.

Worksheet Answer Key

Worksheet 6-1: Label Analysis—Protein

1. a. 10 grams
   b. 10 grams × 4 kcal/gram = 40 calories

2. 55 kilograms × 0.8 grams protein/kilogram = 44 grams of protein (recommended)
   10 grams (product) / 44 grams × 100 = 23%
   23% of the recommended protein would come from this product alone.

3. a. 6 grams × 9 kcal/ gram / 120 total kcal × 100 = 45%
   b. 67 g of broiled 90% lean ground beef provides 7.86 g fat and 145 calories, meaning 49% of its calories come from fat. (It contains more saturated and less polyunsaturated fat than the veggie burger.)

4. a. The 10 milligrams of cholesterol come from cheese-based ingredients.
   b. These ingredients are listed further down in the ingredient list and so are not present in high levels.

5. a. 6%
   b. This may seem low compared to the iron content of a ground beef patty.

6. a. Soy concentrates
   b. Soybeans

7. Cheese-based ingredients

8. a. It is absorbed but not as easily or completely as the protein in a meat-containing product.
   b. The proteins in animal foods are more easily digested by humans than proteins from plant foods, though protein from legumes such as soybeans is nearly as digestible as animal protein.

Worksheet 6-2: Intake Analysis—Protein

1. a. E: Balanced diet with adequate fiber; F: Low-carbohydrate diet; G: Vegan diet
   b. Balanced diet (E): 127.02 grams; low-carbohydrate diet (F): 204.4 grams

2. Reduce the sizes of the meat portions or replace one or two of the meat portions with whole grains, fruits, or vegetables; use skim milk instead of whole milk; use cottage cheese instead of full-fat cheese; replace the blue cheese salad dressing with vinaigrette dressing or another low-fat alternative.

3. a. No; it only provides 30.7 grams

b. It contains no meat or dairy products, which are high in protein.
c. Calories, fat, vitamin B_{12}, thiamin, vitamin E, iron, and zinc
d. Add whole grains for calories and thiamin, more green leafy vegetables and orange juice for iron, nuts for vitamin E and zinc, and monounsaturated fats

Worksheet 6-5: Plant Proteins in Human Nutrition—Myths and Realities

Myth	Reality
Plant proteins are not complete; they lack certain amino acids.	Most dietary combinations of proteins are complete; certain food proteins may be low in specific amino acids. Soy beans and quinoa contain complete proteins.
Plant proteins are lower in quality than animal proteins.	Protein quality depends not only on the source but also on the dietary mixture of plant proteins; plant proteins can be as high in quality as animal proteins when complemented by a variety of foods.
Proteins from different plant foods must be carefully mixed and eaten together in the same meal.	Proteins do not have to been eaten at the same meal; the mixture over a day is important for nutritional value.
Plant proteins are difficult to digest.	Depending on the source and method of food preparation, plant proteins can be easy to digest.
People cannot meet protein needs with plant proteins alone.	Plant protein or animal protein can provide adequate protein for human needs.
Plant proteins are lacking in nutritional value because they are not balanced.	Plant proteins do not create a practical problem in terms of balance; possible imbalances are observed in amino acid supplementation.

Worksheet 6-6: Chapter 6 Review Crossword Puzzle

1. fruitarian
2. tripeptide
3. carbohydrate
4. collagen
5. tryptophan
6. complementary
7. polypeptide
8. kidneys
9. nitrogen
10. denaturation
11. alkalosis
12. ribosome

Learning Activities & Project Ideas

Activity 6-1: Demonstration of Diffusion and Active Transport[3] LO 6.3

Divide the class physically in half with a space down the center (the cellular membrane). Demonstrate diffusion by giving half the class small balloons to bounce up in the air (an area of higher concentration). A line of students can then be placed in the "membrane" space to demonstrate how active transport assists in the process of transferring the "molecule" balloons. The students can take the balloons and move them to the other side of the membrane to show active transport.

Activity 6-2: Protein Comparisons Project LO 6.4, 6.6

This assignment makes students go to the grocery store and actually compare what they see on the shelves and in the stores. Explain to students that, while visiting the store, "Your assignment is to compare natural protein sources from whole foods with protein supplements, such as whey powder, and determine which source is better for your specific situation. The idea here is to get you to understand protein supplementation. Visit your local grocery store and see what you can find out about the protein contents of foods and protein supplements. There are many protein-containing food options out there." Instruct students to take notes while at the store about any available nutrition information, prices, and quantities sold for those prices. Each student should then write a summary of his or her findings, identifying which protein sources would be best for him or her and explaining why.

Chapter Lecture Outline

I. The Structure of Proteins
   A. Overview
      1. The structure of proteins enables them to perform many vital functions.

[3] Contributed by Dorothy G. Herron, Orangeburg-Calhoun Technical College

2. Proteins contain nitrogen, unlike CHO and fat.
3. Amino acids are the building block.
4. 20 different amino acids exist.

B. Amino Acids
1. Each amino acid consists of a single carbon atom attached to a nitrogen-containing amino group and to a carboxyl-containing acid group.
2. The side chains vary among the different amino acids and give the amino acid different sizes, shapes, and charges.
3. Essential Amino Acids
   a. 9 amino acids are essential and must come from the diet.
   b. 11 amino acids are nonessential and can be made by the body.
   c. Under special circumstances, a nonessential amino acid can become essential – conditionally essential amino acids (see Table 6-1)
4. Recycling Amino Acids
   a. The body can recycle amino acids from proteins no longer needed.
   b. These amino acids can be used to build new proteins or provide energy if glucose is lacking in the diet.

C. How Do Amino Acids Build Proteins?
1. Amino acids are linked by peptide bonds into long strands that coil and fold to make a wide variety of different proteins.
   a. A string of 10 or more amino acids is known as a polypeptide.
   b. The side groups of different amino acids may be attracted to each other and form either tough pleated sheets or elastic coils.
2. Several strands may cluster together into a functioning unit, such as an enzyme, or a metal ion (mineral) or a vitamin may join to the unit and activate it.

D. The Variety of Proteins
1. Overview – the shapes of proteins help determine their functions
   a. Some proteins have hollow interiors that allow them to store substances.
   b. Collagen is a long yet strong protein.
   c. Hemoglobin is made up of 4 associated protein strands and carries oxygen in the red blood cells (see Figure 6-4).
   d. Each type of protein has a distinctive sequence of amino acids and so has great specificity.
   e. Like letters in the alphabet, the sequence of amino acids determines the identity of the protein.
   f. The variety of possible sequences for amino acid strands is tremendous.
   g. A single human cell may contain as many as 10,000 different proteins, each one present in thousands of copies.
2. Inherited Amino Acid Sequences
   a. The sequence of amino acids in a protein is determined by heredity.
   b. If an incorrect amino acid is inserted, the result can be disastrous to health.
      1. In sickle-cell disease, a glutamic acid in one strand is replaced with a valine (Figure 6-5).
      2. Analogous to spelling a word wrong – it no longer makes "sense"
   c. Genes determine the sequence of amino acids in each finished protein.
   d. Genetic information in a cell goes from: DNA → RNA → protein (Figure 6-6)
3. Nutrients and Gene Expression
   a. Every cell nucleus contains the DNA for making every human protein, but cells do not make them all.
   b. Some genes are "expressed" and others are not depending on the cell type. For example, only cells of the pancreas express the gene for the protein hormone insulin.
   c. Nutrients do not change DNA structure, but they greatly influence genetic expression.

E. Denaturation of Proteins
1. Proteins can be denatured (distorted in shape) by heat, radiation, alcohol, acids, bases, or the salts of heavy metals.
2. During digestion, stomach acid denatures proteins, permitting digestive enzymes to make contact with the peptide bonds and cleave them.
3. Denaturation also occurs during cooking.

F. Think Fitness: Can Eating Extra Protein Make Muscles Grow Stronger?
1. Athletes need to work hard to stimulate muscle repair and growth.
2. Well-timed protein intakes may further stimulate muscle growth.
3. Amino acid or protein supplements offer no advantage over food.

II. Digestion and Absorption of Protein (Figure 6-8)
A. Protein Digestion
1. In the Stomach
a. Proteins (enzymes) activated by stomach acid digest proteins from food, denatured by acid.
b. The mucus coating secreted by the stomach wall protects its own proteins from attack by either enzymes or acid.
c. pH of stomach acid is 1.5
2. In the Small Intestine – By the time most proteins enter the small intestine, they are denatured and broken into smaller pieces.
a. A few are single amino acids
b. Most are large strands called polypeptides
c. In the small intestine, bicarbonate acts to raise pH and enzymes continue digesting the strands into single amino acids or di- and tripeptides.
3. Common Misconceptions – false claims for supplemental enzymes & predigested proteins since the digestive system is designed to break down complete proteins
B. What Happens to Amino Acids after Protein Is Digested?
1. The cells of the small intestine complete digestion, absorb amino acids and some larger peptides, and release them into the bloodstream for use by the body's cells.
2. These larger pieces may provide the body with information about the outside environment but can also cause food allergies.

III. The Importance of Protein
A. Introduction
1. The body needs dietary amino acids daily to grow new cells and to replace worn-out ones.
2. The entire process of breakdown, recovery, and synthesis is called protein turnover.
B. The Roles of Body Proteins
1. Introduction
a. Proteins are versatile, are unique, and play important roles in the body.
b. Proteins have been called "the primary material of life."
2. Providing Structure and Movement
a. Muscle protein structures permit movement & can release amino acids for energy.
b, Muscle tissue makes up about 40% of all of the body's proteins.
c. Structural proteins strengthen bones, teeth, skin, tendons, cartilage, blood vessels, etc.
3. Building Enzymes, Hormones, and Other Compounds – The body makes enzymes, hormones, and chemical messengers of the nervous system from its amino acids.
a. Figure 6-9 shows how an enzyme functions.
b. Figure 6-10 shows the amino acid sequence and protein structure of insulin.
4. Building Antibodies – Antibodies are proteins produced by white blood cells that defend against foreign proteins and other foreign substances within the body.
a. Each antibody protein is specific for one invader and is made each time the body encounters a new invader.
b. The immune system "remembers" each specific invader and can produce antibody proteins quickly if the body encounters the same invader again.
5. Transporting Substances – Transport proteins include hemoglobin & lipoproteins.
6. Maintaining Fluid and Electrolyte Balance – Proteins, such as albumin in the blood plasma, help regulate the body's electrolytes and fluids.
a. Too much fluid in the tissues is called edema
b. The cells have transport proteins that allow certain molecules into or out of the cells.
7. Maintaining Acid-Base Balance – Proteins buffer the blood against excess acidity or alkalinity.
a. Too much acid in the blood or tissues is called acidosis
b. Too much base is called alkalosis

8. Blood Clotting – Proteins that clot the blood prevent death from uncontrolled bleeding.

C. Providing Energy and Glucose
  1. Amino Acids to Glucose – When amino acids are degraded for energy or made into glucose, the nitrogen part is removed from each amino acid and converted into urea, and the resulting carbon-containing fragment can be used to build glucose or fatty acids.
  2. Drawing Amino Acids from Tissues
     a. Protein is not stored in the body, unlike glucose (stored as glycogen) and fats (stored as triglycerides).
     b. When insufficient carbohydrate and fat are consumed to meet the body's energy need, food protein and body protein are sacrificed to supply energy.
     c. The body will first use protein from the muscles but may need to use protein from organs like the heart if the need arises.
  3. Using Excess Amino Acids
     a. Surplus amino acids are not stored; their amino groups are stripped off first and then the remains can be used to:
        1. Meet immediate energy needs
        2. Make glucose for storage as glycogen
        3. Make fat for energy storage
     b. Energy nutrients compared – Figure 6-12 Three Different Energy Sources

D. The Fate of An Amino Acid
  1. When an amino acid arrives in a cell, it can be:
     a. Used as is to build protein
     b. Altered somewhat to make another needed compound, such as the vitamin niacin
     c. Dismantled to use its amine group to build a nonessential amino acid
  2. The remaining carbon, hydrogen, and oxygen atoms can be converted to glucose or fat.
  3. In a cell starved for energy with no glucose or fatty acids:
     a. The amino acid is stripped of its amine group (nitrogen part) and the remainder of its structure is used for energy.
     b. The amine group is excreted from the cell and then from the body in the urine.
  4. A cell that has a surplus of energy and amino acids:
     a. Takes the amino acid apart
     b. Excretes the amine group
     c. Converts the rest to glucose or fat for storage
  5. Amino acids are "wasted" when:
     a. Energy is lacking from other sources
     b. Protein is overabundant
     c. An amino acid is oversupplied in supplement form
     d. The quality of the diet's protein is too low (too few essential amino acids)

IV. Food Protein: Need and Quality

A. Food protein overview
  1. The body's use of a protein depends in part on the user's health.
  2. To be used efficiently, protein must be accompanied by ample carbohydrate and fat, vitamins and minerals.
  3. Protein quality is influenced by a protein's digestibility and its amino acid composition.

B. A Consumer's Guide to Evaluating Protein And Amino Acid Supplements
  1. Protein Supplements
     a. Athletes take them to build muscle.
     b. Excess amino acids need to be broken down, which generates a surplus of nitrogen that burdens the kidneys.
     c. Dieters may take them to speed weight loss; in fact, many protein bars add calories to the diet and may cause weight gain.
  2. Amino Acid Supplements
     a. People take lysine supplements to reduce the duration of a herpes virus infection but it's not known if these supplements work.

b. People believe that amino acid supplements will stimulate muscle protein synthesis, but any meal with complete proteins will accomplish this just as well.
c. People take protein supplements to strengthen their nails; nails need other vitamins and minerals in addition to sulfur-containing amino acids for their overall health.
d. Because tryptophan is converted into serotonin, a neurotransmitter that regulates sleep, appetite, and mood, tryptophan supplements are taken to relieve pain and depression.

3. What Scientists Say
    a. The body handles whole proteins best and breaks them down in such a way that the individual amino acids are optimal absorbed by shared amino acid transporters.
    b. Excess methionine can be converted to homocysteine, which is associated with inflammation and heart disease.
    c. Supplements may also cause water to flow into the digestive tract from the body's tissues, causing diarrhea and dehydration
    d. Table 6-3 lists people vulnerable to harm from amino acid supplements.
    e. Protein or amino acid supplements may interfere with the action of some medications.
4. Moving Ahead – Select foods that are protein rich and low in saturated fats.

C. How Much Protein Do People Really Need?
1. The DRI recommendation for protein intake depends on size and stage of growth.
    a. DRI recommended intake is 0.8 gram per kilogram of body weight
    b. Minimum is 10% of total calories
    c. See Table 6-4 for protein intake recommendations for healthy adults
2. Athletes may need slightly more (1.2-1.7 grams per kg).
3. To figure your protein need:
    a. Find your body weight in pounds
    b. Convert pounds to kilograms (by dividing pounds by 2.2)
    c. Multiply kilograms by 0.8 to find total grams of protein recommended
4. The Body's Health – needs increased by malnutrition or infection
    a. Malnutrition may cause a reduction of digestive enzyme production, which can impair protein digestion and absorption.
    b. During infection, more protein is needed for enhanced immune functions.
5. Other Nutrients and Energy – adequate energy, macro- & micronutrients are required
6. Protein Quality – DRI assumes a mixed (omnivorous) diet & is generous since not all proteins are used with 100% efficiency by the body

D. Nitrogen Balance – Protein recommendations are based on nitrogen balance studies, which compare nitrogen excreted from the body with nitrogen ingested with food (Figure 6-13).
1. Healthy adults are normally in N equilibrium or zero balance.
2. Positive Nitrogen Balance
    a. Occurs during growth in children or during pregnancy
    b. People need to have more protein in their bodies at the end of the day than what they started with
3. Negative Nitrogen Balance – occurs during injury when skin or muscle tissue can be broken down

E. Protein Quality
1. Introduction
    a. High-quality proteins provide all of the essential amino acids the body needs to make proteins.
    b. If the diet does not provide enough of an essential amino acid, the cells:
        1. Break down internal proteins to get the essential amino acid
        2. Limit their synthesis of proteins to conserve the essential amino acid
2. Limiting Amino Acids
    a. High-quality proteins – provide enough of all of the essential amino acids needed to make new proteins
    b. Low-quality proteins – do not provide all the essential amino acids
    c. If a nonessential amino acid is unavailable from food, the cell synthesizes it.
    d. If the diet fails to provide an essential amino acid, the cells begin to conserve the amino acid and reduce their use of amino acids for fuel.
    e. Amino acids are not stored and will be released from the cell and returned to the circulation to be used by other cells.
    f. The amino acids may also be wasted.

3. Complementary Proteins (Figure 6-15)
    a. If a person does not consume all the essential amino acids he needs, the body's pool of essential amino acids will dwindle until body organs are compromised.
    b. Dietary proteins lacking essential amino acids can be used only if those amino acids are present from other dietary sources.
4. Protein Digestibility
    a. Digestibility of protein varies from food to food.
        1. Amino acids from animal proteins are most easily digested and absorbed (over 90%)
        2. Amino acids from legumes are next (80 to 90%)
        3. Amino acids from plant foods vary (70 to 90%)
    b. Cooking with moist heat can improve digestibility whereas dry heat methods impair it.
5. Perspective on Protein Quality – quality is practically important only in areas where malnutrition is common or protein sources are limited or unreliable

V. Protein Deficiency And Excess
  A. Overview
    1. Protein deficiencies and energy deficiencies are the world's leading form of malnutrition.
    2. Both protein deficiencies and excess are of concern.
  B. What Happens When People Consume Too Little Protein?
    1. Obvious symptoms are slow growth in children, impaired brain and kidney function, weakened immunity, and impaired nutrient absorption
    2. Protein-energy malnutrition (PEM) is the most widespread form of malnutrition in the world today and is discussed more in Chapter 15.
  C. Is it Possible to Consume Too Much Protein ? – There is no benefit from eating excess protein.
    1. How Much Protein Do People Take In?
        a. AMDR = 10-35% of total calories from protein
        b. U.S. average = 16% of calories for adult males; 13-15% for women, children, some elderly
    2. Protein and Weight Loss Dieting
        a. Some diets recommend that 65% of calories come from protein.
        b. This approach may work short term because protein may help control the appetite.
        c. It is the reduction of overall calories with adequate nutrition that brings about the most effective weight loss.
    3. Protein Sources in Heart Disease
        a. Foods rich in animal protein tend to be rich in saturated fats.
        b. Higher fat intakes may correlate with higher body weights, which can increase the risk of heart disease.
    4. Kidney Disease
        a. Animals fed experimentally on high-protein diets often develop enlarged kidneys or livers.
        b. In human beings, a high-protein diet increases the kidneys' workload but this alone does not appear to damage healthy kidneys or cause kidney disease.
        c. In people with kidney problems, a high-protein diet may speed the kidneys' decline.
    5. Adult Bone Loss
        a. Feeding purified proteins to human subjects causes calcium to be spilled from the urine.
        b. Evidence indicates that high protein intakes from foods may not increase calcium loss.
        c. Too little protein may weaken the bones in malnourished elderly individuals.
    6. Cancer
        a. As for heart disease, the effects of protein on cancer causation cannot be easily separated from the effects of fat.
        b. Population studies suggest a correlation between high intakes of fatty and well-cooked red meats and processed meats and some types of cancer, particularly of the digestive tract, breast, and prostate.
    7. Is a Low-Gluten Diet Best for Health?
        a. Gluten is a protein found in grain foods and may cause a range of digestive symptoms in people with celiac disease or gluten allergy.
        b. Gluten has also been blamed for headaches, weight gain, cancer, and Alzheimer's disease but these links have not been established.

D. Food Feature: Getting Enough But Not Too Much Protein
   1. Protein-Rich Foods
      a. Most food groups, with the exception of fruit, can contribute to protein intake each day.
      b. Figure 6-16 shows that many foods contribute protein to the diet.
      c. Figure 6-17 lists the top protein-contributing foods in the U.S. diet.
      d. Too many protein-containing foods in the diet can displace other foods that provide folate and vitamin C.
      e. The American diet contains an ample amount of protein so it is possible to eat meatless meals and still get enough protein.
   2. The Advantage of Legumes (see Figure 6-18)
      a. The protein quality of legumes is almost comparable to that of meat.
      b. Legumes also provide many B vitamins, iron, and other minerals.
      c. Soy protein can be considered equivalent to that of meat.
         1. Soy products can reduce iron absorption.
         2. There are many soy-based products available, such as textured vegetable protein or tofu.
         3. These foods still need to be eaten with a variety of other foods.

VI. Controversy: Vegetarian And Meat-Containing Diets: What Are The Benefits And Pitfalls?
In affluent countries, people who eat well-planned vegetarian diets suffer less often from chronic diseases than people whose diets center on meat and people choose a vegetarian diet for a variety of reasons (Table C6-1 & 2)
A. Positive Health Aspects of Vegetarian Diets – Strong evidence links vegetarian diets with reduced incidences of chronic diseases. Some benefits include:
   1. Defense against Obesity – vegetarians are less likely to be obese
   2. Defense against Heart and Artery Disease
      a. May also be due to the inclusion of more vegetables, fruits, nuts, and whole grains
      b. Without meat or animal products in the diet, the intake of saturated fats may also be lower.
      c. Vegans have the lowest LDL cholesterol levels.
      d. Replacing meat with soy products may significantly reduce the levels of LDL cholesterol.
   3. Defense against High Blood Pressure
      a. Vegetarians tend to maintain a healthy body weight, which helps to control blood pressure.
      b. A diet high in fiber, fruits, and vegetables provides potassium, which may reduce blood pressure as well.
   4. Defense against Cancer
      a. Colon and rectal cancer rates are lower in people who eat more plant-based diets.
      b. People who eat fish have the lowest rate of colon and rectal cancer.
      c. People who eat meat may eat less vegetables and fruits.
   5. Other Health Benefits
      a. Vegetarian food choices may reduce the risk of cataracts, diabetes, diverticulosis, gallbladder disease, and osteoporosis.
      b. May be due to the inclusion of healthier foods rather than just the elimination of meat
B. Positive Health Aspects of the Meat Eater's Diet
   1. A balanced, adequate diet in which lean meats and seafood, eggs, and milk play a part in addition to fruits, vegetables, and whole grains can be very healthy.
   2. True meat lovers who shun all vegetables have no adequate substitutions for these foods (unlike vegetarians who can find suitable replacements for meat).
   3. Support during critical times
      a. Both meat eaters and lacto-ovo vegetarians can rely on their diets during critical times of life.
      b. A vegan diet can pose challenges. Why?
      c. Meat provides abundant iron, zinc, and vitamin B_{12} needed by everyone, but in particular by pregnant women, children, and adolescents.
   4. In Pregnancy and Infancy
      a. Lacto-ovo vegetarians receive enough energy, vitamin B_{12}, vitamin D, calcium, iron, and zinc.
      b. Vitamin B_{12} deficiency is of concern to vegans since only animal foods naturally supply it.
   5. In Childhood
      a. Children who are lacto-ovo vegetarians or meat eaters can get enough protein, iron, zinc, vitamin E, and vitamin B_{12}.

   b. Vegan children may be at risk of deficiency since their foods may make them full before they get all of their essential nutrients.
6. In Adolescence
   a. Vegetarians should choose fruits and vegetables over sweets, fast foods, and salty foods.
   b. Many teens do not plan out their meals and thus lack energy, protein, vitamin B_{12}, calcium, zinc, and vitamin D.
   c. Reduced intakes of vitamin D and calcium could make the bones weaker later in life.
7. In Aging and in Illness – Soft or ground meats in small meals can provided needed nutrients.

C. Planning a Vegetarian Diet – is more than just eliminating foods
1. Poorly planned vegetarian diets typically lack iron, zinc, calcium, omega-3 fatty acids, vitamin D, and vitamin B_{12}.
2. Choosing within the Food Groups – vegetarians should emphasize sources of calcium and iron from green leafy vegetables or dried fruits
   a. Fortified soy milk can be substituted for dairy products.
   b. Legumes, soy products, nuts, and seeds can be used within the protein foods group.
   c. Vegetarians need to selected fortified foods or supplements to get enough vitamin B_{12} and possibly vitamin D.
3. Milk Products and Protein Foods
   a. Consult Figure C6-2 and Appendix E to find foods in these groups as well as USDA Food Patterns for either vegans or lacto-ovo vegetarians
   b. Use the USDA's MyPlate website for planning vegetarian diets
4. Convenience Foods – are easy but it is important to read the labels since some of these products may have a lot of added saturated fat
5. A Word about Protein Foods – The vegetarian protein foods made of textured vegetable protein may be higher in salt, sugar, and other additives.
   a. The ingredients list of the label will show what additives are in the product.
   b. Soy beans or tofu have little unwanted additives.
6. Iron – vegetarians need about 1.8 times more protein than meat eaters since iron in fruits and vegetables is less efficiently absorbed
7. Zinc
   a. Plant sources poorly absorbed; supplementation may be needed for growing children
   b. Zinc deficiencies can increase the risk of infection in the elderly.
8. Calcium is easy to obtain for lacto-ovo-vegetarians, but vegans may have to consume soy products along with a variety of other foods to obtain enough calcium.
9. Vitamin B_{12} – vegans need B_{12}-fortified foods (such as soymilk) or a supplement
10. Vitamin D
   a. Can be obtained from fortified dairy products or by skin exposure to the sun
   b. People in northern climates may need to take a supplement to get enough preformed vitamin D.
11. Omega-3 Fatty Acids – DHA can be obtained from fortified foods or from flaxseed, walnuts but not at the levels found in fish
12. Conclusion
   a. Both a meat eater's diet and a vegetarian's diet are best approached scientifically.
   b. There are many in-between ways of eating that don't fall into strict categories.
   c. Limit foods that are high in sodium, solid fats, and added sugars.

Worksheet 6-1: Label Analysis—Protein

Instructions: Use the pizza burger label to answer the questions that follow.

Flowery Branch Farm
Tomato & Basil Pizza Burger

Nutrition Facts

Serving Size 1 Burger (67g)
Servings Per Container 4

Amount Per Serving	
Calories 120	Calories from Fat ?
	% Daily Value*
Total Fat 6g	**9%**
Saturated Fat 1.5g	**8%**
Trans Fat 0g	
Polyunsaturated Fat 2.5g	
Monounsaturated Fat 1.5g	
Cholesterol 10mg	**3%**
Sodium 280mg	**12%**
Potassium 160mg	**5%**
Total Carbohydrate 7g	**2%**
Dietary Fiber 3g	**10%**
Sugars 2g	
Protein 10g	
Vitamin A 4% •	Vitamin C 10%
Calcium 2% •	Iron 6%

* Percent Daily Values are based on a 2,000 calorie diet. Your Daily Values may be higher or lower depending on your calorie needs.

	Calories	2,000	2,500
Total Fat	Less than	65g	80g
Sat Fat	Less than	20g	25g
Cholesterol	Less than	300mg	300mg
Sodium	Less than	2400mg	2400mg
Total Carbohydrate		300g	375g
Dietary Fiber		25g	30g

100% VEGETARIAN

INGREDIENTS: Textured Soy Protein Concentrate with Water, Onion, Mushrooms, Tomato Paste (Tomatoes, Salt), Textured Wheat Gluten with Water, Corn Oil with TBHQ for Freshness, Mozzarella Cheese (Pasteurized Milk, Cultures, Salt, Enzymes), Provolone Cheese (Pasteurized Milk, Cultures, Salt, Enzymes), Egg Whites, Water, Red Bell Peppers, Dried Tomato, Contains Two Percent or Less of Potato Starch, Methyl-Cellulose, Garlic, Autolyzed Yeast Extract, Cheddar Cheese Powder (Cheddar Cheese [Milk, Salt, Cheese Cultures, Enzymes], Whey, Buttermilk, Salt, Disodium Phosphate), Basil and Other Spices, Paprika for Color, Garlic, Natural and Artificial Flavors from Non-Meat Sources, Maltodestrin, Soybean Oil, Modified Corn Starch with Corn Syrup Solids, Lactic Acid, Salt, Canola Oil, Caramel Color, Soy Lecithin, Torula Yeast, Barley Malt Flour, Triacetin, Citric Acid, Dextrose. **CONTAINS SOY, WHEAT, MILK AND EGG INGREDIENTS.**

1. a. What is the gram amount of protein listed per serving of this product?

   b. How many calories from protein does this represent?

2. What would be the contribution (percentage of total protein) of this product towards the total amount of recommended protein for a person who weighs 55 kilograms?

3. a. What is the percentage of the total calories coming from fat of this product?

   b. How does this compare with a comparable amount of 90% lean ground beef?

4. a. What is the source of cholesterol in this product?

   b. Why is this level so low?

5. a. What is the level of iron in this product?

   b. Is this considered high or low and why?

6. a. What is the most abundant ingredient listed for this product?

   b. What is the source of this ingredient?

7. What are the sources of saturated fat in this product?

8. a. Is this type of protein easily digested and absorbed by the body?

   b. Why or why not?

Worksheet 6-2: Intake Analysis—Protein

Eating Plan E (1 Day's Intake)	Eating Plan F (1 Day's Intake)	Eating Plan G (1 Day's Intake)
¾ cup Nature's Path flax cereal ½ cup soy milk ½ cup acai juice + seltzer water 1 medium banana 12 ounces coffee 6 ounces 6-grain yogurt ½ cup blueberries ¾ cup raspberries 2 Mushroom Lover's Veggie Burgers 1 cup roasted carrot soup ½ cup sweet green peppers 6 carrot sticks 2 whole-wheat wasa crackers 8 ounces Vruit juice 8 ounces soy milk 1 peanut butter Fiber One Bar 6 ounces grilled salmon 10 cooked asparagus spears 6 ounces white wine ½ cup olives ½ cup sun-dried tomatoes ½ cup whole-wheat angel hair pasta ¼ cup mixed nuts	2 scrambled eggs 1 cup whole milk 2 slices bacon 2 1-ounce Slim Jims 6 ounces lean ground beef 2 ounces provolone cheese ¼ cup blue cheese dressing 12 ounces water 2 ounces cheddar cheese cubes 6 ounces grilled chicken breasts 1 scrambled egg 1 cup lettuce ½ cup blue cheese dressing 2 ounces pork rinds 12 ounces water	1 cup honey dew melon 1 cup fresh strawberries 1 large apple ½ avocado ½ cup sweet green peppers ½ cup sweet red peppers ¼ cup black olives 1 medium orange 1 medium banana 1 cup boiled green beans 10 cooked asparagus spears 1 cup sautéed mushrooms 1 cup kidney beans ¼ cup dried apricots ¼ cup dried Craisins 5 dried, pitted dates

Look at Eating Plans E, F, and G:

1. a. What type of diet is represented by each of these eating plans?

   b. Which of these diets may exceed the recommended amount of protein?

2. How can Eating Plan F be modified to reduce the amount of saturated fat and protein?

3. a. Does Eating Plan G provide enough protein?

   b. Why or why not?

   c. What other nutrients are lacking from this eating plan?

   d. How could Eating Plan G be modified (without changing the overall type of diet) to provide the nutrients that are lacking?

Worksheet 6-3: Do You Get Enough or Too Much Protein Each Day?

1. Calculate your protein need:

   a. Your weight = ________ pounds

   b. To convert your weight into kilograms:

   ________ pounds ÷ 2.2 pounds per kilogram = __________ kilograms

   c. DRI recommendation for adults: 0.8 grams of protein/kilogram of body weight/day

   ________ kilograms body weight × 0.8 gram protein/kilogram of body weight = __________

This is your recommended amount of protein per day.

2. Record a day's worth of your food and drink intakes in a table like the one below.

Example of part of a day's intake:

Meal	Food and amount	Protein (grams)
Breakfast	1 cup plain instant oatmeal	6 g
	1 banana	1 g
	2 tablespoons sugar	0 g
	1 cup orange juice	2 g
Lunch	2 fast food bean burritos	14 g
	1 12-oz. can Cherry Coke	0 g

You can determine your protein intake in several different ways. You can use the food composition table in Appendix A of the textbook to help you calculate the total grams of protein. You can also use software such as *Diet Analysis +* that your instructor has chosen for the course. Cell phone "apps" and free online tools like the USDA's Super Tracker (https://www.supertracker.usda.gov/#home) can provide this information as well. These programs automatically calculate the protein amounts.

Analysis:
Was your protein intake higher or lower than your recommended amount? If it was higher or lower, suggest ways that you could change your daily food choices to bring your daily protein intake closer to your recommended level.

You can repeat the exercise above but you can design an improved diet and enter the information into a second table like the one above. You can check to see whether your new diet brings your protein intake closer to the recommended levels.

Worksheet 6-4: Where Are the Proteins? Meats versus Vegetables as Sources

People who eat animal products but no meat are called lacto-ovo vegetarians. They eat eggs and dairy products such as milk, cheese, or eggs. People who eat no animal products are called vegans. They eat beans, grains, nuts, fruits, and vegetables. Both types of vegetarians eat this way for many years and are as healthy as anyone else. How do they do it?

Can you get enough proteins if you don't eat meat? What if you don't eat any animal products? How can you find out? You can try some diet planning and diet analysis to find out where the protein is found in foods.

Design a 1-day diet as if you are a meat eater, lacto-ovo vegetarian, or vegan. You can analyze the food using the food composition table in the back of your textbook, software such as *Diet Analysis* +, a cell phone "app," or the USDA's Super Tracker tool (https://www.supertracker.usda.gov/#home). Prepare a table (or computer printout) including each food/amount, grams of protein, grams of saturated + *trans* fats, and grams of unsaturated fats (polyunsaturated + monounsaturated).

Example of part of a day's intake for a vegan:

Food and amount	**Protein (grams)**	**Sat. + *trans* fat (grams)**	**Poly. + mono. fat (g)**
2 small whole-wheat bagels	24 g	0.6 g	1.6 g
2 cups apple juice	1 g	0 g	0 g
2 slices whole-wheat bread	6 g	0.6 g	1.6 g
1 vegan soy burger patty	16 g	0 g	0.8 g
¼ tomato, sliced	0.25 g	0 g	0.2 g
¼ cup onion, sliced	0.5 g	0 g	0 g

Can you get enough (or too much) protein if you eat a lacto-ovo vegetarian diet? A vegan diet? If you did not get enough protein for your body weight, suggest ways that you could get more. Consider trying food substitutions or adjusting portion sizes.

Compare the fat content of the 3 diets. Which of your diet plans most closely followed dietary recommendations for the amounts and types of fats as presented in your textbook?

Worksheet 6-5: Plant Proteins in Human Nutrition—Myths and Realities

Instructions: Some common myths regarding plant protein sources are listed in the table below. Fill in the right side of the table with the facts to counter each myth.

Myth	Reality
Plant proteins are not complete; they lack certain amino acids.	
Plant proteins are lower in quality than animal proteins.	
Proteins from different plant foods must be carefully mixed and eaten together in the same meal.	
Plant proteins are difficult to digest.	
People cannot meet protein needs with plant proteins alone.	
Plant proteins are lacking in nutritional value because they are not balanced.	

Worksheet 6-6: Chapter 6 Review Crossword Puzzle

Across	Down
1. An individual who only eats raw fruit, nuts, and seeds follows a _____ diet. 6. Proteins from different foods that, together, contain all of the essential amino acids are called _____ proteins. 7. A string of 10 or more amino acids bonded together is known as a _____. 8. Excess protein consumption can lead to large amounts of amino acids being broken down and puts a strain on the _____ if they are already damaged by disease. 10. The process of unfolding a protein from its original 3-dimensional shape 11. The condition in which the blood is too basic (alkaline) is known as _____. 12. Site of protein synthesis in the cell	2. A group of 3 bonded amino acids that is broken down into individual amino acids on the surface of the small intestine 3. Both protein and _____ supply 4 kilocalories/gram. 4. A protein that serves as the building block for ligaments and tendons 5. An amino acid that is commonly sold as a dietary supplement 9. The amount of protein that enters the body and is utilized in the body can be measured by _____ balance studies.

Handout 6-1: Using the Exchange System to Estimate Protein

The exchange system provides an easy way to estimate dietary protein. The foods on the milk and meat lists supply protein in abundance: a cup of milk provides 8 grams of protein; an ounce of meat, 7 grams. The starch and vegetable lists contribute small amounts of protein, but they can add up to significant quantities; fruits and fats provide no protein.

Exchange	Protein (g)
Milks	8
Meats/meat substitutes	7
Starch	3
Nonstarchy vegetables	2
Fruits	---
Fats	---

To estimate the protein in a meal consisting of a bean and cheese burrito, 1 cup of milk, and an apple, you first need to recognize that the burrito contains about ½ cup pinto beans and ½ ounce shredded cheese wrapped in a tortilla. Then you need to translate these portions into exchanges: 1 ½ meats, 1 starch, 1 milk, and 1 fruit, respectively.

Using the exchange system to estimate, this lunch provides about 22 grams of protein. A computer diet analysis program calculated the same. The exchange system sometimes over- or underestimates the protein contents of individual foods, but for most, its estimates of daily intakes are close. In any case, for nutrients eaten in such large quantities as protein, a difference of a few grams in a day's total is insignificant.

Lunch		Exchange	Protein (g)	
			Estimate	Actual
½ cup pinto beans	=	1 meat	7	
½ oz. cheese	=	½ meat	4	} 14
1 tortilla	=	1 starch	3	
1 cup milk	=	1 milk	8	8
1 apple	=	1 fruit	---	---
			22	22

Chapter 7 – The Vitamins

Quick List: IM Resources for Chapter 7

- **Class preparation resources:** learning objectives/key points, suggested activities and projects, lecture outline
- **Assignment materials:** **Related LO**
  - Critical thinking questions (with answer key) 7.3, 7.4, 7.6, 7.8, 7.10
  - Discussion questions (with answers) for Controversy 7 .... 7.12
  - Worksheet 7-1: Label Analysis—Vitamins 7.2, 7.3, 7.4
  - Worksheet 7-2: Intake Analysis—Vitamins 7.11
  - Worksheet 7-3: Factors that Destroy Vitamins[1] 7.1, 7.7, 7.8
  - Worksheet 7-4: Comparing Supplements Label to Label[2] 7.12
  - **New!** Worksheet 7-5: Chapter 7 Review Crossword Puzzle
- **Enrichment materials:** Handout 7-1: Vitamins Do More Than Treat Deficiency Diseases........ 7.3-7.5, 7.8, 7.10

Chapter Learning Objectives and Key Points

7.1 **List the fat-soluble and water-soluble vitamins, and describe how solubility affects the absorption, transport, storage, and excretion of each type.**
Vitamins are essential, noncaloric nutrients that are needed in tiny amounts in the diet and help to drive cellular processes. Vitamin precursors in foods are transformed into active vitamins by the body. The fat-soluble vitamins are vitamins A, D, E, and K. The water-soluble vitamins are vitamin C and the B vitamins.

7.2 **Discuss the significance of the fat-soluble nature of some vitamins to human nutrition.**

7.3 **Summarize the physiological roles of vitamin A and its precursor beta-carotene, name the consequences of deficiencies and toxicities, and list the major food sources of both forms.**
Three active forms of vitamin A and one precursor are important in nutrition. Vitamin A plays major roles in gene regulation, eyesight, reproduction, cell differentiation, immunity, and growth. Vitamin A deficiency causes blindness, sickness, and death and is a major problem worldwide. Vitamin A overdoses and toxicity are possible and cause many serious symptoms. Vitamin A's active forms are supplied by foods of animal origin. Fruits and vegetables provide beta-carotene. The vitamin A precursor in plants, beta-carotene, is an effective antioxidant in the body. Many brightly colored plant foods are rich in beta-carotene.

7.4 **Summarize the physiological roles of vitamin D, name the consequences of deficiencies and toxicities, and list its major food sources.**
Low and borderline vitamin D levels are not uncommon in the United States. When exposed to sunlight, the skin makes vitamin D from a cholesterol-like compound. Vitamin D helps regulate blood calcium and influences other body tissues. A vitamin D deficiency causes rickets in childhood, low bone density in adolescents, or osteomalacia in later life. Some groups of people are more likely to develop vitamin D deficiencies. Vitamin D is the most potentially toxic vitamin. Overdoses raise blood calcium and damage soft tissues. Ultraviolet light from sunshine acts on a cholesterol compound in the skin to make vitamin D. The DRI committee sets recommended intake levels and a Tolerable Upper Intake Level for vitamin D. Food sources of vitamin D include a few naturally rich sources and many fortified foods.

7.5 **Summarize the physiological roles of vitamin E, name the consequences of deficiencies and toxicities, and list its major food sources.**
Vitamin E acts as an antioxidant in cell membranes. Average U.S. intakes fall short of DRI recommendations. Vitamin E deficiency disease occurs rarely in newborn premature infants. Toxicity is rare but supplements may carry risks.

7.6 **Summarize the physiological roles of vitamin K, name the consequences of deficiencies, and list its major food sources.**

---

[1] Contributed by Lori W. Turner, Ph.D., R.D., University of Alabama

[2] Contributed by Mary Ellen Clark and Lori W. Turner

Vitamin K is necessary for blood to clot. Vitamin K deficiency causes uncontrolled bleeding. Excess vitamin K can cause harm. The bacterial inhabitants of the digestive tract produce vitamin K.

7.7 **Describe some characteristics of the water-soluble vitamins.**
Water-soluble vitamins are easily absorbed and excreted from the body, and foods that supply them must be consumed frequently. Water-soluble vitamins are easily lost or destroyed during food preparation and processing.

7.8 **Summarize the physiological roles of vitamin C, name the consequences of deficiencies and toxicities, and list its major food sources.**
Vitamin C maintains collagen, protects against infection, acts as an antioxidant, and aids iron absorption. Ample vitamin C can be easily obtained from foods.

7.9 **Describe some of the shared roles of B-vitamins in body systems.**
As part of coenzymes, the B vitamins help enzymes in every cell do numerous jobs. B vitamins help metabolize carbohydrate, fat, and protein.

7.10 **List and summarize the physiological roles of individual B vitamins in the body, name the consequences of deficiencies, and list their most important food sources.**
Thiamin works in energy metabolism and in nerve cells. Its deficiency disease is beriberi. Many foods supply small amounts of thiamin. Riboflavin works in energy metabolism. Riboflavin is destroyed by ordinary light. Niacin deficiency causes the disease pellagra, which can be prevented by adequate niacin intake or adequate dietary protein. The amino acid tryptophan can be converted to niacin in the body. Low intakes of folate cause anemia, digestive problems, and birth defects in infants of folate-deficient mothers. High intakes can mask the blood symptom of a vitamin B_{12} deficiency. Vitamin B_{12} occurs only in animal products. A deficiency anemia that mimics folate deficiency arises with low intakes or, more often, poor absorption. Folate supplements can mask a vitamin B_{12} deficiency. Prolonged vitamin B_{12} deficiency causes nerve damage. Vitamin B_6 works in amino acid metabolism. Biotin and pantothenic acid are important to the body and are abundant in food. Choline is needed in the diet, but it is not a vitamin, and deficiencies are unheard of outside the laboratory. Many other substances that people claim are vitamins are not.

7.11 **Suggest foods that can help to ensure adequate vitamin intakes without providing too many calories.**

7.12 **Identify both valid and invalid reasons for taking vitamin supplements.**

Critical Thinking Questions

1. *Why can people consume large amounts of foods with beta-carotene without any ill effects but cannot consume large amounts of foods with active vitamin A without risk of serious toxic effects?*

   The liver converts beta-carotene into active vitamin A. The diet must supply 12 micrograms of beta-carotene to produce 1 microgram of active vitamin A, and this conversion is not efficient enough to result in a toxic level of active vitamin A. The only sign of excess beta-carotene intake is a bright yellow color of the skin due to a buildup of beta-carotene in the fat beneath the skin.

   Certain animal foods, such as liver, contain very high levels of active vitamin A. When these foods are ingested, all of the vitamin A is sent directly into the body and its fat tissues. The amount of active vitamin A can quickly reach toxic levels that can cause digestive upset as well as possible damage to the liver.

2. a. *How do vitamin B_{12} and folate function similarly in the body?*

   Both vitamins are coenzymes that support enzymes for new cell synthesis. In particular, both vitamins are needed for red blood cell production. They are also needed together because each allows the other vitamin to function.

   b. *Why is it important that somebody not take high doses of either of these 2 vitamins?*

   If someone consumes very high levels of folate, his red blood cells will be formed well but the folate excess may mask a vitamin B_{12} deficiency, which otherwise would result in oversized, immature blood cells. The vitamin B_{12} is also needed for optimal nerve function. This individual may experience subtle changes in nerve function but will not have the anemia that is more easily detectable.

Vitamin B_{12} does not have any associated toxicities if taken in excess. It does not function in cell development the same way that folate does. However, there is no benefit to taking mega-doses of B_{12} (unless prescribed by a physician to treat poor absorption), so this would be a waste of money.

3. a. *Which 2 vitamins require healthy organ systems for their synthesis in the body?*

Vitamins D and K require the healthy functioning of the body's organ systems.

b. *Describe the impact of any condition that would affect the organ systems responsible for the production of these 2 vitamins.*

Vitamin D production is dependent on healthy skin, liver, and kidneys. Any skin condition may affect the ability of the body to make the vitamin D precursor. Any condition that affects the liver, such as alcoholism, or a condition that affects the kidney tissue can reduce the production of active vitamin D. Over time, this can lead to softening of the bones.

The colon (large intestine) needs to be healthy to support the growth of bacteria that produce about 50% of the body's vitamin K needs each day. A person who has taken antimicrobial drugs will have a large decline in the colonic bacteria that produce vitamin K. This can lead to a deficiency of vitamin K, which can cause prolonged bleeding.

4. a. *Other than vitamin B_{12}, which 2 water-soluble vitamins are important for healthy functioning of the nervous system?*

Thiamin and vitamin B_6 are very important for the healthy functioning of the nervous system.

b. *Describe how each vitamin contributes to the overall function of the nervous system.*

Thiamin is important for the health of the neuronal cell membranes. These cells pass electrical impulses along their membranes, which allow neurons to fire and communicate with each other. Neurons are found within the brain and throughout the entire nervous system.

Vitamin B_6 is necessary for the production of neurotransmitters such as serotonin. These chemicals allow the communication between neurons in the brain and can affect many aspects of nervous system function.

5. *Which 3 vitamins can impact the health of the connective tissue and skeletal systems of the body? How does each of these vitamins contribute to the health of these systems?*

Vitamin A contributes to the health of the bones. This vitamin affects the expression of genes (DNA into protein), which can affect cell development. If vitamin A is deficient, the cells that build bone may not be fully functional. This could affect the quality of the bone tissue.

Vitamin D is essential for bone health. It stimulates the small intestine to absorb more calcium from foods so that the bones can make use of the calcium. Young people who lack vitamin D during growth may have softened, misshapen bones, as is seen with rickets. Older individuals may experience softening of the bones as calcium is released from them as a result of vitamin D deficiency. This condition is known as osteomalacia.

Vitamin C is needed for the formation of collagen, the base material of bones and other connective tissues. Vitamin C deficiency, known as scurvy, leads to poorly formed connective tissue, which can cause bleeding of the gums or rashes on the skin.

6. *Why won't eating high-calorie fast foods make people feel more energetic than eating lower-calorie foods?*

Fast foods provide higher amounts of fats, carbohydrates, and protein. They may not provide high levels of the B vitamins. These vitamins serve as coenzymes, assisting enzymes active in the cell's production of energy. When the diet supplies adequate B vitamins, the cell's energy metabolism enzymes work more efficiently at releasing energy from carbohydrates and fats.

7. *Why have the recommendations for vitamin D recently become a controversial topic among experts?*

Originally, it was thought that vitamin D just helped the body absorb more calcium to strengthen the bones. Within cells, vitamin D interacts with the genes to modulate how the cells function or grow. More current research suggests that higher levels of vitamin D intake may help reduce the risks of some types of cancers and cardiovascular disease. Vitamin D may also influence the function of the immune system in fighting infections and the development of autoimmune diseases like multiple sclerosis.

Controversy Discussion Questions

1. *Give any 2 examples of dietary supplements that could be susceptible to contamination. What foods could replace these 2 supplements?*

   Children's chewable vitamins have been found to contain excess levels of lead and levels of niacin above the UL. Children need to try different fruits and vegetables as well as whole grains to get their nutrients from a safe source. Putting a little bit of cheese on broccoli or drizzling a bit of chocolate on fresh bananas or strawberries may help a child learn to like for fruits or vegetables, for example.

   Herbal supplements may contain toxic plant materials or harmful bacteria. Most people can gain the benefits of some herbal remedies by trying a lot of different spices and herbs in moderation while cooking.

2. *Discuss what foods you could eat that would work as well as the following supplement formulas:*

   a. *"Stress formula"*

   "Stress formula" supplements claim to have higher levels of vitamin C and B vitamins to combat oxidative stress in the body. The person can obtain more benefits by eating more fruits, whole grains, and vegetables each day.

   b. *"For better metabolism"*

   These formulas contain extra biotin that may help the body better metabolize high levels of protein. Most adequate and varied diets contain plenty of biotin-containing foods, making biotin supplements unnecessary. The best alternative to this formula is to follow a diet that is low in refined sugars, not complex carbohydrates.

3. *Give any 2 reasons why people may NOT want to take supplements that contain beta-carotene or vitamin E.*

   Both vitamin E and beta-carotene have antioxidant properties that may help promote cardiovascular health.

   It has been suggested that people who take vitamin E supplements may reduce their risk of cardiovascular disease, but early studies supporting this view may not have accounted for variation in the subjects such as illnesses or smoking histories. A large study that closely examined other studies of vitamin E intake versus cardiovascular disease found that increased vitamin E intakes are not protective and may actually cause more harm.

   It has been suggested that increased intake of beta-carotene may reduce the risk of developing certain cancers such as lung cancer in smokers. Studies have shown that people taking beta-carotene supplements may be at increased risk for damage to their DNA, which can lead to cancer development, and that beta-carotene supplement intake in smokers actually increased the rate of lung cancer.

   Foods provide lower levels of vitamin E and beta-carotene in association with other nutrients; thus, with foods there is less risk of effects from excessive amounts of either of these two nutrients alone.

4. *List any 3 medical conditions or life stages in which a person may need to take a vitamin supplement in addition to eating a varied and adequate diet.*

   Pregnant women may need increased amounts of vitamin B_{12}, iron, and folate to support increased red blood cell development that is needed during pregnancy.

   Some people do not produce enough of intrinsic factor, needed for adequate absorption of vitamin B_{12}, in their stomach. These individuals cannot absorb enough vitamin B_{12}, even when they eat plenty of food sources. They often need injections of vitamin B_{12} to avoid a deficiency, which can result in nerve damage and anemia.

   People who are chronically dieting, such as people with anorexia or bulimia nervosa, would need supplements to ensure that they are getting enough vitamins and minerals.

People who are lactose intolerant may need a vitamin D and calcium supplement if they do not eat a varied diet rich in other sources of vitamin D.

People who are recovering from illness or surgery have increased demands for nutrients in order to repair or rebuild body tissues and essential molecules to restore health. People who have had weight-loss surgery often need supplements long term to obtain adequate amounts of nutrients.

Worksheet Answer Key

Worksheet 7-1: Label Analysis—Vitamins

1. Look up the Daily Value for vitamin A (5000 IU or 1500 RAE) and multiply this by the %DV on the label. If this cereal contributes 10% of the Daily Value, than it contributes 1500 RAE × 0.1 = 150 RAE of vitamin A.
2. The vitamins are added to the cereal (through fortification) because they are listed further down in the ingredients list.
3. a. No, because they are expressed as percentages of Daily Values.
   b. Some vitamins, like vitamin A, have RAE units, which describe an activity or amount of an active version of the vitamin. This is not an actual mass. Also, U.S. food label regulations do not require that quantities of vitamins in a food be included on the Nutrition Facts panel.
4. Vitamin D is increased from 10% to 25% with the addition of milk.
5. a. The B vitamins and vitamin C are more abundant since they appear first in the ingredients list.
   b. The B vitamins and vitamin C are water-soluble vitamins that do not build up in the body. There is not as much of a concern of toxicity from these vitamins as compared to fat-soluble vitamins.

Worksheet 7-2: Intake Analysis—Vitamins

1. a. Eating Plan B (4639 RAE)
   b. Eating Plan C (10 micrograms)
   c. Eating Plan G (280 millograms)
   d. Eating Plan B (700.6 micrograms)
   e. Eating Plan B (26 micrograms)
2. a. Eating Plan G would be deficient since pre-formed (active) vitamin A comes from animal sources.
   b. No, there are plenty of fruits and vegetables that contribute beta-carotene that can be converted into active vitamin A in the liver.
   c. There is enough beta-carotene to compensate for the lack of pre-formed vitamin A in Eating Plan G.
3. a. Include oranges, strawberries, or sweet peppers (also contribute fiber)
   b. Vitamin C is an important antioxidant as well as a supporter of healthy collagen protein in the body's tissues.
4. a. Eating Plans B and C are tied for the highest level of adequacy. They each meet the nutrient requirements for 19 out of 21 nutrients.
   b. Since both Eating Plans B and C have the same level of adequacy, it is necessary to look at the total kilocalories provided by each plan. Eating Plan B has 2994 kilocalories compared to 3746 kilocalories from Eating Plan C. So Eating Plan B has the most nutrient-dense choices based on adequacy versus kilocalorie content.

Worksheet 7-5: Chapter 7 Review Crossword Puzzle

1. energy
2. rickets
3. pellagra
4. antioxidant
5. niacin
6. Beta-carotene
7. Rhodopsin
8. precursor
9. osteoporosis
10. calcium
11. retinal
12. epithelial
13. Intrinsic
14. sunlight

Learning Activities & Project Ideas

Activity 7-1: A Vitamin Interview[3] LO 7.3-7.6, 7.8, 7.10

To help students learn all the vitamins, set up "The Body Company." Have each student "apply" for a job as a vitamin by describing (in an interview) what that vitamin can do for "The Company" and which other nutrients it works best with.

Activity 7-2: Vitamin Vocabulary Worksheets[4] LO 7.3-7.6, 7.8, 7.10

Ask students to write an original sentence using an assigned vitamin term. Then combine all of the students' sentences into a worksheet, removing the term used in the sentence, and replacing it with a blank line. At the end of the worksheet list all of the terms used alphabetically. The students have the fun of seeing their writing in print and are much more likely to enjoy the process than they would filling in the blanks of a "canned" worksheet.

Example ("niacin," the answer to #1, would be one of the key terms at the bottom of the worksheet):

Vitamin Vocabulary Worksheet
1. A deficiency of _________ produces diarrhea, dermatitis, and dementia.

Activity 7-3: Supplement Absorption Experiments[5] LO 7.12

Invite students to bring in their vitamin or mineral supplements. Using clear, plastic 8- to 10-oz. cups, put each supplement into a cup of vinegar, stir over the course of the class, and evaluate after an hour which have dissolved (high chance of being absorbed) and which have not (likely to pass through the GI tract unabsorbed). You can also point out the bright yellow/green color from the riboflavin.

Take liquid iron supplements (sold OTC as pediatric supplements) and add one drop at a time into (1) water; (2) very weak (almost clear) black tea; and (3) a sample of herbal "tea." The black tea almost instantly turns very black, indicating binding of the iron to the tannins and illustrating how/why tannin-containing foods/beverages can inhibit absorption of iron. Specifically, iron supplements shouldn't be taken with tea or other tannin-containing beverages, caffeinated or not.

Activity 7-4: Examination of Nutrition Quackery Via the Internet Project[6] LO 7.12

Instruct students to obtain information about a questionable nutritional product such as a nutrient supplement by performing an Internet search. Next, have students evaluate the claims regarding the product using anti-quackery sites on the Internet. The Internet Health Pilot http://www.ihealthpilot.org/quackery/index.shtml (sponsored by Quackwatch) is a good index to reliable anti-quackery websites.

Chapter Lecture Outline

I. Definition and Classification of Vitamins
   A. Introduction
      1. Vitamins were discovered at the beginning of the twentieth century.
      2. Definition: An essential, noncaloric, organic nutrient needed in tiny amounts in the diet.
      3. Vitamins help the body's metabolic enzymes maximize energy yields from macronutrients as well as help maintain the health of the body's cells, tissues, and organs.
      4. The only disease a vitamin can cure is the one caused by a deficiency of that vitamin.
   B. The Concept of Vitamin Precursors – Some vitamins exist as precursors (or provitamins) that need to be converted to active form in the body.
   C. Two Classes of Vitamins: Fat-Soluble and Water-Soluble – Table 7-2 describes the characteristics of the fat-soluble and water-soluble vitamins.

---

[3] Contributed by Marie E. Carter, St. Louis Community College at Florissant Valley

[4] Contributed by Penny Fredell, Yuba College, Marysville, CA

[5] Contributed by Anne O'Donnell, M.S., M.P.H., R.D., of Santa Rosa Junior College

[6] Contributed by Nancy Cotugna, University of Delaware

II. The Fat-Soluble Vitamins
   A. A, D, E, K
   B. Found in fats and oils of foods
   C. Require bile for absorption
   D. Stored in liver and fatty tissues until needed
   E. Not needed in the diet daily
   F. Can reach toxic levels if too much is consumed
   G. Deficiencies can occur when people eat diets that are extraordinarily low in fat.
   H. Vitamins A and D act similarly to hormones and influence cellular activity.
   I. Vitamin E protects the tissue from oxidative stress.

III. Vitamin A
   A. Forms
      1. Beta-carotene – plant-derived precursor
      2. Retinol – active form stored in the liver
      3. Converted by cells into its other two active forms, retinal and retinoic acid, as needed
   B. Roles of Vitamin A and Consequences of Deficiency
      1. Vitamin A plays a variety of roles in the body such as:
         a. Gene expression
         b. Vision – both for the health of the cornea and for a visual pigment in the retina
      2. Eyesight
         a. Vitamin A plays two roles:
            1. Process of light perception at the retina
            2. Maintenance of a healthy cornea
         b. Vitamin A is part of the rhodopsin molecule, a pigment within the cells of the retina.
         c. When light falls on the eye, it bleaches rhodopsin, which breaks off the vitamin A, initiating a signal that conveys the sensation of sight to the optic center of the brain.
         d. The vitamin then reunites with the pigment, but a little vitamin A is destroyed each time this reaction takes place, and fresh vitamin A must replenish the supply.
      3. Night Blindness – If the vitamin A supply runs low, night blindness can result – a lag before the eye can see again after a flash of bright light at night.
      4. Xerophthalmia and Blindness – A more serious deficiency of vitamin A occurs when the protein keratin accumulates and clouds the eye's outer vitamin A-dependent part, the cornea.
         a. Keratinization of the cornea can lead to xerosis (drying) and then progress to thickening and permanent blindness, xerophthalmia.
         b. 500,000 of the world's vitamin A-deprived children become blind each year due to xerophthalmia.
      5. Gene Regulation
         a. Vitamin A exerts influence on body functions through its regulation of genes.
         b. Hundreds of genes are regulated by the retinoic acid form of vitamin A.
      6. Cell Differentiation
         a. Vitamin A is needed by all epithelial tissue, which includes the protective linings of the lungs, intestines, vagina, urinary tract, and bladder.
         b. If vitamin A is deficient, goblet cells fail to differentiate to make protective mucus and instead secrete keratin, the same protein found in hair and nails.
         c. Keratinization makes the tissues dry, hard, and cracked, which makes them more susceptible to infection.
      7. Immune Function
         a. Vitamin A has a reputation as an "anti-infective" vitamin.
         b. Body's defenses depend on an adequate supply of vitamin A for proper development of immune system cells.
      8. Growth
         a. Vitamin A assists in growth of bone (and teeth).
         b. In children, failure to grow is one of the first signs of poor vitamin A status.
      9. Vitamin A Deficiency Around the World
         a. About 5 million of the world's preschool children suffer from vitamin A deficiency with symptoms of night blindness, diarrhea, appetite loss, and reduced food intakes.

b. About 180 million children suffer from a milder form of vitamin A deficiency that reduces their resistance to infections.
c. The WHO and UNICEF are working to reduce the rates of vitamin A deficiency in children around the world.

C. Vitamin A Toxicity
1. Can occur when excess vitamin A is taken as supplements or fortified foods
2. Chronic use of vitamin supplements providing three to four times the recommended dose for pregnancy has caused birth defects.
3. High vitamin A intakes may also weaken the bones and lead to fractures later in life.
4. Even some bubble gum and candy bars have added vitamin A.
5. With the exception of liver, it is not easy to ingest toxic amounts of vitamin A – 1 oz of beef liver contains 3 times the DRI

D. Vitamin A Recommendations and Sources
1. Overview
a. Vitamin A is not needed every day since it is stored in the body.
b. DRI for man is 900 micrograms
c. DRI for woman is 700 micrograms
d. Tolerable Upper Intake Level is 3,000 micrograms
2. Food Sources of Vitamin A
a. Beta-carotene is found in vegetables and fruits – Orange or muddy green colored
b. Active vitamin A is found in fortified foods and foods of animal origin – Liver, fish oil, milk, fortified cereals, eggs, butter
3. Liver: A Lesson in Moderation – 1 ounce of liver can supply 3-4 times the DRI for vitamin A and a common portion size is 4-6 ounces.
4. Can Fast Foods Provide Vitamin A? – Many fast-food places now offer salads with cheese and carrots as well as other vitamin A-rich foods.

E. Beta-Carotene
1. Overview
a. In plants, vitamin A only exists in its precursor form.
b. Beta-carotene, the most abundant of these carotenoid precursors, has the highest vitamin A activity.
c. Beta-carotene and other carotenoids may protect against macular degeneration, which is a common form of age-related blindness.
2. Does Eating Carrots Really Promote Good Vision?
a. Yes, eating carrots and other rich sources of beta-carotene promotes good vision
b. Dark green vegetables
c. Spinach, broccoli, collard greens
d. Orange fruits and vegetables
e. Carrots, sweet potatoes, pumpkins, mango, cantaloupe, apricots
3. Beta-Carotene, an Antioxidant – Beta-carotene is an antioxidant along with vitamin E, vitamin C, selenium, and many phytochemicals.
4. Measuring Beta-Carotene
a. How are beta-carotene and active vitamin A related?
b. It takes 12 micrograms of beta-carotene to produce 1 microgram of active vitamin A (retinol) in the body.
5. Toxicity
a. Beta-carotene from food is not converted to retinol efficiently enough to cause vitamin A toxicity.
b. Excess beta-carotene is stored the fat under the skin, imparting a yellow cast, which is actually harmless.
6. Food Sources of Beta-Carotene – Dark green vegetables such as spinach, broccoli, & collard greens & orange fruits and vegetables such as carrots, sweet potatoes, pumpkins, mango, cantaloupe, & apricots supply beta-carotene in the diet.

IV. Vitamin D

A. General characteristics
1. Can be self-synthesized with the help of sunlight.

2. Whether made with the help of sunlight or obtained from food, vitamin D undergoes chemical transformations in the liver and kidneys to activate it.
3. There has been a national drop in blood vitamin D levels in the last decades – may be related to higher levels of obesity since excess fat tissue keeps vitamin D less available to the blood

B. Roles of Vitamin D
   1. Calcium Regulation
      a. Vitamin D functions as a hormone to regulate blood calcium and phosphorus levels, thereby maintaining bone integrity.
      b. To replenish blood calcium, vitamin D acts at three body locations to raise blood calcium levels: skeleton, digestive tract, kidneys
   3. Other Vitamin D Roles
      a. Vitamin D stimulates maturation of cells, including immune cells that defend against infectious, cardiovascular disease, vision loss, and cancer.
      b. Deficiencies of vitamin D have been associated with: inflammatory conditions, multiple sclerosis, higher risk of death

C. Too Little Vitamin D—A Danger to Bones
   1. Rickets is a result of vitamin D deficiency in childhood (see Figure 7-6) – The legs are bowed due to the weakened bones' inability to support the body's weight
   2. Preventing Rickets
      a. Still seen in 50% of children in Mongolia, Tibet, and the Netherlands
      b. Not as common in the U.S. except in black, overweight females
   3. Deficiency in Adults
      a. In adults, the poor mineralization of bone results in osteomalacia, which may not have obvious clinical signs.
      b. Later on, deficiencies result in osteoporosis, which can cause bone fractures.
   4. Who Should be Concerned?
      a. In obese individuals, vitamin D may be stored in fat tissue and not accessible to the blood.
      b. People who do not get sunlight may also be at risk of vitamin D deficiency.

D. Too Much Vitamin D—A Danger to Soft Tissues
   1. Vitamin D is the most potentially toxic of all vitamins.
   2. Toxic to bones, kidneys, brain, nerves, heart, and arteries
   3. More likely if supplements are taken

E. Vitamin D from Sunlight
   1. Will not reach toxic levels
   2. Vitamin D Synthesis and Activation – Table 7-4 describes factors that affect vitamin D synthesis
      a. When ultraviolet light from the sun shines on a cholesterol compound in human skin, the compound is transformed into a vitamin D precursor and is absorbed directly into the blood.
      b. Over the next day, the liver and kidneys finish converting the precursor to active vitamin D.
      c. Dark-skinned people need up to 3 hours of direct sun for several days to make enough vitamin D.
      d. Light-skinned people need much less time—10 or 15 minutes.
      e. Many people may not get outside much and may become somewhat deficient in vitamin D.
      f. People who restrict their intake of animal and dairy foods may lack dietary vitamin D.

F. Vitamin D Intake Recommendations
   1. 15 micrograms/day for people ages 1-70 years
   2. 20 micrograms/day for adults over 70 years
   3. UL:100 micrograms/day (4,000 IU on supplement labels)

G. Vitamin D Food Sources – include butter, fortified margarine and milk as well as fortified soy products, cereals and infant formulas (see Snapshot 7-2)

H. Consumer's Guide to Sources of Vitamin D
   1. Finding Vitamin D in Food
      a. Only a handful of foods are naturally high in vitamin D like fatty fish, liver oil, beef liver, or egg yolks
      b. Many foods are fortified with added vitamin D, which is convenient, but a person can ingest too much vitamin D this way – Look at labels carefully
   2. Supplement Speed Bumps – many supplements have very high levels of vitamin D, which could push intakes up past the UL

3. Sunshine—It's Free, but Is It Safe?
   a. Sunlight's ultraviolet radiation contributes to about 1 million skin cancers per year.
   b. Sunscreens help reduce skin cancer risk but also block the ability of the skin to produce the precursor to vitamin D.
   c. Tanning booths are not a safe alternative to sun exposure either.
4. Moving Ahead
   a. Foods rich in vitamin D are the best choices.
   b. Fortified foods or supplements are not a reliable source of vitamin D.
   c. Get some sun exposure but protect your skin from excessive UV exposure.

V. Vitamin E – a.k.a. tocopherol
  A. Roles of Vitamin E
    1. Vitamin E is an antioxidant.
    2. Oxidative damage occurs when highly unstable molecules known as free radicals, formed normally during cell metabolism, run amok and disrupt cellular structures (Figure 7-7).
       a. Oxidative damage can lead to inflammation that is associated with cardiovascular disease and some types of cancer.
       b. The lung tissue is susceptible to oxidative damage due to the high oxygen concentrations found there.
  B. Vitamin E Deficiency
    1. Deficiencies are almost never seen in healthy humans.
    2. A classic vitamin E deficiency occurs in diseases with fat malabsorption or in premature babies born before the transfer of the vitamin from mother to the infant, which takes place in the last weeks of pregnancy.
    3. Infant's RBC rupture and infant becomes anemic
    4. Heart disease and cancer may arise in part through tissue oxidation and inflammation.
    5. People with low blood vitamin E concentrations die more often from these and other causes than do people with higher blood levels.
  C. Toxicity of Vitamin E
    1. No adverse effects arise from consuming foods that naturally provide vitamin E.
    2. Vitamin E supplements may also increase the effects of anticoagulant medication.
    3. An increase in brain hemorrhages, a form of stroke, among smokers taking just 50 mg of vitamin E per day has also been noted.
    4. Vitamin E supplements should be used at low doses so that the UL of 1000 mg/day is not exceeded.
  D. Vitamin E Recommendations and U.S. Intakes
    1. 15 milligrams a day for adults
    2. On average, U.S. intakes of vitamin E fall substantially below the recommendation.
  E. Vitamin E Food Sources
    1. Widely distributed in plant foods; fresh, raw oils, seeds (see Snapshot 7-3)
    2. Processing of foods and their associated vegetable oils can lead to the destruction of vitamin E.

VI. Vitamin K – Have you ever thought about how remarkable it is that blood can clot? What would happen if it didn't?
  A. Roles of Vitamin K
    1. Main function of vitamin K is to help synthesize proteins that help blood clot.
       a. People with heart problems may need a blood thinner, warfarin, that interferes with the effects of vitamin K.
       b. Such individuals may need vitamin K if they encounter excessive bleeding with warfarin use.
    2. Also necessary for the synthesis of key bone proteins
  B. Vitamin K Deficiency
    1. Vitamin K deficiency is rare but can occur if a person is on antimicrobial medicine that destroys intestinal bacteria.
    2. Newborn babies have a sterile intestine and it may take a couple of weeks for the intestinal bacteria to get established.
  C. Vitamin K Toxicity
    1. Toxicity is rare and there is no Tolerable Upper Intake Level.

2. Toxicity causes jaundice and may occur if supplements of a synthetic version are given too enthusiastically.

D. Vitamin K Requirements and Sources
   1. 120 micrograms/day for men, 90 micrograms/day for women
   2. Vitamin K can be made by intestinal bacteria.
   3. Newborns are given a dose of vitamin K at birth.
   4. Food sources: dark leafy greens, cabbage-type vegetables, liver (see Snapshot 7-4)

VII. The Water-Soluble Vitamins
   A. Vitamin C and the B vitamins
   B. Cooking and washing cut foods with water can leach these vitamins out of the food – See Table 7-5 for ways to minimize nutrient losses
   C. Absorbed easily and excreted easily in urine
   D. Foods never deliver a toxic dose of them but large doses concentrated in some vitamin supplements can cause toxicity.

VIII. Vitamin C
   A. History of its discovery
      1. More than 200 years ago, any man who joined the crew of a seagoing ship knew he might contract scurvy, which would end up killing as many as 2/3 of the crew.
      2. The first nutrition experiment was done nearly 250 years ago to find a cure for scurvy:
         a. 4 experimental groups: (1) Vinegar, (2) Sulfuric acid, (3) Seawater, (4) Lemons
         b. Those receiving the citrus fruits were cured.
      3. It took 50 years for the British navy to make use of the information and require all its ships to provide lime juice to every sailor daily – Nicknamed them “limeys”
      4. The name given to the vitamin that the fruit provided, ascorbic acid, literally means “no scurvy acid.”
      5. Today called vitamin C
   B. The Roles of Vitamin C
      1. A Cofactor for Enzymes – Assists enzymes involved in the formation and maintenance of collagen, which forms the base for all of the body’s connective tissues and for scar formation.
      2. An Antioxidant – Acts as an antioxidant, especially protecting the immune system cells from free radicals generated during their assault on invaders
         a. Vitamin C protects iron in the intestines from oxidation and enhances its absorption.
         b. Vitamin C in the blood helps preserve and recycle vitamin E.
      3. Can Vitamin C Supplements Cure a Cold? – Many studies do not show a strong relationship between vitamin C intake and the prevention of colds.
   C. Deficiency Symptoms – Most scurvy symptoms are due to collagen breakdown.
      1. Loss of appetite
      2. Growth cessation
      3. Tenderness to touch
      4. Bleeding gums
      5. Swollen ankles and wrists
      6. Anemia
      7. Red spots on skin
      8. Weakness
      9. Loose teeth
      10. Scurvy is rare; seen in infants fed cow’s milk with no vitamin C supplementation, elderly, severely ill people, alcohol or drug abusers, etc.
   D. Vitamin C Toxicity – Possible adverse effects of taking 2 grams a day:
      1. Alteration of the insulin response to carbohydrate
      2. Interference with blood clotting medications
      3. Increased risk of kidney stones
      4. Gout
      5. Excessive vitamin C can be dangerous for people who have an overload of iron in their systems
      6. Digestive upsets
      7. Doses approaching 10 grams per day are seen as being unsafe.

E. Vitamin C Recommendations
   1. DRI = 90 mg for men, 75 mg for women
   2. Only 10 mg/day needed to prevent scurvy
   3. Recommendation for smokers: 125 mg/day for men, 110 mg/day for women

G. Vitamin C Food Sources – fruits and vegetables (see Snapshot 7-5)

IX. The B Vitamins in Unison

A. Introduction
   1. B vitamins function as part of coenzymes.
   2. Coenzymes help enzymes do their jobs in making chemical reactions occur with less needed energy in the body (see Figure 7-11).

B. B Vitamin Roles in Metabolism
   1. Thiamin, riboflavin, niacin, pantothenic acid, and biotin participate in the release of energy from the energy nutrients.
   2. Vitamin B_6 helps the body use amino acids to synthesize proteins.
   3 Folate and vitamin B_{12} help cells multiply.

C. B Vitamin Deficiencies
   1. In a B vitamin deficiency, every cell is affected.
   2. Symptoms include: Nausea, severe exhaustion, irritability, depression, forgetfulness, loss of appetite and weight
   3. Impairment of immune response, abnormal heart action
   4. Skin problems, swollen red tongue, teary, red eyes, pain in muscles
   5. It may be difficult to determine which B vitamin is deficient since an inadequate diet may be deficient in several of the vitamins (see Figure 7-12).

X. The B Vitamins as Individuals

A. Thiamin Roles
   1. Characteristics
      a. Plays a critical role in the energy metabolism of all cells
      b. Occupies a site on nerve cell membranes
      c. Nerve processes and their responding muscles depend heavily on thiamin.
   2. Thiamin Deficiency – Beriberi
      a. First observed in East Asia, where rice provided 80 to 90% of the total calories most people consumed.
         1. Polished rice became widespread, and beriberi became epidemic.
         2. A physician noted a beriberi-like illness in chickens living in areas where people had beriberi (see Figure 7-14).
         3. Chickens were cured when fed rice bran, which contains thiamin
      b. In developed countries today, alcohol abuse often leads to a severe form of thiamin deficiency, Wernicke-Korsakoff syndrome.
         1. Alcohol impairs thiamin absorption.
         2. Symptoms: Apathy, irritability, mental confusion, memory loss, jerky movement, staggering gait
   3. Recommended Intakes and Food Sources (see Snapshot 7-6)
      a. Men should receive 1.2 milligrams/day of thiamin and women should receive 1.1 milligrams/day.
      b. Pork products, sunflower seeds, enriched/whole-grain cereals, legumes

B. Riboflavin Roles and Sources
   1. Riboflavin plays a role in energy metabolism.
   2. When thiamin is deficient, riboflavin usually deficient as well.
   3. Riboflavin deficiency may be seen in children or the elderly who do not consume milk and meats.
   4. Sources of riboflavin are enriched breads, cereals, pasta, milk, certain vegetables, eggs, and meats (see Snapshot 7-7)

C. Niacin
   1. Participates in energy metabolism (ATP production) of every cell.

2. Niacin Deficiency – Deficiency disease is pellagra, which appeared in Europe in the 1700s when corn from the New World became a staple food.
   a. In the early 1900s in the U.S., pellagra was affecting hundreds of thousands in the South and Midwest.
   b. Pellagra is still common in parts of Africa and Asia.
   c. Pellagra still occurs in the U.S. among poorly nourished people, especially alcohol addicts.
   d. Pellagra symptoms: 4 "D's": Diarrhea, dermatitis, dementia, death
   e. See Figure 7-15 for the skin condition associated with pellagra – Keep in mind that deficiencies of other vitamins can also affect the skin
3. Niacin Toxicity and Pharmacology
   a. Supplements may be taken as a treatment to lower blood lipids associated with cardiovascular disease.
   b. Symptoms of toxicity:
      1. Life-threatening drop in blood pressure
      2. Liver injury
      3. Peptic ulcers
      4. Vision loss
      5. Niacin flush, which can be very painful
4. Niacin Recommendations and Food Sources (see Snapshot 7-8)
   a. The key nutrient that prevents pellagra is niacin.
   b. Or, consuming adequate tryptophan (an amino acid found in proteins), which can be converted to niacin in the body
   c. The amount of niacin in a diet is stated in terms of niacin equivalents (NE), a measure that takes available dietary tryptophan into account.
   d. Most well-fed people rarely show signs of niacin deficiency.

D. Folate Roles – Folate helps synthesize DNA and so is important for making new cells.
   1. Folate Deficiency
      a. Deficiency of folate causes anemia, diminished immunity, and abnormal digestive function.
      b. Deficiencies are related to increased risk of cervical cancer (in women infected with HPV), breast cancer (in women who drink alcohol) and pancreatic cancer (in men who smoke).
      c. Some medicines like aspirin may interfere with the body's ability to use folate.
   2. Birth Defects and Folate Enrichment
      a. Adequate intakes of folate during pregnancy can reduce a woman's chances of having a child with a neural tube defect (NTD).
      b. NTD arise in the first days or weeks of pregnancy, long before most women suspect they are pregnant.
      c. In the late 1990s the FDA ordered fortification of all enriched grain products with an absorbable synthetic form of folate, folic acid.
      d. Since fortification began, the U.S. incidence of NTD dropped by 25 percent (see Figure 7-16).
   3. Folate Toxicity
      a. Tolerable Upper Intake Level for folate is 1,000 micrograms a day for adults
      b. A concern about fortifying the nation's food supply with folic acid is folate's ability to mask deficiencies of vitamin B_{12}.
   4. Folate Recommendations – 400 micrograms/day
   5. Folate Food Sources (see Snapshot 7-9)
      a. Green leafy vegetables, other raw fruits/vegetables, enriched grain products
      b. Folate is also measured in DFE (dietary folate equivalents), which convert the micrograms of all folate sources to be equivalent to that found in foods.

E. Vitamin B_{12} Roles
   1. Vitamin B_{12} and folate are closely related: each depends on the other for activation.
   2. Main roles: helps maintain nerves and is a part of coenzymes needed in new blood cell synthesis
   3. Vitamin B_{12} Deficiency Symptoms
      a. Symptoms of deficiency of either folate or vitamin B_{12} include the presence of immature red blood cells (see Figure 7-17).
      b. Administering extra folate often clears up this blood condition but allows the B_{12} deficiency to continue.

c. Vitamin B_{12}'s other functions then become compromised, and the results can be devastating: damaged nerves, creeping paralysis, and general muscle and nerve malfunctioning.

4. A Special Case: Vitamin B_{12} Absorption – Intrinsic factor is a compound made by the stomach needed for the absorption of B_{12}.
   a. A few people have an inherited defect in the gene for intrinsic factor, which makes B_{12} absorption poor.
   b. Vitamin B_{12} must be injected to bypass the defective absorptive system.
   c. This anemia of the vitamin B_{12} deficiency caused by a lack of intrinsic factor is known as pernicious anemia.
5. Vitamin B_{12} Food Sources – Vitamin B_{12} is generally found in animal foods, so strict vegetarians may need to get vitamin B_{12} from supplements (see Snapshot 7-10).
6. Perspective – exemplifies the importance of professional (not self) diagnosis of deficiencies

F. Vitamin B_6 Roles
   1. Vitamin B_6 participates in more than 100 reactions in body tissues.
   2. Needed to convert one amino acid to another amino acid that is lacking
   3. Aids in conversion of tryptophan to niacin
   4. Plays important roles in the synthesis of hemoglobin and neurotransmitters such as serotonin
   5. Assists in releasing glucose from glycogen
   6. Has roles in immune function and steroid hormone activity
   7. Critical to fetal nervous system development
   8. Vitamin B_6 Deficiency – Deficiencies of vitamin B_6 can show up as changes in the skin, weakness, depression, and neurological symptoms in cases of extreme deficiency (see Figure 7-18).
   9. Vitamin B_6 Toxicity – Toxicity of vitamin B_6 has developed in women taking supplements to relieve premenstrual syndrome.
      a. They developed difficulty walking due to the effects of excess vitamin B_6 on the nerves.
      b. Fortunately, the toxic effects are reversible.
   10. Vitamin B_6 Intake Recommendations and Food Sources – Most whole foods are good sources of vitamin B_6 (see Snapshot 7-11).

G. Biotin and Pantothenic Acid
   1. Biotin and pantothenic acid are also important in energy metabolism and serve as cofactors.
   2. Both vitamins are readily available in foods.

H. Non B Vitamins
   1. Many substances that people claim are B vitamins are not.
   2. Choline – important in fetal development – common in foods
   3. Carnitine, inositol, and lipoic acid – nonvitamins because they are nonessential – common in foods

XI. Food Feature: Choosing Foods Rich in Vitamins
   A. Which Foods Should I Choose? – Foods work in harmony to provide most nutrients.
   B. A Variety of Foods Works Best – to supply all of the essential vitamins and phytochemicals
   C. Figure 7-19 shows the foods that contribute the highest amounts of vitamin A, vitamin E, thiamin, vitamin B_6, folate, and vitamin C

XII. Controversy: Vitamin Supplements: Do the Benefits Outweigh the Risks? – About half of the U.S. population buys nutrient supplements, spending 24 billion dollars each year.
   A. Arguments in Favor of Taking Supplements (see Table C7-1)
      1. People with Deficiencies
         a. In the U.S. and Canada, adults rarely suffer nutrient deficiencies, but they do still occur.
         b. Luckily, deficiency diseases quickly resolve when a physician identifies them and prescribes therapeutic doses (two to ten times the DRI).
      2. People with Increased Nutrient Needs
         a. Nutrient needs increase during certain stages of life and so sometimes nutrient supplementation is needed.
         b. Women who lose a lot of blood and therefore a lot of iron during menstruation each month may need an iron supplement.
         c. Newborns require a single dose of vitamin K at birth.
         d. Women of childbearing age need supplements of folate to reduce the risk of NTD.

3. People Coping with Physical Stress
    a. Any condition that interferes with a person's appetite, ability to eat, or ability to absorb or use nutrients can easily impair nutrition status.
    b. Secondary deficiencies

B. Arguments Against Taking Supplements
1. Introduction
    a. Unlike foods, supplements can easily cause nutrient imbalances or toxicities.
    b. The higher the dose, the greater the risk of harm.
2. Toxicity – No one knows for sure how many people in the U.S. suffer from supplement toxicities but many cases likely go unreported.
3. Supplement Contamination and Safety
    a. FDA identified >140 supplements containing pharmaceutical drugs
    b. Some supplements contained twice the amount of vitamin A that was stated on the label.
    c. The FDA has little control over supplement sales and does not routinely test new supplements.
4. Life-Threatening Misinformation
    a. Another problem arises when people who are ill use high doses of supplements to cure themselves.
    b. Marketing materials are often misleading and false.
5. Unknown Needs
    a. No one knows exactly how to formulate the "ideal" supplement.
    b. Should phytochemicals be added? If yes, how much?
    c. What nutrients should be added?
6. False Sense of Security
    a. Using supplements may lull people into a false sense of security.
    b. People may think food choices are not important because the supplement will take care of any discrepancies.
    c. Self-diagnosing a condition and taking a supplement may postpone an accurate diagnosis.
7. Whole Foods Are Best for Nutrients
    a. Nutrients are absorbed best when ingested with food.
    b. Taken in pure, concentrated form, nutrients are likely to interfere with one another's absorption or with the absorption of nutrients from foods eaten with them.
        1. Zinc hinders copper and calcium absorption.
        2. Iron hinders zinc absorption.
        3. Vitamin C enhances iron absorption.

C. Can Supplements Prevent Chronic Diseases? – Can taking a supplement prevent these killers?
1. Vitamin D and Cancer – Low vitamin D intakes have been associated with some types of cancer but increasing vitamin D intake has not be shown to reduce cancer risk.
2. Oxidative Stress, Subclinical Deficiencies, and Chronic Diseases
    a. Antioxidant nutrients help to quench free radicals, rendering them harmless to cellular structures (see Table C7-3).
    b. Studies with mice have shown that increased vitamin C intake actually increase markers of oxidation in the blood and increase the risk of developing cataracts.
3. Vitamin E and Chronic Disease
    a. After years of recording health data, evidence shows that vitamin E supplements offered no protection against heart attack incidence, hospitalization, or death from heart failure.
    b. In fact, an alarming increased risk for death emerged for people taking vitamin E supplements.
    c. When the data from many studies are pooled and analyzed, it appears that high vitamin E intakes may actually be harmful.
4. The Story of Beta-Carotene—A Case in Point
    a. Similar to the hopeful beginnings of the vitamin E story, beta-carotene showed early promise as a cancer fighter.
    b. Results from controlled clinical human trials reveal no benefit from beta-carotene.
    c. In fact, there was a 38% increase in deadly lung cancer among smokers taking beta-carotene compared with placebos.
    d. Beta-carotene found in foods may not exert the same effects in the body as supplements.

D. SOS: Selection of Supplements – If you cannot meet your needs from foods, a supplement containing nutrients only can prevent serious problems.
   1. Choosing a Type
      a. Don't fall for meaningless labels such as, "advanced formula," "maximum power," "stress formula," "time Release," and the like.
      b. Avoid unknown herbal additions within a supplement.
   2. Reading the Label
      a. What form do you want? (chewable, liquid, pills)
      b. Some supplements may come in high-calorie forms such as a sugary vitamin drink or candy bar.
   3. Targeting Your Needs – Who are you? What vitamins & minerals do you actually need?
   4. Choosing Doses – Watch the dose you select!
      a. Avoid any preparation that in a daily dose provides more than the RDA/AI of vitamin A, vitamin D, or any mineral, or more than the Tolerable Upper Intake Level for any nutrient.
      b. Avoid doses of iron over 10 milligrams per day.
   5. Going for Quality
      a. USP symbol on label
      b. A high-priced supplement may not be higher in quality.
   6. Avoiding Marketing Traps – Avoid marketing hype on the labels such as "stress formula," "high potency formula," "for better metabolism," "organic," "natural," "time release," or claims that food lacks the necessary nutrients.

E. Conclusion
   1. People in developed nations are far more likely to suffer from overnutrition and poor lifestyle choices than from nutrient deficiencies.
   2. Invest energy in eating a wide variety of fruits and vegetables in generous quantities, along with the recommended daily amounts of whole grains, lean protein foods, and milk products every day, and take supplements only when they are needed.

Worksheet 7-1: Label Analysis—Vitamins

Nutrition Facts

Serving Size $^3/_4$ cup (31g)
Servings Per Container 11

Amount Per Serving	Cereal	with $^1/_2$ cup skim milk
Calories	120	160
Calories from Fat	10	10
	% Daily Value**	
Total Fat 1g*	**2%**	**2%**
Saturated Fat 0g	**0%**	**0%**
Trans Fat 0g		
Polyunsaturated Fat 0g		
Monounsaturated Fat 0.5g		
Cholesterol 0mg	**0%**	**1%**
Sodium 270mg	**11%**	**14%**
Potassium 60mg	**2%**	**8%**
Total Carbohydrate 26g	**9%**	**11%**
Dietary Fiber 1g	**5%**	**5%**
Sugars 11g		
Other Carbohydrate 14g		
Protein 2g		
Vitamin A	10%	15%
Vitamin C	10%	10%
Calcium	10%	25%
Iron	25%	25%
Vitamin D	10%	25%
Thiamin	25%	30%
Riboflavin	25%	35%
Niacin	25%	25%
Vitamin B_6	25%	25%
Folic Acid	25%	25%
Vitamin B_{12}	25%	35%
Phosphorus	4%	15%
Magnesium	2%	6%
Zinc	25%	30%

* Amount in cereal. A serving of cereal plus skim milk provides 1g total fat, less than 5mg cholesterol, 340mg sodium, 270mg potassium, 32g total carbohydrate (16g sugars) and 6g protein.
**Percent Daily Values are based on a 2,000 calorie diet. Your Daily Values may be higher or lower depending on your calorie needs.

INGREDIENTS: Whole Grain Wheat, Sugar, Corn Meal, Brown Sugar Syrup, Modified Corn Starch, Canola and/or Rice Bran Oil, Honey, Salt, Baking Soda, Calcium Carbonate, Dextrose, Trisodium Phosphate, Zinc and Iron (Mineral Nutrients), Vitamin C (Sodium Ascorbate), A B Vitamin (Niacinamide), Artificial Flavor, Vitamin B_6 (Pyridoxine Hydrochloride), Vitamin B_2 (Riboflavin), Vitamin B_1 (Thiamin Mononitrate), Vitamin A (Palmitate), A B Vitamin (Folic Acid), Vitamin B_{12}, Vitamin D. BHT Added to Preserve Freshness.

Instructions: Use the cereal label to answer the questions that follow.

1. How would you find out what amount of vitamin A is contributed by a serving of this cereal?

2. What are the sources of vitamins in this cereal?

3. a. Are any actual vitamin amounts (e.g., mass or volume) given on the label?

   b. Why might this be?

4. Which vitamin amount in the cereal is significantly increased by milk?

5. a. What class of vitamins is more abundant in the cereal alone?

   b. Why might this be?

Worksheet 7-2: Intake Analysis—Vitamins

Eating Plan B (1 Day's Intake)	**Eating Plan C (1 Day's Intake)**
6 ounces grapefruit juice 2 scrambled eggs 1 ounce cheddar cheese 20 ounces coffee 2 ounces soy milk 1 cup fresh raspberries 1 cup cantaloupe 1 honey oat granola bar 1 cup vanilla yogurt 6 ounces grilled salmon 10 cooked asparagus spears 1 cup broccoli 4 ounces white wine 4 ounces blueberry juice + seltzer water 20 barbecue flavor soy crisps 1 cup wasabi peas 1 3" x 3" spanakopita 1 cup spinach 1/3 cup feta cheese ¼ cup black olives 5 grape tomatoes 3 Tbsp. oil & vinegar dressing 6 ounces white wine ¼ cup mixed nuts 1 cup vanilla ice cream	6 5"-diameter pancakes 1/3 cup pure maple syrup ¼ pound of bacon 2 scrambled eggs 6 ounces orange juice 8 ounces 1% fat milk 2 slices of unseeded Italian bread 3 ounces of thinly sliced pastrami 2 Tbsp. spicy brown mustard 2 ounces of cheddar cheese 2 cups of Lucky Charms cereal 1 ½ cups 1% fat milk 6 ounces beef tenderloin 1 ½ cups mashed potatoes 1 cup cooked corn 1 cup cooked peas 10 ounces Seltzer water 2 ounces cheddar cheese
Eating Plan F (1 Day's Intake)	**Eating Plan G (1 Day's Intake)**
2 scrambled eggs 1 cup whole milk 2 slices bacon 2 1-ounce Slim Jims 6 ounces lean ground beef 2 ounces provolone cheese ¼ cup blue cheese dressing 12 ounces water 2 ounces cheddar cheese cubes 6 ounces grilled chicken breasts 1 scrambled egg 1 cup lettuce ½ cup blue cheese dressing 2 ounces pork rinds 12 ounces water	1 cup honey dew melon 1 cup fresh strawberries 1 large apple ½ avocado ½ cup sweet green peppers ½ cup sweet red peppers ¼ cup black olives 1 medium orange 1 medium banana 1 cup boiled green beans 10 cooked asparagus spears 1 cup sautéed mushrooms 1 cup kidney beans ¼ cup dried apricots ¼ cup dried Craisins 5 dried, pitted dates

Look at Eating Plans B, C, F, and G:

1. Compare each of these eating plans for their vitamin contents.

    a. Which eating plan has the highest level of vitamin A?

    b. Vitamin D?

    c. Vitamin C?

    d. Folate?

    e. Vitamin B_{12}?

2. a. Which of these eating plans is deficient in pre-formed vitamin A (retinol)?

    b. Is this same eating plan also deficient in beta-carotene?

    c. If not, is there enough beta-carotene to compensate for the reduced level of preformed vitamin A?

3. a. Suggest ways to increase the vitamin C content of Eating Plan F.

    b. Why is this important to do?

4. a. Which of these eating plans has the highest level of adequacy in terms of supplying essential vitamins?

    b. Does the same eating plan that you chose in 4.a. have the most nutrient-dense choices?

Worksheet 7-3: Factors that Destroy Vitamins[7]

Nutrient	Acid	Alkaline	Oxygen	UV Light	Heat
Thiamin		✓	✓		✓
Riboflavin		✓		✓	
Niacin	✓				
Biotin	✓	✓	✓	✓	
Pantothenic acid	✓	✓			✓
Vitamin B_6		✓		✓	✓
Folate	✓		✓	✓	✓
Vitamin B_{12}	✓			✓	
Vitamin C		✓	✓		✓
Vitamin A			✓	✓	✓
Vitamin D	✓		✓	✓	
Vitamin E			✓	✓	
Vitamin K		✓		✓	

Questions for discussion:

1. What types of food processing methods are available that can protect nutrients from the harmful effects of oxygen?

2. What types of food packaging could be used to block the penetration of the food by ultraviolet light?

3. Describe the food sources that can create an acidic or alkaline environment, which can destroy some of the nutrients.

7 Source for table: Adapted from C.D. Berdanier, *Advanced Nutrition: Micronutrients* (Boca Raton, Fla.: CRC Press, 1998).

Worksheet 7-4: Comparing Supplements Label To Label

Instructions: Obtain the labels of 2 multi-nutrient supplements. Compare these 2 different multivitamin preparations for their contributions of each vitamin and mineral to the percent of Daily Values.

- You can look at brand-name supplements as compared to similar generic supplements.
- Or, you can compare a specialty formula (men's/women's formula, stress formula, dieter's formula, etc.) with a general multivitamin.
- Fill in the following table and answer the questions to help you compare different multivitamins.

Supplements you compared: #1 ________________________ #2 ________________________

Vitamin/Mineral	Amount Listed		% Daily Value		UL
	Supp. #1	Supp. #2	Supp. #1	Supp. #2	
Vitamin A					
Riboflavin					
Thiamin					
Niacin					
Folate					
Vitamin B_6					
Vitamin B_{12}					
Vitamin C					
Vitamin D					
Vitamin E					
Vitamin K					
Calcium					
Phosphorous					
Sodium					
Potassium					
Magnesium					
Chromium					
Cooper					
Selenium					
Zinc					

Supplements can safely provide 100% of the Daily Values for most vitamins and minerals.

Answer these questions for supplement #1 on a separate sheet of paper:

1. What is the name of the supplement?
2. What is the cost per pill?
3. Is the supplement complete (does it contain all vitamins and minerals with established DRIs)? If no, what is missing?
4. Are most vitamins and minerals present at or near 100% of the DRIs? Exceptions include biotin, calcium, magnesium, and phosphorus, which are rarely found in amounts near 100% of the DRI. List any vitamins or minerals that are present in low amounts or dangerously high amounts.
5. Does the supplement contain unnecessary nutrients or nonnutrients? If yes, list them.
6. Is there "hype" on the label? Does the label use the terms "natural," "organic," "chelated," "no sugar," "stress-reliever," etc.? List any terms used.

Answer these questions for supplement #2 on a separate sheet of paper:

7. What is the name of the supplement?
8. What is the cost per pill?
9. Is the supplement complete (does it contain all vitamins and minerals with established RDIs)? If no, what is missing?
10. Are most vitamins and minerals present at or near 100% of the DRIs? Exceptions include biotin, calcium, magnesium, and phosphorus, which are rarely found in amounts near 100% of the DRIs. List any vitamins or minerals that are present in low amounts or dangerously high amounts.
11. Does the supplement contain unnecessary nutrients or nonnutrients? If yes, list them.
12. Is there "hype" on the label? Does the label use the terms "natural," "organic," "chelated," "no sugar," "stress-reliever," etc.? List any terms used.

Special Notes:

- Vitamin A should come from beta-carotene with only about 3,000 IU coming from retinal (active vitamin A).
- Older adults may need higher amounts of vitamin D than a multivitamin can provide. They may have to eat additional foods with vitamin D or consult their healthcare provider about taking additional vitamin D supplements.
- Post-menopausal women and men do not need the 100% daily value for iron.
- Doses of manganese (trace mineral) should not exceed 11 mg daily. Excessive doses can cause Parkinson's-like symptoms.
- Doses of zinc above 40 mg/day can interfere with copper absorption. Copper is needed for red blood cell formation in addition to iron.
- Try to get vitamin E in the form of mixed tocopherols instead of just alpha-tocopherol.

Ask Yourself:

13. When would a specialty formula be necessary?
14. Is a brand name vitamin always superior to a generic version?

References:

Why I Take Supplements. *Dr. Andrew Weil's Self Healing.* Premiere Issue, pages 1,6-7.

Does Your Supplement Provide a Nutrient Overdose? *Tuft's University Health and Nutrition Letter.* Volume 19 (2), April 2001, page 4.

Forman, Adrienne. Multis Deliver Nutrition Insurance: EN Helps You Make the Best Choice. *Environmental Nutrition.* Volume 27 (6) June 2004, pages 1, 4-5.

Worksheet 7-5: Chapter 7 Review Crossword Puzzle

Across:	Down:
1. Riboflavin and thiamin are important for _____ production within cells, including nervous system cells. 3. The niacin-deficiency disease causing dermatitis 5. This vitamin can produced in the body if enough tryptophan (an amino acid in proteins) is present 6. _____ is one of the plant-based forms of vitamin A that must be made active in the body. 9. Thinning of bones that occurs in older age and results in serious fractures 10. Active vitamin D acts on 3 key target organs/tissues in the body to raise the blood _____ levels. 12. Type of tissue that lines and protects the digestive tract and respiratory tract and is maintained by vitamin A 13. _____ factor, produced in the stomach, is needed for the body to be able to absorb adequate amounts of vitamin B_{12}. 14. Vitamin D can be produced by exposure of the skin to _____.	2. Vitamin D deficiency in childhood can result in _____, which is associated with weakened, misshapen bones. 4. Vitamin E functions as an _____, which can help protect cells from damage. 7. _____ is a visual pigment that contains vitamin A and is needed for night vision. 8. Stored form of a vitamin that needs to be made active inside the body 11. Another name for the active form of vitamin A involved in low-light vision

Handout 7-1: Vitamins Do More than Treat Deficiency Diseases

Vitamins play many roles in the body from maintaining cells and tissues to helping the body obtain maximum energy from macronutrients. Most people in developed countries do not suffer from diseases related to vitamin deficiencies but people do suffer from diseases such as cancer, cardiovascular disease, and osteoporosis. Vitamins can actually help prevent these chronic conditions if taken at effective and safe doses.

Vitamin	May Help Prevent	Special Notes
Vitamin A	Cancer, cardiovascular disease, macular degeneration	Get from beta-carotene-containing produce that has other protective phytochemicals
Vitamin B_6	Heart disease and reduced immunity	Can cause toxicity, so do not exceed the Tolerable Upper Intake Level
Vitamin B_{12}	Nervous system damage and anemia	
Folate	Heart disease, anemia, neural tube defects, breast cancer, and colon cancer	Stimulates red blood cell production
Vitamin C	Boosts immunity and may prevent cancer and cardiovascular disease	Avoid chewable tablet forms of vitamin C, which is ascorbic acid; it can erode tooth enamel
Vitamin D	Osteoporosis and breast cancer	Vitamin D is fat soluble, so do not exceed the Tolerable Upper Intake Level
Vitamin E	Cancer and cardiovascular disease	May be hard to get enough if one is on a low-fat diet

An adequate and varied diet can provide many of the vitamins in needed amounts. Older adults may need to get more vitamin D than what they can consume in their diets. Vegans may need to get additional vitamin B_{12} from a supplement. Everyone should watch that they do not exceed the Tolerable Upper Intake Level (UL) for vitamin A. This can be done by consuming most of the vitamin A in the form of beta-carotene from brightly colored produce.

References:

Why I Take Supplements. *Dr. Andrew Weil's Self Healing*. Premiere Issue, pages 1,6-7.

Does Your Supplement Provide a Nutrient Overdose? *Tuft's University Health and Nutrition Letter*. Volume 19 (2), April 2001, page 4.

Chapter 8 – Water and Minerals

Quick List: IM Resources for Chapter 8

- **Class preparation resources:** learning objectives/key points, suggested activities and projects, lecture outline
- **Assignment materials:** **Related LO**
  - Critical thinking questions (with answer key) 8.1, 8.4, 8.5
  - Discussion questions (with answers) for Controversy 8 .... 8.7
  - Worksheet 8-1: Label Analysis—Minerals 8.4, 8.5
  - Worksheet 8-2: Intake Analysis—Minerals 8.1, 8.4, 8.5
  - Worksheet 8-3: Iron and Calcium Intakes[1] 8.4, 8.5
  - **New!** Worksheet 8-4: Chapter 8 Review Crossword Puzzle
- **Enrichment materials:**
  - Handout 8-1: Why Does Calcium Accumulate Outside of the Teeth and Bones? 8.4
  - Handout 8-2: Magnesium and Potassium—Often Overlooked but Often Critical 8.4
  - Handout 8-3: Spices to Enhance Salt-Free Dishes 8.4

Chapter Learning Objectives and Key Points

8.1 **Describe the body's water sources and routes of water loss, and name factors that influence the need for water.**
Water makes up about 60 percent of the body's weight. Water provides the medium for transportation, acts as a solvent, participates in chemical reactions, provides lubrication and shock protection, and aids in temperature regulation in the human body. A change in the body's water content can bring about a temporary change in body weight. Water losses from the body must be balanced by water intakes to maintain hydration. The brain regulates water intake; the brain and kidneys regulate water excretion. Caloric beverages add to energy intakes. Dehydration and water intoxication can have serious consequences. Many factors influence a person's need for water. Water is provided by beverages and foods and by cellular metabolism. Sweating increases fluid needs. High-calorie beverages affect daily calorie intakes.

8.2 **Compare and contrast the health effects of various sources of fluid.**
Hard water is high in calcium and magnesium. Soft water is high in sodium, and it dissolves cadmium and lead from pipes. Public drinking water is tested and treated for safety. All drinking water, including bottled water, originates from surface water or groundwater, which are vulnerable to contamination from human activities.

8.3 **Discuss why electrolyte balance is critical for the health of the body.**
Cells regulate water movement by pumping minerals across their membranes; water follows the minerals. Mineral salts form electrolytes that help keep fluids in their proper compartments. Minerals act as buffers to help maintain body fluids at the correct pH to permit life's processes.

8.4 **Identify the major minerals important in human nutrition and their physiological roles in the body, the consequences of deficiencies, and their most important food sources.**
Calcium makes up bone and tooth structure. Calcium plays roles in nerve transmission, muscle contraction, and blood clotting. Calcium absorption adjusts somewhat to dietary intakes and altered needs. Phosphorus is abundant in bones and teeth. Phosphorus helps maintain acid-base balance, is part of the genetic material in cells, assists in energy metabolism, and forms part of cell membranes. Phosphorus deficiencies are unlikely. Magnesium stored in the bones can be drawn out for use by the cells. Many people consume less than the recommended amount of magnesium. U.S. diets often provide insufficient magnesium. Sodium is the main positively charged ion outside the body's cells. Sodium attracts water. Too much dietary sodium raises blood pressure; few diets lack sodium. Potassium, the major positive ion inside cells, plays important metabolic roles and is necessary for a regular heartbeat. Americans take in too few potassium-rich fruits and vegetables. Potassium excess can be toxic. Chloride is the body's major negative ion, is responsible for stomach acidity,

[1] Contributed by Sharon Rady Rolfes

and assists in maintaining proper body chemistry. No known diet lacks chloride. Sulfate is a necessary nutrient used to synthesize sulfur-containing body compounds.

8.5 **Identify the trace minerals important in human nutrition and their physiological roles in the body, the consequences of deficiencies, and their most important food sources.**
Iodine is part of the hormone thyroxine, which influences energy metabolism. Iodine deficiency diseases are goiter and cretinism. Large amounts of iodine are toxic. Most people in the United States meet their need for iodine. Most iron in the body is in hemoglobin and myoglobin or occurs as part of enzymes in the energy-yielding pathways. Iron absorption is affected by the hormone hepcidin, other body factors, and promoters and inhibitors in foods. Iron-deficiency anemia is a problem among many groups worldwide. Too much iron is toxic. Zinc assists enzymes in all cells with widespread functions. Deficiencies cause many diverse maladies. Zinc supplements can interfere with iron absorption and can reach toxic doses; zinc in foods is nontoxic. Selenium works with an enzyme system to protect body compounds from oxidation. Deficiencies are rare in developed countries, but toxicities can occur from overuse of supplements. Fluoride stabilizes bones and makes teeth resistant to decay. Excess fluoride discolors teeth and weakens bones; large doses are toxic. Chromium is needed for normal blood glucose regulation. Whole, minimally processed foods are the best chromium sources. Copper is needed to form hemoglobin and collagen and assists in many other body processes. Copper deficiency is rare. Many different trace elements play important roles in the body. All of the trace minerals are toxic in excess.

8.6 **Outline a plan for obtaining sufficient calcium from a day's meals.**

8.7 **Describe the influence of diet during youth on the risk of osteoporosis later in life.**

Critical Thinking Questions

1. *Why does the body draw calcium out of the bones even if the bones may be thinned?*

   The bones serve as a repository of calcium that can be taken by or returned from the blood as needed. The blood calcium levels are held in a narrow range by the action of hormones. The body requires calcium for nerve function, muscle contraction, blood clotting, hormone secretion, and enzyme function. If the diet does not contain adequate calcium or vitamin D to keep the blood calcium levels in the necessary range, the bones will be required to release calcium to the blood. This will lead to further reduction in bone density.

2. *Why does the body control the amount of iron that is absorbed?*

   Iron is difficult for the body to release and so it can build up to harmful levels. High iron levels can cause oxidative damage to the tissues, which can increase inflammation and decrease their ability to function. Also, infectious bacteria can thrive in the presence of high levels of iron. Thus, the body uses several mechanisms to regulate the amount of iron that is absorbed from the diet.

3. *Describe any three ways to reduce one's sodium intake without radically changing the diet.*

   - People can read food labels carefully and compare products in order to select foods providing up to 2300 mg (or 1500 mg) of sodium a day. If a canned soup has 800 milligrams of sodium, a person can select a different brand of soup or find a lower-salt alternative that may only provide 200-300 milligrams of sodium. A person can keep a "running total" of sodium by reading labels and adding up the sources.
   - People can use spices to make foods taste interesting. Added salt does bring out the flavor in foods, but some spices can, too. People can read labels to select low-sodium condiments since these items often contribute a lot of added salt to a person's diet.
   - People can replace cold cuts or foods preserved in brine with fresh foods that contain less salt.

4. *Explain why people may not recognize mild dehydration and attribute its signs and symptoms to other conditions.*

   Dehydration's effects may resemble those of other conditions (see Table 8-1). For example, dehydration can cause fatigue or a feeling of weakness. People may assume that they have anemia or that they need more carbohydrates in their diet. If they are chronically dehydrated, they may not realize that they would have more strength and energy if they drank more water.

5. *What are the functions of magnesium in the body, and why are so many Americans deficient in magnesium?*

   Magnesium helps the body's enzymes work more efficiently. It is also necessary for the body's ability to uptake and metabolize calcium, vitamin D, and potassium. Magnesium deficiency may result in impaired calcium, vitamin D, and potassium metabolism, which could appear as deficiencies of these essential nutrients as well. People who are severely magnesium deficient may experience neurological symptoms such as weakness or confusion.

   Many Americans eat a large amount of processed foods each day. Magnesium is found in whole foods and is lost during processing. Most Americans only get about 2/3 of their daily recommended magnesium.

6. *How does the body "know" how to adjust the level of iron absorption to match its needs?*

   The body has a feedback system that monitors blood iron levels. When the iron levels are in the right range or a little bit too high, the liver produces and secretes hepcidin, which reduces iron absorption from the body. When blood iron levels are low, hepcidin secretion from the liver is reduced so that the body will absorb more iron from food.

Controversy Discussion Questions

1. *You have a teenaged friend who is a vegan and she has just found out that her mother has osteoporosis. She is very worried about her bone health but will not eat any animal products. Give her any three suggestions that she could follow to ensure the future health of her bones.*

   - She should look for foods and beverages that contain added calcium such as cereals, soy products, or orange juices. She can also eat green leafy vegetables to get more calcium. (Table 8-12 provides tips for boosting calcium in meals.) She could select plant-derived calcium sources such as almond butter.
   - She should also do weight-bearing exercise to encourage maximum bone density. Consult Table C8-3 for more information as to how to prevent osteoporosis.
   - She may want to consider taking a calcium and vitamin D supplement but she should be aware of the risks of taking calcium supplements as described in Table C8-4.

2. *Many people assume that calcium and vitamin D are the only 2 nutrients that are essential to bone health, so they focus on getting enough of these 2 nutrients. List any 3 other nutrients that are important for bone health and describe how they function in the body.*

   Vitamins A, K, and C as well as magnesium and omega-3 fatty acids are also important for bone health. Vitamin A is needed for adequate bone remodeling to maintain the strength of the bones. Vitamin K, which tends to be found in the same green leafy vegetables that contain calcium, is necessary for the production of a key bone protein. Vitamin C, magnesium, and omega-3 fatty acids are needed for maintaining bone density. Magnesium may also help to maintain bone mineral density since it influences calcium use in the body.

3. *Your friend argues that being thin and keeping one's weight down place less stress on the bones. She uses smoking as a way to reduce her appetite so that she doesn't overeat. You have taken a nutrition class and are aware of the risk factors associated with osteoporosis. Discuss what you would tell her about the impact of her strategy on the health of her bones.*

   Table C8-2 lists risk factors for osteoporosis. Both smoking and low body weight are considered modifiable risk factors for osteoporosis. If she is not eating enough to maintain her weight, she is also not likely getting enough vitamins and minerals to support the health of her bones. She could also use weight-bearing exercise to keep her bones strong while avoiding gaining body fat.

4. *Give two reasons why drinking cola beverages can be harmful to the health of the bones.*

   - Young people often drink cola in place of milk or calcium-fortified juices. They don't get the recommended amounts of calcium and vitamin D to attain the maximum bone density.
   - Cola is preserved with phosphoric acid, which may cause the bones to release more calcium instead of retaining calcium. This can lead to bone loss as well.

Worksheet Answer Key

Worksheet 8-1: Label Analysis—Minerals

1. Sodium, potassium, calcium, iron, phosphorous, magnesium, zinc, copper, and manganese.
2. a. People with allergies may not be able to eat mixed nuts.
   b. They could have a life-threatening allergic reaction such as anaphylaxis.
3. a. This product contains the highest Daily Value level of manganese at 35%.
   b. Trace mineral
4. Copper helps the body to produce hemoglobin for the red blood cells for oxygen transport and it helps build strong collagen for the dense, fibrous connective tissue.
5. a. The copper RDA for adults is 900 µg. The DV, 2 mg, is considerably higher than the RDA (over twice the RDA amount). However, since the UL for copper is 10,000 µg (10 mg), this seems safe.
   b. Daily Value × 0.25 = 0.5 mg (500 µg) = amount of copper provided by this product.
6. The DV for magnesium is 400 milligrams.
   400 mg × 0.20 × 2 = 160 milligrams of magnesium contributed by 2 servings of this product.

Worksheet 8-2: Intake Analysis—Minerals

1. a. Eating Plan B (2.5 L)
   b. This plan provides fluids in the way of juices, soy milk, and white wine.
2. a. Eating Plan F could be modified to add more water content.
   b. The water content of Eating Plan F could be improved by adding fruits, vegetables, and juices.
3. a. Eating Plan B supplies enough potassium (5592 milligrams).
   b. Eating Plan B supplies enough magnesium (516.6 milligrams).
   c. Magnesium is important for the function of enzymes and muscles.
   Potassium is important for fluid balance, nerve function, and lowering blood pressure.
4. For Eating Plan A: use low-salt ham, reduce the amount of cheese or use a low-salt cheese, and use a lower-salt enchilada sauce.
   For Eating Plan B: reduce the number of scrambled eggs or the amount of salt added to the eggs, use less cheese or lower-salt cheese.
   For Eating Plan D: reduce the amount of marinara sauce or use a low-salt version. Reduce the amount of mustard and Italian dressing, or use a low-salt version of these condiments. Substitute roast beef for pastrami.
5. a. No there is not (9.9 milligrams).
   b. Iron-fortified cereals, breads, or grain bars could be added. Green peas or vegetable burgers (soy) could also be added to increase iron levels in this vegan eating plan.

Worksheet 8-4: Chapter 8 Review Crossword Puzzle

1. fluorosis
2. solvent
3. dehydration
4. Hypertension
5. selenium
6. Hydroxyapatite
7. Antacids
8. Iodine
9. urination
10. nonheme
11. zinc
12. chromium
13. magnesium

Learning Activities & Project Ideas

Note: Activities 7-1 ("Vitamin Interview") and 7-2 ("Vitamin Vocabulary Worksheets"), which are designed to help students review the characteristics of the individual vitamins, can easily be adapted as mineral review activities.

Activity 8-1: Water Comparison Project[2] LO 8.2

This is a big eye opener for the students who are fanatic about water consumption. Explain: "I'd like to see a brief industry summary on the bottled water industry. Included in this summary would be an explanation of the different types of bottled water, how this water gets to our tables, and the steps that are taken to ensure for the consumer that the product is in fact what it claims to be. Finally, I'd like to see a comparison between at least two bottled water manufacturers."

Activity 8-2: The Great Bone Robbery—Demonstration of Calcium Loss in Osteoporosis[3] LO 8.4, 8.7

Calcium taken out of the body would look like flour. You can use flour to represent the calcium in our bones. (Have flour measured into clear plastic bags or measure out as you talk.)

- Announce: A newborn has only 27 grams of calcium in his or her body, which would look like this. (Display ¼ cup of flour in a small clear plastic bag.)
- Continue: By age 10, the amount of calcium in your body would look like this. (Display 3 ½ cups of flour.) A 10 year old's body contains about 400 grams of calcium.
- Ask: Why has the amount gone up? (Answer: The bones are growing.)
- Continue: By age 15, your body has grown and will grow even more. At this age your bones become longer and wider. Your body has twice as much calcium as at age 10. It would look like this. (Display 7 cups of flour.)
- Continue: By adulthood, your bones will grow even more. As an adult, you have 44 times more calcium than you had when you were born. It would look like this. (Display 11 cups of flour.)
- Summarize: Osteoporosis often is not detected until 30% to 40% of the bone is lost. You can see how significant this calcium loss is by comparing the calcium in healthy adult bones to the calcium in the bones of a person with osteoporosis. (Display 6 ½ cups of flour as an example of someone with osteoporosis. Compare to the healthy adult with 11 cups.)

Activity 8-3: Sodium Intake Demonstration[4] LO 8.4

Ask the students to name high-sodium foods, and then have them look up the amount of sodium in a typical portion. Next, help them translate the milligrams of sodium into salt milligrams (salt is about 40% sodium, so mg Na/0.4 = mg salt) and weigh out this amount of salt using a scale. The students will observe how much salt is contained in a cup of canned soup, for example. You can also take a fast food menu, and show them how much salt we are consuming when we eat out (then compare this with the amount of sodium required for adults). Many of the fast-food establishments publish nutrition information online that can be accessed via the Internet in class.

Chapter Lecture Outline

I. Introduction to water and minerals – "Ashes to ashes, dust to dust" – when we die, what is left behind becomes nothing but a pile of ashes.
   A. Carbon atoms in carbohydrates, fats, proteins, and vitamins combine with oxygen to produce carbon dioxide, which goes into the air.
   B. Hydrogens and oxygens form water, and along with body water, this evaporates.
   C. Ashes are about 5 pounds of minerals
      1. About ¾ is calcium and phosphorus
      2. Less than a teaspoon of iron
   D. Major minerals – 7 minerals – Present in larger quantities than trace minerals
   E. Trace minerals – Present in smaller quantities than major minerals

II. Water
   A. Why Is Water the Most Indispensable Nutrient?
      1. Makes up about 60% of an adult's weight

---

[2] Contributed by Peter C. DuBois, M.Ed., Lorain County Community College

[3] Contributed by the Midland Dairy Council

[4] Contributed by Nancy J. Correa-Matos, Ph.D., R.D., University of North Florida

2. Participates in chemical reactions
3. Carries nutrients throughout the body
4. Solvent – Serves as the solvent for chemicals in the body
5. Cleansing Agent – Cleanses the tissues and blood of wastes
6. Lubricant and Cushion
   a. Acts as a lubricant around joints
   b. Serves as a shock absorber inside eyes, spinal cord, joints, and amniotic sac
7. Coolant – Aids in maintaining the body's temperature

B. The Body's Water Balance
   1. To maintain water balance, a person must consume at least the same amount lost each day to avoid life-threatening losses.
   2. Imbalances can result in dehydration or water intoxication.
   3. A change in the body's water content can bring about a temporary change in body weight.

C. Quenching Thirst and Balancing Losses
   1. The brain's hypothalamus monitors fluid volume, blood particle concentration, and blood pressure.
      a. If blood volume falls, the hypothalamus will register thirst and will send a signal to the pituitary gland.
      b. Pituitary gland releases a hormone that causes the kidneys to retain fluid in the blood instead of releasing it into the urine
   2. Dehydration
      a. Effects of mild dehydration, severe dehydration, and chronic lack of fluid are shown in Table 8-1
      b. Thirst lags behind a lack of water.
         1. To ignore thirst is to invite dehydration.
         2. When a person is thirsty, he may already have lost up to 2 cups of total fluid.
   3. Water Intoxication – occurs when too much plain water floods the body's fluids and disturbs their normal composition
      a. Can occur if several gallons of water are consumed in a few hours' time
      b. Can be fatal due to imbalance in concentrations of critical electrolytes

D. How Much Water Do I Need to Drink in a Day?
   1. Table 8-2 describes factors that increase fluid needs.
   2. Water from Fluids and Foods – About 13 cups/day for men, 9 cups/day for women
   3. The Effect of Sweating on Fluid Needs – Increases needs

E. A Consumer's Guide to Liquid Calories
   1. Mystery Pounds – Many people, like Derek, drink beverages that may cause them to gain weight.
   2. Drinking without Thirst – Few people choose beverages based on their thirst – They seek stimulants like caffeine or think that they need carbohydrates in sports drinks, as well as drinking beverages for pleasure
   3. Weighing in on Extra Fluids – Extra beverages do help to prevent dehydration but sodas can add empty calories.
      a. Beverages can add up to 22% of total calories in a day.
      b. People can choose nutrient-dense beverages like tomato juice versus orange juice.
   4. Seeking an Expert's Advice – track intake of calories, sodium, etc. from beverages
   5. Looking at Labels – Nutrition experts suggest that consumers consult the Nutrient Facts panel of food labels.
   6. Moving Ahead – People can meet their fluid needs with lower-calorie alternatives such as fruit juice mixed with sparkling water or limit serving sizes of caloric beverages.

III. Drinking Water: Types, Safety, and Sources – Water is arguably the most precious resource on the planet.

A. Hard Water or Soft Water—Which Is Best?
   1. Hard water – high concentrations of calcium and magnesium
   2. Soft water – high sodium – may aggravate high blood pressure; dissolves cadmium & lead from pipes

B. Safety of Public Water
   1. Hundreds of contaminants have been detected in public drinking water.
   2. Americans without access to chlorinated water are at risk of water-borne infectious disease.
   3. Testing and Reporting – The Environmental Protection Agency (EPA) is responsible for ensuring that public water systems meet minimum standards for protection of health.

4. Chlorination and Cancer – Public water systems remove some hazards; treatment includes the addition of a disinfectant (usually chlorine) to kill most microorganisms.

C. Water Sources – All drinking water originates from surface water or ground water that is vulnerable to contamination from human activities.
   1. Surface Water
      a. Water from lakes, rivers, reservoirs and fills about half of the nation's need for drinking water
      b. It is exposed to a variety of contamination sources like petroleum products or fertilizers but also to air and sunlight, which may break down some of the contaminants.
   2. Groundwater – From underground aquifers, which could be exposed to gas lines or pollution from dumps
   3. Home Water Purification
      a. People may also rely on water purification systems at home or may drink bottled water.
      b. Some home water purification systems remove lead, chlorine, and other substances while other systems do very little.
   4. Bottled Water
      a. About 7% of U.S. households use bottled water as the main drinking water source.
      b. Costs about 250 to 10,000 times the price of tap water
      c. About $^{1}/_{3}$ of bottled waters were found to be contaminated with bacteria, arsenic, or synthetic organic chemicals
      d. Problems: large input of resources to produce; 80% of bottles enter landfills

IV. Body Fluids and Minerals – Water is inside and outside of the cells – How do cells keep themselves from collapsing when water leaves them and from swelling up when too much water enters them?
   A. Water Follows Salt – Major minerals form salts that dissolve in body fluids; the cells direct where the salts go; and this determines where the fluids flow because water follows salt.
   B. Fluid and Electrolyte Balance – Electrolytes (salts) guide water flow among body compartments.
      1. The body has several homeostatic mechanisms that ensure electrolyte balance within and outside of cells to maintain their health.
      2. People experiencing diarrhea or eating disorders may lose a lot of water from their body's cells, which can cause life-threatening changes in the electrolyte balance.
   C. Acid-Base Balance
      1. Minerals help manage the acid-base balance, or pH of the body's blood and tissues.
      2. The body's proteins and some of its mineral salts act as buffers—molecules that keep a tight control on pH.

V. The Major Minerals – Calcium, chloride, magnesium, phosphorus, potassium, sodium, sulfate
   A. Calcium
      1. Characteristics
         a. Nearly all (99%) of the body's calcium is stored in the bones and teeth.
         b. Two important roles:
            1. Integral part of bone structure
            2. Serves as a bank that can release calcium to the body fluids if the slightest drop in blood concentration occurs
      2. Calcium in Bone and Tooth Formation – Hydroxyapatite and fluorapatite
      3. Calcium in Body Fluids – Only about 1% of the body's calcium is in the fluids that bathe and fill the cells, but this tiny amount plays these major roles:
         a. Regulates the transport of ions
         b. Helps maintain blood pressure
         c. Plays a role in blood clotting
         d. Essential for muscle contraction
         e. Allows for secretion of hormones, digestive enzymes, and neurotransmitters
         f. Activates cellular enzymes
         g. Adequate calcium may also reduce the risk of high blood pressure, diabetes, and colorectal cancer.
      4. Calcium Balance
         a. Skeleton is a bank from which the blood can borrow and return calcium as needed

   b. If more calcium is needed in the body, the body can increase the absorption from the intestine and prevent its loss from the kidneys.
   c. People can go without adequate calcium intake but at the expense of bone density.
5. Calcium Absorption
   a. Adults absorb ~30%, pregnant women 50%, growing children/teens 50-60%
   b. The body absorbs more calcium when intakes are low.
6. Bone Loss
   a. Bone loss is an inevitable consequence of aging.
      1. Sometime around age 30, or 10 years after adult height is achieved, the skeleton no longer adds to bone density.
      2. After about age 40, bones begin to lose calcium but the loss can be slowed somewhat by diet and regular physical activity.
   b. Osteoporosis, or adult bone loss, occurs if a person's calcium savings bank is not sufficient.
      1. As the body requires calcium for the blood, the calcium is removed from the bones, which weakens them.
      2. A diet low in calcium-rich foods during the growing years may prevent a person from achieving peak bone mass.
7. How Much Calcium Do I Need and Which Foods Are Good Sources? (see Snapshot 8-1)
   a. Obtaining enough calcium in childhood helps ensure that the skeleton starts adulthood with a high bone density.
   b. Intakes of calcium from supplements may elevate blood calcium or lead to calcifications.
   c. Higher intakes may not reduce the risk of bone fractures in older women.
   d. RDA = 1,000 mg for adults 19-50 years old, 1,200 mg for adults 51 and older
   e. UL = 2,500 mg for adults

B. Phosphorus
   1. Roles in the Body
      a. Second most abundant mineral in the body
      b. 85% of body's phosphorus is found combined with calcium in the bones and teeth.
      c. Helps maintain-acid base balance
      d. Part of genetic material
      e. Assists in energy metabolism
      f. Forms part of cell membranes
      g. Found in some proteins
   2. Recommendations and Food Sources – Food sources of phosphorous are listed in Snapshot 8-2

C. Magnesium
   1. A major mineral and yet there is only about 1 ounce in a 130-pound person, over half in the bones
   2. Most of the body's magnesium is in the bones and can be drawn out for all the cells to use in building protein and using the energy nutrients.
   3. Roles in the Body – Magnesium is important for the functioning of many enzymes & for normal heart muscle function, & is necessary for proper processing of calcium, vitamin D, & potassium.
   4. Magnesium Deficiency
      a. Can occur with vomiting, diarrhea, alcoholism, or malnutrition
      b. May cause hallucinations, which may be confused with mental illness or drunkenness
   5. Magnesium Toxicity – rare but can occur due to overuse of magnesium-containing laxatives
   6. Recommendations and Food Sources – Sources of magnesium include slightly processed or unprocessed foods (see Snapshot 8-3).

D. Sodium
   1. Roles of Sodium
      a. Salt has been valued throughout recorded history.
         1. "You are the salt of the earth" means you are valuable.
         2. Even the word *salary* comes from the Latin word for salt.
      b. Sodium is the main positively charged ion outside the body's cells.
      c. In 1 gram of table salt, NaCl, there are 400 milligrams of sodium and 600 milligrams of chloride.
      d. Is a major part of the body's fluid and electrolyte balance system.
      e. Helps maintain acid-base balance
      f. Is essential to muscle contraction and nerve transmission

g. 30 to 40% of body's sodium is on the surface of the bone crystals, where it is easily drawn upon to replenish blood concentrations.

2. Sodium Deficiency
   a. Severe diarrhea or vomiting can result in very low levels of sodium in the body's tissues, which can be very dangerous.
   b. Why are people urged to limit sodium? – To understand why, you must first understand how sodium interacts with body fluids.
3. How Are Salt and "Water Weight" Related?
   a. If blood sodium rises, as it will after a person eats salted foods, thirst ensures that the person will drink water until the sodium-to-water ratio is restored.
   b. Then the kidneys excrete the extra water along with the sodium.
   c. Overly strict use of low-sodium diets can deplete the body of needed sodium; so can vomiting, diarrhea, or very heavy sweating.
4. Sodium Recommendations and Intakes
   a. AI = 1,500 mg for adults 19-50 years old, 1,300 mg for age 51-70, 1,200 mg for 71 and older
   b. UL = 2,300 mg for adults 19 and older
   c. *DGA* = 2,300 mg/day or less for healthy adults, 1,500 mg/day if you have or are at risk of hypertension
5. Sodium and Blood Pressure
   a. The relationship between salt intakes and blood pressure is direct—the more salt a person eats, the higher the blood pressure goes.
   b. Stronger effect among people with diabetes, hypertension, kidney disease, African descent, history of parents with hypertension, and anyone over 50 years of age
   c. Higher blood pressure is related to heart disease and strokes.
   d. People have varied blood pressure changes in response to salt intake. The genes that control blood pressure do so by altering the way that the kidneys handle sodium.
6. Can Diet Lower Blood Pressure?
   a. The DASH (Dietary Approaches to Stop Hypertension) diet often achieves a lower blood pressure than restriction of sodium alone.
      1. Calls for greatly increased intakes of fruits and vegetables, with adequate amounts of nuts, fish, whole grains, and low-fat dairy products
      2. Only small amounts of red meat, butter, and other high-fat foods, and sweets are held to occasional small portions
      3. Salt and sodium are greatly reduced.
   b. Low potassium intake on its own raises blood pressure, whereas high potassium intake appears to both help prevent and correct hypertension.
7. Other Reasons to Cut Salt Intakes – Excess sodium intake could increase the excretion of calcium, which could affect the health of the bones.
8. Our Salty Food Supply
   a. People have a hard time keeping their sodium intake under 2300 milligrams.
   b. Experts are calling for a reduction of sodium in the food supply to reduce peoples' risk of cardiovascular disease.
9.. Reducing Sodium Intakes
   a. Only about 15% of sodium comes from the salt shaker; the rest is found in foods.
   b. Table 8-7 shows how to cut sodium from a barbecue lunch.
   c. Figure 8-10 shows the major sources of sodium in the American diet.

E. Potassium
   1. Roles in the Body
      a. Potassium is the principal positively charged ion inside the body's cells.
      b. Plays a major role in maintaining fluid and electrolyte balance and cell integrity, and is critical in maintaining a heartbeat
   2. Potassium Deficiency
      a. More common in that people don't get the recommended amount of potassium
      b. Severe potassium deficiency is due to dehydration, diuretic use or from untreated eating disorders – Leads to heart failure

3. Potassium Toxicity – very rare because the body has a very strong vomiting reflex that will expel excess potassium
4. Potassium Intakes and Food Sources
    a. Sources of potassium include fresh, whole foods as shown in Snapshot 8-4.
    b. Bananas are an enjoyable and reliable source of potassium in the diet.

F. Chloride
1. Chloride is the body's major negative ion.
2. It is responsible for stomach acidity and assists in maintaining body chemistry.
3. No known diet lacks chloride since it is part of the salt molecule.

G. Sulfate
1. Sulfate is the oxidized form of sulfur as it exists in food and water.
2. Used to synthesize sulfur-containing body compounds such as sulfur-containing amino acids
3. Deficiencies of sulfate are unknown.

VI. The Trace Minerals

A. Overview
1. Often difficult to determine their precise roles in humans due to the difficulty of providing an experimental diet lacking in the one element under study
2. Studies are generally done in laboratory animals, which can be fed highly defined diets.
3. Table 8-8 lists the trace minerals.

B. Iodine
1. Iodide Roles – Iodine is part of thyroxine, the hormone made by the thyroid gland that is responsible for regulating the basal metabolic rate.
2. Iodine Deficiency
    a. Goiter
        1. Cells of the thyroid gland enlarge until it makes a visible lump in the neck.
        2. Leads to sluggishness, forgetfulness, and weight gain
        3. Due to the thyroid gland's inability to make hormone due to insufficient dietary iodine
    b. Cretinism – severe iodine deficiency during pregnancy causes fetal death or cretinism
        1. Irreversible mental and physical retardation
        2. The world's most common and preventable causes of mental retardation
3. Iodine Toxicity
    a. Also causes enlargement of thyroid
    b. Iodine may become toxic at levels greater than 800 micrograms/day
4. Iodine Food Sources and Intakes
    a. Iodine in food varies because it reflects the soil in which the plants are grown or on which animals graze.
    b. Most salts are iodized and contain sufficient amounts of iodine to prevent deficiency.
    c. Milk has added iodine due to the use of an iodine disinfectant on the cow's udder.

C. Iron
1. Roles of Iron – Most iron in the body is contained in hemoglobin and myoglobin or occurs as part of enzymes in the energy-yielding pathways.
2. Iron Stores
    a. Iron is a very important element for the health of the body but it can be oxidized, which can lead to free-radical formation and inflammation.
    b. The body has several iron transport proteins that separate reactive iron from the body's tissues.
3. An Iron-Regulating Hormone—Hepcidin
    a. Hepcidin is a hormone secreted by the liver that regulates blood iron concentration by reducing iron absorption from the small intestine.
    b. Hepcidin is secreted at higher levels when the body's iron stores are abundant.
4. Food Factors in Iron Absorption:
    a. Iron occurs in two forms in foods:
        1. Heme iron is part of hemoglobin and myoglobin in meat, poultry, and fish
        2. Nonheme iron found in foods from plants and in the nonheme iron in meats
    b. Question? – Which form of iron do you think is absorbed better? (heme is more easily absorbed at about 23% versus 2-20% for non-heme iron)

   c. The combination of heme iron, nonheme iron, MFP factor, and vitamin C helps to achieve maximum iron absorption.
5. Iron Inhibitors – tannins and phytates – inhibit absorption
6. What Happens in Iron Deficiency?
   a. A mild iron deficiency results in depleted iron stores.
   b. If the iron stores & dietary intake are insufficient, iron-deficiency anemia can result.
   c. Iron-deficiency anemia is a problem worldwide.
   d. Anemia reduces the ability of red blood cells to carry oxygen and can be due to a decline in the number of red blood cells or the amount of hemoglobin in each red blood cell.
   e. Young children are at risk of iron deficiency or anemia if they consume large amounts of milk products.
7. Mental Symptoms of Iron Deficiency – can adversely affect mental activity and energy levels
   a. Children have trouble concentrating in school and may be irritable.
   b. Often confused with learning disabilities or other problems
8. Causes of Iron Deficiency and Anemia
   a. Worldwide, iron deficiency is the most common nutrient deficiency, affecting more than 1.2 billion people.
   b. Usually caused by malnutrition – Either from lack of food or from high consumption of the wrong foods
   c. People who consume high-carbohydrate and highly processed foods may not receive enough iron in their diets.
   d. Blood loss is the leading non-nutritional cause of iron deficiency.
9. Who Is Most Susceptible to Iron Deficiency? – women in their reproductive years, infants, children, teens
10. Can a Person Take in Too Much Iron?
    a. Iron is toxic in large amounts.
    b. Iron overload in healthy people is prevented by absorbing less iron when iron stores are full.
    c. Hereditary iron overload is a fairly common condition in Caucasian people – Intestines absorb iron at a high rate despite the excess iron building up in body tissues
    d. Symptoms:
       1. Early symptoms: fatigue, mental depression, abdominal pain
       2. Late symptoms: liver failure, abnormal heartbeats, diabetes, infections
    e. Iron supplements are a leading cause of fatal accidental poisonings among U.S. children under six years old.
11. Iron Recommendations and Sources
    a. RDA = 8 mg for men & women 51 and older, 18 mg for women 19-50 years old
    b. UL = 45 mg
    c. Vegetarian recommendation = 1.8 × RDA since the non-heme iron in plants is not as well absorbed as heme iron from animal flesh.
    d. Snapshot 8-5 shows foods that are good sources of iron.

D. Zinc – Zinc works with protein in every organ, helping nearly 100 enzymes and regulating gene expression – very important for cell development
1. Zinc is important for metabolism of macronutrients, release of active vitamin A from the liver, immune system function, blood glucose regulation, antioxidant activities, and several other cell functions.
2. Zinc is also needed to help produce the active form of vitamin A needed for night vision.
3. Problem: Too Little Zinc
   a. Impairs healing, sperm production, taste perception, growth & development
   b. Unleavened bread contains intact phytates that block the absorption of zinc.
   c. Too little zinc can impair digestive function and can exacerbate malnutrition.
   d. Zinc deficiency can be seen in young children, the elderly, and pregnant women.
4 Problem: Too Much Zinc
   a. Excess zinc can interfere with iron absorption.
   b. Zinc lozenges and nose sprays can damage the sense of smell as well.
5. Food Sources of Zinc – meats, shellfish, poultry, dairy products, fortified foods (Snapshot 8-6)

E. Selenium
  1. Roles in the Body
    a. Selenium works with an enzyme to protect body compounds from oxidation.
    b. Selenium may also help the thyroid gland hormones function more optimally in the body.
  2. Relationship with Chronic Diseases – studies are examining the role of selenium in reducing the risk of cancer
  3. Deficiency
    a. A deficiency induces a disease of the heart that is serious and warrants the inclusion of selenium as an essential trace mineral.
    b. Subtle deficiencies of selenium may lead to oxidative damage to tissues.
  4. Toxicity – Deficiencies are rare in developed countries because selenium is found in most unprocessed foods, but toxicities can occur from overuse from supplements and can affect hair, nails, bones, joints, and nerves.
  5. Sources – Unprocessed foods

F. Fluoride
  1. Roles in the Body – Fluoride stabilizes bones and makes teeth resistant to decay.
  2. Deficiency – Dental decay
  3. Toxicity – Excess fluoride discolors teeth (fluorosis); large doses are toxic.
  4. Sources of Fluoride – Major source: Fluoridated water from public water systems

G. Chromium
  1. Roles in the Body – Chromium works with the hormone insulin to control blood glucose concentrations.
  2. Chromium Sources
    a. Chromium is present in a variety of unrefined foods such as yeast, liver, and whole grains.
    b. It is estimated that 90% of U.S. adults consume less than the recommended minimum intake of 50 micrograms a day.
    c. Chromium supplements may not deliver promised results such as increased muscle strength.

H. Copper
  1. Copper is needed to form hemoglobin and collagen and may help a key antioxidant enzyme function better.
  2. Babies fed a copper-poor formula may experience disturbed growth and metabolism.
  3. Deficiency is rare but may result in reduced immunity and blood flow through arteries.
  4. Toxicity of copper can occur through intake of supplements.
  5. Good food sources include organ meats, seafood, nuts, and seeds.

I. Other Trace Minerals and Some Candidates
  1. Many different trace elements play important roles in the body.
  2. All are toxic in excess.
  3. Examples: molybdenum, manganese, boron, cobalt, nickel, silicon
  4. Table 8-8 highlights all of the minerals.

VII. Food Feature: Meeting the Need for Calcium

A. Low calcium intakes are associated with:
  1. Adult bone loss
  2. High blood pressure
  3. Colon cancer
  4. Kidney stones
  5. Lead poisoning

B. Milk & Milk Products – contributes nearly half of most Americans' calcium intakes
  1. Many people are lactose intolerant and may need to reduce their dairy product consumption.
  2. Figure 8-16 shows recommended amounts of milk products that should be consumed each day.

C. Vegetables – many green vegetables contain adequate amounts of calcium and the amount of calcium absorbed from them is quite high, as shown in Figure 8-16

D. Calcium in Other Foods – People who cannot tolerate dairy products can get calcium from sardines, almonds, or mineral water.

E. Calcium-Fortified Foods – contain calcium that has been added during processing; e.g., soy products, canned tomatoes, or stone-ground flour

F. Making Meals Rich in Calcium (Table 8-12)
   1. At breakfast – by adding a serving or two of milk and dairy products
   2. At lunch – by adding more leafy green vegetables
   3. At supper – by adding milk or dairy products, canned fish, or vegetables

G. Tracking Calcium
   1. A cup of milk contains about 300 mg of calcium.
   2. Most adults need about 1000-1200 mg calcium a day, which converts into 3.5-4 cups of milk a day.
   3. People can equate their calcium intake from other foods into cups of milk to help them track their calcium intakes.

VIII. Controversy: Osteoporosis: Can Lifestyle Choices Reduce the Risks?

A. Introduction
   1. An estimated 44 million people in the U.S.—the majority of them women over 50—have or are developing osteoporosis.
   2. Each year, ~ 1,500,000 people break a hip, leg, arm, hand, ankle, or other bone due to osteoporosis.
      a. 30% of these people are men
      b. About $^{1}/_{3}$ of people with hip fractures die of complications.

B. Development of Osteoporosis – due to a complex interactions of factors
   1. Bone Basics
      a. Trabecular bone – is more metabolically active than cortical bone and is tapped to raise blood calcium when the day's supply runs short
      b. Cortical bone – is the outer, ivory like bone and is found in shafts – calcium can also be withdrawn but more slowly
   2. Bone Loss (see Figure C8-1)
      a. Loss of trabecular bone begins to be significant for men and women around age 30.
      b. Loss of cortical bone begins at about age 40.
      c. Bone density declines and the vertebrae of the spine can compress and cause a loss of height or dowager's hump in women (See Figure C8-2).

C. Toward Prevention—Understanding the Causes of Osteoporosis
   1. Overview of causes:
      a. Gender, advanced age
      b. Genetics, environment
      c. Poor calcium and vitamin D nutrition as well as reduced absorption with age
   2. Bone Density and the Genes
      a. A strong genetic component contributes to osteoporosis, reduced bone mass, and the increased risk of fragility of bones.
      b. Over 170 genes are under investigation and each may interact with others and with environmental factors, such as vitamin D and calcium nutrition.
      c. Genes can influence the bone-building and bone-dismantling cells.
      d. Genes may influence the activity of cells that produce collagen.
      e. Genes may impact the mechanisms for absorbing and using vitamin D.
      f. Caucasians are at higher risk for developing osteoporosis than African Americans.
   3. Calcium and Vitamin D
      a. Vitamin D and calcium affect bone deposition and withdrawal.
      b. Most girls in their bone-building years fail to meet their calcium needs.
      c. Higher levels of calcium and vitamin D in the later years can slow down the rate of bone loss but cannot replenish the bone as well as in the younger years (see Figure C8-3).
   4. Gender and Hormones
      a. Declining estrogen levels in women may lead to increased bone loss.
         1. This bone loss accelerates in the 6-8 years after the onset of menopause.
         2. Younger women who do not produce enough estrogen may also lose bone more rapidly during menopause.
         3. Low estrogen production can be due to diseased ovaries but is often due to eating disorders in which the body weight is too low.
      b. Declining testosterone levels in older men may also lead to bone loss and increased risk of fractures.

5. Body Weight – women who are thinner may be at higher risk of developing osteoporosis
6. Physical Activity – weight-bearing exercise keeps the bones more dense
   a. .Table C8-2 shows that the harm from inactivity to the bones is comparable to that of nutrient deficiencies that result from smoking.
   b. Preventing falls in the elderly is key for reducing the risk of fractures.
7. Tobacco Smoke and Alcohol
   a. Smoking and increased alcohol consumption may increase the rate of bone loss.
   b. Smoking cessation may allow the bones to become denser over time.
   c. Excess alcohol consumption can cause the kidneys to excrete calcium that is needed for bone health.
   d. Alcohol can be toxic to the bone-building cells as well.
8. Protein
   a. May help build bones after a fracture but excess dietary protein may not be beneficial to the bones
   b. Diets low in protein may also be low in nutrients needed for bone health such as vitamin D, vitamin K, and calcium.
   c. The effects of excess protein intake on bones are being studied.
   d. Vegans may have lower bone density since they do not consume dairy products.
   e. The role of soy phytochemicals in bone health is being studied.
9. Sodium, Caffeine, Soft Drinks
   a. Soft drinks contain high levels of phosphoric acid (a preservative), which may increase the rate of bone loss.
   b. More studies are needed but a concern is that soft drinks are displacing milk and other calcium-rich beverages.
10. Other Nutrients Important to Bones
    a. Vitamin K is needed for a bone maintenance protein.
    b. Vitamin A is needed for bone remodeling.
    c. Vitamin C is needed for collagen maintenance.
    d. Table C8-2 shows both risk factors and protective factors related to the development of osteoporosis.

D. Diagnosis and Medical Treatment
1. Diagnosis includes measuring bone density using an advanced form of X-ray (DEXA) or ultrasound.
2. Several drugs also reverse bone loss – they inhibit the activities of the bone-dismantling cells or stimulate the bone-building cells
3. Estrogen therapy can help nonmenstruating women prevent further bone loss and reduce the incidence of fractures.

E. Calcium Intakes and Recommendations
1. 25% of U.S. children over age 3 do not get even 400 mg of calcium per day.
2. Only 10% of young women and men get the DRI recommendation of 1000 mg of calcium per day.
3. Those who cannot consume dairy products as a source of vitamin D and calcium and may need to take supplements or eat other foods to supply calcium.
4. Table C8-3, A Lifetime Plan for Healthy Bones
5. Calcium intake alone cannot reverse bone loss so supplementation may be necessary.
6. Calcium supplementation is not without risks (see Table C8-4).

F. Calcium Supplements
1. Calcium supplements come in a variety of forms such as calcium carbonate, citrate, gluconate, and others.
2. People should not exceed the UL of 2000-3000 milligrams.
3. Most calcium supplements contain between 250 & 1000 milligrams.
4. Some calcium supplements may dissolve more easily in the body than others.
5. Test this by placing a pill in 6 ounces of vinegar and seeing if it dissolves within 30 minutes.
6. The body absorbs calcium carbonate, calcium citrate, or calcium phosphate equally well.
7. Dividing the calcium supplement dose in half may improve absorption with each dose.
8. Table C8-5 describes supplement terminology.
9. People can take calcium supplements but should also get as much calcium from foods as possible.

Worksheet 8-1: Label Analysis—Minerals

Instructions: Use the mixed nuts label to answer the questions that follow.

Nutrition Facts	Amount/Serving	% DV*	Amount/Serving	% DV*
Serving Size 1 oz (28g/about 21 pieces)	**Total Fat** 15g	**23%**	**Sodium** 110mg	**5%**
	Saturated Fat 2g	**10%**	**Potassium** 180mg	**5%**
Servings Per Container about 40	*Trans* Fat 0g		**Total Carbohydrate** 6g	**2%**
Calories 170	Polyunsaturated Fat 3.5g		Dietary Fiber 2g	**8%**
Calories from Fat 130	Monounsaturated Fat 9g		Sugars 1g	
	Cholesterol 0mg	**0%**	**Protein** 5g	
* Percent Daily Values are based on a 2,000 calorie diet.	Vitamin A 0% • Vitamin C 0% • Calcium 4% • Iron 8% • Vitamin E 10%			
	Phosphorus 15% • Magnesium 20% • Zinc 8% • Copper 25% • Manganese 35%			

INGREDIENTS: CASHEWS, ALMONDS, PECANS, BRAZIL NUTS, HAZELNUTS (FILBERTS), PEANUT AND/OR COTTONSEED OIL, SALT.

1. What minerals are listed on the label for this product?

2. a. Who may not be able to eat this product?

   b. Why?

3. a. Which mineral has the highest percent Daily Value contributed by this product?

   b. Is this a major or trace mineral?

4. What are the functions of copper in the body?

5. a. What is the recommended intake of copper for an adult? How does this compare to the Daily Value?

   b. How much actual copper does 1 ounce of this product contribute?

6. What actual amount of magnesium in grams is contributed by 2 servings of this product?

Worksheet 8-2: Intake Analysis—Minerals

Eating Plan A (1 Day's Intake)

1 cup of Corn Flakes cereal
1 cup of 1% fat milk
2 cups of coffee
2 slices of whole-wheat bread
2 ounces thinly sliced baked ham
2 ounces cheddar jalapeño cheese
8 ounces chocolate milk
3 12-ounce beers
2 beef and cheese enchiladas

Eating Plan B (1 Day's Intake)

6 ounces grapefruit juice
2 scrambled eggs
1 ounce cheddar cheese
20 ounces coffee
2 ounces soy milk
1 cup fresh raspberries
1 cup cantaloupe
1 honey oat granola bar
1 cup vanilla yogurt
6 ounces grilled salmon
10 cooked asparagus spears
1 cup broccoli
4 ounces white wine
4 ounces blueberry juice + seltzer water
20 barbecue flavor soy crisps
1 cup wasabi peas
1 3" x 3" spanakopita
1 cup spinach
1/3 cup feta cheese
¼ cup black olives
5 grape tomatoes
3 Tbsp. oil & vinegar dressing
6 ounces white wine
¼ cup mixed nuts
1 cup vanilla ice cream

Eating Plan D (1 Day's Intake)

1 cup of Corn Flakes cereal
¾ cup 1% fat milk
6 ounces orange juice
12 ounces coffee
1 honey nut granola bar
6 ounces chocolate milk
2 slices rye bread
2 ounces pastrami
2 Tbsp. hot mustard
1 ounce Swiss cheese
1 cup 2% fat milk
1 large apple
8 Ritz crackers
2 Tbsp. peanut butter
12 ounces Diet Coke
1 cup angel hair pasta
¾ cup marinara sauce
1 cup lettuce & 1 sliced tomato
1/3 cup shredded cheddar cheese
5 cucumber slices
¼ cup Italian dressing
1/6 of a devil's food cake
6 ounces red wine

Eating Plan F (1 Day's Intake)

2 scrambled eggs
1 cup whole milk
2 slices bacon
2 1-ounce Slim Jims
6 ounces lean ground beef
2 ounces provolone cheese
¼ cup blue cheese dressing
12 ounces water
2 ounces cheddar cheese cubes
6 ounces grilled chicken breasts
1 scrambled egg
1 cup lettuce
½ cup blue cheese dressing
2 ounces pork rinds
12 ounces water

Eating Plan G (1 Day's Intake)

1 cup honey dew melon
1 cup fresh strawberries
1 large apple
½ avocado
½ cup sweet green peppers
½ cup sweet red peppers
¼ cup black olives
1 medium orange
1 medium banana
1 cup boiled green beans
10 cooked asparagus spears
1 cup sautéed mushrooms
1 cup kidney beans
¼ cup dried apricots
¼ cup dried Craisins
5 dried, pitted dates

Look at Eating Plans B, F, and G:

1. a. Which of these diets supplies the most water for the body?

   b. What are the major water sources in this meal plan?

2. a. Which of the eating plans could be modified to increase the water content?

   b. What food or drink choices would be included to increase the water content of the particular eating plan?

Look at Eating Plans A, B, and D:

3. a. Which of these eating plans supplies enough potassium?

   b. Enough magnesium?

   c. Why are these 2 minerals important for the health of the body?

4. Suggest ways to reduce the sodium content of each of these eating plans.

Look at Eating Plan G:

5. a. Is there enough iron in this eating plan?

   b. How could this eating plan be modified to increase the iron but maintain the mission of this eating plan?

Worksheet 8-3: Iron and Calcium Intakes

The two minerals most likely to fall short in the diet are iron and calcium. Interestingly, both are found in protein-rich foods, but not in the same foods. Meats, fish, and poultry are rich in iron but poor in calcium. Conversely, milk and milk products are rich in calcium but poor in iron. Including meat or meat alternates for iron and milk and milk products for calcium can help defend against iron deficiency and osteoporosis, respectively. Determine whether these food choices are typical of your diet.

Food choices	Frequency per week
Calcium-fortified foods (such as corn tortillas, tofu, cereals, or juices)	
Dark green vegetables (such as broccoli)	
Iron-fortified foods (such as breads or cereals)	
Legumes (such as pinto beans)	
Meats, fish, poultry, or eggs	
Milk or milk products	
Nuts (such as almonds) or seeds (such as sesame seeds)	
Small fish (such as sardines) or fish canned with bones (such as canned salmon)	
Whole or enriched grain products	

1. Do you eat a variety of foods, including some meats, seafood, poultry, or legumes, daily?

2. Do you drink at least 3 glasses of milk—or get the equivalent in calcium—every day?

3. How would you obtain these minerals if you followed a vegan diet?

4. How would you obtain these minerals if you needed to restrict the protein in your diet due to kidney disease?

Worksheet 8-4: Chapter 8 Review Crossword Puzzle

Across:	Down:
2. Water is a medium in which salt, amino acids, and sugars dissolve. It is known as (almost) a universal _____.	1. Excess fluoride intake can cause _____, which is a weakening and discoloration of the enamel of teeth.
6. _____ is what gives bones their hardness and is made up of calcium and phosphorous.	3. Thickening of blood, a weak, rapid pulse, and disorientation can be the result of severe _____.
9. The body loses most of its water through _____.	4. _____ is another term for high blood pressure, which can be aggravated by excessive sodium intake.
12. This mineral may assist insulin in maintaining blood glucose levels	5. A mineral that serves as an antioxidant
13. Calcium and _____ work together to ensure proper functioning of muscles.	7. _____ contain calcium and can relieve heartburn.
	8. _____ is needed for the thyroid gland to make its hormone thyroxine.
	10. Iron that comes from plant sources is _____ iron.
	11. Non-iron mineral that functions in DNA and heme production and energy metabolism

Handout 8-1: Why Does Calcium Accumulate Outside of the Teeth and Bones?

Q: What are calcifications?

A: Calcifications are inappropriate deposits of calcium found in soft tissues outside of the bones and teeth. They can be made of calcium phosphate salts, calcium oxalate, and octacalcium phosphates.

Q: Where can calcifications be found?

A: Calcifications can be found in kidney stones, skin, tendons, blood vessels, and heart valves (including prosthetic valves).

Q: What causes calcifications?

A: Calcium deposits can occur due to injury, disease, and the aging process. Calcification in the blood vessels and the heart valves may be due to inflammation, which can stimulate white blood cells known as macrophages to secrete substances that encourage calcium deposits.

Arteriosclerosis is the stiffening of arteries that can be due to the build-up of fatty plaques. These plaques can cause local inflammation of the blood vessels that can attract fiber-producing white blood cells. The resulting plaques can develop calcifications due to the build-up of calcium deposits around the fatty plaques. The calcium deposits in the arteries certainly contribute to the stiffening of the arteries that can lead to cardiovascular disease.

Q: How are calcifications treated?

A: Most calcifications in the blood vessels are not treated but can be detected by imaging techniques that can detect the hard calcium deposits in soft tissue. Heart valves that have a large amount of calcification may not function properly and may need to be replaced.

Kidney stones can be removed surgically if they are larger. Smaller stones can be broken up by high-energy waves that are directed at the stones from outside of the body. The broken-up calcium deposits can pass into the urine.

Q: How can calcifications be prevented?

A: People at risk of forming kidney stones are encouraged to limit their intake of organ meats that contain oxalate molecules. The oxalate molecule combines with calcium to produce the kidney stones. Calcium restriction is not necessary in order to prevent kidney stones.

People at risk for developing calcifications in their arteries are encouraged to eat a healthy diet that emphasizes fruits, vegetables, whole grains, and fish. These people may need to limit their intake of saturated fats and cholesterol as well. These dietary practices may limit inflammation of the blood vessels as well.

Some people have overactive parathyroid glands that may cause calcium levels in the blood to be too high. Such individuals can have surgery to remove some of the parathyroid gland.

Intake of calcium in the diet has very little impact in the development of calcium deposits.

References: (1.) www.mayoclinic. com. (2.) Giachelli, Cecila M., Ectopic Calcification: Gathering Hard Facts about Soft Tissue Mineralization. *American Journal of Pathology*. Volume 154. 1999, pages 671-675. (3.) Shioi, Atsushi, et al. Induction of Bone-Type Alkaline Phosphatase In Human Vascular Smooth Muscle Cells. *Circulation Research.* Volume 91 (9) 2002.

Handout 8-2: Magnesium and Potassium—Often Overlooked but Often Critical

Magnesium Fact Sheet

What is it?	It is a mineral that is needed for many body functions.
What can it do?	• Adequate levels may reduce the risk of developing diabetes. • Adequate levels may reduce the risk of arrhythmias. • Adequate levels may reduce blood pressure. • Adequate levels may ensure strong bones.
How much per day?	310 milligrams for women, 400 milligrams for men
Sources?	Whole, unprocessed foods such as spinach, yogurt, brown rice, almonds, salmon, whole-wheat bread, skim milk.
Do we get enough?	Not usually—especially since people eat a lot of processed foods that have magnesium removed from them during processing.
Ways to get more?	• One should eat a lot of whole foods since any one food does not contain a large amount of magnesium. • Eating a variety of whole foods will help ensure that enough magnesium is consumed.
Why it is so important?	• Enzymes that help produce energy (ATP) and synthesize DNA need magnesium to function. • Magnesium also helps to transport calcium and potassium into cells.
Used in treatment of:	High blood pressure, preeclampsia of pregnancy, heart attack, diabetes mellitus, osteoporosis, migraines, and acute asthma attacks

Potassium Fact Sheet

What is it?	It is a mineral that is needed for a wide variety of body functions.
What can it do?	• It helps maintain the heartbeat. • It helps maintain electrolyte and fluid balance. • It may help reduce blood pressure.
How much per day?	4700 milligrams
Sources?	Whole, unprocessed foods such as bananas, almonds, spinach, and cantaloupe.
Do we get enough?	Not usually—especially since people eat a lot of processed foods that have potassium removed from them during processing.
Ways to get more?	• One should eat a lot of whole foods since any one food does not have contain a large amount of potassium. • Eating a variety of whole foods will help ensure that enough magnesium is consumed.
Why it is so important?	• Potassium is the predominant positively charged ion within the body's cells and helps maintain the flow of ions and water into and out of cells. • Nervous and muscle tissue rely on potassium to maintain membrane charges needed for electrical impulse transmission.
Used in treatment of:	High blood pressure and electrolyte imbalances

References:

Tuft's University Health & Nutrition Letter, Volume 22 (4), June 2003, page 1.
Tuft's University Health & Nutrition Letter, Volume 21 (4), June 2003, page 1.
http://lpi.oregonstate.edu/infocenter/minerals/magnesium/
Sizer, F. & Whitney, E. *Nutrition: Concepts and Controversies* 12e.

Handout 8-3: Spices to Enhance Salt-Free Dishes

For general seasoning purposes, use these mixed herbs (place in shaker):

Saltless Surprise	2 tsp garlic powder; 1 tsp each of basil, oregano, and powdered lemon rind (or dehydrated lemon juice). Blend, mix well, store in glass container with rice to prevent caking.
Pungent Salt Substitute	3 tsp basil; 2 tsp each of savory, celery seed, ground cumin seed, marjoram, sage, lemon thyme. Mix well, then powder with a mortar and pestle.
Spicy Salt Substitute	1 tsp each of cloves, pepper, and crushed coriander seed; 2 tsp paprika; 1 tbsp rosemary. Mix in a blender and store in an airtight container.

For specific seasoning purposes, use these herbs. Store together mixtures of those you especially like, and label them "soup blend," "beef blend," etc.

When you serve:	Use:
Beef	Bay, chives, cloves, cumin, garlic, hot pepper, marjoram, rosemary, savory
Bread	Caraway, marjoram, oregano, poppy seed, rosemary, thyme
Cheese	Basil, chervil, chives, curry, dill, fennel, garlic chives, marjoram, oregano, parsley, sage, thyme
Fish	Chervil, dill, fennel, garlic, parsley, tarragon, thyme
Fruit	Anise, cinnamon, cloves, coriander, ginger, lemon verbena, mint, rose geranium
Lamb	Garlic, marjoram, oregano, rosemary, thyme
Pork	Coriander, cumin, garlic, ginger, hot peppers, pepper sage, savory, thyme
Poultry	Garlic, oregano, rosemary, sage, savory
Salads	Basil, borage, burnet, chives, garlic chives, parsley
Soups	Bay, chervil, marjoram, parsley, rosemary, savory
Vegetables	Basil, burnet, chervil, chives, dill, marjoram, mint, parsley, pepper, thyme

Source: Adapted from H. H. Shimizu, Do yourself a favor, *FDA Consumer*, April 1984, pp. 16-19.

Chapter 9 – Energy Balance and Healthy Body Weight

Quick List: IM Resources for Chapter 9

- **Class preparation resources:** learning objectives/key points, suggested activities and projects, lecture outline
- **Assignment materials:** **Related LO**
    - Critical thinking questions (with answer key) 9.1, 9.2, 9.3, 9.4, 9.6, 9.8
    - Discussion questions (with answers) for Controversy 9 .... 9.10
    - Worksheet 9-1: Breakfast Shake Label Analysis 9.8
    - Worksheet 9-2: Intake Analysis—Energy Balance and Body Weight 9.8
    - Worksheet 9-3: How Many Minutes or Miles for that Doughnut? 9.2
    - Worksheet 9-4: Exploring Eating Habits 9.6, 9.9
    - Worksheet 9-5: Behaviors that Influence Weight Status[1] 9.6, 9.8, 9.9
    - Worksheet 9-6: How to Get Your 150 Minutes a Week! 9.8
    - Worksheet 9-7: Evaluation of a Weight-Loss Plan or Program[2] 9.8, 9.9
    - Worksheet 9-8: Eating Attitudes Test 9.10
    - **New!** Worksheet 9-9: Chapter 9 Review Crossword Puzzle
- **Enrichment materials:** Handout 9-1: Medical Problems Associated with Obesity 9.1

Chapter Learning Objectives and Key Points

9.1 **Delineate the health risks of too little and too much body fatness, with emphasis on central obesity and its associated health risks.**
Deficient body fatness threatens survival during a famine or when a person must fight a disease. Obesity raises the risks of developing many chronic diseases and other illnesses. Central obesity is particularly hazardous to health. Adipokines are hormones produced by visceral adipose tissue that contribute to inflammation and diseases associated with central obesity. Health risks from obesity are reflected in BMI, waist circumference, and a disease risk profile. Fit people are healthier than unfit people of the same body fatness. Overweight people face social and economic handicaps and prejudice.

9.2 **Describe the roles of several factors, including BMR, in determining an individual's daily energy needs.**
The "energy in" side of the body's energy budget is measured in calories taken in each day in the form of foods and beverages. No easy method exists for determining the "energy out" side of a person's energy balance equation. Two major components of energy expenditure are basal metabolism and voluntary activities. A third component of energy expenditure is the thermic effect of food. Many factors influence the basal metabolic rate. The DRI Committee sets Estimated Energy Requirements for a reference man and woman, but individual energy needs vary greatly. The DRI Committee has established a method for determining an individual's approximate energy requirement.

9.3 **Calculate the BMI for various people when given their height and weight information, and describe the health implications of any given BMI value.**
The BMI values mathematically correlate heights and weights with health risks. The BMI concept is flawed for certain groups of people. Central adiposity can be assessed by measuring waist circumference. The percentage of fat in a person's body can be estimated by using skinfold measurements, radiographic techniques, or other methods. Body fat distribution can be revealed by radiographic techniques. No single body composition or weight suits everyone; needs vary by gender, lifestyle, and stage of life.

9.4 **Identify several factors, including hormones, that contribute to increased appetite and decreased appetite.**
Hunger outweighs satiety in the appetite control system. Hunger is a physiologic response to an absence of food in the digestive tract. The stomach hormone ghrelin is one of many contributors to feelings of hunger. Satiation ends a meal when the nervous and hormonal signals inform the brain that enough food has been

---

[1] Contributed by Sharon Rady Rolfes, modified by Mary Ellen Clark

[2] Contributed by Lori W. Turner, Ph.D., R.D., University of Alabama

eaten. Satiety postpones eating until the next meal. The adipokine leptin suppresses the appetite and regulates body fatness. Protein, carbohydrate, and fat play various roles in satiation and satiety.

9.5 **Describe some inside-the-body factors and theories of obesity development.**
Metabolic theories attempt to explain obesity on the basis of molecular functioning. A person's genetic inheritance greatly influences, but does not ensure, the development of obesity.

9.6 **Summarize some outside-the-body factors that may affect weight-control efforts.**
Studies of human behavior identify stimuli that lead to overeating. Food environments may trigger brain changes that lead to overeating. Too little physical activity, the built environment, and a lack of access to fresh foods are linked with overfatness. National antiobesity efforts are underway.

9.7 **Briefly describe metabolic events occurring in the body during both feasting and fasting.**
When energy balance is negative, glycogen returns glucose to the blood and fat tissue supplies fatty acids for energy. When fasting or a low carbohydrate diet causes glycogen to run out, body protein is called upon to make glucose, while fats supply ketone bodies to help feed the brain and nerves. When energy balance is positive, carbohydrate is converted to glycogen or fat, protein is converted to fat, and food fat is stored as fat. Alcohol delivers calories and encourages fat storage.

9.8 **Construct a weight-loss plan that includes controlled portions of nutrient-dense foods and sufficient physical activity to produce gradual weight loss while meeting nutrient needs.**
Setting realistic weight goals provides an important starting point for weight loss. Many benefits follow even modest reductions in body fatness among overweight people. Successful weight management takes time and effort; fad diets can be counterproductive. To achieve and maintain a healthy body weight, set realistic goals, keep records, eat regularly (especially at breakfast), and expect to progress slowly. Watch energy density, make the diet adequate and balanced, eliminate excess calories, and limit alcohol intakes. Physical activity greatly augments weight-loss efforts. Weight gain requires an eating pattern of calorie-dense foods, eaten frequently throughout the day. Physical activity helps to build lean tissue. For people whose obesity threatens their health, medical science offers drugs and surgery. The effectiveness of herbal products and other gimmicks has not been demonstrated, and they may prove hazardous. People who succeed at maintaining lost weight keep to their eating routines, keep exercising, and keep track of calorie intakes and body weight.

9.9 **Defend the importance of behavior modification in weight loss and weight maintenance over the long term.**

9.10 **Compare and contrast the characteristics of anorexia nervosa and bulimia nervosa, and outline strategies for combating eating disorders.**

Critical Thinking Questions

1. *Why is central obesity of such concern as regards the health of an individual?*

   Central obesity is the accumulation of visceral fat beneath the muscles of the abdominal area. The fat in this region is very hormonally active and releases into the blood fatty acids that may change the blood lipid profile negatively, resulting in metabolic syndrome and increased chronic disease risks.

2. *Describe 3 major ways that the body uses energy and discuss how an individual may influence one of them.*

   Basal metabolic rate is the largest consumer of energy. This is the energy used for vital body functions such as respiration, heart beat, brain functioning, and heat production. It is influenced by lean body mass, gender, height, and thyroid hormone levels.

   The thermic effect of food is the energy used to process foods. The digestive system must break down and assimilate nutrients as well as eliminate wastes. This thermic effect of food represents about 5-10% of daily energy expenditure.

   The energy used by voluntary activities above and beyond the basal metabolic rate can be influenced by the individual's activity level. If a person walks more or exercises more each day, he will expend more calories that day. Anywhere from 25-50% of the body's energy use is necessitated by physical activity.

3. *Martha is 5'10" tall and weighs 125 pounds. What is her BMI, and is it considered healthy?*

   If you use the formula on page 343, BMI = weight in kilograms/height in $meters^2$

   Martha is 70 inches tall. 70 inches × 2.54 centimeters/inch = 177.8 centimeters
   177.8 centimeters / 100 centimeters per meter = 1.78 meters
   $(1.78 \text{ meters})^2 = 3.2 \text{ meters}^2$
   Her weight is 125 pounds / 2.2 pounds per kilogram = 56.8 kilograms
   Her BMI = 56.8 kilograms / 3.2 $meters^2$ = 17.75

   Or: BMI = weight (lb) × 703 / height (in^2) = 125 × 703 / $(70)^2$ = 87875/4900 = 17.9

   Martha would be considered underweight. Her BMI should be between 18.5 and 24.9 as shown in Table 9-1.

4. a. *Describe how hunger and appetite differ from each other.*

   Hunger is the physiological need for food. The empty digestive system and the reduced levels of glucose and amino acids in the bloodstream will send a hunger signal to the hypothalamus. One of these signals is a hormone, known as ghrelin, that is produced in the stomach and stimulates hunger. People notice that their stomach begins to grumble or hurt a bit if they are experiencing true hunger.

   Appetite is the psychological need for food and is not dependent on the internal physiological state of the body. The appetite can be triggered by food customs, preferences for sweet or salty foods, the sight or smell of appealing foods, or social interactions, to name a few factors.

   b. *Which of these can be associated with obesity and why?*

   Appetite can be associated with "outside of the body" obesity because appetite can be stimulated in the absence of hunger, which can lead to overeating. Some people may take medicines that stimulate their appetite in the absence of true hunger as well. If someone overeats on a regular basis, he or she will take in more calories than he or she expends, which could lead to obesity.

5. *Your friend has gone to the doctor and has found out that she has borderline-high blood pressure and high blood cholesterol. She would like to avoid taking medicine to control these conditions but she is not happy about having to diet to lose weight since she is only 21 years old. You have successfully completed a basic nutrition course and want to give her some general suggestions to help her to lose weight and to maintain her weight loss. Describe any three measures that she could take to lose weight and keep it off.*

   You could suggest that she modify her diet to reduce her total calories by 500-1000 per day if her BMI is 35 or greater or 300-500 per day if her BMI is between 27 and 35. She may find that this reduction is far easier to follow than a drastic reduction of calories. She is less likely to feel deprived and is less likely to overeat. A total calorie intake of 1000-1200 cal/day will permit her to consume a nutritionally adequate diet. She still needs minerals such as magnesium and potassium to help control her blood pressure.

   You could suggest that she increase her physical activity to expend 100-200 more calories per day. She will not have to add a major fitness routine and will be more likely to be able to follow this. An increase in activity of 200 calories per day coupled with an intake reduction of 300-500 calories per day will create a deficit of energy that will result in the loss of body fat. She could take the stairs instead of the elevator and she could park her car a little bit farther out.

6. *Why can't people speed up their basal metabolic rate (BMR) with exercise or with supplements?*

   The level of thyroxine hormone, produced by the thyroid gland, has the most influence on the BMR. People with higher levels of thyroxine have higher BMRa. There is little anyone can do to change the level of thyroxine production by the thyroid gland.

   Moderate-intensity exercise will increase the amount of calories used during the activity but not immediately afterwards. People can increase energy expenditure by being more active. Over time, an active lifestyle increases the amount of lean tissue (muscle) somewhat, which could increase their BMR as well.

Foods do not speed up the BMR. The body does use about 5-10% of the daily calories to process foods (thermic effect of food) but this will not lead to an increase in the BMR. Supplements that claim to increase the BMR do not work and can have serious side effects as well.

Controversy Discussion Questions

1. *Why do so many young women aspire to be thin like models in magazines when they may realize that these individuals do not eat a healthy diet?*

   Many magazine models may also suffer from anorexia nervosa but the American culture highly values thinness. Women are rewarded for being too thin in that they often win beauty pageants or appear on the cover of magazines. Very young girls are very impressionable and want to be thin even if they are aware of the dangers of being underweight. In other cultures in which body leanness is not key to self-worth, very few people take serious risks in trying to lose weight.

2. *List any 3 serious health consequences of anorexia nervosa and explain how this eating disorder can cause these consequences.*

   People suffering from anorexia nervosa are often anemic due to insufficient iron intake; suffer from reduced body temperature and insomnia; have reduced heart muscle mass and function; have electrolyte imbalances; experience changes in thought processes; and can suffer from kidney failure. Anorexia nervosa is self-starvation that results in protein-energy malnutrition, and thus anorexia has the same consequences as the PEM associated with food poverty. Energy deficit results in wasting of lean body mass—muscles, and eventually organs—and this, combined with micronutrient deficiencies, causes malfunctioning of various tissues, organs, and organ systems.

3. *How are the self-perceptions of a person with bulimia nervosa different from those of a person with anorexia nervosa? How are they similar?*

   People with anorexia nervosa are often very self critical. They tend to be perfectionists and view their bodies as fat even if they are emaciated. They tend to be outwardly very agreeable, but they exert what control they can through reducing their body weight.

   People with bulimia nervosa tend to have low self-esteem and are impulsive. They deal with stress by eating large amounts of food. They feel guilty about bingeing and then they purge.

   People with both anorexia nervosa and bulimia nervosa use food to deal with uncertainty in their lives. Anorexics avoid food (constantly restrict) to exert control over their bodies and lives and bulimics use large amounts of food to deal with stressful situations. Bulimic individuals, however, feel guilty about their bingeing/purging behaviors and recognize them as abnormal, whereas anorexics are unable to perceive their behavior as such.

4. *How do eating disorders in male athletes compare, in terms of self-perception, to anorexia nervosa in a female?*

   Young athletes with low self-esteem see their bodies as poorly developed even if they have exceptional muscles. These men become obsessed with their bodies and weigh themselves constantly. They also may weight train and use anabolic steroids to increase their muscle mass. Many eating disorders in male athletes, like anorexia nervosa, are disorders of body image. Men with eating disorders are also perfectionists and control their bodies by building up their muscle mass even beyond what it may already be.

Worksheet Answer Key

Worksheet 9-1: Breakfast Shake Label Analysis

1. The product appears to be a weight-loss product due to the term "Lean" on the big label.
2. This product is meant to be a food supplement or meal replacement.
3. a. The major source of fat is high-oleic sunflower oil.
   b. Mono- and polyunsaturated fat

4. a. "Use this product as a food supplement only. Do not use for weight reduction."
   b. If someone eats 3-4 servings of this product a day to achieve a 1200-kilocalorie diet for weight loss, the intake of vitamins and minerals will exceed the safe, recommended limits.

5. a. Molybdenum and manganese are present in greater than 100% DV.
   b. These are trace minerals and do not need to be consumed at high levels from a supplement, especially if other sources of these minerals are being consumed in other meals.

6. People depend on simple substitutions to help them lose weight. They need to learn how to eat a variety of foods in moderation for an extended period of time to maintain a weight loss.

Worksheet 9-2: Intake Analysis—Energy Balance and Body Weight

1. a. Find sources of food to increase the following nutrients: fiber, thiamin, riboflavin, niacin, vitamin B_6, folate, vitamin C, vitamin A, vitamin E, calcium, iron, magnesium, potassium, and zinc.

   Suggested foods:
   1 cup of iron-fortified cereal
   ½ cup of skim milk
   6 ounces of grapefruit juice
   1 medium banana
   1 honey-nut granola bar
   4 ounces of broiled haddock
   1 cup of boiled green beans
   1 large apple
   ¼ cup of mixed nuts

   b. 1 cup of mashed potatoes, 1 cup of 1% fat milk, 4-6 ounces of lean beef, and 1 cup of broccoli

2. a. The eating plan promises to help the person lose fat weight quickly by reducing carbohydrate intake. This carbohydrate restriction supposedly causes the body to burn fat and reduces appetite and insulin levels.

   In reality, this eating plan forces the body to use protein as fuel, which leads to dehydration and glycogen depletion. This results in a quick but reversible weight loss.

   b. As long as some carbohydrates are eaten, this will prevent the build-up of ketone bodies. The main concern with high-protein diets is that many of the high-protein foods included are rich in solid fats that are associated with CVD-promoting changes in blood lipids (such as increased LDL).

   c. Choose more whole-grain products, non-fat dairy products, lean meats, fruits, legumes, and vegetables to "round out" this eating plan, while eliminating high-fat meats and whole-fat dairy.

3. a. Eating plan A has the best proportion of carbohydrates, fats, and proteins: 40% cal from carbohydrate, 30% cal from lipids, and 18% cal from protein.

   b. This depends on the person's lifestyle, beliefs, or other factors.

   c. Many people would find Eating Plan A easy to follow since it includes meats, milk, and prepackaged foods. Others might find Eating Plan G easier to follow if they are strict vegetarians.

Worksheet 9-5: Behaviors that Influence Weight Status

Promote weight gain:
Drink plenty of juice.
Eat energy-dense foods.
Eat large portions.
Eat peanut butter crackers between meals.
Eat three or more large meals a day.

Promote weight loss:
Drink plenty of water.
Eat nutrient-dense foods.
Eat slowly.
Eat small portions.
Limit snacks to healthful choices.
Limit television watching.
Participate in physical activity.
Select low-fat foods.
Share a restaurant meal or take home leftovers.

Worksheet 9-9: Chapter 9 Review Crossword Puzzle

1. composition
2. orlistat
3. leptin
4. bulimia
5. amenorrhea
6. deserts
7. thermogenesis
8. ghrelin
9. portion
10. protein
11. overweight
12. cognitive
13. waist

Learning Activities & Project Ideas

Activity 9-1: Food Diary and Examination of Eating Habits[3] LO 9.6, 9.9
Provide a food diary form for students to fill out. Have them calculate their kcalorie intakes for the day. To examine eating patterns and habits, have students complete Worksheet 9-4: Exploring Eating Habits. This handout examines when, where, and why foods are generally eaten. After students have completed these sections, instruct them to write changes they want to make in their food behavior patterns. Discuss the major changes that students want to make and encourage a discussion to provide suggestions for making changes.

Activity 9-2: Evaluation of a Weight-Loss Program[3] LO 9.8, 9.9
Provide students with Worksheet 9-7: Evaluation of a Weight-Loss Plan or Program. This form covers issues related to flexibility, adaptability, variety, cost, use of special foods, nutritional soundness, and long-term effectiveness. Instruct students to select a weight-loss book or program and use the worksheet form to evaluate its safety and effectiveness. Discuss different programs and their usefulness and effectiveness in terms of helping people lose weight while still getting balance and adequacy in their diet.

Activity 9-3: Evaluating the Impact of the Media on Body Image[4] LO 9.10
Before class, have students bring photos of models that appear in fashion magazines that they commonly read. Some examples of magazines include *Seventeen*, *Self*, *Shape*, and *Redbook*. For men, magazines pertaining to men's health or body building can be examined.

Present information about the eating disorders anorexia nervosa and bulimia nervosa. Discuss how society influences body image and fosters, through advertising, an unhealthy desire to be overly thin.

Have students analyze magazines and look for anorexic appearances that contribute to pressures to be overly thin. Discuss the implications and the prevalence of eating disorders in our society. Discuss other ways that students internalize pressure to have perfect bodies. Next, have students present ways that these pressures affect self concept and how students can achieve a realistic body image.

Chapter Lecture Outline

I. Introduction
   A. Both overweight and underweight present risks to health.
   B. It isn't your weight you need to control; it's the fat in your body in proportion to the lean—your body composition.
   C. This chapter will describe how the body manages its "energy budget."
   D. Various causes of obesity are also discussed and sound, scientific strategies for maintaining a healthy body composition are discussed.

II. The Problems of Too Little or Too Much Body Fat
   A. Introduction
      1. In 1960, about 13% of adults in the U.S. were obese.
      2. 68% of U.S. adults are now overweight or obese.
      3. 17% of children and adolescents are obese and many more are overweight.
   B. What Are the Risks from Underweight?
      1. Deficient body fatness threatens survival during a famine or disease epidemic.
      2. Underweight also increases the risk for any person fighting a wasting disease.

---

[3] Contributed by Lori W. Turner, Ph.D., R.D., University of Alabama

[4] Contributed by Jody Yates-Taylor, Portland Community College

C. What Are the Risks from Too Much Body Fat?
   1. Most obese people suffer illnesses, and obesity is considered a chronic disease.
   2. An estimated 300,000 people in the U.S. die each year from obesity-related diseases and 147 million dollars is spent on obesity-related health care.
   3. Chronic Diseases – disorders that can result from obesity include:
      a. Diabetes, heart disease, hypertension, gallstones, liver disease, some cancers, and stroke
      b. Excess body fat is associated with 50% of cases of hypertension, which increases the risk of heart attacks and strokes.
      c. Obesity makes it 3 times more likely for someone to develop diabetes.
   4. Obesity and Inflammation
      a. Fat tissue produces hormones called adipokines that regulate the inflammatory response and energy use by the tissues.
      b. Obesity causes the adipokines to exert an inflammatory effect as well as to make the cells resistant to the effects of insulin.
      c. Leads to the development of diabetes and cardiovascular disease
   5. Other Risks – Obesity elevates the risk of these conditions/diseases:
      a. Hernias, flat feet, sleep apnea, and respiratory problems
      b. Some cancers
      c. High accident rate
      d. Arthritis
      e. Many of these conditions improve with a 5-10% loss in body weight.

D. What Are the Risks from Central Obesity?
   1. Visceral fat – Located deep within the central abdominal area of the body versus subcutaneous fat that is found beneath the skin
   2. Raises the risks of: Hypertension, heart disease, stroke, diabetes
   3. Fatty acids are released from the visceral fat and may lead to metabolic syndrome.
   4. Central obesity and inflammation – Is also associated with increased inflammation and increased risk of insulin resistance
   5 Who develops central obesity? – Factors affecting body fat distribution: Gender, menopause, smoking, alcohol intake, physical activity

E. How Fat Is Too Fat?
   1. Evaluating Risks from Body Fatness
      a. Obesity experts evaluate risks to health from obesity using three indicators:
         1. BMI (body mass index) as listed in Table 9-1 – a measure of average relative weight for height in people older than 20 years
         2. Waist circumference
         3. Disease risk profile and family medical history
      b. Physically fit people are healthier than unfit people of the same body fatness.
   2. Social and Economic Costs of Body Fatness
      a. Overfatness presents social and economic handicaps as well as physical ills.
      b. 30-40% of women and 20-25% of men spend over $50 billion to try to lose weight.
      c. Judging people by their body weight is a form of prejudice in our society.

III. The Body's Energy Balance

A. Overview
   1. When more food is consumed than is needed, excess fat accumulates in the fat cells in the body's adipose tissue where it is stored.
   2. When energy supplies run low, stored fat is withdrawn.
   3. Change in energy stores = energy in – energy out

B. Energy In and Energy Out
   1. Foods and beverages are the only contributors to the "energy in" side of the equation.
   2. The "energy out" side is more difficult to determine and has to do with lifestyle and metabolism.
   3. The amount of fat lost with calorie restriction varies based on individuals' metabolic tendencies.

C. How Many Calories Do I Need Each Day?

1. Major components of the "energy out" side of the body's energy budget are basal metabolism, voluntary activities, and to a lesser extent the thermic effect of food.
    a. The BMR is related to the number of calories that the body uses to maintain temperature, pulse, respiration, and other vital activities.
    b. Table 9-3 shows various factors that can affect the BMR.
    c. People can increase energy expenditure by increasing their physical activity levels.
2. A third component of energy expenditure is the thermic effect of food, which describes the amount of energy needed to ingest, digest, absorb, and eliminate food.

D. Estimated Energy Requirements (EER) – see inside front cover of textbook

1. The DRI Committee sets Estimated Energy Requirements for a reference man and woman.
2. People's energy needs vary greatly.
3. Tall people need more calories due to increased heat loss from a larger skin surface area.
4. Reference man: "active" physical activity level, 22.5 BMI, 5 ft 10 in tall, 154 lbs
5. Reference woman: "active" physical activity level, 21.5 BMI, 5 ft 4 in tall, 126 lbs

E. The DRI Method of Estimating Energy Requirements – The DRI committee developed an equation for estimating energy needs that includes:

1. Gender – women have less lean mass than men and expend fewer calories
2. Age – BMR declines by an average of 5% per decade
3. Physical activity
4. Body size and weight
5. Growth – younger people use more calories to support tissue growth

IV. Body Weight vs. Body Fatness

A. Introduction

1. For most people, weighing on a scale provides a convenient and accessible way to measure body fatness.
2. Researchers and healthcare providers rely on more accurate assessments.

B. High Body Mass Index (BMI)

1. BMI correlates significantly with body fatness but does not measure body composition or fat distribution.
2. To determine your BMI: weight (lbs) × 703 / height $(in)^2$ or weight (kg)/height $(m)^2$
3. Your weight should fall within the range that best supports your health.
4. General guidelines:
    a. BMI < 18.5 = underweight
    b. BMI 18.5 to 24.9 = normal weight
    c. BMI 25 to 29.9 = overweight
    d. BMI ≥30 = obese
5. BMI is not an accurate measure for body builders or pregnant women and may vary between different ethnic groups of people.

C. Measures of Body Composition and Fat Distribution – Techniques for estimating body fatness include (Figure 9-7):

1. Anthropometry – Skinfold test, waist circumference
2. Conductivity – Bioelectrical impedance
3. Radiographic techniques – Dual energy X-ray absorptiometry (DEXA)
4. Figure 9-6 shows the average body composition of men and of women.

D. How Much Body Fat Is Ideal?

1. After you have a body fatness estimate, the question arises: What is the "ideal" body fat for a body to have? Ideal for what? Society's approval or health?
2. For health: People need enough fat to support their lifestyle and health

V. The Appetite and Its Control

A. Food used to be scarce so the body's appetite-regulating systems are skewed in favor of food consumption.

B. Hunger and Appetite—"Go" Signals

1. Eating behavior seems to be regulated by signals that fall into two broad categories: "go" mechanisms that stimulate eating and "stop" mechanisms that suppress eating (see Figure 9-8).

2. Hunger
    a. Hunger is stimulated by an absence of food in the digestive tract.
    b. Ghrelin is a hormone produced by the stomach that signals the hypothalamus of the brain to stimulate eating.
        1. Ghrelin may also promote efficient energy storage.
        2. Lack of sleep may trigger the release of ghrelin.
3. Appetite
    a. Appetite – the psychological desire for food that can be influenced by the use of drugs, cultural habits, hormones, environmental influences, and other factors
    b. Can you experience appetite without hunger? (yes)

C. Satiation and Satiety—"Stop Signals"
1. Satiation – occurs when the digestive organs signal the brain that enough food has been consumed
    a. When the stomach is full, stretch receptors send signals to the brain.
    b. Nutrients entering the small intestine stimulate the release of hormones that "give the hypothalamus information about the meal eaten."
2. Did My Stomach Shrink? – The stomach adjusts to meals of larger or smaller sizes but does not itself change size.
3. Satiety
    a. Is the feeling of fullness that lasts until the next meal
    b. The adipose tissue hormone leptin suppresses the appetite in response to a gain in body fat.
4. Energy Nutrients and Satiety – Some foods, such as low-GI foods, may confer greater satiety than others, but these effects are not yet well established scientifically.

VI. Inside-the-Body Theories of Obesity – Some peoples' bodies use or store every calorie with efficiency while others' bodies may expend calories more freely.

A. Set-Point Theory – states that the body's metabolism may adjust to maintain the body weight within a narrow range

B. Thermogenesis
1. The production by enzymes of heat that is released, expending energy in the process
2. Brown adipose tissue (BAT) may use a lot of calories to produce heat.

C. Genetics and Obesity
1. A person's genetic inheritance greatly influences, but does not ensure, the development of obesity.
2. For someone with at least one obese parent, the chance of becoming obese is estimated to fall between 30 and 70%.
3. The overfeeding or underfeeding of a pregnant woman may affect the risk of her child developing obesity later in life.

VII. Outside-the-Body Theories of Obesity – Food is a source of pleasure and tends to influence people's behavior and food choices.

A. Environmental Cues to Overeating
1. Studies of human behavior identify stimuli that lead to overeating.
2. People can override signals of satiety and hunger and eat whenever they wish.
3. Variety and availability are strong influences to eat when not hungry.
4. Stress can cause overeating, especially of comfort foods.
5. External stimuli such as the time of day promote eating.
6. Large portions encourage overeating.

B. Is Our Food Supply Addictive?
1. Intake of fat- and sugar-rich foods may stimulate the reward centers of the brain and cause the release of dopamine.
2. When people restrict intake of their favorite foods, they crave and eat them more.

C. Physical Inactivity
1. Some people may be obese not because they eat too much, but because they move too little.
2. Table 9-4 shows the amount of calories that are expended by various physical activities.
3. People need to limit their screen time and be more active on the job.

D. Can Your Neighborhood Make You Fat?
1. The physical layout of buildings and roads may discourage physical activity.

2. Food deserts – areas where there are few or no grocery stores selling affordable, healthful foods
3. High-calorie foods are relatively inexpensive, widely available, heavily advertised, and wonderfully delicious, but a steady diet of them correlates with obesity.
4. The National Academies' Institute of Medicine has suggested several goals to reverse the trend of obesity in the U.S.:
   a. Make physical activity a part of daily living.
   b. Make healthy foods and beverages available for all.
   c. Market what is important for a healthy life.
   d. Get employers and healthcare providers involved.
   e. Strengthen health education efforts in schools.

VIII. How The Body Loses and Gains Weight

A. Overview
   1. The body's energy balance is straightforward.
   2. The type of tissue lost or gained depends on how you go about losing or gaining it.
   3. To maintain weight, energy intake = energy out

B. Moderate Weight Loss vs. Rapid Weight Loss
   1. Introduction
      a. Eating periodically, storing fuel, and then using up that fuel between meals is a great advantage.
      b. If a person eats a balanced diet that meets protein and carbohydrate needs, and moderately restricts calories, the body will use stored fat for energy.
      c. Gradual weight loss will occur and will be easier to maintain in the long run.
   2. The Body's Response to Fasting
      a. If a person goes without food for 3 days, the body makes several adjustments:
         1. Less than a day into the fast, the liver's glycogen is used up.
         2. Where can the body obtain glucose to keep its nervous system going?
            a. Not from fat, because fat cannot be converted to glucose.
            b. Not from muscle glycogen, because muscles keep it for their own use.
         3. The body sacrifices the protein in its lean tissue to supply raw materials from which to make glucose.
      b. If the body were to continue consuming its lean tissue unchecked, death would occur in about 10 days. (Death occurs when either fat stores are depleted or half the body's lean tissue is gone.)
      c. To prevent death, the body converts fat to ketones to help feed the nervous system and help spare tissue protein.
   3. Ketosis
      a. After about 10 days of fasting, the brain and nervous system can meet most of their energy needs using ketone bodies.
      b. Thanks to ketosis, a healthy person starving with average body fat content can live totally without food for as long as six to eight weeks.
      c. In summary: The brain and nervous system need glucose, body fat cannot be converted to glucose, protein can be converted to glucose, and ketone bodies can feed some nervous system tissue and preserve protein.
   4. Is Fasting Harmful?
      a. Fasting does not cleanse the body.
      b. Fasting can lead to increased fat storage.
      c. Fasting may result in slowed metabolism as the body adjusts to conserve energy.
      d. Fasting may deprive tissues of nutrients that they need to regenerate or function.
      e. Ketosis upsets the acid-base balance of the blood.
      f. Fasting promotes excessive mineral losses in urine.
      g. Fasting may lead to overeating when food is available.
      h. Intestinal lining loses its integrity

C. Weight Gain – When energy balance is positive:
   1. Dietary protein is broken down into amino acids that are absorbed and used if needed.
   2. Excess amino acids are stripped of their nitrogens and converted to fat.
   3. Carbohydrate is converted to glycogen first and then to fat.
   4. Alcohol is detoxified and then used for fuel, which can encourage fat storage.

5. Too little physical activity encourages body fat accumulation.
6. Figure 9-10 outlines the effects of fasting and feasting on the body's use of nutrients.

IX. Achieving and Maintaining a Healthy Body Weight
   A. Introduction
      1. Consider your motivation for losing weight: people have more success when losing weight for health reasons.
      2. Modest weight loss of 5 to 10 pounds can produce gains in quality of life as well as improvements in chronic conditions
      3. First, a Reality Check – Excess weight takes years to accumulate so losing it takes time as well.
      4. Set Achievable Goals
         a. Start by not gaining more weight.
         b. Lose 5-10% of your body's weight in a year's time.
         c. Start by eliminating all sugar-containing beverages.
         d. Aim to lose 1 to 2 pounds of body fat per week.
      5. Keep Records – Keeping records of food intakes to spot trends or notice behaviors that need improvement
   B. What Food Strategies Are Best for Weight Loss?
      1. Choose an Appropriate Calorie Intake – In 2009, the Academy of Nutrition and Dietetics recommended that calorie reductions should be based on BMI.
         a. People with a BMI >35 should reduce calories by 500-1000 per day.
         b. People with a BMI between 27 and 35 should reduce calories by 300-500 per day.
         c. As weight loss progresses, the number calories needed to lose more weight may increase, possibly because metabolism slows and calorie expenditure during physical activity declines.
         d. Table 9-8 shows eating plans that will allow men and women to safely lose weight while obtaining adequate nutrients.
      2. Make Intakes Adequate
         a. Balance carbohydrates, fats, and proteins and get foods from all of the major food groups to provide the necessary nutrients.
         b. Consider a supplement to ensure adequacy.
      3. Avoid Portion Pitfalls – Learn how to measure portions and keep them smaller to control calories.
      4. Meal Spacing – Some people eat 3 meals a day while others eat several smaller meals.
         a. Eat regularly before you get really hungry.
         b. Snacks low in solid fats and added sugars should be selected.
      5. Identify Calorie Excesses
         a. Small daily calorie excesses add up over a year's time.
         b. Each meal eaten away from home increases the daily intake by 134 calories.
      6. Choose Foods Low in Energy Density – Foods high in fat and low in water content tend to be high energy density.(Figure 9-10).
      7. Consider Nonnutritive Sweeteners – some successful weight-loss maintainers use them but beverages containing them may displace more nutritious beverages like milk or juice
      8. Demonstration Diet – Figure 9-11, Meal Makeover – to reduce the calories in meals, reduce portion sizes and added sugars
   C. A Consumer's Guide to Fad Diets
      1. Table 9-7 describes some common fantasies and truths about fad diets.
      2. Are Fad Diets All Nonsense? – Most fad diets will allow the person to restrict calories and lose weight for a short period of time.
      3. Are Fad Diets Nutritious? – Many fad diets restrict entire groups of foods such as grains, vegetables, or fruits (e.g., as do low-carbohydrate diets).
      4. Are the Diets Safe? – Some low-carbohydrate diets can adversely affect the pH balance of the blood or the linings of the blood vessels.
      5. Moving Ahead – Many fad diets do not work because they don't incorporate lifestyle changes that are long lasting.
   D. Physical Activity in Weight Loss and Maintenance
      1. Advantages of Physical Activity, and a Warning
         a. Physical activity does not increase appetite.

   b. Physical activity builds lean muscle, which then burns more calories per pound than body fat.
   c. Physical activity may prevent bone loss and may promote restful sleep.
   d. People who reward their exercise with high-calorie treats negate any calorie deficits.
2. Which Activities Are Best?
   a. Choose those that can be enjoyed and performed regularly.
   b. Everyday activities can count towards physical activity.

E. What Strategies Are Best for Weight Gain? (see Table 9-9)
1. Choose Foods with High Energy Density – Weight gain requires a diet of calorie-dense foods, eaten frequently throughout the day.
2. Portion Sizes and Meal Spacing – Increase portion sizes.
3. Physical Activity to Gain Muscle and Fat
   a. Physical activity builds lean tissue, and no special supplements can speed the process.
   b. It is important to consume enough calories to support muscle activity and weight gain.

F. Medical Treatment of Obesity
1. Obesity Medications
   a. Table 9-10 describes pharmaceutical treatments of obesity.
   b. The FDA noted that many OTC weight-loss pills, powders, herbs, and other supplements contain unproven experimental drugs or even banned drugs.
   c. Several prescription drugs can be used but their effects may only be temporary.
2. Obesity Surgery – used for people with BMI above 40 or 35 with coexisting disease (Figure 9-12)
   a. Over 90% of patients achieve a weight loss of over 50% of their excess body weight.
   b. This may lead to improvement of conditions such as diabetes, high cholesterol, high blood pressure, heart disease, or sleep apnea.
   c. Complications of surgery can occur.
   d. Patients may experience deficiencies of zinc, iron, copper, vitamin B_{12}, vitamin A, and vitamin C.
   e. People need to continue to eat smaller portions and make other changes long term.

G. Herbal Products and Gimmicks
1. Herbals and botanicals – The effectiveness of herbal products and other gimmicks has not been demonstrated, and some herbal remedies may prove to be dangerous.
2. Supplements like ephedra can cause high blood pressure and other serious cardiovascular side effects.
3. Other gimmicks such as cellulite reducers do not work either.

H. Once I've Changed My Weight, How Can I Stay Changed?
1. A lifelong commitment – People who succeed at maintaining lost weight keep to their eating routines, keep exercising, and keep track of calorie and fat intakes and body weight.
2. Self-Efficacy and Other Keys to Success – The more traits related to positive self-image and self-efficacy a person possesses or cultivates, the more likely that person will succeed.
   a. People monitor their intakes and address lapses to prevent major ones
   b. People need a plan for long-term weight loss so that they do not experience weight cycling—repeated loss and regain of weight.
3. Seek Support
   a. Groups like TOPS (Take off Pounds Sensibly) or Weight Watchers can help people make permanent lifestyle changes.
   b. Cell phones "apps" to track diets along with many Internet resources are available.

I. Food Feature: Behavior Modification for Weight Control – Supporting diet and exercise is behavior therapy
1. How Does Behavior Modification Work? – Involves changing behaviors and thought processes
   a. Keeping a food and activity diary helps identify eating cues (see Figure 9-13).
   b. Once behaviors are identified, they should be changed one at a time, not all at once.
2. Modifying Behaviors (see Table 9-12) –6 elements that may help people change eating and activity habits are:
   a. Eliminate inappropriate eating and activity cues
   b. Suppress cues that cannot be eliminated
   c. Strengthen cues to appropriate eating and activities
   d. Repeat the desired eating and physical activity behaviors
   e. Emphasize negative consequences of inappropriate eating or sedentary behaviors
   f. Emphasize positive consequences of appropriate eating and exercise behaviors

3. Cognitive Skills
   a. Changes in conscious thought that improve adherence to modifications
   b. One has to belief in oneself to make a change.

X. Controversy: The Perils of Eating Disorders
   A. Introduction
      1. About 5 million people in the U.S., mostly females, suffer from the eating disorders anorexia nervosa and bulimia nervosa.
      2. Many more suffer from binge eating disorder or related conditions (see Table C9-1).
   B. Society's Influence
      1. Eating disorders may have many causes: Sociocultural, psychological, heredity, neurochemical
      2. Media Messages – Suggest that in order to be happy, one needs to be thin
      3. Dieting as Risk – Severe food restriction often precedes an eating disorder.
   C. Eating Disorders in Athletes
      1. Risk factors among athletes include:
         a. Adolescence
         b. Pressure to excel at chosen sport
         c. Focus on achieving "ideal weight" or body fat percentage
         d. Participation in sports that emphasize a lean appearance
         e. Unhealthy, unsupervised weight-loss dieting at an early age
         f. Table C9-2 provides suggestions to athletes to protect themselves against eating disorders.
      2. The Female Athlete Triad – Disordered eating, amenorrhea, osteoporosis (see Figure C9-1)
         a. 2-5% of all premenopausal women do not have periods.
         b. Up to 66% of female athletes may not have periods.
      3. Male Athletes and Eating Disorders
         a. On average, wrestlers, gymnasts, and figure skaters strive to be too thin.
         b. Muscle dysmorphia
            1. A weight gain problem, in which young men with well-muscled bodies falsely see themselves as underweight and weak.
            2. Can lead to obsessive weighing, excessive exercise, overuse of special diets or protein supplements, or even steroid abuse.
   D. Anorexia Nervosa
      1. Characteristics of Anorexia Nervosa
         a. Restriction of energy intake relative to body's needs, which leads to weight loss
         b. Intense fear of gaining weight or becoming fat
         c. Disturbances in body image perception
      2. The Role of the Family – some members may overvalue outward appearances and be critical
      3. Self-Starvation – may cause a person to deny hunger, feel full even after a few bites, and exercise excessively
      4. Physical Perils
         a. Anorexia nervosa damages the body in the same way classic protein-energy malnutrition does.
         b. About 1,000 women die of anorexia nervosa a year, mostly from heart abnormalities brought on by malnutrition or from suicide.
      5. Treatment of Anorexia Nervosa
         a. Treatment requires a multidisciplinary approach that addresses food and weight and also involves relationships with oneself and others.
         b. Cognitive therapy, behavior modification, and nutrition guidance may help people with lower malnutrition risks.
         c. Severely underweight people are hospitalized and stabilized medically; they may relapse as well.
   E. Bulimia Nervosa
      1. Characteristics of Bulimia Nervosa
         a. Eating a larger amount of food than most people would eat in a given period of time
         b. A sense of lack of control over eating during the episode
         c. Recurrent behaviors to prevent weight gain such as vomiting or abuse of laxatives
         d. Binge-purge cycles that occur once weekly for 3 months (Figure C9-2)

2. The Role of the Family – women may notice body dissatisfaction in a parent and families may be unsupportive and critical of body shape or weight
3. Binge Eating and Purging
   a. Cyclic binging and purging – a typical binge consists of easy-to-eat, low-fiber, smooth-textured, high-calorie foods
   b. Purging with laxatives or emetics (vomiting-inducing agents) is common.
4. Physical and Psychological Perils
   a. Abnormal heart rhythms
   b. Swollen neck glands
   c. Urinary tract infections
   d. Irritation and infection of the throat
   e. Tears of the stomach and/or esophagus
   f. Dental caries
   g. Shame, guilt
5. Treatment of Bulimia Nervosa – Table C9-3 shows diet strategies for combating bulimia nervosa

F. Binge Eating Disorder – occurs when people restrict their food intakes for several days and then binge on high-calorie treats

G. Toward Prevention – prevention strategies include:
1. Encourage positive eating and physical behaviors that can be maintained.
2. Promote a positive body image.
3. Encourage family meals eaten together.
4. Help children to nurture their bodies through healthy eating, physical activity, and positive self talk.
5. Talk to children about mistreatment due to body weight or size.

Worksheet 9-1: Breakfast Shake Label Analysis

Instructions: Use the instant breakfast shake label to answer the questions that follow.

Nutrition Facts

Serving Size 1 Packet
Servings Per Container 20

Amount Per Serving	
Calories 360	Calories from Fat 60
	% Daily Value*
Total Fat 7g	**11%**
Saturated Fat 3g	**15%**
Trans Fat 0g	
Cholesterol 55mg	**18%**
Sodium 130mg	**5%**
Potassium 880mg	**25%**
Total Carbohydrate 35g	**12%**
Dietary Fiber 7g	**28%**
Sugars 7g	
Protein 40g	**80%**
Phosphorus 300mg	30%
Magnesium 240mg	60%
Calcium 300mg	30%
Iron 10.8mg	60%
Vitamin A 3000IU	60%
Vitamin E 18IU	60%
Thiamin 0.9mg	60%
Niacin 12mg	60%
Folate 240μg	60%
Biotin 180μg	60%
Selenium 35μg	50%
Manganese 2.6mg	130%
Molybdenum 82.5μg	110%
Vitamin C 360mg	60%
Vitamin K 36μg	45%
Riboflavin 1.36mg	80%
Vitamin B_6 1.2mg	60%
Vitamin B_{12} 3.6μg	60%
Pantothenic Acid 6mg	60%
Iodine 90μg	60%
Zinc 9mg	60%
Copper 1.2mg	60%
Chromium 60μg	50%

* Percent Daily Values are based on a 2,000 calorie diet. Your Daily Values may be higher or lower depending on your calorie needs.

Mix one packet of Lean Machine Instant Breakfast Shake with 2 cups (16 fl oz) of cold water or skim milk. Stir or blend until smooth. Use up to 4 times daily.

Other Ingredients: Lean Pro (Whey Protein Concentrate, Calcium Caseinate, Milk protein Isolate, Whey protein Isolate), High Oleic Sunflower Oil, Fibersol-2, banana powder, Natural and Artificial Flavor, FOS (Fructooligosaccharides), Soy Lecithin, Salt, Sucralose, Potassium Phosphate, Spices, Acesulfame-K, Xanthan Gum, Mono & Diglycerides, Guar Gum, cream, Medium Chain Triglycerides, Cellulose Gum, Banana, Calcium Caseinate, Whole Carb (Brown Rice Flour, Hydrolyzed Oat Flour, Rice Bran), Ascorbyl Palmitate, tocopherols added to protect flavor., Beta Carotene (for color), Rice Bran

No Artificial Colors, No Artificial Flavors

Warning: Use this product as a food supplement only. Do not use for weight reduction.

1. What type of product does this appear to be based on the big label on the box?

2. What type of product is this based on reading the fine print on the label?

3. a. What is the major source of fat in this product?

   b. Is this fat source saturated or unsaturated?

4. a. What is the warning listed?

   b. Why is this warning necessary?

5. a. What minerals are present at greater than 100% of the DV for one serving of this product?

   b. Why could this be a concern?

6. What are the shortcomings of using this product as part of a weight reduction plan?

Worksheet 9-2: Intake Analysis—Energy Balance and Body Weight

Eating Plan A (1 Day's Intake)	**Eating Plan B (1 Day's Intake)**	**Eating Plan C (1 Day's Intake)**
1 cup of Corn Flakes cereal 1 cup of 1% fat milk 2 cups of coffee 2 slices of whole-wheat bread 2 ounces thinly sliced baked ham 2 ounces cheddar jalapeño cheese 8 ounces chocolate milk 3 12-ounce beers 2 beef and cheese enchiladas	6 ounces grapefruit juice 2 scrambled eggs 1 ounce cheddar cheese 20 ounces coffee 2 ounces soy milk 1 cup fresh raspberries 1 cup cantaloupe 1 honey oat granola bar 1 cup vanilla yogurt 6 ounces grilled salmon 10 cooked asparagus spears 1 cup broccoli 4 ounces white wine 4 ounces blueberry juice + seltzer water 20 barbecue flavor soy crisps 1 cup wasabi peas 1 3" x 3" spanakopita 1 cup spinach $^1/_3$ cup feta cheese ¼ cup black olives 5 grape tomatoes 3 Tbsp. oil & vinegar dressing 6 ounces white wine ¼ cup mixed nuts 1 cup vanilla ice cream	6 5"-diameter pancakes $^1/_3$ cup pure maple syrup ¼ pound of bacon 2 scrambled eggs 6 ounces orange juice 8 ounces 1% fat milk 2 slices of unseeded Italian bread 3 ounces of thinly sliced pastrami 2 Tbsp. spicy brown mustard 2 ounces of cheddar cheese 2 cups of Lucky Charms cereal 1 ½ cups 1% fat milk 6 ounces beef tenderloin 1 ½ cups mashed potatoes 1 cup cooked corn 1 cup cooked peas 10 ounces Seltzer water 2 ounces cheddar cheese
Eating Plan F (1 Day's Intake)	**Eating Plan J (1 Meal)**	
2 scrambled eggs 1 cup whole milk 2 slices bacon 2 1-ounce Slim Jims 6 ounces lean ground beef 2 ounces provolone cheese ¼ cup blue cheese dressing 12 ounces water 2 ounces cheddar cheese cubes 6 ounces grilled chicken breasts 1 scrambled egg 1 cup lettuce ½ cup blue cheese dressing 2 ounces pork rinds 12 ounces water	1 medium French fries 1 Quarter Pounder with cheese 20 ounces root beer	

Look at Eating Plan J:

1. a. How could this meal be complemented with other food choices that increase the nutritional adequacy of the daily intakes but also control the calorie intake for the day?

   b. Suggest an alternative eating plan to Eating Plan J.

Look at Eating Plan F:

2. a. How might this eating plan help a person lose body weight?

   b. How long can this type of eating plan be safely followed?

   c. How could this eating plan be modified to increase its balance, adequacy, and calorie control?

Look at Eating Plans A, B, and C:

3. a. Which of the eating plans has the best balance of carbohydrates, lipids, and proteins?

   b. Which one of these plans may be the easiest for a person to incorporate?

   c. Why?

Worksheet 9-3: How Many Minutes or Miles for that Doughnut?

1. Pick a food from the list below or pick your own favorite food. Your instructor may also include other possible food types.

   1 chocolate chip cookie
   2 ounces of regular potato chips
   2 slices of pepperoni pizza
   2 cups of chocolate ice cream
   1 large croissant
   2 glazed Krispy Kreme doughnuts

2. Look up how many calories are contained in the particular food by looking up the information in Appendix A of the textbook or by using a cell phone nutrition "app," *Diet Analysis* +, or http://ndb.nal.usda.gov/ndb/search/list. You can also consult the label on the package if you picked a food that is not on the list.

3. Pick an activity from the list below or any other activities provided by your instructor:

   Biking—10 miles per hour
   Jogging—7 miles per hour
   Swimming
   Walking—5 miles per hour
   Weight lifting
   Aerobics
   Housework
   Yard work
   Sitting

   You can look up the number of calories burned per minute or per hour for each of the activities. This information is available through online resources such as *Diet Analysis* +, https://www.supertracker.usda.gov/physicalactivitytracker.aspx, and many nutrition- or physical education-related web sites. Your instructor can also provide the information for you.

4. Calculate the number of minutes of the activity you chose for #3 that you would need to perform to use up the calories provided by the food you chose in #1. Your instructor can give you different combinations of foods and activities to choose from!

Worksheet 9-4: Exploring Eating Habits[5]

Instructions: To explore your eating habits, check all the answers that describe your food intake patterns. Then, consider possible areas for improvement.

When do I usually eat?

- ☐ At mealtime.
- ☐ While studying.
- ☐ While preparing meals or clearing the table.
- ☐ When spending time with friends.
- ☐ While watching TV or participating in other activities.
- ☐ Anytime.

Where do I usually eat?

- ☐ At home at the kitchen or dining room table.
- ☐ In the school cafeteria.
- ☐ In fast-food places.
- ☐ In front of the TV or while studying.
- ☐ Wherever I happen to be when I'm hungry.

Why do I usually eat?

- ☐ It's time to eat.
- ☐ I'm hungry.
- ☐ Foods look tempting.
- ☐ Everyone else is eating.
- ☐ Food will get thrown away if I don't eat it.
- ☐ I'm bored or frustrated.

Changes I want to make:

[5] Source: U.S. Department of Agriculture, *Dietary Guidelines and Your Health: Health Educator's Guide to Nutrition and Fitness* (Washington, DC, US Government Printing Office, 1992).

Worksheet 9-5: Behaviors that Influence Weight Status

Does your BMI fall between 18.5 and 24.9? If so, you may want to maintain your weight. If not, you may need to gain or lose weight to improve your fitness and health. Determine whether these food and activity choices are typical of your lifestyle, and indicate whether you think each choice promotes weight loss/maintenance or weight gain.

Food and activity choices	Weight Loss	Weight Gain	Frequency per week
Select low-fat foods.	☐	☐	
Drink plenty of water.	☐	☐	
Share a restaurant meal or take home leftovers.	☐	☐	
Eat energy-dense foods.	☐	☐	
Eat slowly.	☐	☐	
Eat large portions.	☐	☐	
Limit snacks to healthful choices.	☐	☐	
Eat three or more large meals a day.	☐	☐	
Eat small portions.	☐	☐	
Limit television watching.	☐	☐	
Eat peanut butter crackers between meals.	☐	☐	
Participate in physical activity.	☐	☐	
Drink plenty of juice.	☐	☐	
Eat nutrient-dense foods.	☐	☐	

1. On the average, do your lifestyle choices promote weight gain, weight loss, or weight maintenance?

2. If you feel that changing any of these behaviors is necessary, how would you go about changing them?

Worksheet 9-6: How to Get Your 150 Minutes a Week!

The *Physical Activity Guidelines* published by the DHHR recommend that everyone get at least 150 minutes of moderate activity (or 75 minutes of vigorous activity) each week to maintain their weight. How can you do this if you are a typical, busy person? Perhaps you should take a look at how active you are and then think about how you can add activity to your day to stay healthy and maintain your weight.

You can track your activity using a log. You can consult an exercise calorie expenditure table that lists the amount of calories that you burn per pound of body weight for a given activity. You can also use this table to add activities to your day if you are not getting enough activity. You can consult Appendix H in the textbook to help you define what a "moderate" level of activity is. You can also consult the activity calculator of any diet analysis program.

Physical Activity Log		
Activity	**Amount of Time**	**Calories Used**

There are many excellent sources of information. You can consult the American Heart Association website at www.heart.org to find a physical activity calorie use chart. The USDA's Super Tracker (https://www.supertracker.usda.gov/physicalactivitytracker.aspx) allows users to track energy expenditure for a large number of activities.

1. Use one of these resources to help you determine how much activity you engage in and calories that you use per day.

2. You can also design a physical activity plan using these resources. You can pick activities that you can do in "spurts" so that you can get 60 minutes of activities into each day.

Physical Activity Plan Table	
Activity	**Amount of Time**

You may find that it is easier to engage in 150 minutes of weekly moderate activity than you originally thought. It just takes some observation and patience!

Worksheet 9-7: Evaluation of a Weight-Loss Plan or Program

1. Describe the food program promoted by the publication or organization. Is the program flexible enough to allow people with different food choice preferences and lifestyles to use it successfully? Is it adaptable and easy to follow? Does it provide variety? Does the program provide for weight maintenance after the goal weight is achieved?

2. Describe how the plan works. Does it require substantial registration fees, mandatory purchase of various items or foods, attendance at a minimum number of meetings?

3. Evaluate whether the plan offers a nutritionally sound way to lose weight. What characteristics make it sound or unsound?

4. Describe any "case histories" that you hear or read about and your impressions of them. Do the stories sound authentic? Do they sound as though the person's weight loss was achieved sensibly? Do they present facts? Do they contain any "magic bullets?"

5. Describe your overall impressions of the meeting or plan, telling whether they were positive or negative and why. If you had a weight problem, would you consider membership in this organization/following this plan?

Worksheet 9-8: Eating Attitudes Test[6]

Instructions: Answer these questions using the following responses:
A=Always U=Usually O=Often S=Sometimes R=Rarely N=Never

_____ 1. I am terrified about being overweight.

_____ 2. I avoid eating when I am hungry.

_____ 3. I find myself preoccupied with food.

_____ 4. I have gone on eating binges where I feel that I may not be able to stop.

_____ 5. I cut my food into very small pieces.

_____ 6. I am aware of the calorie content of the foods I eat.

_____ 7. I particularly avoid foods with a high carbohydrate content.

_____ 8. I feel that others would prefer if I ate more.

_____ 9. I vomit after I have eaten.

_____ 10. I feel extremely guilty after eating.

_____ 11. I am preoccupied with a desire to be thinner.

_____ 12. I think about burning up calories when I exercise.

_____ 13. Other people think I am too thin.

_____ 14. I am preoccupied with the thought of having fat on my body.

_____ 15. I take longer than other people to eat my meals.

_____ 16. I avoid foods with sugar in them.

_____ 17. I eat diet foods.

_____ 18. I feel that food controls my life.

_____ 19. I display self-control around food.

_____ 20. I feel that others pressure me to eat.

_____ 21. I give too much time and thought to food.

_____ 22. I feel uncomfortable after eating sweets.

_____ 23. I engage in dieting behavior.

_____ 24. I like my stomach to be empty.

_____ 25. I enjoy trying new rich foods.

_____ 26. I have the impulse to vomit after meals.

Scoring: 3 for never, 2 for rarely, 1 for sometimes, 0 for always, usually and often. Total scores under 20 points indicate abnormal eating behavior.[7]

---

[6] Source: J. A. McSherry, Progress in the diagnosis of anorexia nervosa, *Journal of the Royal Society of Health* 106 (1986): 8-9. (Eating Attitudes Test developed by Dr. Paul Garfinkel.)

[7] Note: This is a survey only, not a diagnostic tool. Any mental or physical health concerns should be brought to the attention of a medical professional.

Worksheet 9-9: Chapter 9 Review Crossword Puzzle

Across:	Down:
1. Assessment of body _____ is more revealing for determining potential health risks because it measures the proportion of lean muscle to body fat as compared to measuring a number on a scale. 4. A psychiatric condition in which a person alternates eating large amounts of food and vomiting or abusing laxatives 7. The body's enzymes release energy in the form of heat. This varies between individuals and is known as _____. 10. If the body does not have enough glycogen or stored fat, it will use _____ as a source of energy. 11. A body mass index of 25-29.9 is considered _____. 12. People who develop new _____ skills often are the most aware of their eating patterns and often have the most success with weight loss and weight loss maintenance. 13. A simple way to determine whether a person has central obesity is to do a _____ measurement.	2. A drug that blocks fat absorption in the intestine 3. A hormone that can suppress the appetite 5. Underweight female athletes often experience _____ as a result of reduced body fat stores and levels of hormones such as estrogen or progesterone. 6. People living in the city often do not have access to fresh, whole foods or supermarkets with a variety of foods. These areas are often referred to as food _____. 8. A hormone released by the stomach that stimulates the drive to eat 9. A simple yet effective way to safely lose or gain weight is to adjust _____ sizes at each meal or snack.

Handout 9-1: Medical Problems Associated with Obesity

- ✓ Abnormal plasma lipid and lipoprotein concentrations
- ✓ Cancer of certain types (endometrial, colon, kidney, gallbladder, postmenopausal breast cancer)
- ✓ Congestive heart failure
- ✓ Coronary heart disease
- ✓ Flat feet and infection in fat folds
- ✓ Gallbladder disease
- ✓ Gastroesophageal reflux disease
- ✓ Hypertension
- ✓ Impaired heat tolerance
- ✓ Menstrual irregularities and toxemia of pregnancy
- ✓ Non-alcoholic fatty liver disease
- ✓ Organ compression by adipose tissue
- ✓ Osteoarthritis and gout
- ✓ Problems with anesthesia during surgery
- ✓ Psychological trauma
- ✓ Pulmonary disease
- ✓ Renal disease
- ✓ Sleep apnea
- ✓ Urinary bladder control problems

Sources: Art Gilbert, Director, Wellness Fitness Institute, University of California, Santa Barbara, with permission.

American Medical Association: *Roadmaps for Clinical Practice—Case Studies in Disease Prevention and Health Promotion: Assessment and Management of Adult Obesity: A Primer for Physicians*

Chapter 10 – Nutrients, Physical Activity, and the Body's Responses

Quick List: IM Resources for Chapter 10

- **Class preparation resources:** learning objectives/key points, suggested activities and projects, lecture outline
- **Assignment materials:** **Related LO**
  - Critical thinking questions (with answer key) 10.1, 10.2, 10.3
  - Discussion questions (with answers) for Controversy 10 .... 10.7
  - Worksheet 10-1: Sports Bar Label Analysis 10.3, 10.6
  - Worksheet 10-2: Intake Analysis—Athletes 10.3, 10.5, 10.6
  - Worksheet 10-3: Activity Diary Evaluation[1] 10.1, 10.5
  - Worksheet 10-4: Developing Performance-Enhancing Eating Plans 10.4, 10.6
  - **New!** Worksheet 10-5: Chapter 10 Review Crossword Puzzle
- **Enrichment materials:** Handout 10-1: I'm in Shape But Why Can't I Perform? 10.3, 10.4, 10.5

Chapter Learning Objectives and Key Points

10.1 **Provide examples of how regular physical activity benefits the body, and explain how the *Physical Activity Guidelines for Americans* can be incorporated into a healthy person's lifestyle.**
Physical activity and fitness benefit people's physical and psychological well-being and improve their resistance to disease. Physical activity improves survival and quality of life in the later years. Hormone-like communication molecules generated by working muscles may trigger healthy changes in body tissues. The U.S. *Physical Activity Guidelines for Americans* aim to improve physical fitness and the health of the nation. Other guidelines meet other needs.

10.2 **Describe in brief how fitness develops, and explain the beneficial effects of both resistance and cardiorespiratory exercise on the body.**
The components of fitness are flexibility, muscle strength, muscle endurance, and cardiorespiratory endurance. Muscle protein is built up and broken down every day; muscle tissue is gained when synthesis exceeds degradation. Physical activity builds muscle tissues and metabolic equipment needed for the activities they are repeatedly called upon to perform. Resistance training can benefit physical and mental health. Sports performance, appearance, and body composition improve through resistance training; bulky muscles are the result of intentional body building regimens. Cardiorespiratory endurance training enhances the ability of the heart and lungs to deliver oxygen to body tissues. Cardiorespiratory training activities elevate the heart rate for sustained periods of time and engage the body's large muscle groups.

10.3 **Explain the importance of glucose, fatty acids, and amino acids to a working athlete before, during, and after vigorous exercise.**
Food energy needs vary by the goals and activities of the athlete. Excess postexercise oxygen consumption (EPOC) can pose weight-loss problems for some athletes but most weight-loss seekers do not achieve significant calorie deficits from EPOC. During activity, the hormone glucagon helps to prevent a drop in blood glucose. Glycogen stores in the liver and muscles affect an athlete's endurance. When glucose availability limits performance, carbohydrate taken during training or competition can support physical activity. Anaerobic breakdown of glucose yields energy and becomes particularly important in high-intensity activity. The more intense an activity, the more glucose it demands for anaerobic metabolism. Lactate accumulates during anaerobic metabolism but does not appear to cause fatigue. Glycogen is used at a rapid rate early in exercise but the rate slows with continued activity. When glycogen depletion reaches a certain point, continued activity of the same intensity is impossible. Highly trained muscles use less glucose and more fat than do untrained muscles to perform the same work. Carbohydrate recommendations for athletes are stated in grams per kilogram of body weight per day. Carbohydrate before, during, and after physical exertion can help to support the performance of certain kinds of activities but not others. The intensity and duration of activity, as well as the degree of training, affect fat use. A diet high in saturated or trans fat raises an athlete's risk of heart disease. Physical activity stimulates muscle cells to both break down and synthesize proteins,

[1] Contributed by Sharon Rady Rolfes

resulting in muscle adaptation to activity. Athletes use amino acids for building muscle tissue and for energy; dietary carbohydrate spares amino acids. Diet, intensity and duration of activity, and degree of training affect protein use during activity. Although certain athletes may need some additional protein, a well-chosen diet that provides ample energy and follows the USDA food patterns provides sufficient protein, even for most athletes.

10.4 **Outline reasons why iron is of special significance for some athletes, and describe the proper roles for nutrient supplements.**
Vitamins and minerals are essential for releasing the energy trapped in energy-yielding nutrients and for other functions that support physical activity. Active people can meet their vitamin and mineral needs if they follow the USDA eating patterns and eat enough nutrient-dense food to meet their energy needs. Iron-deficiency anemia impairs physical performance because iron is the blood's oxygen handler. Sports anemia is a harmless temporary adaptation to physical activity.

10.5 **Identify hazards associated with inadequate fluid replacement in the exercising body, and compare the fluid needs of a casual exerciser and an endurance athlete.**
Evaporation of sweat cools the body, regulating body temperature. Heat stroke is a threat to physically active people in hot, humid weather, while hypothermia threatens exercisers in the cold. Water is the best drink for most physically active people, but some endurance athletes may need the glucose and electrolytes of sports drinks. During events lasting longer than four hours, athletes need to pay special attention to replacing sodium losses to prevent hyponatremia. Most exercising people get enough sodium in their normal foods to replace losses. Carbonated beverages can limit fluid intake and cause discomfort in exercising people. Alcohol use can impair performance in many ways and is not recommended.

10.6 **Plan a nourishing and adequate diet for an athlete, including snacks and pregame meals.**

10.7 **Evaluate whether dietary ergogenic aids are useful for increasing sports performance or obtaining an ideal body composition for sports.**

Critical Thinking Questions

1. a. *Your friend knows that it is important to exercise each day but he doesn't really like to be active. Describe any 3 short-term benefits that he will enjoy if he becomes physically active.*

He may notice that he sleeps better at night. He may also feel more self-confident knowing that he is doing something positive for his health. He may also notice that he can eat more without gaining weight.

b. *Describe any 3 longer-term benefits that he will gain from being more physically active.*

He will be at less risk of developing type 2 diabetes since exercise may help his cells be more sensitive to insulin. His risk of cardiovascular disease may also be lower since exercise may help increase HDL cholesterol and reduce blood pressure. He may have higher bone density, stronger muscles, and better mobility as he ages. His quality of life in his later years may be better due to the absence of chronic conditions.

2. *Why is weight training an important part of a fitness program to ensure optimal health for the body?*

Weight training may not lead to excessive muscle buildup but can lead to an increase in the lean muscle mass that will enable the body to expend more calories during rest, which could help with weight management. Muscles that are not used will start to break down (atrophy).

Weight training can also strengthen the abdominal muscles so that they support the back better. This would reduce the risk of back injury. Weight training also keeps the bones strong throughout life by putting stress on them, which causes them to accrue more calcium and phosphate salts. Weight training strengthens the muscles needed for particular sports, which will increase a person's enjoyment and participation in that sport.

3. *Why do endurance athletes load up on carbohydrate-containing foods before a big event? Why don't they just fill up on fat and protein as well?*

Athletes eat carbohydrates to maximize the stored glycogen in their livers and muscles. Athletes' muscles use glucose from glycogen alongside fats throughout the duration of the activity. If the glycogen stores are depleted, the muscles will have difficulty using energy from fats or from any other source. Muscles can use protein for energy but it is metabolically "costly" to the body and does not supply glucose to the blood as efficiently as stored glycogen. Also, a severe depletion of glycogen can affect the nervous system, which can make the activity difficult to continue.

4. *Why do athletes' muscles need to be trained in order to burn fat most efficiently?*

   Most people's muscles will begin to use fats from the bloodstream after 20 minutes of activity. At this point, the stored glycogen levels may be reduced. Studies have shown that muscles will use fatty acids more efficiently when they are trained. The levels of enzymes that break down fats are higher in trained muscles than in untrained muscles. Aerobic athletes have a stronger heart and lungs that can deliver more oxygen to the muscles. This allows them to break down fats aerobically to produce more energy.

5. *Do athletes need protein powders to increase their muscle mass or athletic performance? Why or why not?*

   Table 10-6 shows the protein needs of athletes. Most people can obtain these quantities of protein by eating high-quality food sources of protein. Foods contain the ideal ratio of all of the amino acids as well as other essential nutrients that would not be found in protein powders. Athletes can ingest lean proteins in the form of fish, chicken, nuts, or beans without taking in excessive levels of saturated fats.

6. *How do nutrition and exercise scientists know that carbohydrates work best for supplying energy to an endurance athlete?*

   A study was done in which athletes ate either a high-carbohydrate, a high-fat, or a normal mixed diet and were tested for how long they could continue an activity at the initial intensity (endurance time). The athletes who ate the high-carbohydrate diets could sustain the activity almost 3 times longer than the athletes who ate a high-fat diet. This may seem odd since fat supplies 9 calories per gram. It turns out that the muscles require a steady supply of glucose to make ATP (energy). The stored glycogen is most easily broken down but is not all used up at the same time. The muscles also break down fatty acids in conjunction with glucose to provide energy to the muscle cells for a long time. People who ate more carbohydrates in their pre-event meal stored more glycogen that their muscles could use as fuel, along with fatty acids, for sustained aerobic activity.

Controversy Discussion Questions

1. *Discuss why Paige's use of carnitine and protein powders will not give her an advantage in terms of muscle performance as compared with DJ's more adequate diet and regular exercise.*

   Carnitine is a substance that shuttles fats across the mitochondrial cell membrane. In theory, an increased use of fats in the citric acid cycle within the mitochondria could lead to more energy release. However, studies have shown that taking carnitine supplements does not increase the carnitine or energy levels in the muscle tissue. A side affect of increased carnitine intake is diarrhea. Carnitine can be found in milk, which DJ may drink, and milk supplies many other essential nutrients as well.

   Consuming protein powders increases the total amount of dietary protein. Most people get enough dietary protein from foods to support their athletic performance. Athletes that take protein powders may see an increase in their muscle mass but this increase may not improve their performance.

2. *Why are amino acid supplements not recommended for athletes?*

   Amino acid supplements usually supply one given amino acid at a much higher level or proportion than would normally be found in the diet. The body needs to absorb 9 essential amino acids from foods. The amino acid transporter mechanisms in the small intestine are shared among several amino acids. If any one amino acid is present in excessively high levels, it may block the absorption of other essential amino acids. Ammonia can also build up from the excess breakdown of the wasted amino acids, and this can lead to fatigue. A balanced diet can provide foods with ample amounts of essential amino acids in optimal proportions for the body to take up.

3. *Why might the use of anabolic steroids actually work against the athlete in terms of enhancing performance?*

   Steroids can cause weight gain and changes in body composition that may impair athletic performance. Anabolic steroids can cause long-term harm to many organs whose functions need to be optimal for athletic performance.

4. *Why do athletes take antioxidant supplements, and what concerns do experts have about them?*

   Aerobic exercise uses a lot of oxygen and speeds up metabolism, potentially producing more free radicals. Antioxidant supplements are thought to reduce the levels of damaging free radicals formed during athletic events. Studies suggest that free radical formation may stimulate the body's beneficial responses to physical activity. Antioxidant supplements may block or suppress the body's beneficial responses to exercise.

Worksheet Answer Key

Worksheet 10-1: Sports Bar Label Analysis

1. a. 34 grams × 4 kcal/gram = 136 kilocalories
   b. 25 grams × 4 kcal/gram = 100 kilocalories
2. Simple sugars enter the blood stream quickly and can provide a quick burst of energy for an athlete who sprints or needs a burst of strength for their athletic efforts.
3. High-fructose corn syrup, other corn by-products, and maltodextrins.
4. Vitamins C and E are antioxidants that may protect an athlete's tissues (muscles and respiratory surfaces) from free radical damage due to high levels of cell energy production and oxygen consumption. This product provides a large portion of these vitamins to supplement the contributions of these vitamins from other foods in the athlete's diet.
5. a. Chromium may help improve the performance of an athlete's body.
   b. Chromium helps the body make the most efficient use of glucose for energy production for the muscles.
6. a. 16 grams protein / 55 grams (average) × 100 = 29%
   b. This is a significant proportion of the daily recommended amount of protein.

Worksheet 10-2: Intake Analysis—Athletes

1. a. Eating Plan C (390.7 grams of carbohydrates and 165.5 grams sugar)
   b. The number of pancakes could be reduced as well as the portion of maple syrup. The bacon, cheese, and pastrami portions could be reduced to lower the amount of saturated fat and calories.
2. Eating Plan E would be the best choice since it supplies ample protein with the least amount of fat (127 grams of protein and 79.4 grams of fat).
3. a. Eating Plan B is the best choice (2.5 L).
   b. An elite endurance athlete could easily lose 1 kilogram (1 L) of fluid during a work-out.

Worksheet 10-5: Chapter 10 Review Crossword Puzzle

1. A: agility; D: Anabolic
2. Caffeine
3. intensity
4. flexibility
5. folate
6. leucine
7. endurance
8. ergogenic
9. carbohydrate
10. recovery
11. Glycogen
12. Resistance

Learning Activities & Project Ideas

Activity 10-1: Enhancing Understanding of Metabolism[2] LO 10.3

To explain human metabolism, an analogy based on the automobile can be offered. The oxidation of gasoline produces heat and energy (measured in miles per gallon) and carbon dioxide and water are waste products. Nutrients and gasoline are both fuels that are oxidized in the presence of oxygen to produce energy, carbon dioxide, and water.

---

[2] Contributed by Samantha Logan, DrPH, University of Massachusetts, Amherst

Ask students to consider a car having a manual transmission with only two gears: first and high. First gear is beneficial for rapid acceleration. If you do not shift out of first gear, the car will no longer accelerate, and it will use gasoline very inefficiently. You must shift into high gear to keep the car running efficiently at a higher speed. Human beings obtain energy from two analogous processes: anaerobic metabolism and aerobic metabolism. Anaerobic metabolism (using glucose) serves the need for quick energy to accomplish an intense activity for a short duration of time. For endurance activities, additional energy must be obtained from aerobic metabolism (using fat and glucose). Explain that the choice of activity determines the proportion of fat and glucose burned during the activity.

	Energy Obtained	Measure of Energy	Advantage	Disadvantage
Car	First gear	Miles/gallon	Quick acceleration	Can only be used for a few seconds of acceleration
Human beings	Anaerobic metabolism	Energy (calories)	Quick, intense muscle activity	Can only be used for a few seconds as lactate is produced
Car	High gear	Miles/gallon	Used to sustain desired velocity over maximum amount of time	Depends on rate of oxygen delivery to fuel source; better tuned engines achieve maximum miles/gallon
Human beings	Aerobic metabolism	Energy (calories)	Used to sustain desired amount of muscle activity over maximum amount of time	Depends on rate of oxygen delivery to fuel source; better conditioning improves rate of oxygen delivery

Activity 10-2: Fitness Quackery Evaluation[3] LO 10.7

For a fitness quackery activity, ask students to bring in newspaper and magazine advertisements and brochures for food supplements and products they believe represent exercise and fitness quackery. Ask what characteristics of the advertisement led them to this conclusion, and whether the use of this food product might pose a danger to one's health. The importance of this activity is that this is an area of quackery that has become a booming business in America. As consumers, students not only should be aware that these problems exist but should know how to distinguish between health-promoting products and those that are fraudulent.

Chapter Lecture Outline

I. Introduction
   A. To understand the interactions between physical activity and nutrition, you must first know a few things about fitness, its benefits, and training to develop fitness.
   B. Later, we will discuss how to fuel physical activities with food and fluids.

II. Fitness
   A. Definitions
      1. Fitness depends on a certain minimum amount of physical activity or exercise.
      2. Exercise is a vigorous, structured, and planned type of physical activity.
      3. In this chapter, both words will be used interchangeably since the muscles are at work in either situation.
   B. The Nature of Fitness
      1. The Nature of Fitness – fit people move easily; have balance, endurance, strength, better emotional health
      2. Longevity and Disease Resistance – inactivity is a potent disease risk factor
      3. Some Benefits of Fitness – Compared with unfit people, physically fit people enjoy:
         a. More restful sleep
         b. Improved nutritional health
         c. Improved body composition
         d. Improved bone density

[3] Contributed by Lori W. Turner, Ph.D., R.D., University of Alabama

e. Enhanced resistance to infectious diseases
f. Lower risk of some cancers
g. Stronger circulation and lung function
h. Lower risk of cardiovascular disease
i. Lower risk of type 2 diabetes & improved control of existing type 2 diabetes
k. Reduced risk of gallbladder disease (women)
l. Lower incidence and severity of anxiety and depression
m. Stronger self-image
n. Longer life and higher quality of life in the later years

C. *Physical Activity Guidelines for Americans* (Figure 10-1) – You can use these guidelines developed by the DHHR & USDA to gain the benefits of physical activity.
   a. People should engage in enough aerobic activity to improve or maintain cardiovascular health.
   b. People should also perform resistance training.
   c. The amount of time spend on each activity varies with the intensity.
   2. Guidelines for Sports Performance – Table 10-2

III. The Essentials of Fitness – To be physically fit, you need to develop enough flexibility, muscle strength, muscle endurance, and cardiorespiratory endurance to allow you to meet the demands of everyday life with some to spare, and you need to have a reasonable body composition. Athletes need muscle power, quick reaction time, agility, and resistance to muscle fatigue in addition to basic fitness.

A. How Do Muscles Adapt to Physical Activity?
   1 Muscle cells respond to an overload of physical activity by gaining strength and size, a response called hypertrophy.
   2. A Balance of Activities
      a. Balanced fitness comes from performing a variety of physical activities such as stretching, aerobic activity, and resistance training each day.
      b. Table 10-3 illustrates a balanced work out program.
      c. Muscles also need rest to replenish their fuel supply and repair themselves.
   3. Resistance Training for Muscle Strength, Size, Power, & Endurance
      a. Progressive weight training may help reduce the risk of chronic conditions such as back problems or enhance an athlete's performance in her sport.
      b. Muscles adapt to activities they are called upon to perform repeatedly.
      c. Swim to be a better swimmer; bike to be a better biker.

B. How Does Aerobic Training Benefit the Heart?
   1. Improvements to Blood, Heart, & Lungs
      a. Cardiorespiratory endurance training enhances the ability of the heart and lungs to deliver oxygen to the muscles.
      b. The heart becomes stronger, breathing becomes more efficient, and the health of the entire body improves.
      c. The accepted measure of a person's cardiorespiratory fitness is maximal oxygen uptake (VO_2 max).
      d. As the heart muscle becomes stronger, its cardiac output increases.
      e. The heart's stroke volume also increases, i.e., the heart pumps more blood per beat.
      f. The blood pressure may be reduced.
      g. See Figure 10-2 and Table 1-4
   2. Cardiorespiratory Training Activities – elevate heart rate for sustained periods of time, use most large-muscle groups

IV. The Active Body's Use of Fuels – Physical activity is supported by different mixtures of glucose, fatty acids, and to a small extent amino acids, depending on the intensity and duration of its activities and on the body's prior training.

A. The Need for Food Energy
   1. Many athletes may need 1,000 to 1,500 extra calories a day to avoid weight loss.
   2. Most people do not need extra calories and should get 30 minutes of moderate-intensity exercise to efficiently produce energy deficits.

B. Glucose: A Major Fuel for Physical Activity
   1. Introduction
      a. When physical activity starts, the muscles use glucose from their own glycogen stores.
      b. The muscles also get glucose from the blood.
      c. The pancreas will release glucagon, which stimulates the liver to break down more glycogen.
      d. Glycogen stores are limited to less than 2,000 calories of energy.
      e. Fat stores are theoretically unlimited and can provide more than 70,000 calories and fuel hours of activity.
   2. Glycogen and Endurance – Total glycogen stores affect an athlete's endurance.
      a. Athletes who start out with more glycogen will have more glucose for sustained exercise.
      b. Runners who ate different diets (normal mixed with 55% of calories coming from carbohydrates, a high-carbohydrate diet [83% of calories], and a high-fat diet [94% calories from fat]) were compared for endurance.
      c. The runners who ate the high-carbohydrate diet had the best endurance (see Figure 10-3).
   3. Glucose from the Digestive Tract
      a. Athletes who eat carbohydrates during an endurance event also can perform longer.
      b. Consider the type of sport to determine if extra carbohydrate is needed
   4. The Aerobic and Anaerobic Difference (see Figure 10-4)
      a. Refers to 2 parts of the body's metabolic system for extracting energy from macronutrients
      b. The aerobic part gets more energy from each glucose and can draw on fatty acids as a fuel source.
      c. The anaerobic part just uses glucose without oxygen and gets less energy from each molecule.
   5. Aerobic Use of Fuel – Aerobic activity:
      a. Moderate physical activity, such as easy jogging, uses glycogen slowly.
      b. The person breathes easily and the heart beats faster than at rest, but steadily.
      c. Muscles get energy from both glucose and fatty acids (this conserves glycogen stores).
   6. Lactate—A Glucose Breakdown Product
      a. Lactate is produced by the anaerobic breakdown of glucose during intense activity.
      b. Lactate travels from muscles to the liver, where it is converted back to glucose.
      c. When the rate of lactate production exceeds the rate of clearance, intense activity can be maintained for only one to three minutes.
      d. Lactate accumulation is associated with fatigue but is not the cause of it.
      e. Depletion of muscle glycogen by 80% will cause fatigue.
   7. Exercise Duration Affects Glycogen Use (Figure 10-5) – Glucose use during physical activity depends on the duration of the activity and its intensity.
      a. First 10 minutes – glycogen used by muscles
      b. First 20 minutes of moderate activity – about $^{1}/_{5}$ of available glycogen used up
      c. A person who exercises for longer than 20 minutes begins to use less glucose & more fat for fuel.
      d. Glycogen depletion occurs after ~2 hours of vigorous exercise.
      e. After that, vigorous activity can continue for a short time as the liver converts lactate and some amino acids into glucose.
      f. Finally, hypoglycemia develops, which brings the nervous system almost to a halt, making intensive activity impossible.
      g. This is what marathon runners call "hitting the wall."
   8. Degree of Training Affects Glycogen Use – Trained muscles can store more glycogen, burn more fat, and use less glucose.

C. Carbohydrate Recommendations for Athletes (Table 10-5)
   1. A certain amount of carbohydrate (expressed in grams per kilogram body weight) is needed to achieve maximum glycogen storage.
   2. Glucose before Activity – Glucose taken a few hours before training or competition may "top off" glycogen stores.
   3. Glucose during Activity
      a. Glucose ingested before and during endurance or intense intermittent activities (lasting more than 45 minutes) makes its way to the working muscles and adds to the glycogen stores.
      b. Athletes should consume smooth-textured foods that are low in fat and fiber.
      c. Some athletes can drink high-carbohydrate energy drinks or eat high-carbohydrate gels.

5 Glucose after Activity – Eating high-carbohydrate foods within 2 hours after physical activity also enlarges glycogen stores.

D. Lipid Fuel for Physical Activity
1. Introduction
a. Body fat is a virtually unlimited source of energy.
b. Early in activity, muscles draw on fat stored within them and under the skin.
c. "Spot reducing" does not work; muscles do not own the fat that surrounds them.
2. Activity Intensity and Duration Affect Fat Use
a. Fat is broken down aerobically, so if the intensity is too high for aerobic metabolism, glucose must be used instead (anaerobically).
b. Moderate exercise >20 min. in duration = greater use of fatty acids & shrinking of fat cells
3. Degree of Training Affects Fat Use – trained muscles develop more fat-burning enzymes; greater availability of oxygen with cardiorespiratory training allows more fat to be used (aerobically)
4. Fat Recommendations for Athletes
a. High-fat, low carbohydrate-diets are not recommended for endurance athletes because their glycogen stores will be depleted.
b. Athletes should get 20-35% of calories from fat, especially from vegetable oils, nuts, olives, and fatty fish.
c. Inflammation can impair athletic performance.

E. Protein for Building Muscles and for Fuel – The body uses amino acids to build protein and can use a small amount for energy.
1. Amino Acids Stimulate Muscle Protein Synthesis
a. The muscles will reach a maximum rate of protein synthesis even when essential amino acids like leucine, are supplied.
b. Taking protein supplements will not force the muscles to make new protein.
2. Does Timing of Protein Matter?
a. The rate of muscle protein synthesis is greatest in the 2 hours following activity but synthesis can stay higher for 1 to 2 days.
b. Increased rate of muscle protein synthesis is supported by the intake of all of the essential amino acids
3. Protein Fuel Use in Physical Activity
a. The body increases its rate of amino acid use for fuel during physical activity as with glucose and fatty acids,
b. The factors that regulate protein during activity are: diet, exercise intensity and duration, and degree of training.
c. Endurance athletes, who train for over an hour a day, engaging in aerobic activity of moderate intensity and long duration, may deplete their glycogen stores by the end of their training and use more protein for fuel.
d. In strength athletes, the higher the degree of training, the less protein a person uses during activity at a given intensity.
4. Protein Recommendation for Athletes – Most athletes can get all of the protein that they need from a balanced diet.

F. How Much Protein Should an Athlete Consume?
1. Table 10-6 lists recommendations in grams of protein/kilogram of body weight/day.
2. Athletes can easily get all of their proteins and the essential amino acids within from whole foods.

V. Vitamins and Minerals—Keys to Performance – Many vitamins and minerals assist in releasing energy from fuels and transporting oxygen.

A. Do Nutrient Supplements Benefit Athletic Performance?
1. Nutrient supplements do not enhance the performance of well-nourished athletes or active people in a timely fashion.
2. More Food Means More Nutrients – Active people eat more food; if they choose correctly, they will get more nutrients.
3. Preventing Deficiencies – deficiencies may result when athletes starve themselves to "make weight"

B. Iron—A Mineral of Concern
1. Iron is needed to deliver oxygen to working muscles.

2. High-impact endurance training can cause the destruction of red blood cells; this can lead to sports anemia—an adaptive, temporary response to endurance training that results in a reduced number of red blood cells.
3. Physically active young women are especially prone to iron deficiency because of:
    a. Habitually low intakes of iron-rich foods
    b. High iron losses through menstruation
    c. High demands of muscles for iron
4. Vegetarian athletes may lack iron since non-heme iron from plants is less well absorbed than heme iron.
5. Consuming vitamin C with non-heme iron sources may enhance iron absorption.

VI. Fluids and Temperature Regulation in Physical Activity

A. Water Losses during Physical Activity Physically active people lose fluids and must replace them to avoid dehydration.

1. Dehydration has varying degrees of severity:
    a. A water loss of 2% can lead to a decrease in performance.
    b. A water loss of 7% is likely to lead to collapse.
2. Sweat and Temperature Regulation – evaporation of sweat cools the skin and underlying blood
3. Heat Stroke
    a. A dangerous accumulation of body heat with a loss of fluid
    b. Symptoms (see Table 10-7):
        1. Clumsiness, confusion
        2. Body temp above 104°F
        3. Nausea, dizziness, headache, stumbling
        4. Sudden cessation of sweating (hot, dry skin)
    c. If you or someone you know is experiencing heat stroke, try to cool off and get immediate medical attention.
4. Hypothermia – Loss of body heat during exposure to cold weather, which can be serious

B. Fluid and Electrolyte Needs during Physical Activity

1. Water
    a. Water is the best drink for most physically active people, but endurance athletes need drinks that supply glucose as well as fluids.
    b. See Table 10-5 for recommended hydration schedule for activities
2. Electrolyte Losses and Replacement
    a. The body loses sodium, potassium, and chloride through sweat.
    b. The trained body adapts to compensate for sweat losses of electrolytes.

C. A Consumer's Guide to Selecting Sports Drinks

1. There are a variety of sports drinks available such as flavored waters, nutritionally enhanced beverages, and recovery drinks (see terms in Table 10-9).
2. First: Fluid – is most important to replace during an event in which a lot is lost due to sweating
2. Second: Glucose – Endurance athletes who engage in a moderate or vigorous activity for more than 1 hour may benefit from added carbohydrates.
    a. Most sports drinks contain 7% glucose, which does not interfere with water absorption.
    b. Too much glucose can slow down water delivery to tissue and can cause cramps, nausea, or diarrhea.
    c. Bananas also provide a good source of glucose as well as vitamins and minerals.
3. Third: Sodium and Other Electrolytes
    a. Some sports drinks have about 55-110 mg of sodium per serving.
    b. Other electrolytes are not needed in sport drinks and can be replenished during meals.
4. Moving Ahead – Most people only need fluid and not extra glucose or electrolytes but if a sport drink increases confidence, it is likely to cause no harm.

D. Sodium Depletion and Water Intoxication

1. Hyponatremia – a dangerous condition of sodium depletion
2. Can occur when endurance athletes drink such large amounts of water over the course of a long event that they overhydrate, diluting the body's fluids to such an extent that the sodium concentration becomes too low

3. Some athletes lose more sodium in their sweat than others.
4. To prevent hyponatremia, sports drinks are more helpful than water.
5. In the days before the event, athletes should not restrict salt in their diets.

E. Other Beverages
1. Carbonated drinks produce gas bubbles that may limit a person's ability to drink enough liquid.
2. Alcohol can impair performance in many ways and is not recommended.

F. Putting it All Together – Table 10-11 is an overview of performance nutrition recommendations

VII. Food Feature: Choosing a Performance Diet

A. Nutrient Density – Athletes should eat a variety of whole foods to get the maximum amount of vitamins and minerals.

B. Carbohydrate (Figure 10-7) – Full glycogen stores are critical to athletes and other active people.
1. High-intensity athletes may not need higher levels of carbohydrates.
2. Endurance athletes need much higher levels of carbohydrates.
3. Athletes should try new combinations of nutrient-dense foods.

C. Protein – Most athletes should get protein from lean sources to avoid taking in too much saturated fat.

D. Pregame Meals – should be small, easily digestible, high in carbohydrates, & moderate in protein, & provide ample amounts of fluid
1. Figure 10-8 shows good pre-game meals from restaurants.
2. Athletes should choose meal plans that work for them.

E. Recovery Meals – allow athletes to rebuild their energy & glycogen stores as well as their muscles
1. Balanced meals such as a turkey sandwich and a fruit smoothie will provide the glucose needed for glycogen stores as well as the protein needed to speed up muscle protein synthesis.
2. Chocolate milk is an ideal recovery snack since it contains lactose (sugar) and protein and tastes good.

F. Commercial Products – Meal replacers are often expensive, may be too high in calories or fat, and are not necessary if an athlete is eating an adequate, varied, and balanced diet.

VIII. Controversy – Ergogenic Aids: Breakthroughs, Gimmicks, or Dangers?

A. Paige and DJ – Paige & DJ are two college athletes that have different approaches to training. The large majority of legitimate research has not supported the claims made for ergogenic aids.

B. Ergogenic Aids (Table C10-2)
2. Antioxidant Supplements
   a. Exercise increases metabolism, which could cause the buildup of free radicals (oxidative stress).
   b. Supplements marketed to reduce these free radicals have not been shown to work.
   c. Within the body, free radicals may signal a physiological response related to some of the benefits of physical activity.
2. Caffeine – seems to provide a physical boost during endurance sports
   a. Caffeine may trigger fat acid release and reduce an endurance athlete's feelings of fatigue.
   b. Little or no positive effect for athletes in short-duration sports
   c. Caffeine can raise blood pressure and cause headaches, diarrhea, and other undesirable short-term effects.
3. Carnitine – a nonessential nutrient often marketed as a "fat burner"
   a. Carnitine supplementation neither raises muscle carnitine levels nor enhances exercise performance.
   b. Large amounts of this supplement can lead to diarrhea in some people.
4. Chromium Picolinate
   a. Chromium picolinate promises to burn fat from the body.
   b. Chromium is an essential trace mineral involved in lipid and carbohydrate metabolism.
   c. Majority of studies showed no effect on body fatness, lean body mass, strength, or fatigue.
5. Creatine
   a. Power athletes often use creatine supplements in the belief that they enhance stores of the high-energy compound creatine phosphate in muscles.
   b. Creatine may enhance performance of high-intensity strength activities such as weight lifting or competitive swimming that is of brief duration.
   c. Creatine does not appear to benefit endurance activity.

d. No long-term studies for safety have been reported and children as young as 9 years of age are taking creatine at the urging of their coaches.

6. Buffers
   a. Sodium bicarbonate (baking soda) has been taken to reduce the level of acid produced during exercise.
   b Ingestion of sodium bicarbonate can be associated with diarrhea and gas as well as sensations of pins and needles.
7. Amino Acid Supplements
   a. To best build muscle protein, all the essential amino acids must be in the blood prior to physical work.
   b. The best source for these amino acids is food, not supplements.
      1. All amino acids are included in a well-balanced diet.
      2. Supplements may not provide the ideal balance.
   c. Only a few grams of amino acids are needed; heavy doses from supplements are not needed.
   d. An overabundance of any one amino acid can disturb the uptake of other essential amino acids by the body.
8. Whey Protein
   a. Such supplements do not provide a better balance of amino acids than that found in whole foods.
   b. Muscles require physical activity and resistance to become stronger for athletic performance.

C. Hormones and Hormone Imitators
1. Anabolic Steroids
   a. Anabolic steroid hormones produce muscle size and strength far beyond that attainable by training alone, but are very dangerous.
   b. Anabolic steroids have many side effects such as: changes in personality, swollen face, jaundice, increased risks of CVD, liver damage, kidney damage, loss of fertility in both sexes, and many others
2. Human Growth Hormone – not a steroid but it can cause overgrowth of the bones, diabetes, thyroid disorder, heart disease, and reproductive issues
3. Steroid Alternatives
   a. These products may be as risky as steroid drugs and provide no competitive edge in sports.
   b. Some herbal remedies that are converted into steroids in the body may contain other harmful toxins.
   c. "Andro" (androstenedione) or DHEA produces unpredictable results.
   d. Illegal to sell and banned by many sports organizations including the International Olympic Committee
4. Drugs Posing as Supplements
   a. A potent thyroid hormone known as TRIAC has been recalled by the FDA.
   b. TRIAC has caused heart attacks and strokes.
   c. DMAA is a stimulant that is sold as a fat destroyer and acts like adrenaline in the body.
   d. DMAA may be linked to stroke, heart attack, seizures, & panic attacks, as well as other harmful effects.

D. Conclusion
1. The scientific response to ergogenic claims is "let the buyer beware."
2. Touted heavily in bodybuilding and health magazines even though none have been scientifically shown to be effective

Worksheet 10-1: Sports Bar Label Analysis

Instructions: Use the sports bar label below to answer the questions that follow.

Nutrition Facts

Serving Size 1 Bar
Servings Per Container 24

Amount Per Serving	
Calories 260	Calories from Fat 60
	% Daily Value*
Total Fat 7g	**11%**
Saturated Fat 3.5g	**17%**
Trans Fat 0g	
Cholesterol 20mg	**7%**
Sodium 370mg	**15%**
Potassium 200mg	**6%**
Total Carbohydrate 34g	**11%**
Dietary Fiber 0g	**0%**
Sugars 25g	
Protein 16g	**32%**
Vitamin A 1250IU	25%
Vitamin C 30mg	50%
Calcium 100mg	10%
Iron 1.44mg	8%
Vitamin E 15IU	50%
Riboflavin 0.51mg	30%
Niacin 6mg	30%
Vitamin B_6 0.6mg	30%
Folate 80μg	20%
Vitamin B_{12} 1.5μg	25%
Biotin 75μg	25%
Pantothenic Acid 3mg	30%
Phosphorus 150mg	15%
Magnesium 16mg	4%
Chromium 60μg	50%
Chloride 340mg	10%

* Percent Daily Values are based on a 2,000 calorie diet. Your Daily Values may be higher or lower depending on your calorie needs.

	Calories	2,000	2,500
Total Fat	Less than	65g	80g
Sat Fat	Less than	20g	25g
Cholesterol	Less than	300mg	300mg
Sodium	Less than	2400mg	2400mg
Total Carbohydrate		300g	375g
Dietary Fiber		25g	30g

Other Ingredients: High Fructose Corn Syrup, Corn Syrup Solids, Fructose, Lecithin, Salt, Artificial Flavor, Natural Flavors, Glycerine, Peanut Flour, Pro Crunch™ Vitamin/Mineral Blend (Ascorbic Acid, d-alpha Tocopheryl Succinate (Natural Vitamin E), Maltodextrin, Niacinamide, D-Calcium Pantothenate, Pyridoxine Hydrochloride, Chromium Polynicotinate, Riboflavin, Vitamin A Palmitate, Biotin, Folic Acid, Cyanocobalamin), Pro Crunch™ coating (Maltitol, Palm Kernel Oil, Cocoa, Whey Powder, Lecithin, Natural Flavors), Pro Crunch™ Crisp Rice (Milled Rice, Sugar, Salt, Corn Syrup, Barley Malt), Pro Crunch™ Protein Blend (Calcium Caseinate, Soy Protein Isolate, Whey Protein Isolate, Whey Protein Concentrate), Pro Crunch™ Peanut Butter (Roasted Peanuts, Dextrose, Vegetable Monoglycerides, Salt)

Storage Instructions: Store in a cool dry place.

Warning: Product contains dairy and soy.

May contain traces of seeds and nuts.

1. a. How many calories come from all carbohydrates in this product?

   b. How many calories come from sugar?

2. Are there any circumstances for which a product with more sugar would be advantageous for an athlete?

3. What are the major sources of sugar in this product?

4. Why are vitamins C and E present in levels up to 50% of the Daily Value in this product?

5. a. Why is chromium present at 50% of the daily value in this product?

   b. What is the function of chromium in the body?

6. a. Does this product contribute a lot of protein to the daily intake?

   b. Why or why not?

Worksheet 10-2: Intake Analysis—Athletes

Eating Plan B (1 Day's Intake)	Eating Plan C (1 Day's Intake)	Eating Plan E (1 Day's Intake)
6 ounces grapefruit juice	6 5"-diameter pancakes	¾ cup Nature's Path flax cereal
2 scrambled eggs	⅓ cup pure maple syrup	½ cup soy milk
1 ounce cheddar cheese	¼ pound of bacon	½ cup acai juice + seltzer water
20 ounces coffee	2 scrambled eggs	1 medium banana
2 ounces soy milk	6 ounces orange juice	12 ounces coffee
1 cup fresh raspberries	8 ounces 1% fat milk	6 ounces 6-grain yogurt
1 cup cantaloupe	2 slices of unseeded Italian bread	½ cup blueberries
1 honey oat granola bar	3 ounces of thinly sliced pastrami	¾ cup raspberries
1 cup vanilla yogurt	2 Tbsp. spicy brown mustard	2 Mushroom Lover's Veggie Burgers
6 ounces grilled salmon	2 ounces of cheddar cheese	1 cup roasted carrot soup
10 cooked asparagus spears	2 cups of Lucky Charms cereal	½ cup sweet green peppers
1 cup broccoli	1 ½ cups 1% fat milk	6 carrot sticks
4 ounces white wine	6 ounces beef tenderloin	2 whole-wheat wasa crackers
4 ounces blueberry juice + seltzer water	1 ½ cups mashed potatoes	8 ounces Vruit juice
20 barbecue flavor soy crisps	1 cup cooked corn	8 ounces soy milk
1 cup wasabi peas	1 cup cooked peas	1 peanut butter Fiber One Bar
1 3" x 3" spanakopita	10 ounces Seltzer water	6 ounces grilled salmon
1 cup spinach	2 ounces cheddar cheese	10 cooked asparagus spears
⅓ cup feta cheese		6 ounces white wine
¼ cup black olives		½ cup olives
5 grape tomatoes		½ cup sun-dried tomatoes
3 Tbsp. oil & vinegar dressing		½ cup whole-wheat angel hair pasta
6 ounces white wine		¼ cup mixed nuts
¼ cup mixed nuts		
1 cup vanilla ice cream		

Look at Eating Plans B, C, and E:

1. a. Which of these eating plans would an athlete choose to maximize his or her stored glycogen before an endurance event?

   b. How could the eating plan chosen in 1.a. be further modified to ensure an adequate supply of carbohydrates while maintaining moderation in calories consumed?

2. Which of these eating plans supplies an adequate amount of protein for muscle repair while achieving moderation in terms of fat content?

3. a. Which of these eating plans is the best choice for restoring fluid balance in the body?

   b. Why?

Worksheet 10-3: Activity Diary Evaluation

Fitness depends on a certain minimum amount of physical activity. Ideally, the quantity and quality of the physical activity you select will improve your cardiorespiratory endurance, body composition, strength, and flexibility. Examine your activity choices by keeping an activity diary for one week. For each physical activity, be sure to record the type of activity, the level of intensity, and the duration. In addition, record the times and places of beverage consumption and the types and amounts of beverages consumed. Now compare the choices you made in your one-week activity diary to the guidelines for physical fitness (see Figure 10-1 or http://health.gov/paguidelines).

1. How often were you engaged in aerobic activity to improve cardiorespiratory endurance? Was the intensity of aerobic activity either moderate or vigorous based on Table 10-1? Was the duration for each session at least 20 minutes?

2. How often did you participate in resistance activities to develop strength or muscular endurance? Was the intensity enough to enhance muscle strength and endurance and improve body composition? Did you perform 8 to 10 different exercises, completing at least 2 to 4 sets of 8 to 12 repetitions?

3. How often did you stretch to improve your flexibility? Were the types of movements sufficient to develop and maintain a full range of motion? Did you hold each stretch 15 to 30 seconds and repeat each stretch at least 2 to 4 times?

4. Do you drink plenty of fluids daily, especially water, before, during, and after physical activity?

5. What changes could you make to improve your fitness?

Worksheet 10-4: Developing Performance-Enhancing Eating Plans

Scene: You are an athletic trainer's assistant who has been asked to help develop the best meal plans for athletes at an area college. You have 3 student athletes that you need to give nutrition advice to.

Athlete #1: Brent is a promising baseball player who is training to be a pitcher. Brent is 6 feet tall and weighs 150 pounds. He is 19 years old. He wants to add weight and strength for the baseball season. He does not cook and he does not have a car but he does eat at the campus cafeteria.

Athlete #2: Kelly is a cross-country runner who is also a vegan. She is 21 years old. She is 5 feet 6 inches tall and she weights 125 pounds. She has been noticing that she is very tired after races. She wants to try to eat better to help her improve her endurance. She likes to cook when she can find the time.

Athlete #3: Frank is a weight lifter who needs to lose some body fat but wants to maintain his strength. He is 20 years old. He is 5 feet 8 inches tall and he weighs 225 pounds. He would like to have more energy during his weight lifting events. Frank has a kitchen and he loves to eat lots of pasta.

Assignment: You have been asked to develop an eating plan for each of these athletes that incorporates adequacy, balance, moderation, and variety. You may have to adjust the calorie counts based on the individual athlete's needs.

Using the information that you have learned in Chapter 10 of the textbook to help you, design a typical daily eating plan for each of these athletes.

Needs: Brent needs to gain lean body mass (muscle) and increase his calorie counts. You can determine what his basal metabolic rate and activity level are to determine his daily calorie needs. You need to increase his number of calories each day. Be careful about the types of foods that you select to help Brent gain weight. He should still eat nutrient-dense foods and increase his portion sizes.

Kelly does not eat any animal products, so consider how she can get enough protein, fat, essential vitamins, and iron in her diet. She will need to eat nuts, beans, and whole grains along with fruits and vegetables to get all of the nutrients that she needs. She needs to get plenty of water, iron, and carbohydrates in her diet. This could help with her fatigue.

Frank needs to lose body fat but maintain or gain muscle mass. Consider how he can reduce his total calories while maintaining his energy level. Again, you will need to determine what his basal metabolic rate and activity level are to determine his daily calorie needs. Frank should reduce his calories very modestly and increase his physical activity to maintain his muscle mass.

Your diet plan for each athlete should include:

- Athlete's name
- Calories used per day
- Calories needed per day
- Meal plan (typical 1 day)

Check out your diet plan by using the tools at www.supertracker.usda.gov, a diet analysis program such as *Diet Analysis +*, a sports nutrition website, or a cell phone "app." You can enter your athlete's profile (age, sex, height, and weight) in a dietary analysis program and obtain daily goals based on the Dietary Reference Intakes (DRI). You can enter your suggested meal plan to see if it meets the DRI recommendations for your athlete.

Worksheet 10-5: Chapter 10 Review Crossword Puzzle

Across:	Down:
1. Preserving _____, the ability to quickly change directions, may help older people avoid falls.	1. _____ steroids are used to increase muscle mass and strength beyond what is possible with training alone.
5. A vitamin that is needed for the production of red blood cells and will help them carry oxygen to working muscles	2. _____ in some beverages may help reduce fatigue in athletes as well as trigger fatty acid release to the muscles for energy.
7. The ability of a muscle to contract and relax repeatedly without fatigue is known as muscular _____.	3. The degree of effort needed to perform a particular exercise
9. A high-_____ diet is best for supporting athletes who participate in endurance events such as running or bicycling.	4. Exercises that help joints go through their full range of motion and are often overlooked in fitness programs
10. Drinks that athletes consume after a sports event to help them replenish energy and muscle tissue	6. Athletes may take supplements of _____, which is an amino acid that will help increase the rate of protein synthesis to rebuild muscles.
11. _____ is stored in the muscle fibers for quick access so that the muscles can make ATP (energy) throughout an extended period of aerobic activity.	8. Athletes sometimes turn to _____ aids to help them improve their performance quickly.
12. _____ exercise develops muscle strength, power, endurance, and mass.	

Handout 10-1: I'm in Shape But Why Can't I Perform?

Many athletes spend a long time getting into shape. They may train for that 10K run or 20-mile bike race. After a period of time, they may notice that they suddenly cannot train at the same level anymore. Many athletes are not aware of the cause of their symptoms or how they can prevent such symptoms. The table lists common causes of athletic performance decline; a list of dietary suggestions is provided to help an athlete avoid such signs and symptoms and better enjoy his or her sport.

Symptoms or signs	Causes
Headache	• Dehydration • Lack of carbohydrates
Fatigue	• Anemia • Dehydration • Deficiency of carbohydrates • Electrolyte deficiency
Rapid pulse	• Anemia • Dehydration
Muscle cramps	• Dehydration • Electrolyte deficiency
Muscle exhaustion	• Deficiency of carbohydrates
Reduced cold tolerance	• Anemia
Dizziness	• Anemia • Dehydration
Shortness of breath	• Anemia
Reduced exercise tolerance	• Anemia • Deficiency of protein • Dehydration • Deficiency of carbohydrates

Dietary Suggestions:

- ***To combat dehydration:*** Drink plenty of fluids before, during, and after the activity
- ***To avoid a deficiency of carbohydrates:*** Get plenty of complex carbohydrates from whole grains, breads, and pastas for several days before the athletic event
- ***To prevent anemia:*** Get enough folate, vitamin B_{12}, and heme or non-heme iron from a variety of whole food sources
- ***To avoid a deficiency of protein:*** Select low-fat sources of protein such as skim milk, fish, lean cuts of meat, soy products, and beans
- ***To avoid an electrolyte deficiency:*** Drink plenty of fluids and eat whole foods like fruits, vegetables, whole grains, and mixed nuts

Chapter 11 – Diet and Health

Quick List: IM Resources for Chapter 11

- **Class preparation resources:** learning objectives/key points, suggested activities and projects, lecture outline
- **Assignment materials:** **Related LO**
    - Critical thinking questions (with answer key) 11.1, 11.2, 11.3, 11.5
    - Discussion questions (with answers) for Controversy 11 .... 11.7
    - Worksheet 11-1: Organic Granola Label Analysis 11.3, 11.5
    - Worksheet 11-2: Intake Analysis—Diet and Disease 11.3, 11.4, 11.5
    - **New!** Worksheet 11-3: Chapter 11 Review Crossword Puzzle
- **Enrichment materials:**
    - Handout 11-1: Functions of the Body's White Blood Cells[1] 11.1
    - Handout 11-2: Effects of Malnutrition on the Body's Immune System[1] 11.1
    - Handout 11-3: Causes of Malnutrition in HIV Infection[1] 11.1
    - Handout 11-4: Designing an Anti-Inflammatory Diet 11.1, 11.3
    - Handout 11-5: High Blood Pressure—How to Deal With It 11.4

Chapter Learning Objectives and Key Points

11.1 **Describe relationships between immunity and nutrition, and explain how malnutrition and infection worsen each other.**
Adequate nutrition is necessary for normal immune system functioning. Both deficient and excessive nutrients can harm the immune system. Inflammation is part of the body's immune defense system. Sustained inflammation can worsen a number of chronic diseases.

11.2 **Identify several risk factors for chronic disease, and explain the relationship between risk factors and chronic diseases.**
The same diet and lifestyle risk factors may contribute to several chronic diseases. A person's family history and laboratory test results can reveal elevated disease risks and suggest strategies for disease prevention.

11.3 **Identify dietary factors that increase and decrease CVD risks, and explain the association between high blood LDL and HDL cholesterol concentrations and CVD risk.**
Atherosclerosis begins with the accumulation of soft, fatty streaks on the inner walls of the arteries. The soft, fatty streaks gradually enlarge and become hard plaques. Plaques of atherosclerosis trigger hypertension and abnormal blood clotting, leading to heart attacks or strokes. In most people, atherosclerosis progresses steadily as they age. Major risk factors for CVD are age, gender, family history, high LDL cholesterol and low HDL cholesterol, hypertension, diabetes, physical inactivity, smoking, an atherogenic diet, and obesity. Lifestyle changes to lower the risk of CVD include increasing physical activity, achieving a healthy body weight, reducing exposure to tobacco smoke, and eating a heart-healthy diet. Dietary measures to lower LDL cholesterol include reducing intakes of saturated fat, *trans* fat, and cholesterol, along with consuming enough nutrient-dense fruits, vegetables, legumes, fish, and whole grains.

11.4 **Outline a general eating and exercise plan for a person with prehypertension, and justify the recommendations.**
Hypertension silently and progressively worsens atherosclerosis and makes heart attacks and strokes likely. All adults should know whether or not their blood pressure falls within the normal range. Blood pressure pushes the blood through the major arteries into smaller arteries and capillaries to exchange fluids between the blood and the tissues. Blood pressure rises when cardiac output or peripheral resistance increases. Obesity, age, family background, and race contribute to hypertension risks, as do salt intake and other dietary factors, including alcohol consumption. For most people, maintaining a healthy body weight, engaging in regular physical activity, minimizing salt and sodium intakes, limiting alcohol intake, and eating a diet high in fruits,

[1] Contributed by Lori W. Turner, Ph.D., R.D., University of Alabama, and Mary Ellen Clark

vegetables, fish, and low-fat dairy products work together to keep blood pressure normal. Certain nutrient deficiencies may raise blood pressure.

11.5 **Describe the associations between diet and cancer observed in research, both positive and negative.** Cancer arises from genetic damage and develops in steps, including initiation and promotion, which may be influenced by diet. Contaminants and naturally occurring toxins can be carcinogenic but they are monitored in the U.S. food supply and the body is equipped to handle tiny doses of most kinds. Obesity, physical inactivity, alcohol consumption, and diets high in red and processed meats are associated with cancer development. Foods containing ample fiber, folate, calcium, many other vitamins and minerals, and phytochemicals may be protective.

11.6 **Make specific recommendations for including sufficient fruits and vegetables in a health-promoting diet.**

11.7 **Describe some recent advances in nutritional genomics with regard to the health of the body through life.**

Critical Thinking Questions

1. *Describe how a deficiency of vitamin A and protein can compromise the body's defenses against infection.*

   A vitamin A deficiency causes a decline in the integrity of the skin, lessoning its ability to serve as a barrier to pathogenic, disease-causing microbes. Vitamin A deficiency can also impair the membranes that protect the body's passages from infectious pathogens. Vitamin A helps cells, including the antibody-producing cells as well as the T lymphocytes and phagocytes, to develop normally and function fully.

   Table 11-3 describes the impact of protein-energy malnutrition on the body's defenses. The immune system needs an adequate amount of protein to produce antibodies and white blood cells to protect the body against pathogens that cause infectious diseases. Proteins are not stored in the body and must be supplied by the diet each day.

2. a. *Describe in your own words how obesity can increase the risk of diabetes and cardiovascular disease.*

   Figure 11-3 shows the interrelationships among several chronic conditions. Obesity, especially central obesity, is associated with insulin resistance (which can lead to type 2 diabetes) and atherosclerosis (which typically leads to heart disease). The abdominal fat of central obesity may release into the blood fatty acids that can increase inflammation in the arteries (leads to atherosclerosis) and insulin resistance.

   b. *How can diabetes increase the risk of cardiovascular disease?*

   Poorly controlled diabetes can increase the risk of high blood pressure (due to changes in the blood vessels that make them less elastic) and atherosclerosis, which can cause changes within the blood vessels that could increase blood clot formation due to the effects of excess blood glucose and inflammation.

   Table 11-2 describes risk factors that can lead to the development of several chronic conditions.

   c. *How does high blood pressure increase the risk of stroke?*

   High blood pressure can cause the arteries to become less elastic and can place an added stress on the blood vessels. This could result in an aneurysm or weakening of the blood vessel, leading to the loss of blood flow to areas of the brain tissue. Death of areas of brain tissue is the cause of strokes.

3. a. *Describe how elevated LDL levels can increase the risk of atherosclerosis.*

   LDL can form deposits on the walls of the arteries. These areas of the blood vessels can become vulnerable to oxidative stress and inflammation. These processes often attract white blood cells to the area of the blood vessel damage, and they engulf LDL and become part of the fatty deposits in the vessel walls. This can cause stiffening and narrowing of the blood vessels as seen in atherosclerosis.

b. *What other diseases are more likely as a result of developing atherosclerosis?*

High blood pressure, strokes, and heart attacks are more likely as a result of unresolved atherosclerosis. Also, reduction of blood flow to the kidneys can lead to damage and kidney failure.

4. *List any 3 lifestyle factors that can contribute to the development of cardiovascular disease and discuss how people can adjust their lifestyles to reduce the risks.*

Some lifestyle factors can include inactivity, smoking, eating a diet high in saturated fats, diabetes, or atherosclerosis.

Table 11-7 describes strategies to reduce the risks for cardiovascular disease. Some of the strategies are easier to employ than others. Many people find it difficult to quit smoking but there are a lot of smoking cessation programs that people can follow in consultation with their health care providers. People may not find it too difficult to add activity to their daily lives. They can take simple measures such as walking for 10 minutes more each day. People can reduce their intake of saturated fats by reducing their intake of animal products such as beef gradually, to avoid feeling deprived.

5. a. *List any 2 dietary excesses that can increase the risk of cancer development and explain how these excesses exert their effects.*

Alcohol, red meats, and even excess calories could increase the risk of cancer development. Alcohol can cause irritation in the mouth, esophagus, or stomach that could lead to changes in the tissues. It may also displace the intake of fruits and vegetables that may protect against cancer development.

Red meats may contain substances that cause changes in the wall of the colon that could lead to the development of colon cancer. Nitrites and nitrates in processed meats may be carcinogenic. Grilled meats may release fats that can become potential carcinogens when they are burned.

b. *List any 2 dietary deficiencies that can increase the risk of cancer development and explain how these deficiencies exert their effects.*

A diet that is low in fiber, antioxidant vitamins, calcium, and vitamin D may increase a person's risk of developing cancer. Fiber may be protective since it helps foods pass through the intestines more quickly. This could result in less irritation of the walls of the colon, which may reduce cancer risks. Antioxidant deficiencies may cause the tissues to be more susceptible to the effects of free radicals. Such molecules may cause mutations in cells' DNA that can lead to cancer development in those cells. Studies suggest that adequate intakes of calcium and vitamin D may also be protective against the development of cancer; research is underway.

6. *Why is a total blood cholesterol of 190 mg/dL not necessarily indicative of a low risk of heart disease?*

Healthcare providers evaluate the proportions of HDL and LDL that comprise this total. Thus, 2 people who have a total cholesterol level of 190 mg/dL, may still have very different risks for developing heart disease.

One person might have an HDL level of 30 mg/dL and an LDL level of 150 mg/dL (VLDL makes up the rest of the cholesterol). This person has a high level of LDL, which may lead to atherosclerosis, and a low level of HDL, which may be less protective against the buildup of plaque in the blood vessels.

The other person might have an HDL level of 70 mg/dL and an LDL level of 110 mg/dL. This person has LDL levels that do not put them at higher risk of atherosclerosis and HDL levels that are more protective against the development of heart disease.

Controversy Discussion Questions

1. *What exactly is the field of "epigenetics," and how can epigenetics affect the function of the body's cells?*

Epigenetics is the study of how genes are expressed without associated changes in the DNA sequence. Some genes are not made into proteins all of the time so there are active mechanisms to "silence" these genes. Histone proteins associated with DNA as well as methyl groups that can bind to the DNA directly can silence genes. Epigenetics examines how and when genes are silenced. For example, proteins needed for cell division are silenced when cells do not have to divide. Genes for hemoglobin protein production are silenced in nerve cells.

2. *Describe any 3 controversies that could arise if genetic testing of everyone were to become routine and required.*

   - It is possible that people's genetic information could be distributed to third parties unintentionally. Many computer databases are susceptible to infiltration by individuals with computer "hacking" skills.
   - It is possible that nutritional supplement companies could get access to people's genetic information and try to sell them expensive supplements that may not be proven to work.
   - It is also possible that medical insurance companies could use the genetic information to deny coverage to individuals who may be at higher risk of a disease with a genetic component.

3. a. *How do B vitamins affect the way genes may be expressed in cells?*

   B vitamins are important for transferring methyl groups to the DNA. When genes are methylated, they are not expressed. The B vitamins do not change the DNA sequences, they just affect how the genes are expressed or suppressed. Genes that trigger cells to divide need to be silenced at times so that cells do not divide too often.

   b. *Give an example of how B vitamins could exert their effects on genes in the cells.*

   Folate may be responsible for transferring methyl groups to key growth genes to "silence" them (keep them from making proteins). A study was done in which pregnant mice were fed folate supplements or a normal diet. The pregnant mice that received folate supplements had pups that were lean with brown fur. The folate silenced the genes that cause body fat to accumulate on the pups. The pregnant mothers fed a normal diet had pups that were fatter with yellow fur.

4. *What is a "SNP," and how can they interact with the diet to contribute to diseases?*

   A "SNP" is a single nucleotide polymorphism. This is a variation in a sequence for a gene. If a SNP occurs in the DNA in regions where it does not encode for a protein, there may not be a pronounced effect on the protein function or cell. If the SNP occurs in an important region of a gene, the resulting protein may not function correctly and the effect on the cell would be great. The Controversy points out that a SNP in the gene that encodes for a key metabolic enzyme can result in PKU.

   People can have thousands of SNPs in their DNA sequence and some of the SNPs that may have subtle effects (as described above) may work with factors from the environment such as diet and environmental exposures to result in the development of chronic diseases. A SNP in fat metabolism genes can change the body's response to the intake of dietary fats. Some people's LDL levels fall when their PUFA intakes increase and rise when their intakes decrease, suggesting that the SNP interacts with PUFA to reduce LDL production in the body.

Worksheet Answer Key

Worksheet 11-1: Organic Granola Label Analysis

1. The vegetarian claim may help a person reduce the amount of cholesterol or saturated fats that would come from animal products.
   The no *trans*-fats claim would help a person avoid such fats, which may contribute to elevated LDL levels in the blood or to cardiovascular disease.
   The low sodium claim may help a person pick foods to keep their blood pressure down.
   The whole grain claim would allow someone to get more fiber and less of a spike in their blood glucose levels after eating a meal.
2. The organic claim would suggest that there are no hormones or pesticides added to the product. This may help reduce the risk of developing some types of cancer.
3. There are no animal products in this product.
4. The soy oil and coconut flakes do contribute saturated fat to this product.
5. a. Lower levels of saturated fat may decrease the levels of LDL, which is associated with cardiovascular disease.

b. Reduced blood LDL levels may slow the build-up of plaques in the blood vessels, and thus the progression of atherosclerosis. When blood flows freely, less stress is placed on the heart and there is less chance that a clot will become lodged in a narrowed blood vessel and cut off blood flow to some part of the body.

c. Lower saturated fat intake may reduce the risks of some types of cancers.

Worksheet 11-2: Intake Analysis—Diet and Disease

1. a. After evaluating all of the plans for adequate potassium, adequate magnesium, reduced sodium, and adequate water intake, it appears that Eating Plan E is the best.

   b. It has levels of water, potassium, and magnesium that are more than adequate and may help lower blood pressure.

   c. Eating Plan E has a lower level of sodium, which helps to reduce blood pressure.

2. a. Eating Plan F is likely the most atherogenic because it has the lowest level of fiber (which may lower cholesterol), a higher level of saturated fat, and a lower level of vitamin C, which is an antioxidant.

   b. Replace whole-fat dairy products and high-fat meats with whole-grain products, non-fat dairy products, lean meats, fruits, legumes, and vegetables to "round out" this eating plan.

3. a. Eating Plan E is highest in fiber.

   b. Whole-grain cereal, carrots, veggie burgers, and tomatoes are the sources of fiber.

   c. Diverticulosis, constipation, colon polyps, hemorrhoids, or blood glucose spikes.

4. a. Eating Plan F has the most (1357 mg).

   b. The sources of calcium are milk, cheese, and blue cheese dressing.

   c. Calcium at adequate levels may be able to prevent osteoporosis, hypertension, and colon polyps.

5. a. The levels of saturated fats can be reduced and the levels of fiber, vitamins C and E, and water can be increased.

   b. The cheese and meat products can be reduced in portion size or replaced with a lower-fat substitute.

Worksheet 11-3: Chapter 11 Review Crossword Puzzle

1. Histones
2. systolic
3. Vitamin A
4. diabetes
5. soluble
6. A: metastasis; D: methylation
7. diastolic
8. atherosclerosis
9. chronic
10. atherogenic
11. epigenetics
12. stroke

Learning Activities & Project Ideas

Activity 11-1: What Disease Term Am I?[2] LO 11.1, 11.3, 11.4, 11.5

Before class, prepare "Post-its," index cards, or slips of paper by writing one new disease term on each post-it, card, or slip of paper. (You may also include other terms that appear in the chapter.) Tape an index card to the back of each student. The goal of the activity is for students to find out what disease or related term is written on their backs.

To discover "What disease term am I?" have students circulate throughout the room asking other students questions about the term written on their backs. They are permitted to ask each student two "yes or no" type questions. After asking a student two questions, they approach another student and ask two more questions. For example, one question could be "Do I often result from consuming too much saturated fat?" After each student has discovered what term is on their card, they can tell the class how they figured it out and what questions they asked during the activity.

Activity 11-2: Low-Sodium Diet Project[2] LO 11.4

To help students develop empathy for people who must consume modified diets, instruct them to consume a special diet for 1-2 days. A 2-gram sodium diet is an excellent choice. Students soon learn how difficult it is to consume a

---

[2] Contributed by Lori W. Turner, Ph.D., R.D., University of Alabama

diet without the flavoring of salt. Remind students to check the sodium content of each product on the Nutrition Facts panel of the label. Instruct students to keep a record of their food choices and responses to the special diet. You may want to distribute Handout 8-3, "Spices to Enhance Salt-Free Dishes," to help them make this diet more enjoyable.

Chapter Lecture Outline

I. Introduction
   A. Can a well chosen diet protect you from developing a disease?
   B. It depends on the disease. There are two main kinds:
      1. Infectious diseases such as H1N1 influenza or tuberculosis – Antimicrobial drugs have reduced death from these diseases but drug-resistant microbes pose a serious threat.
      2. Degenerative (a.k.a. chronic) such as diabetes and heart disease that can arise from genetics, prior or current diseases, and lifestyle choices
   C. Figure 11-1 shows the leading causes of death in the USA in 2012

II. The Immune System, Nutrition, and Diseases
   A. Adequate nutrition is a key component in maintaining a healthy immune system to defend against infectious disease and these tissues are the first to be impaired in the course of vitamin or mineral deficiencies or toxicities.
   B. The Effects of Malnutrition
      1. Malnutrition and Disease Worsen Each Other – Impaired immunity can result in diseases that can further disrupt the functioning of the digestive system, leading to impaired ability to assimilate nutrients from the diet.
      2. Impairment of Immune Defenses (see Table 11-1)
         a. The tissues and cells of the immune system can get smaller in size and number and don't work as well at protecting the body against infection.
         b. Lack of vitamin A weakens the body's skin and mucous barriers to infection.
         c. Lack of vitamin C prevents white blood cells from killing invaders.
         d. Lack of zinc lowers the number and effectiveness of the white blood cells.
      3. Disease Can Worsen Malnutrition – AIDS, cancer, or cancer's treatments can suppress one's appetite and lead to wasting of the body's tissues.
   C. The Immune System and Chronic Diseases
      1. Acute inflammation in which the immune system's white blood cells rush to a site of infection to clear it up is an important and needed response.
      2. Lower-level chronic inflammation can cause harmful changes in the tissues.

III. The Concept of Risk Factors
   A. Cause versus Increased Risk – Risk factors show a correlation with a disease—that is, they occur together with the disease.
      1. A diet may contribute to several degenerative diseases.
      2. Studies will suggest that a particular diet is associated with a chronic condition but will NOT say that a particular diet causes a chronic condition.
      3. Table 11-3 identifies diet-related behaviors that may be related to chronic diseases.
      4. Figure 11-3 shows the interrelationships between chronic diseases.
   B. Estimating Your Risks
      1. A person's family history and laboratory test results can reveal strategies for disease prevention.
      2. See Table 11-4 for risk factors for chronic diseases
      3. For example, if a person has a family history of type 2 diabetes, that individual should avoid becoming overweight by eating a nutritious calorie-controlled diet.
      4. Always ask for test results from your doctor since these can be predictors of disease.

IV. Cardiovascular Diseases
   A. Prevalence
      1. In the U.S., more than 82 million men and women suffer some form of heart disease (CVD) such as heart attack and stroke.

2. The heart does not regenerate and so damage to the muscle is permanent.
3. Almost 1 million people die each year from CVD.
4. In all its forms, CVD kills more U.S. women than any other cause.
5. People have quit smoking and are eating less *trans* fats and saturated fats but they are still over-consuming calories and sodium, under-consuming fruits and vegetables, and failing to engage in enough physical activity.

B. Atherosclerosis – the root of CVD
   1. How Plaques Form
      a. Most people have well developed plaques by the time they are 30 years old.
      b. A diet high in saturated fat is a major contributor.
      c. Inflammation of the artery is also involved; it comes from different factors such as:
         1. High LDL cholesterol
         2. Hypertension
         3. Toxins from cigarette smoking
         4. High blood levels of homocysteine
         5. Certain viral or bacterial infections
      d. Inflammation causes the immune system to:
         1. Send white blood cells (macrophages) to remove the oxidized LDL cholesterol
         2. As the macrophages engulf the LDL, they become known as foam cells, which themselves become oxidized, attracting more immune scavengers to the scene.
      e. Muscle cells of the arterial walls divide in an attempt to heal the damage, but they mix with foam cells to form hardened plaques.
      f. Mineralization increases the hardening of the plaques.
   2. Plaque Rupture and Blood Clots
      a. A spike in blood pressure or a spasm of the artery may cause a plaque to rupture.
      b. The most vulnerable plaques have a large lipid core with thin fibrous cap.
      c. Abnormal blood clotting also threatens life.
      d. Platelets are involved in blood clotting, under normal circumstances, to prevent excessive blood loss from a blood vessel.
      e. In atherosclerosis, platelets clot the blood in an injured, hardened artery.
         1. A stationary clot is called a thrombus.
         2. If a thrombus closes off a blood vessel, it is known as a thrombosis.
         3. If the clot breaks loose, it is known as an embolus.
         4. If the embolus becomes stuck in a blood vessel (embolism), it can lead to heart attack (when lodged in a heart artery) or stroke (when lodged in the brain).
      f. Opposing the clot-forming actions of platelets is one of the eicosanoids, an active product of an omega-3 fatty acid in fish oils.
   3. Plaques and Blood Pressure
      a. Arteries hardened and narrowed by plaques cannot expand as blood flows through, which raises blood pressure.
      b. This further damages the artery walls.
      c. If the pressure causes the wall to weaken and balloon out, it is called an aneurysm.
      d. An aneurysm can be fatal if occurs in the aorta since a large volume of blood will be lost.

C. Risk Factors for CVD
   1. Many risk factors for a heart attack are also risk factors for a stroke.
   2. The Department of Health and Human Services has launched the Million Hearts campaign with the goal of preventing 1 million heart attacks and strokes over the next 5 years.
   3. Age, Gender, and Genetic Inheritance – are three major risk factors for CVD that cannot be modified by lifestyle choices (see Table 11-5)
      a. The rate of atherosclerosis progression may be influenced by the presence or absence of risk factors like high blood pressure, diabetes, high blood cholesterol, and smoking.
      b. Men (at age 55) with 2 major risk factors were 6 times more likely to die from CVD by age 80.
      c. Women of the same age were 3 times more likely to die from CVD with 2 risk factors.
      d. CVD tends to run in families, especially if people are affected at a younger age.
   4. LDL and HDL Cholesterol – can be modified by lifestyle factors
      a. Figure 11-5 shows the relationship of LDL and HDL levels to risk of heart disease.

b. HDL carries cholesterol away from the cells to the liver for use elsewhere in the body.
c. Higher levels are thought to be protective for the heart.
d. LDL can be deposited in artery walls and become oxidized, which leads to inflammation of the arteries and an increased risk of CVD.
e. Figure 11-6 shows the adult standards for blood lipids, body mass index, and blood pressure.
f. Figure 11-7 provides an assessment tool for determining cardiovascular disease risk.

5. Hypertension and Atherosclerosis Worsen Each Other
   a. Hypertension worsens atherosclerosis since high pressure can further weaken stiffened arteries.
   b. Atherosclerosis worsens high blood pressure because plaque stiffens the walls of the arteries, which raises internal pressures.
   c. Atherosclerosis & hypertension worsen each other & put an increased strain on the heart as well.
6. Diabetes
   a. Diabetes, a major independent risk factor for all forms of CVD, increases the risk of death from these causes.
   b. In diabetes, atherosclerosis progresses rapidly, blocking blood vessels and diminishing circulation.
   c. Risk of a future heart attack with diabetes is equivalent to a person, without diabetes, who has already had a heart attack
7. Physical Inactivity
   a. Physical activity expands the heart's capacity to pump blood to the tissues with each beat, thereby reducing the pulse.
   b. Activity also stimulates development of new arteries to nourish the heart muscle.
   c. Activity favors a leaner body.
   d. 30 minutes or more of moderate exercise on 5 or more days/week can improve the odds against heart disease.
   e. Even 15 minutes of more vigorous activity 5 days a week can yield similar benefits.
8. Smoking
   a. Cigarette smoking powerfully increases the risk for CVD.
   b. It damages the heart directly with toxins.
   c. Raises blood pressure
   d. Makes clots more likely by damaging platelets
   e. Deprives the heart of oxygen
   f. Damages the lining of blood vessels
9. Atherogenic Diet
   a. Diet influences the risk of CVD.
   b. An "atherogenic diet" is high in saturated fat, *trans* fat, and cholesterol – increases LDL cholesterol, which can increase the risk of CVD
10. Obesity and Metabolic Syndrome
    a. A distinct array of risk factors often occurs with CVD.
    b. Metabolic syndrome includes central obesity and at least two of the following:
       1. High fasting blood glucose or type 2 diabetes
       2. Hypertension
       3. Low blood HDL
       4. High blood triglycerides
    c. Metabolic syndrome may increase inflammation in the blood vessels and increase the risk of thrombus formation.
    d. More than one third of the U.S. adult population meets the criteria for metabolic syndrome (Table 11-6).
11. High Blood Triglycerides – High triglycerides don't directly cause CVD but may be associated with higher levels of VLDL that may be associated with CVD.

D. Recommendations for Reducing CVD Risk – involve lifestyle adjustments (see Table 11-7)
   1. Diet to Reduce CVD Risk
      a. Lowering intakes of saturated fat and *trans* fat lowers blood LDL cholesterol and this reduces heart disease (see Table 11-8).
      b. When diets are rich in whole grains, vegetables, and fruits, rates of CVD are low and life expectancies are long.

c. A heart-healthy diet provides abundant complex carbohydrates in the form of whole grains, vegetables, and fruit.
d. Eating more whole grains helps improve blood lipids.
e. A meal of fish twice a week can help favor the right balance of fatty acids so that clot formation is less likely.
2. Other Dietary Factors
a. Sterol and stanol esters that are added to certain kinds of margarines, orange juice, and other foods help lower blood cholesterol levels.
b. Getting a majority of protein from soy products may reduce the levels of LDL for some people.
c. Diet and exercise can lower blood pressure and lead to needed weight loss.

V. Nutrition and Hypertension
A. Introduction
1. Hypertension is silent, progressively worsens atherosclerosis, and makes heart attacks and strokes likely.
2. 76 million Americans have high blood pressure, which results in more than 1 million heart attacks and 795,000 strokes each year.
3. All adults should know their blood pressure.
4. Two numbers are important:
a. The systolic pressure measured during ventricular contraction
b. The diastolic pressure measured during relaxation phase of the heart muscle
5. Ideal resting blood pressure is lower than 120 over 80.
B. How Does Blood Pressure Work in the Body?
1. Blood pressure is vital to life.
2. When the pressure is right, the cells receive a constant supply of nutrients and oxygen and can release their wastes (see Figure 11-8).
3. Blood pressure increases due to increases in:
a. Cardiac output – goes up when heart rate or blood volume increases
b. Peripheral resistance – goes up when arteries are narrowed (vasoconstriction, atherosclerosis)
4. Regulated by nervous system (heart muscle contractions, arteries' diameters) and kidneys, which release hormones to constrict vessels & retain water & salt in response to low BP
C. Risk Factors for Hypertension – In addition to atherosclerosis, several major risk factors predict the development of hypertension.
a. Age – about two thirds of U.S. adults over 65 have high blood pressure
b. Genetics – high blood pressure tends to run families and is more prevalent in some races
c. Obesity – 60% of people with high blood pressure have obesity
d. Salt intake
e. Alcohol (more than 2 drinks per day)
f. Other dietary factors (low fruit, vegetable, nut, and non-/low-fat milk intake)
D. How Does Nutrition Affect Hypertension? – see Table 11-9 for prevention strategies
1. The DASH (Dietary Approaches to Stop Hypertension) Diet – emphasizes fruits, vegetables, nuts, whole grains, legumes, fish, & low-fat dairy
a. The DASH diet may also lower total cholesterol, LDL cholesterol, and inflammation.
b. The DASH diet ensures adequate intakes of fiber, potassium, magnesium, and calcium.
2. Weight Control and Physical Activity
a. For people who have hypertension and are overweight, a weight loss of as little as 10 pounds can significantly lower blood pressure.
b. Moderate physical activity can lower almost everyone's blood pressure, even people without hypertension.
3. Salt, Sodium, and Blood Pressure
a. High intakes of salt and sodium are associated with hypertension.
b. As salt intakes decrease, blood pressure drops in a stepwise fashion.
c. African Americans, people with a family history of hypertension, people with kidney problems or diabetes, and older people respond more sensitively to a reduction in salt.
d. No one should consume more than the UL, which is 2,300 mg of sodium per day.
e. People aged 51 and older should reduce their sodium intakes to 1500 mg per day.

4. Alcohol
    a. In moderate doses, alcohol initially relaxes the arteries and so reduces blood pressure.
    b. In higher doses, alcohol raises blood pressure.
    c. Moderation:
        1. No more than 2 drinks a day for men
        2. No more than 1 drink a day for women (this amount raises a woman's risk of breast cancer)
5. Calcium, Potassium, Magnesium, and Vitamin C
    a. Increasing calcium, potassium, and magnesium often reduces blood pressure
    b. Eating a diet with a lot of fruits, vegetables, and low-fat dairy products may help control blood pressure even better than supplements.

VI. A Consumer's Guide to Deciding about CAM
- A. U.S. consumers spent about $34 billion on complementary and alternative medicine (CAM) each year.
    1. CAM treatments range from folk remedies to fraud.
    2. CAM treatments have been used for a long time but may not have been tested by the scientific method.
- B. CAM Best Bets
    1. Dozens of herbal medicines contain effective natural drugs.
    2. Willow bark contains aspirin and valerian contains a tranquilizing oil.
    3. Atemisinin (Chinese herb) is used to kill the malaria parasite in some places.
    4. Herbs can have risks (see Table 11-11).
    5. The National Institutes of Health's NCCAM organization conducts research to distinguish useful from harmful alternative therapies.
- C. A CAM Worst Case – Laetrile, an ineffective drug marketed for cancer in the 1970s that contains cyanide (a poison) is still sold on the Internet to unsuspecting people.
- D. A Curious Case of Anosmia
    1. A zinc nose spray was advertised without FDA approval.
    2. The FDA received over 130 complaints from people who had lost their sense of smell.
    3. The manufacturer was forced by the FDA to take the product off of the market.
    4. The permanent loss of smell can impact many areas of a person's life and well-being.
- E. Mislabeled Herbs
    1. Many herbal remedies may not have the amount of active ingredient listed and may also contain unsafe drugs.
    2. Many herbs can interact with prescription drugs.
    3. Use only herbs with "U.S. Pharmacopeia" or "Consumer Lab" on the label since these products have been tested and shown to contain only the active ingredients.
- F. Lack of Knowledge
    1. Many people get information about herbs on the Internet or from herb sellers.
    2. Many herb sellers do not have training in pharmacology, botany, or human physiology.
    3. Many patients hide their herb use from their doctors.
- G. Moving Ahead
    1. Using unproven treatments may have unpredictable consequences.
    2. Let your doctor know what you are using and seek out reliable sources of scientific information about a particular treatment.

VII. Nutrition and Cancer
- A. Prevalence and introduction
    1. Cancer ranks second to heart disease as a leading cause of death and disability in the U.S.
    2. More than 1.6 million new cancer cases and about 600,000 deaths from cancer are projected in the U.S. in 2012.
    3. Early detection of some common cancers has resulted in the cure or long-term management of the cancer versus certain death.
    4. Question? Can an individual's chosen behaviors affect the risk of contracting cancer? (in many cases, yes, but this varies depending on the particular type of cancer—see Table 11-12)
    5. For most cancers, lifestyle factors and environmental exposures become the major risk factors.
    6. An estimated 30-40% of cancers are influenced by diet.
        a. Foods or their components may cause cancer.

   b. Foods or their components may promote cancer.
   c. Foods or their components may protect against cancer.

B. How Does Cancer Develop?
   1. Cancer arises in the genes when a cell's DNA sustains damage from a carcinogen, such as a free-radical, radiation, and other factors.
      a. Damage occurs daily, but most is repaired.
      b. Occasionally, a damaged cell loses its ability to self-destruct and replicates uncontrollably, resulting in a mass of abnormal tissue—a tumor.
   2. Life-threatening cancer occurs if the tumor tissue, which cannot perform its normal functions, overtakes the healthy organ in which it developed or disseminates its cells through the bloodstream to other parts of the body.
   3. Cancer develops through these steps as shown in Figure 11-9:
      a. Exposure to a carcinogen
      b. Entry of the carcinogen into a cell
      c. Initiation of cancer as the carcinogen damages or changes the cell's genetic material (carcinogenesis), followed by promotion
      d. Acceleration by promoters that stimulate tumor formation; disruption of body functions
      e. Spread of cancer to other body regions through the blood or lymph (metastasis)
   4. Researchers think that the first 4 steps of tumor formation are also key points at which prevention could have a big impact on cancer development.
   5 Contaminants and naturally occurring toxins can be carcinogenic, but they are monitored in the U.S. food supply.
   6. Food additives are safe and should not increase risks of cancer.

C. Which Diet Factors Affect Cancer Risk?
   1. Diet factors substantially influence cancer development.
   2. The degree of cancer risk imposed by the food depends partly on the eater's genetic inheritance, but the exact nature of this relationship is not yet known.
   3. Energy Intake
      a. When calorie intakes are reduced, cancer rates fall.
      b. In animal experiments, this caloric effect proves to be one of the most effective dietary interventions to prevent cancer.
      c. No evidence yet that this is true for humans, too
      d. When a population's calorie intake rises, cancer rates rise in response.
      e. Once cancer has started, the reduced caloric effect may not prevent its progression.
   4. Obesity
      a. Obesity-related cancers include: colon, breast (in postmenopausal women), endometrial, kidney, esophageal; possibly ovarian and prostate
      b. Excess body fat is associated with higher levels of estrogen, which may promote breast cancer in some women.
   5. Physical Activity – Regular physical activity may reduce the risk of colon and breast cancer.
   6. Alcohol
      a. Cancers of the head and neck correlate strongly with the combination of alcohol and tobacco use and low intakes of green and yellow fruits and vegetables.
      b. Alcohol alone is associated with cancers of the mouth, throat, and breast.
   7. Fat and Fatty Acids
      a. Fat appears to be a cancer promoter in animals.
      b. Evidence remains mixed about whether this is also true in humans.
      c. Type of fat may be important – e.g., omega-3 fatty acids from fish may protect against some cancers and may support recovery during treatment for cancer.
   8. Red Meats
      a. Evidence links diets high in red meat with a moderately elevated risk of cancers of the digestive tract, breast, and prostate.
      b. Processed meats may be of special concern due to the presence of additives (nitrites or nitrates) that in the digestive tract form possible carcinogens.
      c. Broiled, fried, grilled, or smoked meats also generate carcinogens as they cook.
      d. These foods should be eaten infrequently and in moderation.

   e. To minimize carcinogen formation during cooking: roast or bake meats, line the grill with foil, try not to burn the foods, and marinate meat before cooking
9. Fiber–Rich Foods
   a. Much evidence now weighs in favor of eating a diet rich in high-fiber, low-fat foods.
   b. Increases in fiber may lower the risk of colon cancer by binding, diluting, and removing potential carcinogens from the colon.
10. Folate and Antioxidant Vitamins
   a. Folate may protect against cancer of the esophagus and colon, but more studies are needed.
   b. Vitamin C and E supplements may promote cancer progression once cancer is established.
11. Calcium and Vitamin D
   a. Some scientific evidence suggests a beneficial effect of sufficient dietary calcium (600 to 1000 mg per day) against colon cancer.
   b. Vitamin D may help protect against cancer but no conclusive evidence has been found.
   c. Adequate vitamin D intake is still necessary for many other health benefits.
12. Iron – may promote colon cancer since it could be oxidized and damage the cellular DNA of the colon
13. Foods and Phytochemicals
   a. Some phytochemicals in fruits and vegetables are thought to be anticarcinogens.
   b. Infrequent intake of cruciferous vegetables is common among people with colon cancer.
   c. A first step in preventing cancer is to consume the recommended number of servings of fruits and vegetables each day.
14. See Table 11-13 for recommendations for reducing cancer risks.

VIII. Conclusion – Nutrition is often associated with promoting health, and medicine with fighting disease, but no clear line separates nutrition and medicine.

IX. Food Feature – The Dash Diet: Preventive Medicine – "If you do not smoke or drink excessively, your choice of diet can influence your long-term health prospects more than any other action you might take," states a former surgeon general.
   A. Dietary Guidelines and the DASH Diet – The DASH diet is presented in Table 11-14.
      1. People who follow the DASH diet see a reduction in their blood pressure, LDL, and total cholesterol levels.
      2. The DASH diet emphasis a variety of fruits, vegetables, whole grains, and low-fat milk products.
      3. The DASH diet also emphasizes eating more fish, nuts, and poultry in place of red meats.
      4. The DASH diet ensures adequate intake of calcium, potassium, and magnesium, which have been shown to reduce blood pressure.
      5. If people restrict their sodium intake in addition to following the DASH diet, they may see an even more significant drop in their blood pressure.
      6. The DASH diet also incorporates more fiber and protein for added health benefits.
   B. Fruits and Vegetables: More Matters
      1. Include fruits, vegetables, legumes, and whole grains not just for nutrients but also for the phytochemicals that combine synergistically to promote health.
      2. People can find out the number of servings that they need by visiting the website: http://www.fruitsandveggiesmorematters.org.
      3. Table 11-15 offers suggestions for increasing intakes of fruits and vegetables.
   C. Conclusion – An occasional snack, such as a banana split, won't be harmful but people should make a point to enjoy the sight, taste, and smell of their foods.

X. Controversy – Nutritional Genomics: Can It Deliver on Its Promises?
   A. Nutritional Genomics Research
      1. New trends in health care promise to help reduce the risk of people developing chronic diseases by designing customized eating plans for each individual, based on their genetic profile or tendency to develop chronic diseases later in their life.
      2. Nutritional genomics researchers are attempting to determine which genes that may play roles in the development of disease can be regulated by diet.

3. Nutritional genomics researchers are also determining which bioactive agents in foods can modify the actions of disease-causing genes and exploring which diets or foods might prevent or relieve chronic diseases by modifying associated gene activity.
4. Researchers use DNA microarray technology, which allows them to determine which DNA gene sequences are actively making proteins and which ones are "silent."

B. DNA Variations, Nutrition, and Disease – Small variations in DNA sequences (mutations) dictate many of the differences seen between people.
   1. SNPs and Diseases
      a. People have single nucleotide (base pair) variations in their DNA called SNPs.
      b. About 10 million possible SNPs are known to exist.
      c. SNPs found within a gene sequence that encodes an important protein will usually cause a serious disease with profound effects.
      d. SNPs may not cause a disease on their own but may work with environmental factors like diet to increase the risk of developing a chronic disease.
   2. Complexity of SNP-Disease Relationships – SNPs may be found in multiple genes that may interact with many environmental factors.

C. Epigenetics
   1. Study of the epigenome, which consists of proteins and other molecules that associate with DNA and may regulate the expression of genes (turning them on or off)
   2. The DNA is written in indelible ink so that the sequence is permanent and the epigenome is written in pencil to allow erasures and changes.
   3. A Cell Differentiation Specialist – epigenome turns genes off or on to direct which proteins different types of cells make, which determines the cell type/function
      a. All cells contain the full complement of genes but only the proteins needed in a particular cell are made in that cell.
      b. Example would be hemoglobin that is made in red blood cells
   4. How Epigenetic Regulation Works
      a. The epigenome consists of histone proteins and methyl groups that can interact with the DNA in such a way that certain gene sequences are actively making protein and others are silent.
      b. Chromosome Structural Proteins in Gene Expression
         1. Histone proteins were thought to be just "spools" that condense DNA but now researchers realize that histones actively control gene expression (see Figure C11-1).
         2. Perhaps the diet can influence how the histone proteins control DNA gene expression.
      c. A Broccoli Phytochemical Example
         1. Studies examine how the anticancer agent sulforafane in broccoli may affect the histone proteins in cancerous cells.
         2. Histone proteins silence DNA gene sequences that should be active in controlling cell growth, which leads to the cells becoming cancerous.
         3. The sulforafane in broccoli apparently reverses the cancerous alterations in the behavior of the histone proteins and reinstates control of cell division.
         4. Other phytochemicals may also affect epigenetic activities in a way that prevents cancer.
      d. DNA Methyl Groups and Gene Regulation
         1. Methyl groups are organic molecules that silence DNA gene sequence expression.
         2. When methyl groups are absent from a gene, it is expressed (makes proteins).
      e. B Vitamins and Methyl Groups
         1. Too little or too much folate in the diet may lead to too little methylation of DNA, which may make gene sequences more active than they should be.
         2. Such genes could be active and cause a cell to grow when it should not grow.
         3. The 2 mice in the photo on p. 460 have identical DNA but they don't look alike.
            a. Both produce a gene that produces fat, yellow pups but their gene expression was altered during gestation.
            b. The mother of the lean brown mouse received folate and vitamin B_{12}.
            c. The gene for yellow and fat was silenced but its DNA sequence was not changed!

5. Can Adults Modify Their Epigenome? – Eating a nutritious diet throughout life may influence the epigenome such that the correct set of DNA gene sequences is active, cells grow normally, and other disease processes can be prevented.
   a. Adults who ingest aflatoxin from mold develop liver cancer at a higher rate.
   b. The aflatoxin may remove methyl groups from both histone proteins and the DNA, which may trigger the cancer.
   c. Identical twins have very similar DNA but develop different diseases as a result of environmental impacts on their epigenomes.
   d. Figure 11-3 shows an epigenome timeline.

D. Arguments Surrounding Genetic Testing (see Table C11-2)
   1. In order for people to take advantage of nutritional genomics, they will need to undergo genetic testing.
   2. Who should have access to this genetic information?
   3. Is genetic testing a cost-effective way to improve public health?
   4. Could DNA information be misused?

E. Nutritional Genomics Fraud
   1. There is concern that unethical companies could get people's genetic information and coerce them into buying expensive, useless supplements.
   2. As noted in Chapter 1, people need to exercise caution when purchasing supplements.

F. Conclusion
   1. Information from genomics will likely reinforce the need for a well-planned diet of whole foods.
   2. Registered dieticians may be able to customize an eating plan based on genomics and a person's risk for a variety of diseases.

Worksheet 11-1: Organic Granola Label Analysis

Instructions: Use the granola cereal label to answer the questions that follow on a separate sheet of paper.

Nutrition Facts

Serving Size 1/2 cup (30g)
Servings Per Container about 11

Amount Per Serving	Cereal	+ 125 ml fortified skim milk
Calories	130	170
Calories from Fat	40	45
	% Daily Value**	
Total Fat 4.5g*	**7%**	**7%**
Saturated Fat 1g	**5%**	**5%**
Trans Fat 0g		
Cholesterol 0mg	**0%**	**0%**
Sodium 35mg	**1%**	**4%**
Total Carbohydrate 21g	**7%**	**9%**
Dietary Fiber 2g	**8%**	**8%**
Sugars 7g		
Protein 2g		
Vitamin A	0%	6%
Vitamin C	0%	0%
Calcium	2%	15%
Iron	6%	6%

* Amount in cereal. One half cup skim milk contributes an additional 40 calories, 65mg sodium, 6g total carbohydrate (6g sugars), and 4g protein.

**Percent Daily Values are based on a 2,000 calorie diet. Your Daily Values may be higher or lower depending on your calorie needs.

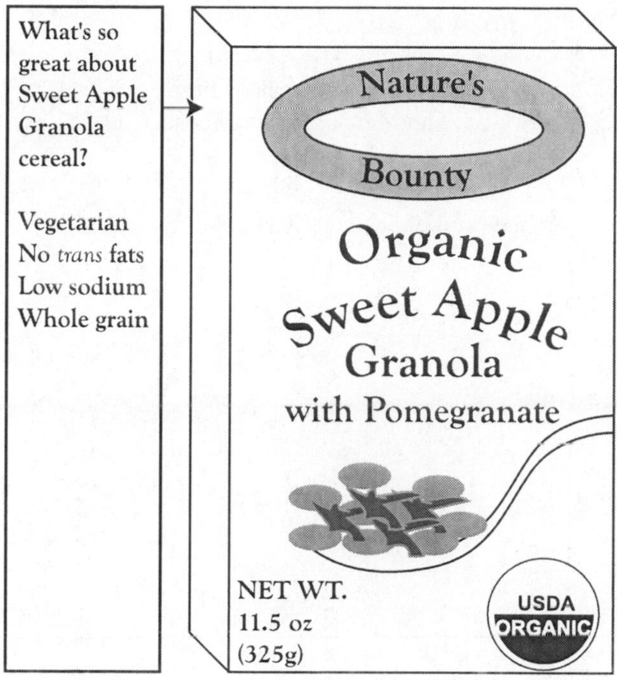

INGREDIENTS: Organic rolled oats, organic evaporated cane juice, organic crispy rice (organic brown rice flour, organic evaporated cane juice, sea salt, organic molasses, organic rice bran extract) organic soy oil, organic diced apple, organic pomegranate juice concentrate, organic oat syrup solids, organic dried coconut, organic acai powder.

May contain traces of peanuts, tree nuts or soy.

1. Explain how each of the claims on the side panel of this label can impact health in the body.
2. How might the organic claims made by this product benefit the health of the body in the long term?
3. Why is the amount of cholesterol in this product listed as 0%?
4. What are the sources of saturated fat in this product?
5. a. Why are lower intakes of saturated fat important to maintain the health of the body?
   b. What are the benefits for the cardiovascular system?
   c. What are any other benefits?

Worksheet 11-2: Intake Analysis—Diet and Disease

Eating Plan A (1 Day's Intake)	**Eating Plan E (1 Day's Intake)**
1 cup of Corn Flakes cereal 1 cup of 1% fat milk 2 cups of coffee 2 slices of whole-wheat bread 2 ounces thinly sliced baked ham 2 ounces cheddar jalapeño cheese 8 ounces chocolate milk 3 12-ounce beers 2 beef and cheese enchiladas	¾ cup Nature's Path flax cereal ½ cup soy milk ½ cup acai juice + seltzer water 1 medium banana 12 ounces coffee 6 ounces 6-grain yogurt ½ cup blueberries ¾ cup raspberries 2 Mushroom Lover's Veggie Burgers 1 cup roasted carrot soup ½ cup sweet green peppers 6 carrot sticks 2 whole-wheat wasa crackers 8 ounces Vruit juice 8 ounces soy milk 1 peanut butter Fiber One Bar 6 ounces grilled salmon 10 cooked asparagus spears 6 ounces white wine ½ cup olives ½ cup sun-dried tomatoes ½ cup whole-wheat angel hair pasta ¼ cup mixed nuts
Eating Plan F (1 Day's Intake) 2 scrambled eggs 1 cup whole milk 2 slices bacon 2 1-ounce Slim Jims 6 ounces lean ground beef 2 ounces provolone cheese ¼ cup blue cheese dressing 12 ounces water 2 ounces cheddar cheese cubes 6 ounces grilled chicken breasts 1 scrambled egg 1 cup lettuce ½ cup blue cheese dressing 2 ounces pork rinds 12 ounces water	**Eating Plan G (1 Day's Intake)** 1 cup honey dew melon 1 cup fresh strawberries 1 large apple ½ avocado ½ cup sweet green peppers ½ cup sweet red peppers ¼ cup black olives 1 medium orange 1 medium banana 1 cup boiled green beans 10 cooked asparagus spears 1 cup sautéed mushrooms 1 cup kidney beans ¼ cup dried apricots ¼ cup dried Craisins 5 dried, pitted dates

Look at Eating Plans A, E, and F:

1. a. Which of these eating plans could help lower blood pressure or reduce the risk of developing high blood pressure?

   b. What nutrients does the chosen eating plan provide that could lower blood pressure?

   c. What nutrient does the chosen eating plan limit that could also help lower blood pressure through its restriction?

2. a. Which of these eating plans is considered atherogenic and why?

   b. How could this chosen eating plan be modified to reduce its atherogenic potential?

Look at Eating Plans A, E, F, and G:

3. a. Which of these eating plans contains the greatest amount of fiber?

   b. What are the sources of fiber in the eating plan chosen in 3.a.?

   c. What conditions can be prevented by adequate fiber intake?

4. a. Which of these eating plans contributes the most calcium?

   b. What are the sources of calcium in the selected eating plan?

   c. What health conditions can adequate calcium levels possibly prevent?

5. a. How could Eating Plans A and F be modified to reduce their cancer causing potential?

   b. To reduce their saturated fat contents?

Worksheet 11-3: Chapter 11 Review Crossword Puzzle

Across:	Down:
1. _____ are structural proteins associated with chromosomes that can also influence whether a gene is expressed (made into an active protein) or silenced. 4. A condition in which the body's cells are resistant to the effects of insulin from the pancreas in the majority of cases 5. A diet with adequate _____ fibers may help reduce the risk of cardiovascular disease. 6. The spread of cancerous cells beyond the point of tumor formation 8. A condition in which blood lipids like cholesterol can be deposited in the walls of the blood vessels 10. A diet that increases LDL levels in the blood and can also increase the risk of cardiovascular disease 11. The study of changes in how genes function without any changes in the sequence of the genes 12. The sudden shutting off of the blood flow to the brain by a thrombus, embolism, or the bursting of a vessel	2. The _____ blood pressure number is the pressure against the artery wall when the heart muscle is contracting. 3. _____ deficiency can weaken the body's skin and membrane defenses against infection. 6. DNA _____ can influence how a gene is expressed (turned on or off) in a developing individual. 7. The _____ blood pressure number is the pressure against the artery wall when the heart muscle is relaxing. 9. A type of disease that results from the interaction of genetics, nutrition, and past or current diseases

Handout 11-1: Functions of the Body's White Blood Cells

Phagocytes	Lymphocytes		Granulocytes
	T-Cells (cell-mediated immunity)	**B-Cells (humoral immunity)**	**Neutrophils, Basophils, and Eosinophils**
• Engulf foreign organisms • Activate lymphocytes • Suppress appetite • Induce fever and malaise • Display antigens	• Recognize antigens and send chemical signals • Stimulate T-cell development • Release chemicals that kill pathogens • Suppress immune response when battle against infection has been won	• Produce antibodies • Kill invaders directly or make them easy targets for phagocytic white blood cells	• Destroy any pathogen by phagocytosis (neutrophils) • Allow easier movement of white blood cells to the site of injury (basophils) • Destroy parasites (eosinophils)

Handout 11-2: Effects of Malnutrition on the Body's Immune System

Immune System Component	Effects of Malnutrition	Nutrient Deficiencies that Cause These Conditions
Skin	Thinned or cracked on the surface, with less connective tissue	Vitamin A, vitamin C, copper
Mucous membranes	Microvilli in small intestine flattened; antibody secretions reduced	Vitamin A, protein
GI tract	Atrophy of intestinal cells	Protein
Lymph tissues	Thymus gland, lymph nodes, and spleen reduced in size; T-cell areas depleted of lymphocytes	Vitamin A, vitamin C, protein
Phagocytosis	Pathogen kill time prolonged	Vitamin A, vitamin C, protein
Cell-mediated immunity	Circulating, active T-cells reduced	Vitamin A, vitamin C, protein
Humoral immunity	Circulating immunoglobulin levels normal; antibody response possibly impaired	Vitamin A, vitamin C, protein, vitamin B_{12}, and folate

Handout 11-3: Causes of Malnutrition in HIV Infection

Reduced Food Intake	Accelerated Nutrient Losses
Drug therapy causes anorexia, nausea, and vomiting; food aversions arise	Cancers of the GI tract and cancer therapy lead to malabsorption
Lethargy and exhaustion drain the energy to eat	Chronic or recurrent diarrhea interferes with nutrient absorption
Fever, pain, and infection cause anorexia	Malabsorption limits nutrient absorption
Psychological stresses such as fever and depression make eating seem unimportant	Low serum albumin levels provide too few nutrient carriers
Oral infections (thrush) alter taste sensations, cause pain, and reduce saliva flow	Malnutrition leads to diarrhea and malabsorption
Oral infections (herpes virus) cause painful mouth ulcers and problems with chewing and swallowing	Drug therapy causes diarrhea and malabsorption
Esophageal infections and lesions make swallowing difficult	High gastric pH limits absorption and promotes bacterial growth, leading to infections
Kaposi's sarcoma (a cancer associated with AIDS) causes esophageal lesions and obstructions	Infections and fever accelerate metabolism (high BMR)

Handout 11-4: Designing an Anti-Inflammatory Diet

What Is Inflammation?

- Inflammation is the body's natural response against injury.
- When there is an injury to the tissues, the body responds with an acute inflammation response in which:
  1) Blood vessels dilate.
  2) Fluid leaks out of the blood vessels and into the injured tissue area.
  3) Hormones, proteins, and white blood cells travel to the area to destroy harmful bacteria or substances and then heal the tissue.
- Inflammation produces pain, redness, heat, and swelling in an area where injury has occurred.

Why Is Inflammation a Problem?

- Acute inflammation is a short-term, protective response that is not bad for the body. It can help the body kill microbes by allowing white blood cells to access the site of infection, can help remove damaged tissue, and promotes healing.
- Chronic inflammation is a low-level inflammation that persists and is not often felt by the person. It may occur deep in the body's tissues or blood vessels. Inflamed tissues produce hormone-like molecules, free radicals, blood clotting factors, and other chemical mediators that affect the function of the body's tissues.
- Chronic inflammation has been associated with some cancers, cardiovascular disease, arthritis, asthma, high blood pressure, insulin resistance, and diabetes.
- Chronic inflammation may cause plaque in the arteries to dislodge, travel through the blood, and cause blockage of blood flow in the heart or brain.

How Can Chronic Inflammation Be Detected?

- A protein called C-reactive protein (CRP) has been associated with increased risk of cardiovascular disease.
- An increased level of a protein called interleukin-6 (IL-6) is associated with increased immune response activity and chronic inflammation.
- Increased levels of a protein called tumor necrosis factor (TNF) may also be associated with chronic inflammation.
- CRP, IL-6, and TNF can be detected by blood tests.

How Can Diet or Lifestyle Affect the Occurrence of Chronic Inflammation?

- Vitamins A (beta-carotene), C, and E are antioxidants that may reduce the levels of inflammation in the blood vessels. Antioxidants neutralize free radicals that can react with low-density lipoprotein (LDL) deposits in the blood vessels. These protective vitamins can be obtained by eating fruits and vegetables every day. Supplements of vitamins C and E are not recommended.
- Consume more linolenic acid, EPA, and DHA (omega-3 fatty acids) that produce the anti-inflammatory group of prostaglandins found in cell membranes of the body's tissues. These nutrients can be found in cold-water fish, flaxseed, nuts, seeds, tofu, and leafy greens.
- Reduce the amount of linoleic acid (omega-6 fatty acids) in the diet. These fatty acids come from corn, cottonseed, safflower, and sunflower oils found in processed foods.
- People should take in omega-3: omega-6 fatty acids in a 1:1 ratio if possible.
- Decrease intake of saturated fatty acids that can compete with omega-3 fatty acids that reduce inflammation.
- Lose excess weight, especially fat around the abdomen, because this visceral fat may increase the level of inflammatory compounds in the blood and blood vessels.

References:

Special Supplement: *Tuft's University Health & Nutrition Letter*. Volume 20 (3) May 2002

The Truth About Inflammation: *Dr. Andrew Weil's Self-Healing Letter*. November 2004, pages 4-5

Aubertin, Amy, M.S., R.D., Inflammation May Be Key Cause of Heart Disease and More. *Environmental Nutrition*. Volume 27 (7), pages 1 & 4.

Anti-Inflammatory Eating: *Tuft's University Health & Nutrition Letter*, Volume 21 (12), February 2004, pages 4-5.

Handout 11-5: High Blood Pressure—How to Deal With It

What Is High Blood Pressure?	• Consistent readings of >140/90 mm Hg
What Do the Numbers Mean?	• The higher number (systolic reading) measures the pressure on the blood vessels as the heart muscle is contracting • The lower number (diastolic reading) measures the pressure on the blood vessels as the heart muscle is relaxed
What Are the Risks of High Blood Pressure?	• Untreated high blood pressure can increase the risk of strokes, peripheral blood vessel disease, heart disease, or decreased mental function
What Is the Standard Medical Treatment?	• Diuretics, which increase the release of water from the body to decrease the blood volume • Beta-blockers, which decrease the force of the heart beat • Calcium channel blockers, which open the blood vessels and decrease the force of the heart beat • ACE (angiotensin-converting enzyme) inhibitors, which block the ACE from constricting blood vessels and increasing fluid volume to increase blood pressure
What Are Dietary or Lifestyle Treatments?	• Lose weight • Try the D.A.S.H. (Dietary Approaches to Stop Hypertension) plan that encourages one to eat fruits, vegetables, and whole grains; these foods supply a lot of calcium, magnesium, potassium, fiber, and vitamin C that may help reduce blood pressure • Get physically active, which may reduce stress, help with weight loss, and help make the blood vessels more elastic • Reduce sodium intake by reading labels carefully • Consume alcohol in moderation
What Is the Best Treatment?	• Doctors will encourage people to try to make diet or lifestyle changes; in many cases, these changes can significantly reduce blood pressure and may make medications unnecessary, at least initially • If medication is needed to control high blood pressure, lifestyle changes should still be carried out; this may reduce the required dosage of medication, which may in turn reduce any side-effects

References:

Castleman, Michael. *Blended Medicine: The Best Choices In Healing*. Rodale Press. 2000, pages 373-374.
Special Report: *Tufts University Health and Nutrition Letter*, Volume 21 (5). July 2003, pages 4-5.
Help For Hypertension: Lowering Blood Pressure: *Dr. Andrew Weil's Self Healing*. March 2003, pages 4-5.
Moore, Thomas, M.D. *The D.A.S.H. Diet for Hypertension*. Pocket Books. 2001

Chapter 12 – Food Safety and Food Technology

Quick List: IM Resources for Chapter 12

- **Class preparation resources:** learning objectives/key points, suggested activities and projects, lecture outline
- **Assignment materials:** **Related LO**
  - Critical thinking questions (with answer key) 12.1, 12.3, 12.4, 12.6
  - Discussion questions (with answers) for Controversy 12 .... 12.8
  - Worksheet 12-1: Label Analysis—Food Safety and Technology 12.5, 12.6
  - Worksheet 12-2: Intake Analysis—Food Safety 12.2, 12.4
  - Worksheet 12-3: Nutrient Additives—Can You Spot Them on the Label? 12.6
  - **New!** Worksheet 12-4: Chapter 12 Review Crossword Puzzle
- **Enrichment materials:**
  - Handout 12-1: How to Detect and Avoid Spoiled Foods[1] 12.1, 12.2
  - Handout 12-2: Why Salty and Sugary Foods Last 12.6

Chapter Learning Objectives and Key Points

12.1 **Describe two ways in which foodborne microorganisms can cause illness in the body, and describe ways, from purchase to table, in which consumers can reduce their risks of foodborne illnesses.**
Each year in the United States, tens of millions of people suffer mild to life-threatening symptoms caused by foodborne illnesses. These people are especially vulnerable to suffer serious harm from foodborne illnesses: pregnant women, infants, toddlers, older adults, and people with weakened immune systems. Despite government and industry efforts to safeguard the food supply, outbreaks of foodborne illnesses continue to occur. Consumers should carefully inspect foods before purchasing them. Foodborne illnesses are common, but the great majority of cases can be prevented. To protect themselves, consumers should remember the four cores: clean, separate, cook, chill.

12.2 **Identify foods that often cause foodborne illnesses, and describe ways of increasing their safety.**
Raw meats and poultry pose special microbial threats and so require special handling. Consuming raw eggs, milk, or seafood is too risky. Produce causes more foodborne illnesses today than in the past. Proper washing and refrigeration can minimize risks. Cooking ensures that sprouts are safe to eat. The FDA is working to improve the safety of imported foods. Honey should never be fed to infants. Leftovers can be safely stored when safety rules are followed.

12.3 **Name some recent advances aimed at reducing microbial food contamination, and describe their potential contribution to the safety of the U.S. food supply.**
Food irradiation kills bacteria, insects, molds, and parasites on foods. Consumers have concerns about the effects of irradiation on foods, workers, and the environment. Irradiation controls mold, sterilizes spices and teas, controls insects, extends shelf life, and destroys disease-causing bacteria. Scientific advances, such as research on high pressure processing, continuously improve food safety.

12.4 **Describe how pesticides enter the food supply, and suggest possible actions to reduce consumption of residues.**
Natural foods contain natural toxins that can be hazardous under some conditions. To avoid harm from toxins, eat all foods in moderation, treat toxins from all sources with respect, choose a variety of foods, and respect bans on seafood harvesting. Pesticides can be part of a safe food production process but can also be hazardous if mishandled. Consumers can take steps to minimize their ingestion of pesticide residues in foods. FDA-approved hormones, antibiotics, and other drugs are used to promote growth or increase milk production in conventionally grown animals. Antibiotic resistant bacteria pose a serious and growing threat. Persistent environmental contaminants present in food pose a small but significant risk to U.S. consumers. Mercury and other contaminants pose the greatest threat during pregnancy, lactation, and childhood.

12.5 **Discuss potential advantages and disadvantages associated with organic foods.**

---

[1] Contributed by Lori W. Turner, Ph.D., R.D., University of Alabama

12.6 **Name some functions served by food additives approved for use in the United States, and provide evidence concerning their safety.**
Food additives must be safe, effective, and measurable in the final product for FDA approval. Approved additives have wide margins of safety. Sugar and salt have the longest history of use as additives to prevent food spoilage. Nitrites and sulfites have advantages and drawbacks. People with PKU should avoid the nonnutritive sweetener aspartame. The flavor enhancer MSG may cause reactions in people with sensitivities to it. Fat replacers and artificial fats reduce the fat calories in processed foods, and the FDA deems them safe to consume. Olestra in large amounts can cause digestive distress. Incidental additives enter food during processing and are regulated; most do not constitute a hazard. Consumers should use only microwave-safe containers and wraps for microwaving food.

12.7 **Discuss several ways that food-processing techniques affect nutrients in foods.**

12.8 **Compare and contrast the advantages and disadvantages of food production by way of genetic modification and conventional farming.**

Critical Thinking Questions

1. *Distinguish between a foodborne infection and a food intoxication in terms of how they are caused.*

   A foodborne infection is caused by the ingestion of a pathogenic microbe and its subsequent growth within the body. For example, the *Salmonella* bacterium enters the small intestine, invades the walls of the small intestine, and causes an intense dysentery illness.

   A food intoxication is caused by the ingestion of a preformed toxin that is secreted by a living pathogenic microorganism. *Clostridium botulinum* produces a toxin that can cause paralysis. If someone ingests the bacteria before it produces toxin, they may not get sick, but if they ingest the toxin, they will get very ill. *Staphylococcus aureus*, a bacterium associated with skin infections, can also produce a toxin that cause food poisoning as well. See Table 12-2 for more examples of foodborne infections and intoxications.

2. *Describe any 3 precautions that consumers can take to protect themselves from foodborne infections or intoxications.*

   Customers can inspect food packages to ensure that they are intact. Cans should not be dented and plastic wrap should not be broken.

   Customers can also look at labels for freshness dates (as described in Table 12-4) and then determine the safest way to store the food item as shown in Table 12-7. As a rule, foods like meats that are ground and handled more are likely to have more bacteria or viruses in them and need to be used more quickly.

   Figure 12-4 illustrates safe cooking of foods to ensure that all foodborne pathogens or their toxins are destroyed. This ensures food safety. Foods need to be cooked at high temperatures to kill all bacteria or viruses. Foods also need to be stored in the refrigerator or freezer to stop the growth of any remaining bacteria. Foods should not be held at room temperature, at whicih many bacteria can grow and release toxins.

3. *Describe any 3 advances in food processing technology or packaging that can reduce the risk of foodborne illness.*

   Foods can be irradiated with high-energy beams of cobalt 60 that will kill microbes within the foods by destroying bacterial DNA. Irradiation also preserves foods.

   Modified atmosphere packaging (MAP) ensures that microbes or toxins from the air cannot get into a food. Some disease-causing bacterial species grow well in the absence of oxygen within MAP, so it is very important to store perishable foods in MAP in the refrigerator or freezer.

   Some food wraps also contain antimicrobial substances that can prevent the growth of disease-causing pathogens on food as well.

4. *Describe why foods imported from other countries may pose a greater pesticide hazard than locally grown foods or foods from other regions within the U.S.*

   The FDA (Food and Drug Administration) and the EPA (Environmental Protection Agency) regulate the levels of pesticides found within foods and out in the environment. The EPA sets limits for pesticides in foods and both the FDA and the USDA (U.S. Department of Agriculture) will test foods to see if they meet the EPA standards for pesticides. Other countries may have fewer restrictions on pesticide levels, and pesticides can remain on the crops even after transport. The USDA guidelines set strict standards for foods that can or cannot bear the "organic" label based on the presence or absence of pesticides in the food itself or its contributing ingredients. See Table 12-12 for a list of conventional produce items that contain the most pesticides.

5. *Why would food manufacturers use food additives on the GRAS list as opposed to introducing new additives to foods?*

   The FDA's GRAS (Generally Recognized as Safe) list names over 700 food additives that have been proven to not cause harm in people. A food manufacturer need not submit a food additive that is already on the GRAS list to safety testing. If they introduce a new additive, they have to provide results from extensive studies that prove that the additive is safe for human consumption. A new additive that involves any risk can only be used at a concentration at least 100 times lower than the highest concentration at which the risk is still zero (1/100).

6. *Why are antibiotics in animal feed such a big concern to the health of people?*

   Antibiotics are administered in animal feed to help reduce the risk of infection in large herds that are crowded together and to promote faster growth and greater meat production. The concern is that similar antibiotics are used to treat infections in people. Bacteria grow quickly and can mutate into strains resistant to the killing effects of the antibiotic drugs. If an *E. coli* bacterium becomes resistant to a particular antibiotic, the bacterium will continue to grow even if the drug is present. If this bacterium enters a person and causes an infection, the drugs used to treat the infection may not work because the bacterium is resistant to the drugs.

Controversy Discussion Questions

1. *Describe how a plant can be altered to have a pesticide "built" right into its cells.*

   Scientists can extract a piece of genetic information that encodes for a protein that can repel insects. They can place this gene into an expression vector (piece of DNA that produces proteins within a cell) and transfer it into a plant embryo such that the plant incorporates the pesticide protein. This protein can then be found in the leaves of the new plant and can act as a pesticide, which reduces the need for sprayed-on chemical pesticides. See Figure C12-2 for an illustrated explanation of rDNA technology.

2. *Why might pesticides that grow within a genetically modified plant be more of a concern than pesticides that are sprayed onto a conventional plant?*

   The answer to question one above explains how a pesticide can be placed into a plant using genetic engineering. The chemical pesticides that are sprayed onto a plant can be removed by washing and rinsing it. A pesticide protein or molecule that is part of a plant's structure cannot easily be removed since it is part of the cell. It is unknown whether such genetically engineered pesticide proteins can have harmful effects in people.

3. *Give an example of how selective breeding can change a typical food-bearing plant such as corn.*

   Selective breeding is the process by which plants that have desirable physical traits are purposefully cross-pollinated to produce offspring that have desirable traits as well. The original corn plants produced few seeds/kernels per ear of corn, but by finding plants that produced more seeds/kernels and cross-pollinating them over successive generations, it was possible to produce new corn plants with more seeds/kernels per ear of corn. This increases the nutrition that each ear of corn can provide to livestock or to people. Natural pollination of plants is more random and there is not as much selective pressure to produce plants with the desired traits in a short amount of time. (Natural selection favors traits conducive to the plant's survival as opposed to traits desirable to human consumers.)

4. a. *Why is out-crossing of genetically modified plants and wild weeds of concern?*

Out-crossing is the accidental pollination of a wild plant by a genetically engineered plant that has a pesticide protein within its cellular structure. This is a concern because pollen from GE crops can be spread to neighboring fields where wild plants grow. This would result in the natural pollination of the GE plant with the wild plant and would generate offspring with the GE trait and with the wild plant traits.

b. *What could be the consequence of such out-crossing?*

It might produce pesticide-resistant "super-weeds" if the plants pick up the genetically engineered protein gene from their GE plant parent along with the ability to grow quickly from their natural weed parent. They would then be resistant to insects and would need stronger chemical pesticides to control their growth.

Worksheet Answer Key

Worksheet 12-1: Label Analysis—Food Safety and Technology

1. "USDA organic" suggests that the ingredients that go into this product were grown without the use of synthetic pesticides or fertilizers and hormones, and had not been genetically engineered.
2. a. Salt, natural sodium phosphate, and annatto extract. (The first two cannot be "organic" because they are mineral compounds, not agricultural products.)
   b. They are called "organic" in the ingredients list.
3. Use organic milk and butter products.
4. a. Salt
   b. Salt prevents bacteria or other microorganisms from growing in the product during storage.
5. There is no *trans* fat and this product is a good source of protein and calcium.
6. a. This product contains milk and wheat ingredients and is made on equipment that is used to process eggs and soy products.
   b. Some people cannot digest milk or tolerate wheat gluten. Other people are allergic to egg, milk, and soy products.

Worksheet 12-2: Intake Analysis—Food Safety

1. a. Eating Plan H.
   b. This plan includes shellfish and seafood that can harbor bacterial or other types of contamination if they are not properly cooked.
2. The ground beef is a source of food-borne illness and should be cooked thoroughly. It could also be substituted with a piece of whole beef, chicken, or fish (well cooked).
3. a. heavy metal contamination: Salmon
   b. pesticide contamination: raspberries, blueberries, and carrots
   c. bacterial contamination: salmon, raspberries, and carrots
   d. The salmon can be purchased from a body of water with proven low levels of contamination. The salmon could be replaced with chicken or another source of protein (a).
   The berries and carrots could be purchased as organic or washed very well (b).
   The salmon and carrots should be cooked thoroughly, and the raspberries washed very well (c).
4. There is a good variety of fruits and vegetables. There are whole grains and yogurts included and protein from lower-fat sources.

Worksheet 12-4: Chapter 12 Review Crossword Puzzle

1. A: antibiotic; D: aspartame
2. norovirus
3. pesticides
4. somatotropin
5. Extrusion
6. A: bioaccumulation; D: botulism
7. foodborne
8. cyanogens
9. separate
10. aflatoxin
11. organic
12. stevia
13. nonnutritive

Learning Activities & Project Ideas

Activity 12-1: Food Safety[2] LO 12.1, 12.2
This activity gets students thinking about the potential hazards of the foods they eat.

Step one: Ask students to identify foods that they eat regularly and list them on the board or using projection equipment. Then ask students to name the potential hazards associated with these foods. These are to be specific microbial illnesses (bacteria or other contamination of foods that could make you ill).

Step two: Choose one of these foods and ask students to name at least three critical control points, from growing to consumption, at which a contaminant might enter ("Think about how you obtain this food and identify points at which it might become contaminated or allow microbial growth").

Step three: Finally, have students describe the preventative measures for each control point. Emphasize that the consumer's food handling practices are often the cause of food-borne illnesses.

Activity 12-2: Name that Food[3] LO 12.6
Students enjoy the classroom game of guessing a product from reading its ingredients label. This is especially effective when students bring in food labels. The instructor reads a vitamin supplement label, or a list of the chemicals in a natural food, such as an orange. (For example, water is hydrogen oxide and citric acid is 2-hydroxy-1,2,3-propanetricarboxylic acid.) Students quickly learn that a chemical name may sound formidable, but that the ingredient is not necessarily "bad." This activity could also be used in Chapter 4 when discussing the different names for sugar—many of which sound like scary chemical names.

Activity 12-3: Comparing Different Foods[4] LO 12.7
Have students make a table of values of selected nutrients such as vitamins for several foods that compares fresh, frozen, canned, dried, or other processes. Have students draw conclusions about how processing affects the contributions a food makes to a day's nutrient requirements.

Activity 12-4: Estimate Vitamin Losses[4] LO 12.7
Using a 24-hour recall, have students calculate the percent of daily requirement of the B vitamins and vitamin C that they consume if typical vitamin losses occur. For example, if a student consumes 85% of the daily requirement for vitamin C and there is a 10% loss from poor food storage, she only consumed 75% of the requirement for that day.

Chapter Lecture Outline

I. Introduction – The U.S. and Canada have some of the safest food supplies in the world but the importation of food from other parts of the world present a challenge.
   A. The Food and Drug Administration (FDA) is the major agency charged with monitoring the U.S. food supply. (Other agencies that monitor the U.S. food supply are noted in Table 12-1.)
   B. The FDA's ongoing areas of concern regarding the safety of our food supply include:
      1. Microbial foodborne illness, which has affected 48 million U.S. people
      2. Natural toxins in foods
      3. Residues in foods, which can be of 3 types:
         a. Environmental contaminants
         b. Pesticide residues
         c. Animal drugs such as hormone and antibiotics
      4. Nutrients in foods, which may include artificial colors and preservatives
      5 Intentional approved food additives
      6. Genetically modified foods

[2] Contributed by Peter C. DuBois, M.Ed., Lorain County Community College

[3] Contributed by I. K. Howard of Houghton College

[4] Contributed by Lori W. Turner, Ph.D., R.D., University of Alabama

II. Microbes and Food Safety
  A. Many people assume that foodborne illnesses are not serious but in fact they can be life threatening.
    1. Some infections do not respond to antimicrobial drugs.
    2. Foodborne illnesses can be lethal in people who are malnourished or who have diminished immunity.
  B. How Do Microbes in Food Cause Illness in the Body?
    1. Microorganisms (Table 12-2) can cause foodborne illness by infection or by intoxication.
      a. Infection – When the microorganism (e.g., *Salmonella* bacteria, hepatitis virus) gets past the body's defenses, infects the tissues of the human body, and multiplies there
      b Intoxication – When the microorganism in the food produces enterotoxins or neurotoxins, poisonous substances that cause harm ranging from stomach pain to death
        1. *Staphylococcus aureus* and *Clostridium botulinum* produce toxins.
        2. *Clostridium botulinum* grows in anaerobic conditions and produces a toxin.
        3. Botulism can paralyze muscles and requires immediate medical attention.
      c. Table 12-3 describes dangerous symptoms of foodborne illnesses.
  C. Food Safety from Farm to Table
    1. Figure 12-1 summarizes the path that food takes from the farm to the table.
      a. Commercially prepared food is usually safe, but an outbreak of illness from this source often makes the news because outbreaks can affect many people at once.
      b. Dairy farmers rely on pasteurization to make milk safe to consume but it still needs refrigeration because all bacteria are not killed.
      c. Microbes from animal wastes or sick farm workers could contaminate foods from the fields.
    2. Attention on *E. coli*
      a. The dangerous types of *E. coli* are those that produce Shiga toxin such as O157:H7.
      b. Causes bloody diarrhea, severe cramps, dehydration, and sometimes hemolytic-uremic syndrome
      c. Associated with eating tainted meat, raw milk, or contaminated produce
      d. Strains of Shiga toxin-producing *E. coli* (STEC) have caused outbreaks of foodborne illness from raw foods or ground beef.
    3. Food Industry Controls – include daily inspection of meat processing plants by USDA inspectors
      a. A Hazard Analysis Critical Control Point (HACCP) plan must be developed and followed by all food manufacturers to prevent foodborne illness outbreaks at the source.
      b. The HACCP system has reduced the rate of *Salmonella* outbreaks and *E. coli* contaminations.
    4. Grocery Safety for Consumers
      a. Includes checking expiration dates on packages and making sure that food packaging is not damaged and frozen items are solidly frozen
      b. Make sure that egg shells are not cracked.
  D. Safe Food Practices for Individuals
    1. Introduction
      a. Three requirements of disease-causing bacteria: Warmth, moisture, nutrients
      b Any food with an "off" appearance or smell should not be consumed.
    2. Core Practice #1: Clean
      a. Proper hand washing with soap and water as shown in Figure 12-3 prevents illness.
      b. To eliminate microbes on surfaces, utensils, and cleaning items, you can:
        1. Use 1 tsp bleach per quart of water for washing sponges and surfaces
        2. Wash with soapy hot water (at least 140°F)
        3. Use an automatic dishwasher, which uses heat and the chlorine in the water to reduce the number of microbes
        4. Use a microwave to kill microbes on sponges
    3. Core Practice #2: Separate
      a. Keeping raw foods separate means preventing cross-contamination of foods.
      b. Use separate cutting boards so that the juices of one raw food don't contaminate other foods.
      c. Put cooked burgers on a clean plate, not the plate used for raw meat.
    4. Core Practice #3: Cook
      a. Keep hot foods hot and make sure that the food reaches a hot enough temperature on the inside.
      b. Use a food thermometer to test the temperature of cooked foods as shown in Figure 12-4.
      c. Keep foods at 140°F until they are ready to serve.

5. Core Practice #4: Chill
    a. Use an insulated bag to keep foods cold during the ride home from the grocery store.
    b. Always chill prepared or cooked foods in shallow containers, not deep ones.
    c. Keep perishable buffet items on ice.
    d. Table 12-7 shows recommended storage times for foods in the refrigerator.

III. Which Foods Are Most Likely to Cause Illness?
  A. Protein Foods – are susceptible to bacterial contamination due to processing and to the moisture and nutrients found in the meat
    1. Follow these safety rules (see Figure 12-5):
        a. Cook all meat and poultry to the suggested temperatures.
        b. Never defrost meat or poultry at room temperature or in warm water since bacteria can grow.
        c. Never microwave a large meatloaf since cool spots can allow bacteria to grow.
        d. Do not use the same utensils for handling raw meat & foods that are eaten raw like tomatoes.
        e. Wash hands well after handling raw meat.
        f. Not related to sanitation, but animal diseases like "mad cow disease" or, more properly, bovine spongiform encephalopathy (BSE), can pose a worry for meat eaters
    2. Ground Meats – A safe hamburger is cooked well-done (internal temperature of 160°F) and has juices that run clear.
    3. Stuffed Poultry – Stuffing within a turkey or chicken could become contaminated by bacteria within the bird's cavity.
        a. Follow the Fight Bac principles of clean, separate, cook, and chill.
        b. Cook any raw meat, poultry, or shellfish before adding it to the stuffing.
        c. Cook the stuffing to 165°F.
    4. Eggs
        a. *Salmonella* or other bacteria from the digestive tract of normal chickens may contaminate raw, unpasteurized eggs, or other foods such as fresh juices, salsas, meats, sprouts, fruit, and salads.
        b. About 30% of *Salmonella* infections come from eating undercooked eggs.
        c. The FDA requires egg farmers to use methods to control *Salmonella* bacteria on and in the eggs.
        d. Raw cookie dough is hazardous but the slice- and-bake dough is pasteurized and so safe to eat raw.
    5. Seafood
        a. Properly cooked fish and other seafood sold in the U.S. and Canada are safe from microbial threats.
        b. Raw seafood can cause illness from viruses, worms, flukes, bacteria
        c. These pathogens are more common due to the increase in the population along the shorelines.
        d. 90% of waters off of the U.S. coast contain disease-causing viruses.
        e. People who eat sushi need to be very careful to avoid pathogens.
        f. See Table 12-8 for raw seafood myths and truths.
    6. Raw Milk Products
        a. Unpasteurized milk, sold as "health food," causes a majority of the dairy-related foodborne illnesses.
        b. Milk sterilized by an ultra-high temperature treatment doesn't need refrigeration until it is opened.
  B. Raw Produce
    1. Introduction
        a. Foods consumed raw, such as lettuce, spinach, tomatoes, and scallions, that grow close to the ground are susceptible to contamination from animal waste runoff.
        b. In 2011, 30 people died from an infection caused by *Listeria*-contaminated cantaloupe.
        c. Produce may need to be scrubbed because rinsing may not dislodge the biofilm created by *E. coli.*
    2. Precut Salads and Vegetables – triple-washed, often treated with chlorine or ozone but should refrigerated until they are opened
    3. Melons and Berries – have crevices that can contain bacteria
        a. It is important to rinse berries for at least ten seconds to remove bacteria (see Table 12-9).
        b. Figure 12-7 depicts the warning displayed on unpasteurized juice containers.
    4. Sprouts – Alfalfa, radish, and clover sprouts may contain *E. coli* or *Salmonella* and should be cooked before consumption.

C. Other Foods
1. Imported Foods and Travel – Produce may be imported from countries that do not adhere to safe growing practices.
   a. About two thirds of produce and 80% of seafood is imported into the U.S. but only 1% of it is subject to inspection.
      1. Such fresh produce may be irrigated with water containing human-borne pathogens.
      2. Most canned and processed foods are safe to consume.
      3. Regulators require certain foods to have a country of origin label.
   b. People who travel to places with lower sanitation standards have about a 50% chance of getting traveler's diarrhea.
      1. It is important to wash hands frequently, drink only bottled or canned beverages, peel one's own fruits, and skip salads.
      2. So boil it, cook it, peel it, or forget it
2. Honey
   a. Can contain spores of *Clostridium botulinum* that can germinate and grow in the human body to produce the deadly *botulinum* toxin
   b. Adults are usually protected by stomach acid but infants under 1 year of age should never be fed honey.
3. Picnics and Lunch Bags – are convenient but there are some simple steps to keep their contents safe:
   a. Choose foods that are safe without refrigeration like whole fruits, vegetables, breads, crackers, and canned foods to open and use right away.
   b. Keep meat, egg, cheese, or seafood sandwiches cold until eaten.
   c. Use thermal lunch bags; freeze beverages to pack with the foods.
   d. Mayonnaise does not actually spoil easily due to its higher acid content.
4. Take-Out Foods and Leftovers
   a. Store leftovers promptly and properly.
   b. Reheat them to 165°F.
   c. Follow the 2, 2, and 4 rules of leftover safety: Within 2 hours of cooking, refrigerate food in shallow containers about 2 inches deep, and use it up within 4 days or toss it out.
   d. Table 12-10 lists more food safety myths and truths.

IV. Advances in Microbial Food Safety – These advances may offer benefits, but some also often raise concerns among consumers.

A. Is Irradiation Safe?
1. Food irradiation has been extensively evaluated over the past 50 years, approved in over 40 countries, and approved by numerous health agencies, including the World Health Organization (WHO) and the American Medical Association.
2. Low doses protect consumers from foodborne illnesses by:
   a. Controlling mold in grains that can produce aflatoxin
   b. Sterilizing spices and teas
   c. Controlling insects
   d. Extending shelf life in fresh fruits and vegetables
   d. Destroying disease-causing bacteria in fresh and frozen meats
3. How Irradiation Works
   a. Irradiation exposes foods to gamma rays from a cobalt 60 source.
   b. Disrupts bacterial DNA, protein, and other structures and so kills them
   c. It delays ripening in fresh fruits and vegetables.
4. Irradiation Effects on Foods
   a. Does not make foods radioactive or change taste/texture of approved foods
   b. Dried herbs can withstand sterilization.
5. Consumer Concerns about Irradiation – Concerns include:
   a. Fear that food will be radioactive and cause harm (which is false)
   b. Requires transporting radioactive materials, training workers to handle them safely and dispose of spent wastes
   c. Unscrupulous food manufacturers might use the technology to make old or tainted food seem wholesome.

d. Labeling of irradiated foods: The "radura" logo is the international symbol for foods treated with irradiation.

B. Other Technologies – Several other technologies have potential to resolve some of the threat from contamination of food products:
   1. Improved Testing and Surveillance – Improved automated testing and surveillance methods have reduced the risks of foodborne illnesses, especially *E. coli* illnesses.
   2. Modified Atmosphere Packaging
      a. Modified atmosphere packaging (MAP) uses plastics that prevent oxygen in the air from affecting the foods.
      b. By excluding oxygen, the MAP:
         1. Reduces the growth of oxygen-dependent microbes
         2. Prevents discoloration of produce
         3. Prevents spoilage of fats by rancidity
         4. Slows ripening of produce
      c. Foods in MAP still need to be refrigerated to prevent the growth of anaerobic bacteria.
   3. High Pressure and Ultrasound
      a. Used on deli meats, applesauce, and orange juice to kill norovirus and hepatitis virus
      b. Limited use due to expensive equipment and potential flavor and texture changes in meat with extensive treatment
   4. Antimicrobial Wraps and Films – may kill bacteria that come in contact with foods
      a. A biodegradable wrap from milk whey protein is in use.
      b. Other films are made of fruit or vegetable purees with a dose of cinnamon or oregano extract, which is a natural antimicrobial.

V. Toxins, Residues, and Contaminants in Foods – The FDA, along with the Environmental Protection Agency (EPA), regulates many chemicals that occur in foods as a result of human activities.

A. Natural Toxins in Foods
   1. Some toxins occur naturally too.
   2. Nature has provided many plants with natural poisons to fend off diseases, insects, and other predators.
   3. Herbs and Cabbages
      a. The herb sassafras contains a carcinogen and liver toxin.
      b. Cabbage, turnips, mustard greens, radishes – goitrogens
   4. Foods with Cyanogens – precursor to cyanide in cassava, fruit seeds/pits
   5. Potatoes – contain solanine, a powerful, bitter, narcotic-like substance; peeling the potato will remove the solanine
   6. Seafood Red Tide Toxin – Seafood that has been exposed to red tide toxin from algal blooms contains a potent toxin that can cause paralysis.
   7. To avoid poisoning, eat all foods in moderation and choose a variety.

B. Pesticides
   1. Pesticides help ensure the survival of food crops but the damage pesticides do to the environment and humans is considerable and increasing.
      a. Farmers are still losing large amount of crops to insects
      b. Pesticides can pose additional hazards to people who manufacture, transport, and apply pesticides to crops.
   2. Do Pesticides on Foods Pose a Hazard to Consumers?
      a. Pesticide residues on agricultural products can survive processing and are often present in and on foods served to people.
      b. Laboratory animals, given large doses of pesticides, can develop birth defects, sterility, tumors, organ damage, and central nervous system issues
      c. Figure 12-8 shows how pesticides can accumulate in the foods as they get processed.
   3. Especially Vulnerable: Infants and Children
      a. Children have immature detoxifying systems.
      b. Infants and children are particularly susceptible to pesticides due to their small body size.
      c. Children are more apt to play on lawns that are treated with pesticides.
      d. Children consume more food relative to their body weight and so pesticide toxins can build up quickly in their systems.

   e. Table 12-11 lists ways to reduce pesticide residue intakes.
4. Regulation of Pesticides
   a. The EPA sets a reference dose for the maximum pesticide residues allowable on foods.
   b. There are reference doses set for more than 300 pesticides allowed on U.S. crops.
   c. The limits generally represent between 1/100 & 1/1,000 of the reference dose that is found to cause no adverse health effects in laboratory animals.
5. Pesticide-Resistant Insects
   a. There are insect pests that have become resistant to the effects of the pesticides.
   b. This illustrates the need to find alternatives to more powerful pesticides.
6. Natural Pesticides
   a. Natural pesticides found in some plants leave less persistent residues in the environment than most man-made ones.
   b. Nicotine in tobacco plant leaves is a natural insecticide.
   c. Advances in biotechnology have reduced the need for pesticides sprayed on many crops.
   d. People should choose organic foods, which don't utilize pesticides.

C. A Consumer Guide to Understanding Organic Foods
1. Introduction
   a. Sales of certified organic foods have risen and totaled $28.6 billion in 2011.
   b. Consumers are willing to pay 10 to 40% more since organic food does not have pesticides added and is not genetically modified.
2. Organic Rules
   a. Foods are certified "organic" if the producer of the food adheres to strict guidelines at every step of production from the seeds in the ground to the type of fertilizer that is used.
   b. Figure 12-9 defines terms found on organic food labels.
   c. The National Organic Program develops, implements, & administers standards for organic foods.
   d. Compliance problems are common and this group is working to close loopholes.
3. Pesticide Residues—They're Everywhere
   a. A diet of organic foods measurably reduces pesticide exposure.
   b. About 25% of organic foods may be grown in soil that contains pesticides due to a prior application of a pesticide that did not easily break down or to spray drift from nearby conventional farms.
   c. Not known if the tolerance limit set for a pesticide is of any risk to a sensitive individual
   d. A typical pesticide exposure in the U.S. is 10,000 times below the level at which risks begin to rise.
   e. Children are more sensitive to the effects of pesticides.
4. To Bean or Not To Bean
   a. Table 12-12 lists the 12 foods that are most likely to be contaminated with pesticides.
   b. It may be wise to buy organic versions of these if the budget allows but conventional foods are safe.
5. Nutrient Composition
   a. There are no significant differences in nutrient composition between organic and conventional foods.
   b. Organic foods may contain more phytochemicals than conventionally grown foods since these crops need the phytochemicals to fight off insects.
   c. Organic candy bars and fried snack chips are no more nutritious (or less fattening) than ordinary treats.
6. Environmental Benefits – Organic foods are grown by using the techniques of sustainable agriculture that produce food without environmental harm.
   a. Producers rotate crops and use predators to eliminate insect pests.
   b. Poultry can be produced by animals that are allowed to live in more natural surroundings.
   c. Animals do not need antibiotics and growth hormones to produce high-quality meat and eggs.
5. Organics' Potential Pitfalls
   a. For microbial safety, certified organic foods test about the same as conventionally produced foods.
   b. Consumers may still be exposed to dangerous microorganisms if manure is not sterilized before use.
   c. Organic ingredients from other countries are cheaper but the farms are difficult to inspect.

   d. Shipping organic ingredients over long distances violates principles of sustainability.
6. Moving Ahead
   a. Buy conventional produce and wash well.
   b. If you can afford organics, enjoy them.
   c. Ultimately, choose nutritious produce in abundance.

D. Animal Drugs—What Are the Risks?
1. Introduction
   a. Consumer groups express concern about drugs given to livestock that produce food.
   b. Of particular concern: Hormones, antibiotics, drugs that contain arsenic compounds
2. Livestock and Antibiotic-Resistant Microbes
   a. Farmers administer antibiotics to animals to prevent infections in crowded conditions and to promote faster growth.
   b. Antibiotic overuse fosters antibiotic resistance in bacteria, threatening human health.
   c. New federal voluntary guidelines urge farmers to use antibiotics only in cases of infection.
3. Growth Hormone in Meat and Milk
   a. Bovine somatotropin (bST) causes cattle to produce more meat and milk on less feed than untreated cattle.
   b. This may have an environmental benefit if fewer cattle are grazing.
   c. The FDA and WHO have both deemed products from treated cattle to be safe.
   d. Another drug, IGF-I (insulin-like growth factor), is also used.
   e. Tests of conventional milk, hormone-free milk, and organic milk reveal no differences in the levels of antibiotics, bacteria, hormones, or nutrients.
4. Arsenic in Food Animals
   a. Arsenic drugs are used to promote growth in chickens and other livestock.
   b. Chickens are given small doses of arsenic that inhibit the growth of parasites that would otherwise inhibit the growth of the chicken.
   c. Rice can also be a source of arsenic.

E. Environmental Contaminants (Table 12-13)
1. Harmfulness of Contaminants
   a. Persistent environmental contaminants pose a significant, but generally small, threat to the safety of food.
   b. These contaminants can accumulate within species further up the food chain (known as bioaccumulation), as shown in Figure 12-10.
   c. The toxic effect of a chemical depends on its inherent toxicity and the degree of human exposure to the chemical.
2. Mercury in Seafood
   a. Minamata disease – The effects of mercury contamination can be severe, as when 120 people in Minamata, Japan developed a strange illness.
      1. They developed blindness, deafness, loss of coordination, progressive mental impairment
      2. Due to discharge of mercury into the water from a manufacturing plant
   b. The FDA and EPA warn people to limit intake of fish from mercury-contaminated waters.

VI. Are Food Additives Safe? – The 3,000 or so food additives approved for use in the U.S. are strictly controlled and well-studied for safety.

A. Regulations Governing Additives
1. Overview – a manufacturer must test a new additive and satisfy the FDA that the additive is effective and can be detected and measured in the final food product
   a. The manufacturer has to prove that the additive is safe to consume.
   b. The FDA has the responsibility for deciding which additives are permitted in foods.
   c. Manufacturers must comply with many regulations that ensure safety for consumers.
   d. Table 12-14 lists examples of food additives.
2. The GRAS List
   a. Many additives were exempted from complying with rules set by the FDA because they had been in use for a long time and their use entailed no known hazards.
   b. Some 700 substances are on the GRAS List (generally recognized as safe).
   c. No additives are permanently approved; all are periodically reviewed.

3. The Margin of Safety
    a. A food additive is supposed to have a wide margin of safety.
    b. Most additives that involve risk are allowed in foods only at levels 100 times below those at which the risk is still known to be zero.
4. Risks and Benefits of Food Additives
    a. Benefits far outweigh or justify risks
    b. Food colors are another story in that only 10 of the original 80 colors are still approved by the FDA.

B. Additives to Improve Safety and Quality – A few food additives receive the most publicity because people ask questions about them most often.
1. Salt and Sugar
    a. Salt and sugar are widely used as preservatives: they remove water from the food and microbes need water to grow.
    b. These can be overused because they make food taste better to many people.
2. Nitrites
    a. Nitrites are added to:
        1. Preserve the pink color of hot dogs and other cured meats
        2. Inhibit rancidity
        3. Prevent bacterial growth, especially the deadly *C. botulinum* bacterium
    b. In the stomach, nitrites can be converted to nitrosamines, chemicals linked to colon cancer.
    c. Other sources of nitrosamines include beer and cigarette smoke.
3. Sulfites
    a. Sulfites prevent oxidation in many processed foods, in alcoholic beverages, and in drugs.
    b. For most people, sulfites are harmless, but some people are allergic.
    c. FDA prohibits sulfites on food meant to be eaten raw (except grapes)
    d. Sulfites can destroy thiamin in foods.

C. Flavoring Agents
1. Nonnutritive Sweeteners (Table 12-15)
    a. Nonnutritive sweeteners can make foods taste sweet without the added empty calories of sugar.
    b. Also reduce the risk of tooth decay
    c. The FDA approves of the use of nonnutritive sweeteners within acceptable daily intake (ADI) levels.
    d. Aspartame consists of two amino acids connected together and has been extensively studied.
    e. Aspartame poses a risk for people with phenylketonuria (PKU) since aspartame contains phenylalanine that can build up to toxic levels in these individuals (see Figure 12-11).
2. Monosodium Glutamate (MSG)
    a. MSG is a flavor enhancer widely used in restaurants, especially Asian restaurants.
    b. MSG also has a basic taste (termed *umami*).
    c. In sensitive people, MSG produces adverse reactions known as the MSG symptom complex.
    d. These individuals may be able to reduce these symptoms by consuming adequate amounts of carbohydrates.

D. Fat Replacers and Artificial Fats
1. Carbohydrate-based fat replacers are used as thickeners.
2. Protein-based fat replacers are used in ice cream and give it a creamy consistency.
3. Olestra is a fat that cannot be broken down by the body's enzymes so it passes through the digestive system unabsorbed.
4. Olestra does not cause serious harm but products containing it must be fortified with vitamins A, D, E, and K.
5. See Table 12-16 for a list of fat replacers.

E. Incidental Food Additives
1. Incidental food additives are contaminants that are unintentionally added to foods.
    a. They end up in food during production, processing, storage, packaging, or consumer preparation.
    b. Include: Tiny bits of paper, plastic, glass, tin and the solvent used to decaffeinate some coffee
    c. Adverse effects are rare.
    d. Well regulated and their safety confirmed by strict procedures like those governing intentional additives

2. BPA – can leach into foods from plastic-lined cans and clear, hard, plastic water bottles
   a. BPA has been banned for use in baby bottles and sippy cups due to potential disease risks.
   b. The body can break down BPA and so exposure is lower than originally thought.
   c. More research on the safety of BPA is underway and many people avoid products in containers made with BPA.
3. Microwave Packages – use microwave-safe containers
   a. Microwave pizzas have a container with a thin coat of metal that heats the pizza but may get into the pizza; the particles are tested for safety.
   b. Reusable plastic tubs like margarine tubs may not be safe to use in the microwave.
4. Methylene Chloride – used to decaffeinate coffee beans, extract flavor from spices or hops

VII. Conclusion – U.S. food supply is safe; hazards are rare

VIII. Food Feature: Processing and the Nutrients in Foods

A. The Choice of Orange Juice
   1. People can get fresh, frozen, or canned.
   2. Each 100 calories of fresh squeezed juice has 98 mg of vitamin C, as compared to 82 mg in reconstituted and 82 mg in canned juice.
   3. People need 75 mg of vitamin C, which can be supplied by the one serving of orange juice.
   4. Freezing and canning the orange juice may destroy some of the vitamin C but also makes the juice available for more people to drink.

B. Processing Mischief
   1. As foods are processed, the levels of sodium, fats, and sugars are often increased – e.g., nuts or raisins covered with yogurt sounds healthy but 75% of the yogurt coating is sugar and fat
   2. Table 12-17 shows the effects of food processing on nutrients.
   3. Grains and legumes are ground and heated under pressure in the process of extrusion, which strips such foods of many of their nutrients.
   4. In general, the more heavily processed a food is, the less nutritious it becomes.

C. Best Nutrient Buys – The nutrient density of processed foods exists on a continuum:
   1. Whole-grain bread > refined white bread > doughnuts
   2. Milk > fruit-flavored yogurt > canned pudding
   3. Corn on the cob > canned cream corn > caramel corn
   4. Oranges > orange juice > orange-flavored drink
   5. Baked ham > deviled ham > fried bacon
   6 Purchase mostly whole foods or those that processing has benefited nutritionally
   7. Choose whole foods to the greatest extent possible.
   8. Use foods that processing has improved or left intact such as nonfat milk.
   9. Short cooking times with little water (like steaming) will preserve the nutrients of vegetables

IX. Controversy – Genetically Modified Foods: What Are the Pros and Cons?

A. Although genetic engineering (GE) technologies are relatively new to farming, their roots lie in naturally-occurring genetic events and centuries-old breeding techniques.
   1. Figure C12-1 shows that 90% of U.S. soybeans and 88% of feed corn are genetically engineered organisms.
   2. Food additives like HFCS come from plant materials.
   3. Biotechnology strives to solve current food and energy problems.

B. Selective Breeding
   1. Wild plants cross-pollinate randomly.
   2. Farmers change the genetic makeup of crops and farm animals through selective breeding.
   3. The original ear of corn shown in the Controversy section bears little resemblance to ears of corn today.
   4. DNA from successful plant seedlings is analyzed by the computer and seedlings with the right genes are grown to maturity and reproduced to yield new breeds in a short time.

B. Recombinant DNA Technology
   1. Figure C12-2 compares the genetic results of selective breeding and rDNA technology.

2. Obtaining Desired Traits
    a. Scientists can insert genes for pest resistance right into a crop's stem cell.
    b. This transgenic plant can then grow and clones of this same transgenic plant can be produced.
    c. An example is a potato that has a virus gene inserted into its cells; this protein can help the potato resist attack from the real virus in the field.
3. Suppressing Unwanted Traits – Scientists are finding ways to turn off genes that encode for unwanted proteins such as the protein in peanuts that is responsible for people's severe allergies.

C. The Promises and Problems of rDNA Technolgoy – The Academy of Nutrition and Dietetics takes the position that agricultural and food biotechnology can enhance the quality, safety, nutritional value, and variety of the food supply, while helping to solve problems of production, processing, distribution, and environmental and waste management.
1. Human Nutrition – Golden Rice contains a gene for making beta-carotene that will allow rice planted anywhere in the world to help people get enough vitamin A in their diets.
    a. Golden Rice yields 35 micrograms of beta-carotene per gram of rice.
    b. Other rice types have 80% more iron and zinc than ordinary rice.
2. Molecules from Microbes
    a. Human insulin produced by bacteria is far safer for human use than insulin from pigs & cows.
    b. Transgenic bacteria can cheaply produce the rennin enzyme (from cows) used in cheese manufacture, which was previously harvested from the stomachs of calves.
    c. Animals may be engineered to secrete vaccines in their milk.
3. Greater Crop Yields – GE crops fall into 2 categories
    a. Herbicide resistant: plants can be altered by genes that protect them against herbicides (to eliminate weeds)
    b. Insecticide-resistant plants make pesticides to protect themselves from pests like the corn-destroying worm.
4. Food from Cloned Animals – can produce safe meat and dairy products but animal cloning is very expensive and is not often done

D. Issues Surrounding GE Foods
1. Nutrient Composition
    a. Identical with that of conventionally grown food crops unless intentionally modified
    b. Over-ingestion of Golden Rice could result in overdoses of beta-carotene.
2. Accidental Ingestion of Drugs from Foods – If plants that contain genes for drugs are accidentally released into the environment, they could contaminate the natural food supply.
3. Pesticide Residues & Resistance – Pesticide residues that arise from a protein within the transgenic crop cannot be as easily removed as externally applied pesticides.
4. Unintended Health Effects – e.g., an increasing level of a natural pesticide in celery was discovered when harvesters of the celery developed a severe skin allergy
5. Environmental Effects – due to unpredictable effects of genetically engineered plants interacting with the natural plant and weed population
    a. Outcrossing is the accidental cross-pollination of plant pesticide crops with wild weeds.
    b. If the weed inherits the pesticide resistance gene, it could be impossible to eliminate and would crowd out crops.
6. Ethical Arguments about Genetic Engineering – revolve around religious views that nature should not be manipulated but others argue that people need genetic engineering to ensure an adequate supply of food
7. The FDA's Position on GE Foods
    a. They are safe unless they differ a lot from their conventional counterparts.
    b. Foods from GE animals must be marketed with FDA approval.

E. The Final Word – It is important to eat produce regardless of its source.

Worksheet 12-1: Label Analysis—Food Safety and Technology

Instructions: Use the macaroni and cheese mix label to answer the questions that follow.

Nutrition Facts

Serving Size 2.5 oz. (71g)
About 1 cup prepared
Servings Per Container about 2.5

Amount Per Serving	Mix	As prepared
Calories	270	280
Calories from Fat	30	35
	% Daily Value**	
Total Fat 3.5g*	**5%**	**6%**
Saturated Fat 2g	**10%**	**10%**
Trans Fat 0g		
Cholesterol 10mg	**3%**	**3%**
Sodium 570mg	**24%**	**24%**
Total Carbohydrate 47g	**16%**	**16%**
Dietary Fiber 2g	**8%**	**8%**
Sugars 5g		
Protein 10g	**11%**	**13%**
Vitamin A	2%	2%
Vitamin C	0%	0%
Calcium	10%	15%
Iron	4%	4%
Thiamin (Vit. B_1)	10%	10%
Folic Acid	10%	10%

* Amount in mix. Prepared with 1/4 cup lowfat milk adds 10 calories (5 fat cal.), 0.5g total fat, 10mg sodium, 1g total carb. (1g sugars), 1g protein.
**Percent Daily Values are based on a 2,000 calorie diet. Your Daily Values may be higher or lower depending on your calorie needs.

Best Ingredients:
Organic semolina pasta shells from durum wheat, organic cheddar cheese (organic cultured pasteurized milk, salt, non-animal enzymes), organic whey, salt, natural sodium phosphate, annatto extract for natural color.

Contains milk and wheat ingredients.
Made on shared equipment that also processed eggs and soy.

1. What is meant by the term *USDA organic*?

2. a. Are there any non-organic ingredients listed?

   b. How can you tell that the ingredients are organic?

3. How would you prepare this product to maintain its organic claims?

4. a. Are there any natural preservatives in this product?

   b. What is the function of the preservative listed?

5. What nutrition claims can be made about this product based on the label information?

6. a. What warning about this product is listed near the ingredients?

   b. Why are these warnings significant in terms of food safety?

Worksheet 12-2: Intake Analysis—Food Safety

Eating Plan E (1 Day's Intake)	**Eating Plan H (1 Meal)**
¾ cup Nature's Path flax cereal ½ cup soy milk ½ cup acai juice + seltzer water 1 medium banana 12 ounces coffee 6 ounces 6-grain yogurt ½ cup blueberries ¾ cup raspberries 2 Mushroom Lover's Veggie Burgers 1 cup roasted carrot soup ½ cup sweet green peppers 6 carrot sticks 2 whole-wheat wasa crackers 8 ounces Vruit juice 8 ounces soy milk 1 peanut butter Fiber One Bar 6 ounces grilled salmon 10 cooked asparagus spears 6 ounces white wine ½ cup olives ½ cup sun-dried tomatoes ½ cup whole-wheat angel hair pasta ¼ cup mixed nuts	1 cup New England clam chowder 1 2-ounce cheesy biscuit 4 ounces broiled lobster tail 4 ounces broiled scallops 3 Tbsp. drawn, melted butter 1 cup rice pilaf 1 cup boiled carrot and green beans 12 ounces sweetened ice tea 1 cup vanilla ice cream
Eating Plan J (1 Meal)	**Eating Plan K (1 Meal)**
1 medium French fries 1 Quarter Pounder with cheese 20 ounces root beer	6 ounces meat loaf 1 cup mashed potatoes 1 cup cooked peas 12 ounces 1% fat milk 1/6 (slice) apple pie

Look at Eating Plans H, J, and K:

1. a. Which of these eating plans has the greatest potential for causing food-borne illnesses?
   b. Why is this so?
2. How could Eating Plan J be modified to reduce the risk of food-borne illnesses?

Look at Eating Plan E:

3. Select the sources of each of the following from Eating Plan E:
   a. heavy metal contamination.
   b. pesticide contamination.
   c. bacterial contamination.
   d. Suggest ways to reduce each of these threats (a., b., and c.) in an alternative eating plan.
4. What are the strengths of this eating plan in terms of the types of foods consumed?

Worksheet 12-3: Nutrient Additives—Can You Spot Them on the Label?

When you buy prepared foods at the store, do you know what is in them? Are there words on the ingredients list of the label that you don't recognize? There are many types of food additives such as added vitamins, preservatives, gums, sulfites, food colorings, sweeteners, and fat substitutes. Many of these additives give food a more appealing texture, appearance, or taste, and prolong shelf life.

Label-Reading Exercise:

1. Select 3 different brands of a given food such as cookies, bread, or another type of snack food. Pick an organic version, a low-fat/-sodium version, and a typical version of this food.
2. List the ingredients on the label that you do not recognize in the table below and categorize the type of additive that each ingredient represents. Also note how it benefits the food that it is part of or if there are any health concerns associated with this additive in the comments section.
3. The Center for Science in the Public Interest (CSPI) has a website with an excellent article with a comprehensive listing of additives. You can locate this article by searching for "Food Additives" on the website at www.cspinet.org.
4. Fill out a table for each of the food's ingredient labels that you are studying. Consider whether a certain type of food contains more preservatives or other additives to give the food a certain texture, taste, or appearance. Use the website to help you learn about the additives in any food that you may consider buying and consuming.

Food item ____________________________ Version of food ______________________________

Ingredient	Type of Additive	Comments

Food item ____________________ Version of food ____________________

Ingredient	Type of Additive	Comments

Food item ____________________ Version of food ____________________

Ingredient	Type of Additive	Comments

Types of Additives:

Preservatives	BHA or BHT preserves the oils in foods to prevent them from tasting bad. Sodium nitrates are used to preserve the flavor and color of prepared deli meats as well as inhibit the growth of harmful bacteria. Sulfites prevent oxidation in may processed foods, wine, and some drugs. Sulfites are used to keep dried produce from getting discolored.
Artificial Colors	Blue 1 & 2, Citrus Red 2, Green 3, Red 3 & 40, Yellow 5 & 6 are used to give foods a more desirable or striking appearance.
Gums	Carrageenan, guar, locust bean, or xanthans are used to thicken and keep foods from separating.
Nonnutritive Sweeteners	Aspartame, saccharin, mannitol, stevia, sorbitol, or sucrolose provides a high level of sweetening power for a small amount. This reduces the calories in a food (see Table 12-15).
Sweeteners	High-fructose corn syrup or corn syrups are used in food to give them sweetness at a reasonable cost to the food manufacturer. These additives do add calories to the food.
Olestra	A fat substitute that gives foods a "fatty" feel without the calories.
Vitamins and Minerals	Many enriched foods such as baked goods have additional vitamins or minerals added to increase their nutrient content. Beta-carotene or retinal (vitamin A), alpha-tocopherol (vitamin E), ascorbic acid (vitamin C), and thiamin mononitrate (vitamin B_1) are examples of added vitamins. Phosphates and sodium chloride are found in foods.

There are other additives and more types than what are listed above.

References:

"CSPI's Guide to Food Additives" on the website at www.cspinet.org.

Girard-Eberle, Suzanne, Common Food Additives: Safe at the Plate. *Delicious Living* Dec00.

Worksheet 12-4: Chapter 12 Review Crossword Puzzle

1 2 3 4 5 6 7 8 9 10 11 12 13 14 15

(clues provided on following page)

Across:	Down:
1. Bacteria that are not killed by medicines are called _____ resistant. 3. Chemicals applied to crops that keep insects from destroying the crops 6. The increased levels of contaminants (heavy metals or toxic chemicals) that are seen in higher levels of the food chain are known as _____. 8. Naturally occurring poisons in foods that can be converted to cyanide 12. A very powerful sweetener derived from a plant source 13. Foods can be sweetened by the addition of _____ sweeteners, which do not contribute to the calorie content of the food. 14. A genetically identical plant or animal organism 15. A nonnutritive sweetener that can be used in baking and is often used by diabetics	1. A commonly used nonnutritive sweetener that contains amino acids and should be restricted in people with PKU 2. An infection that is spread from person to person easily, can be transmitted through produce, and has caused illness on cruise ships 4. Another name for growth hormone for cows is bovine _____. 5. _____ is a food processing step that involves the grinding and cooking of whole food ingredients under high heat and pressure. 6. An infection that can cause paralysis and is due to the ingestion of a bacterium and its associated toxin 7. A _____ illness is caused by an infectious agent that can be found in certain foods. 9. The second core (safe food) practice that people should follow is to _____ their foods to prevent the risk of exposure to disease-causing microbes. 10. A dangerous substance that can be secreted by molds 11. In agriculture, crops grown and processed according to USDA regulations defining the use of fertilizers, herbicides, insecticides, fungicides, preservatives, and other chemical ingredients

Handout 12-1: How to Detect and Avoid Spoiled Foods

These Foods...	Are Risky When:
Fresh poultry	• stored raw in the refrigerator for longer than 1-2 days (3-4 days for cooked poultry) • left unrefrigerated for more than 2 hours either before or after cooking
Fresh meat	• stored raw in the refrigerator for longer than 3-5 days (1-2 days for hamburger) • discolored, smelling, slimy • left unrefrigerated for more than 2 hours either before or after cooking
Fresh fish	• stored for longer than 1-2 days in the refrigerator • dried at edges, smelly • left unrefrigerated for more than 2 hours either before or after cooking
Milk, cream, egg products	• left unrefrigerated for more than 2 hours • stored in the refrigerator longer than 5-7 days
Frozen meats, poultry, fish, casseroles	• thawed at room temperature • allowed to thaw and be refrozen • eaten without thorough cooking
Canned foods*	• liquid spurts out when can is opened • can is corroded, rusty, or leaky, swollen on top or bottom, dented on side seams • contents have off-odors, a foamy or mushy texture • stored at temperatures above 100° F or allowed to freeze and thaw
Fresh fruits and vegetables	• unwashed, moldy
Cereal products, flour	• moldy, infested with insects

*Home-canned foods should never be used in family day care, congregate meal sites, or other food service operations.

Handout 12-2: Why Salty and Sugary Foods Last

What causes food to spoil?

- Bacteria and fungi can land on food, grow even in the refrigerator, and secrete substances that make the food taste bad and can make people sick when they eat the food

What environments bacteria like:

- Like warm places like the body
- Like solutions with a small amount of salt (called saline) containing 99.1% water and 0.9% salt
- Bacteria have the same saline-like solution within them
- Like solutions with a small amount of sugar similar to the saline solution

Why don't salty/sugary foods spoil easily?

- They contain a higher amount of salt/sugar in water than a saline-like solution and thus draw water out of the bacteria
- The bacteria shrivel up and die and cannot spoil the food

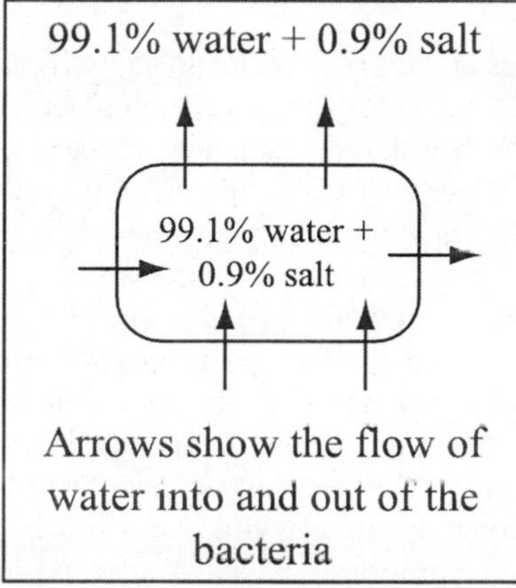

Isotonic (saline) solution has the same salt concentration as found inside the bacteria, so water moves in and out at equal rates

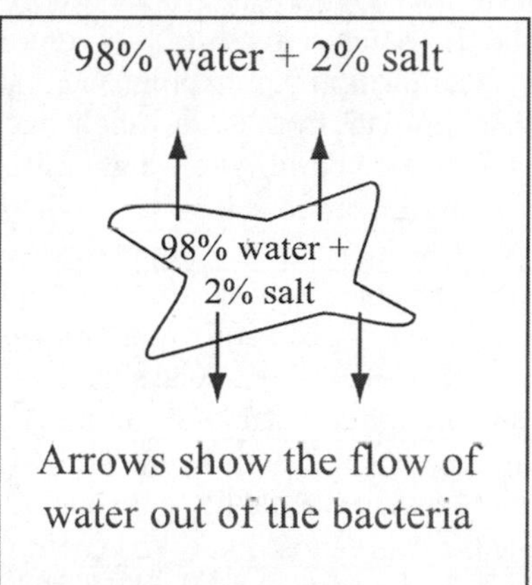

Brine solution (higher salt) draws water out of the bacteria toward the area of greater salt concentration (water follows salt)

Chapter 13 – Life Cycle Nutrition: Mother and Infant

Quick List: IM Resources for Chapter 13

- **Class preparation resources:** learning objectives/key points, suggested activities and projects, lecture outline
- **Assignment materials:** **Related LO**
  - Critical thinking questions (with answer key) 13.1, 13.3, 13.5
  - Discussion questions (with answers) for Controversy 13 .... 13.7
  - Worksheet 13-1: Infant Formula Label Analysis 13.5
  - Worksheet 13-2: Intake Analysis—Pregnancy and Lactation 13.1, 13.2, 13.4
  - **New!** Worksheet 13-3: Chapter 13 Review Crossword Puzzle
- **Enrichment materials:**
  - Handout 13-1: Effects of Nutrient Deficiencies during Pregnancy[1] 13.1
  - Handout 13-2: Feeding Infants around the World[1] 13.5
  - Handout 13-3: Why Breast Milk Is the Best Food[1] 13.5

Chapter Learning Objectives and Key Points

13.1 **Explain why a nutritionally adequate diet is important before and during a pregnancy, and identify the special nutritional needs of a pregnant teenager.**

Adequate nutrition before pregnancy establishes physical readiness and nutrient stores to support placental and fetal growth. Both underweight and overweight women should strive for appropriate body weights before pregnancy. Newborns who weigh less than 5 ½ pounds face greater health risks than normal-weight babies. Implantation, fetal development, and critical period development depend on maternal nutrition status. The effects of malnutrition during critical periods are irreversible. Pregnancy brings physiological adjustments that demand increased intakes of energy and nutrients. A balanced nutrient-dense diet is essential for meeting nutrient needs. Folate and vitamin B_{12} play key roles in cell replication and are needed in large amounts during pregnancy. Folate plays an important role in preventing neural tube defects. Adequate vitamin D and calcium are indispensable for normal bone development of the fetus. Iron supplements are recommended for pregnant women. Zinc is needed for protein synthesis and cell development during pregnancy. Physicians routinely recommend daily prenatal multivitamin–mineral supplements for pregnant women. Prenatal supplements are most likely to benefit women who do not eat adequately, are carrying twins or triplets, or who smoke cigarettes, drink alcohol, or abuse drugs. Food assistance programs such as WIC can provide nutritious food for pregnant women of limited financial means. Participation in WIC during pregnancy can reduce iron deficiency, infant mortality, low birthweight, and maternal and newborn medical costs. Appropriate weight gain is essential for a healthy pregnancy. Appropriate weight gain is influenced by prepregnancy BMI, maternal nutrient needs, and the number of fetuses in the pregnancy. Physically fit women can continue physical activity throughout pregnancy but should choose activities wisely. Pregnant women should avoid sports in which they might fall or be hit and avoid becoming overheated or dehydrated. Pregnant teenage girls have extraordinarily high nutrient needs and an increased likelihood of problem pregnancies. Adequate nutrition and appropriate weight gain for pregnant teenagers can substantially improve outcomes for mothers and infants. Food cravings usually do not reflect physiological needs, and some may interfere with nutrition. Nausea arises from normal hormonal changes of pregnancy. Smoking during pregnancy delivers toxins to the fetus, damages DNA, restricts fetal growth, and limits delivery of oxygen and nutrients and the removal of wastes. Smoking and other drugs, contaminants such as mercury, foodborne illnesses, large supplemental doses of nutrients, weight-loss diets, and excessive use of artificial sweeteners and caffeine should be avoided during pregnancy.

13.2 **Evaluate the statement that "no level of alcoholic beverage intake is safe or advisable during pregnancy."**

Alcohol crosses the placenta and is directly toxic to the fetus. Alcohol limits oxygen delivery to the fetus,

---

[1] Adapted from L. K. DeBruyne and S. R. Rolfes, *Life Cycle Nutrition: Conception Through Adolescence*, ed. E. N. Whitney (St. Paul, Minn.: West, 1989), p. 68.

slows cell division, and reduces the number of cells organs produce. The severe birth defects of fetal alcohol syndrome arise from damage to the fetus by alcohol. Lesser conditions, ARND and ARBD, also arise from alcohol use in pregnancy. Alcohol's damaging effects on the fetus are dose dependent, becoming greater as the dose increases. Abstinence from alcohol in pregnancy is critical to preventing irreversible damage to the fetus.

13.3 **Describe the impacts of gestational diabetes and preeclampsia on the health of a pregnant woman and on the fetus.**
If discovered early, many diseases of pregnancy can be controlled—an important reason early prenatal care is recommended. Gestational diabetes, hypertension, and preeclampsia are problems of some pregnancies that must be managed to minimize associated risks.

13.4 **Describe maternal nutrition needs for lactation, the impact of malnutrition on breast milk, and contraindications to breastfeeding.**
The lactating woman needs extra fluid and adequate energy and nutrients for milk production. Malnutrition diminishes the quantity of the milk without altering quality. Breastfeeding is not advised if the mother's milk is contaminated with alcohol, drugs, or environmental pollutants. Most ordinary infections such as colds have no effect on breastfeeding infants, but HIV may be transmitted through milk.

13.5 **Identify characteristics of breast milk that make it the ideal food for human infants, and discuss the introduction of solid foods into the diet.**
An infant's birthweight doubles by about 5 months of age and triples by 1 year. Infants' rapid growth and development depend on adequate nutrient supplies, including water from breast milk or formula. With the exception of vitamin D, breast milk provides all the nutrients a healthy infant needs for the first 6 months of life. Breast milk offers the infant unsurpassed protection against infection—including antiviral agents, anti-inflammatory agents, antibacterial agents, and infection inhibitors. Infant formulas are designed to resemble breast milk in nutrient composition. After the baby's first birthday, reduced-fat or low-fat cow's milk can replace formula. At 6 months, an infant may be ready to try some solid foods. By 1 year, the child should be eating foods from all food groups. The early feeding of the infant lays the foundation for lifelong eating habits. The most important single measure to undertake during the first year is to encourage eating habits that will support continued normal weight as the child grows.

13.6 **List some feeding guidelines that encourage normal eating behaviors and autonomy in the child.**

13.7 **Discuss some relationships between childhood obesity and chronic diseases, and develop a healthy eating and activity plan for an obese child of a given age.**

Critical Thinking Questions

1. *Why is it particularly important for a pregnant woman to obtain all of the essential nutrients (or have adequate stores of them) during the critical periods of embryonic/fetal development?*

   These critical periods are called so because organs such as the brain or heart develop in a definite time period, and if essential nutrients are lacking, these structures may not develop completely, which will compromise their function. Once the heart forms, it cannot "reform" at a later time. The nutrients to support optimal tissue and organ development need to be present at just the right time. Early malnutrition at around 10 weeks' gestation may impair the development of the heart and brain.

2. *Explain how folate serves "double duty" during pregnancy and why deficiencies of this vitamin can be devastating.*

   Folate directs the synthesis of the cells' DNA molecules and also helps cells develop appropriately. The mother's blood volume increases 50% during the last 2 trimesters of pregnancy, so the bone marrow must be able to manufacture enough red blood cells to support the mother's circulatory needs as well as those of the fetal circulation. Deficiencies of folate can result in anemia, which can jeopardize both the mother's and fetus's health.

Folate is also essential for proper spinal column development in the embryo and fetus. A deficiency of folate can result in the incomplete closure of the spinal column, which can cause spina bifida (shown in Figure 13-5). This condition can result in permanent physical and/or mental disability in the child.

3. *Describe any two problems that can develop in the pregnant woman during pregnancy. How can they affect her future health and that of her baby?*

   Gestational diabetes can result when the hormones of pregnancy interfere with the woman's cells' ability to respond to insulin. This results in high blood glucose in the mother that can increase the weight of her infant. Some infants of diabetic mothers also suffer from physical or mental conditions as well as respiratory difficulties. Women with gestational diabetes are at greater risk of developing type 2 diabetes later in life. If women are diagnosed with type 2 diabetes during pregnancy and their blood glucose levels are actively controlled, they (mother, fetus, and newborn) are less likely to experience complications.

   Preeclampsia in mothers results in very high blood pressure. It can cause the mother's organs to fail, which can lead to death for both the mother and the fetus. Detection of maternal high blood pressure can reduce the risk of maternal or fetal/infant mortality.

4. *Discuss any 3 reasons why breast milk is the best nutrition for an infant less than 6 months old.*

   Table 13-10 lists benefits of breastfeeding for infants. Breast milk contains antibody proteins and white blood cells from the mother that can protect the infant against pathogens that could cause gastrointestinal and respiratory infections. Breast milk contains a protein called alpha-lactalbumin that is easy for the infant to digest, which may lead to fewer stomach upsets. Breastfed infants may also have a reduced risk of developing serious food allergies. Breast milk is ready to drink and does not depend on a safe water supply like formula does. This decreases the risk of an infant getting a foodborne illness.

5. *Describe any 3 clues that an infant or small child is ready to try a new food with a different texture.*

   See Table 13-13, which lists infant feeding skills and the foods these skills permit them to safely eat. Babies are ready for solid foods when they show a diminished extrusion reflex (spitting food out of the mouth) in the first 4-6 months. This suggests that an infant can swallow solid foods more successfully.

   Infants can eat Cheerios or other finger foods at 6-8 months of age as they develop coordination in their fingers and thumb. An infant can handle a spoon at 10-12 months and may be ready to feed herself oatmeal and other simple foods.

   It is very important that infants are supervised while eating since they are at substantial risk for choking.

6. *Why are overweight or obese women discouraged from losing weight during pregnancy?*

   Though overweight/obese women have excess body fat, they still need adequate nutrition to support a healthy pregnancy. All women need adequate protein from a variety of food sources to support the development of the placenta and fetal tissues. Women need a variety of foods to provide all of the vitamins and minerals that are needed for a healthy pregnancy. For example, a woman needs enough vitamin A, vitamin B_{12}, and folate to support the development of cells for the fetus and for her red blood cell supply. She also needs enough vitamin D and calcium to support the development of fetal bones and to maintain her bone density. She needs enough iron and zinc to support blood health and cell development.

Controversy Discussion Questions

1. *Describe 3 ways that you could start to modify Gabby's diet or a child like Gabby's diet to help her maintain her current weight as she gets taller.*

   - Firstly, don't restrict calories to the extent that Gabby loses weight. Gabby still needs adequate nutrients such as essential fatty acids, vitamin D, and calcium from a variety of foods.
   - Limit Gabby's sweet treats and replace one or two of them with healthier treats such as fresh fruit.
   - Make sure that Gabby eats appropriate portions regularly. She should not feel deprived because she will have cravings and end up possibly eating more than she needs to maintain her weight.

- Introduce Gabby to new fruits and vegetables to help increase her tastes for healthy foods. Make it a fun adventure that she will look forward to. Eating healthy is NOT punishment. Perhaps Gabby can select fruits or vegetables with her parents at the store.

2. *How do TV food advertisements directed at children increase the risk for childhood obesity?*
   - Food manufacturers enlist stars that children admire (e.g., animal friends in "advergames") to endorse foods that provide excess calories from added sugars and solid fats.
   - The number of commercials during programming breaks is quite high. Children may see as many as 40,000 TV commercials a year. Children are exposed to a variety of foods and products, become familiar with such foods, and then request and often are allowed to eat them. Whether the high-calorie foods replace or are added to nutritious foods, they provide excess calories that contribute to unwanted weight gain.

3. *Why is it important for children to adjust their diets and activity levels before resorting to medications to control their blood cholesterol or their weight gain?*

   It is important that children avoid the medications that are used to control blood cholesterol because such medications can act on liver metabolism and affect how their bodies handle fats and other nutrients. Children still need essential fatty acids for tissue development and moderate total fat intakes for energy. If a child's blood cholesterol levels remain high in spite of changes in their diet and activity over 6 months or longer, then certain drugs may be used to lower their cholesterol levels.

4. *How can a school nurse distinguish whether a child is just a bit "chubby" or is truly overweight or obese?*

   The body mass index (BMI) chart is often used to distinguish overweight and obesity from a healthy weight. Children's BMI values are compared to percentile charts for their age and gender groups as well. Children whose BMI values are above the 85th percentile are considered overweight; those with BMI values at or are above 95th percentile are considered obese. The school nurse could also find out what the child's diet is like and whether they get any exercise. Both environment and genetics play roles in the development of obesity.

Worksheet Answer Key

Worksheet 13-1: Infant Formula Label Analysis

1. The body cannot make these particular amino acids. This formula is the only source of nutrition for a small infant.
2. a. Yes, soy isolates do provide all of the essential amino acids.
   b. It is a complete protein.
3. Major sources of energy are the corn maltodextrin (carbohydrate) and vegetable oils (fat). They are similar in that fat and carbohydrate provide energy in both breast milk and the formula, but different in that breast milk provides carbohydrate as lactose and this formula is lactose free.
4. a. The listing per 100 kilocalories would demonstrate the nutrient density of this formula. This could be compared to other formulas.

   b. The listing per 100 grams may be useful if someone is preparing this formula at a different strength. They could still figure out how much of the nutrients are in the fluid given to the infant.

   c. The listing per 1 liter is useful for a person who wants to know how much of the nutrients an infant is getting from multiple feedings throughout the day.
5. Lactose is a milk sugar, and whey protein comes from the whey of milk.
6. a. No, technically breast milk is not vegan.
   b. It comes from an animal.

Worksheet 13-2: Intake Analysis—Pregnancy and Lactation

1. a. Eating Plan B has the highest level of folate.

b. Folate helps cells produce their genetic material and divide well. This helps prevent neural tube defects in infants.

c. Eating Plan B has the highest level of B_{12}.

d. Eating Plan B has the highest level of iron.

e. Iron, folate, and vitamin B_{12} help in the development and production of red blood cells and the accumulation of adequate iron stores in the fetal liver. Red blood cells can transport oxygen to the tissues of the mother and fetus, which ensures the best outcome for both.

2. a. White wine may not be safe to ingest during pregnancy.

   b. The threshold for an infant to develop fetal alcohol effect or fetal alcohol syndrome is not known. Some fetuses may be more sensitive to the effects of alcohol than others. It is best to avoid alcohol during pregnancy and during breastfeeding as it may pass into the milk.

3. a. It has not been established that any one food type may enter the breast milk and irritate the infant. White wine from Eating Plan B could get into the breast milk. The large amount of fruits and vegetables consumed in Eating Plan B may affect the breast milk and cause irritability in some infants.

   b. If an infant seems irritated after drinking breast milk, the mother may wish to eliminate a food to see if future feedings irritate the infant.

4. a. Both of the eating plans supply enough of these nutrients due to the variety of fruits and vegetables either in the form of whole fruits or juices.

   b. These eating plans do not need additional foods to increase the levels of these nutrients.

Worksheet 13-3: Chapter 13 Review Crossword Puzzle

1. heartburn
2. allergies
3. gestational
4. MyPlate
5. trimesters
6. implantation
7. iodine
8. vitamin D
9. folate
10. amniotic
11. underweight
12. protein

Learning Activities & Project Ideas

Activity 13-1: Role Playing Project[2] LO 13.1, 13.6, 13.7
Have students write a play that portrays people discussing nutrition issues with medical professionals. A very popular topic may be weight gain in infants or children. Roles in the play could include: a student, physician, nutritionist, parent, child, and/or professor. Each character asks questions, makes statements based on myths, and/or describes a questionable eating pattern. Volunteers may read the play out loud.

Activity 13-2: Controversial Topics Debate Project[3] LO 13.1, 13.5
Have students research and debate a controversial topic such as breastfeeding versus bottle feeding, sugar in the diet, water fluoridation, or federal programs such as WIC. Greater interest in such topics is often generated by debates than by straight lectures.

Chapter Lecture Outline

I. Pregnancy: The Impact of Nutrition on the Future – A pregnant woman must understand that her nutrition today is critical to the health of her future child throughout life.
   A. Preparing for Pregnancy
      1. The nutrient demands of pregnancy are extraordinary.
         a. Before she becomes pregnant, a woman must establish eating habits that will optimally nourish both the growing fetus and herself.

---

[2] Contributed by Lori W. Turner, Ph.D., R.D., University of Alabama

[3] Contributed by Virginia A. Beal, University of Massachusetts

b. The embryo undergoes significant and rapid developmental changes that depend on good nutrition.

2. Certain lifestyles, such as reduced fruit and vegetable intake or excess alcohol intake, can impair fertility in the father.
3. Prepregnancy Weight
    a. A woman who starts out underweight and who fails to gain sufficiently during pregnancy is likely to have a low-birthweight baby (< 5 ½ pounds).
    b. Low birthweight babies are associated with: Lower adult IQ, short stature, chronic diseases
    c. Obese women are also urged to achieve a healthy weight before pregnancy.
    d. Babies born to obese mothers are more likely to have heart defects, neural tube defects, and other problems.
    e. Obese women are at higher risk for developing high blood pressure or diabetes during pregnancy.
4. A Healthy Placenta and Other Organs – as shown in Figure 13-2
    a. A major reason the mother's nutrition before pregnancy is so crucial is that it determines whether her uterus will be able to support the growth of a healthy placenta during the first month of gestation.
    b. The placenta is critical for the fetus to obtain nutrients and oxygen from the mother's bloodstream and for removal of fetal wastes to the mother's bloodstream (see Figure 13-2).
    c. The placenta also produces hormones that act in many ways to maintain pregnancy and prepare the mother's breasts for lactation.

B. The Events of Pregnancy
1. Fertilization and implantation
    a. The newly fertilized ovum, called a zygote, begins as a single cell and divides many times during the days after fertilization.
    b. Within 2 weeks, the zygote embeds itself in the uterine wall in a process known as implantation.
    c. Adverse influences such as drug abuse, smoking, and malnutrition can lead to abnormalities such as neural tube defects.
2. The Embryo and Fetus – The 40 or so weeks of pregnancy are divided into thirds, each of which is called a trimester.
3. A Note about Critical Periods
    a. Each organ and tissue type grows with its own characteristic pattern and timing.
    b. The development of each takes place only at a certain time—the critical period.
    c. If the development of an organ is limited during a critical period, recovery is impossible.
    d. Any deficiencies in nutrition during these critical periods may increase the risk of chronic disease development in the future adult.
    e. Figure 13-3 shows the major periods of embryonic, fetal, and neonatal development.
    f. Table 13-1 describes factors that can lead to a high risk pregnancy

C. Increased Need for Nutrients – are shown in Figure 13-4
1. Energy, Carbohydrate, Protein, and Fat
    a. Pregnancy brings physiological adjustments that demand increased intakes of energy and nutrients.
    b. Women need 340 additional calories per day during the second trimester and 450 additional calories per day during the third trimester.
    c. Women need at least 135 g of carbohydrate a day for optimal fetal growth and brain function.
    d. A balanced diet that includes more nutrient-dense foods from the five food groups can help to meet these needs for both the mother and the fetus.
    e. Protein supplements during pregnancy may be harmful to fetal development.
2. Of Special Interest: Folate and Vitamin B_{12}
    a. Due to their key roles in cell reproduction, folate and vitamin B_{12} are needed in large amounts during pregnancy.
    b. Folate plays an important role in preventing neural tube defects.
        1. One type is anencephaly, in which the brain fails to develop.
        2. Another is spina bifida, in which the membranes covering the spinal cord protrude from the spine as a sac, as shown in Figure 13-5.
        3. Pregnant women need at least 400 micrograms/day of folate to help reduce the risk of neural tube defects.

c. Folate and vitamin B_{12} are also needed for increased red blood cell development in the mother's body during pregnancy.

3. Vitamin D and Calcium
    a. Among the minerals, calcium, phosphorus, and magnesium are in great demand during pregnancy because they are necessary for normal development of the bones and teeth.
    b. Vitamin D is needed for adequate calcium metabolism for both the mother and the developing infant.
        1. Earlier in pregnancy, the calcium absorbed is doubled and is deposited on the mother's bones.
        2. Later in the pregnancy, the calcium is released from the mother's bones and goes to the fetus where bone formation is taking place.
        3. Adequate calcium intake is directed at preserving the mother's bone density and meeting the needs of the fetus.
        4. Many pregnant women under 25 years of age need to make sure that they get the DRI for calcium since their bones are still actively depositing minerals.
4. Iron
    a. During pregnancy, the body avidly conserves iron and absorption increases up to threefold.
    b. Iron needs of fetus have priority over those of the mother since the fetus must have sufficient iron stores for the first 4 to 6 months of life.
    c. Women can lose a lot of iron during birth, especially with a Cesarean section.
    d. Women should choose foods with heme iron, as well as iron-rich vegetables and legumes, and consume vitamin C-rich foods to enhance iron absorption.
5. Zinc – Zinc, required for protein synthesis and cell development, is vital during pregnancy and can be obtained from a variety of foods.
6. Prenatal Supplements – Women most likely to benefit from prenatal multivitamin-mineral supplements during pregnancy include those who do not eat adequately, those carrying twins or triplets, and those who smoke cigarettes or are alcohol or drug abusers.

D. Food Assistance Programs
1. Food assistance programs such as Special Supplemental Food Program for Women, Infants and Children (WIC) can provide nutritious food for pregnant women of limited financial means.
2. More than 9 million people (mostly women and children) receive WIC benefits each month.

E. How Much Weight Should a Woman Gain during Pregnancy?
1. Weight gain is essential for a healthy pregnancy for any woman of any BMI.
2. A woman's prepregnancy BMI, her own nutrient needs, and the number of fetuses she is carrying help to determine appropriate weight gain, as shown on Table 13-5.
    a. BMI $<18.5 = 28\text{-}40$ lb.
    b. BMI 18.5-24.9 = 25-35 lb.
    c. BMI 25-29.9 = 15-25 lb.
    d. BMI $\geq 30 = 11\text{-}20$ lb.
3. Most weight gained is lean tissues such as the placenta, uterus, blood, mammary glands, and fetus.
4. The fat weight gained is needed to support lactation later on.

F. Weight Loss after Pregnancy
1. Women who gain weight beyond the recommended amounts will store most of this weight as fat.
2. To avoid cumulative, unhealthy gains, women should achieve a healthy weight.

G. Should Pregnant Women Be Physically Active?
1. Physically fit women can continue to be physically active throughout pregnancy.
2. Pregnant women should be cautious in their choices of activities in order to minimize the risk of impacts or excessive physical exertion.
3. High internal body temperatures can lead to dehydration and could harm the fetus.
4. Figure 13-8 shows guidelines for physical activity for pregnant women.

H. Teen Pregnancy
1. In 2010, more than 367,000 infants were born to teenage mothers.
2. Of all the population groups, pregnant teens have the highest nutrient needs due to their own bodies' continuing development.
    a. Many teens are deficient in vitamin B_{12}, D, folate, iron, & calcium, which can impair fetal growth.
    b. Also, more teens may smoke, which can result in an increased likelihood of poor pregnancy outcomes like low infant birthweight.

c. A pregnant teenager of normal BMI status should gain 35 pounds.

I. Why Do Some Women Crave Pickles and Ice Cream While Others Can't Keep Anything Down?
1. Food cravings usually do not reflect physiological needs, and some may interfere with nutrition.
2. Nausea arises from hormonal changes of pregnancy and simple measures can reduce its severity in most women.
3. Table 13-6 lists tips for relieving common discomforts.
4. As the fetus grows and takes up more space, women may notice more heartburn or constipation.
5. Heartburn can be relieved by elevating the head of the bed; constipation can be prevented by consuming more fiber and water.

J. Some Cautions for the Pregnant Woman – Some choices that pregnant women make or substances they encounter can harm the fetus, sometimes severely.
1. Cigarette Smoking – about 10-12% of pregnant women smoke
   a. A surgeon general's warning states that parental smoking can kill an otherwise healthy fetus or newborn.
   b. Nicotine and cyanide in cigarettes are toxic to the fetus.
   c. Smoking limits the oxygen delivered to the fetus.
   d. Can damage fetal chromosomes
   e. Risk of low-birthweight baby
   f. Increased risk of asthma and sudden infant death syndrome (SIDS)
   g. Even environmental tobacco smoke is unhealthy.
2. Medicinal Drugs and Herbal Supplements
   a. Medicinal drugs taken during pregnancy can cause serious birth defects.
   b. Herbal supplements have not been adequately tested for safety or effectiveness during pregnancy.
3. Drugs of Abuse – Illicit drugs such as marijuana and cocaine can cause serious health problems in the fetus, including nervous system disorders and other developmental delays.
4. Environmental Contaminants
   a. Infants and young children of pregnant women exposed to lead show signs of delayed mental and psychomotor development.
   b. Mercury in some fatty fish can damage the developing brain and nervous system of the fetus.
   c. Pregnant women are advised to restrict their intake of fish to 12 ounces per week.
5. Foodborne Illness
   a. Vomiting and diarrhea caused by foodborne illnesses can leave a pregnant woman exhausted and dangerously dehydrated.
   b. Listeriosis can cause miscarriage, stillbirth, or severe damage to the fetus.
      1. A blood test can detect listeriosis and antibiotics can be given to the mother to prevent fetal infection.
      2. Listeriosis can be prevented by consuming only pasteurized juices and dairy products, eating well-cooked luncheon or deli meats, washing produce, & avoiding refrigerated pates or smoked seafood that is not canned.
6. Vitamin-Mineral Megadoses
   a. Many vitamins are toxic when taken in excess, and minerals are even more so.
   b. A single megadose of vitamin A has caused birth defects.
7. Restrictive Dieting
   a. Weight-loss dieting, even for short periods, is hazardous during pregnancy.
   b. Low-carbohydrate diets or fasts that cause ketosis deprive the fetal brain of needed glucose and may impair its development.
   c. Energy restriction during pregnancy is dangerous, regardless of the woman's prepregnancy weight or the amount of weight gained the previous month.
8. Sugar Substitutes
   a. Artificial sweeteners have been studied extensively and found to be acceptable during pregnancy if used within the FDA's guidelines.
   b. Women with phenylketonuria should not use aspartame.
9. Caffeine – Research studies:
   a. Have not indicated that caffeine (even in high doses) causes birth defects in human infants
   b. Have found that moderate or heavy caffeine intake during pregnancy may affect fetal growth

II. Drinking during Pregnancy – Alcohol is the most hazardous drug to future generations because it is legally available, heavily promoted, and widely abused.
   A. Alcohol's Effects
      1. Women of childbearing age need to know about alcohol's harmful effects on a fetus.
      2. Alcohol crosses the placenta freely and is directly toxic. Alcohol:
         a. Limits oxygen delivery to the fetus
         b. Slows cell division, which can cause abnormalities in organs
         c. Affects fetal brain cell division, which occurs at a rate of 100,000 new cells a minute
         d. Interferes with nutrient transport to fetus
      3. Before fertilization, alcohol can damage the ovum or sperm, leading to abnormalities in the child.
   B. Fetal Alcohol Syndrome
      1. Abstinence from alcohol is critical to prevent irreversible damage to the fetus.
      2. Fetal alcohol spectrum disorders (FASD) cause a range of physical, behavioral, & cognitive symptoms.
      3. Fetal alcohol syndrome (FAS) is at the most severe end of the spectrum (see Figure 13-10).
      4. The mental problems seen with fetal alcohol exposure are called ARND or alcohol-related neurodevelopment disorder.
      5. The physical malformations seen with fetal alcohol exposure are called ARBD or alcohol-related birth defects.
   C. Experts' Advice
      1. Despite the warnings, 1 out of 8 pregnant women drinks alcohol some time during pregnancy.
      2. 1 out of 75 report "binge" drinking (four or more drinks on one occasion).
      3. Abstinence from alcohol is critical to prevent irreversible damage to the fetus.

III. Troubleshooting – Disease during pregnancy can endanger the health of the mother and fetus, but if discovered early, many diseases can be controlled—another reason early prenatal care is recommended.
   A. Diabetes – Women with type 1 or 2 diabetes may experience hypoglycemia or hyperglycemia that could lead to pre-term labor and pregnancy-related high blood pressure.
      1. Gestational diabetes is a pregnancy-related form of diabetes.
      2. Usually resolves after delivery but some women go on to develop type 2 diabetes
      3. Can lead to fetal or infant sickness or death
      4. More commonly leads to surgical birth and high infant birthweight
      5. All women are screened for this during the first trimester.
   B. Hypertension – chronic hypertension and gestational hypertension pose risks to mother/fetus
   C. Preelampsia
      1. Hypertension in pregnancy may signal the onset of preeclampsia, a condition characterized by high blood pressure, protein in the urine, and edema (especially in the hands and face).
      2. Affects all the mother's organs and can progress to eclampsia, which can be fatal.

IV. Lactation – A woman decides to feed her baby breast milk, infant formula, or both—these are the only foods recommended for the first 4 to 6 months of life; she can work with a certified lactation consultant.
   A. Nutrition during Lactation
      1. A nursing mother produces about 25 ounces of milk a day.
      2. Energy Cost of Lactation
         a. Producing this milk costs a woman almost 500 calories per day above her regular need during the first six months of lactation.
         b. She should eat an extra 330 calories of food and the other 170 calories can be drawn from her fat stores (see Table 13-2 on page 516 for a sample menu).
      3. Fluid Need – Lactating women need extra fluid (about 13 cups total) and enough energy and nutrients to make sufficient milk each day.
      4. Variations in Breast Milk
         a. The effect of nutritional deprivation of the mother is to reduce the quantity, not the quality, of her milk.
         b. If a woman is lacking a nutrient, such as calcium, in her diet, the nutrient will be put into her breast milk at the expense of her bones or other nutrient stores.
         c. Undernourished women who breastfeed may benefit from taking a supplement.
         d. Some spicy foods that the mother eats may cause distress in the infant.

   e. Infants from families with a strong history of allergies may benefit from breastfeeding.
5. Lactation and Weight Loss – Women can slowly lose body fat while lactating but quick weight loss may reduce the amount of breast milk that is produced.

B. When Should a Woman Not Breastfeed?
1. Breastfeeding is not advised if the mother's milk is contaminated with alcohol, drugs, or environmental pollutants such as mercury from fish.
2. Alcohol and Illicit Drugs – can be transferred to the baby and should be avoided
3. Tobacco and Caffeine
   a. Tobacco should be avoided, & caffeine used in moderation.
   b. Breast milk from smoking mothers contains less fat and results in less weight gain in the infant.
4. Medications – some are secreted in breast milk & can be harmful to the infant so a woman should discuss the safety of taking a medicine while breastfeeding with her healthcare provider
5. Environmental Contaminants – benefits of breastfeeding generally outweigh risks; most women do not experience substantial exposures to environmental contaminants
6. Maternal Illness
   a. Most ordinary infections such as colds have no effect on breastfeeding.
   b. Where safe alternatives are available, HIV-infected women should not breastfeed their infants.
   c. In areas of the world that lack access to clean water, HIV positive women are encouraged to breastfeed for the first 6 months.

V. Feeding the Infant – Early nutrition affects later development, and early feedings establish eating habits that influence nutrition throughout life.

A. Nutrient Needs
1. An infant's birthweight doubles by about 5 month of age and triples by 1 year; a baby's length increases by 10 inches in the first year (see Figure 13-11).
2. In the second year of life, an infant gains 10 pounds and 5 inches in height.
3. An infant needs 100 calories/kilogram of body weight versus 40 calories/kilogram for an adult
4. Infants need a lot of water to prevent dehydration.
2. See Figure 13-12 for some comparisons between adults' and infants' nutritional needs.

B. Why Is Breast Milk So Good for Babies? – The Academy of Nutrition and Dietetics and the and American Academy of Pediatrics recognize exclusive breastfeeding for 6 months, and breastfeeding with complementary foods for at least 12 months, as an optimal feeding pattern for infants.
1. Breastfeeding Tips
   a. Breast milk is more easily and completely digested than infant formula, so breastfed infants usually need to eat more frequently than formula-fed infants do.
   b. During the first few weeks, the newborn will need approximately 8 to 12 feedings a day, on demand.
   c. As the infant gets older, there are longer intervals between feedings.
2. Energy Nutrients in Breast Milk
   a. For infants, breast milk is the most nearly perfect food.
   b. Lactose, the carbohydrate in breast milk, enhances calcium absorption.
   c. Contains a generous proportion of the essential fatty acids as well as their longer-chain derivatives, arachidonic acid and DHA
   d. DHA helps stimulate infant brain development and is found in the retina.
   e. The protein is largely alpha-lactalbumin and lactoferrin, which helps absorb iron into the infant's blood stream.
3. Vitamins and Minerals in Breast Milk – With the exception of vitamin D, the vitamin content of the breast milk of a well-nourished mother is ample.
4. Supplements for Infants (Table 13-11)
   a. The AAP recommends a vitamin D supplement for exclusively breast-fed infants.
   b. At six months of age, an exclusively breast-fed baby needs additional iron.
   c. If the water supply is low in fluoride, fluoride supplementation is needed after 6 months.
5. Immune Factors in Breast Milk
   a. During the first two or three days of lactation, the breasts produce colostrum, a premilk substance containing antibodies and white cells from the mother's blood.

   b. Breastfed infants may have:
      1. Fewer ear and respiratory infections
      2. Fewer allergies and less incidence of asthma
      3. Less risk of SIDS
6. Other Potential Benefits
   a. May protect against obesity in childhood and later years
   b. May have a positive effect on later intelligence
   c. See Table 13-10 for all of the benefits of breastfeeding.

C. Formula Feeding – an acceptable alternative to breastfeeding & allows others to feed the infant as well
1. Infant Formula Composition
   a. Infant formulas are designed to resemble breast milk and must meet an AAP standard for nutrient composition (see Figure 13-14).
   b. Formulas are usually iron fortified.
2. Special Formulas
   a. Special formulas are available for premature infants, allergic infants, and others.
   b. Soy-based formulas or formulas containing hydrolyzed proteins may be appropriate.
3. The Transition to Cow's Milk
   a. Formulas should be replaced with milk after the baby's first birthday.
   b. Cow's milk in excess can reduce an infant's iron status because it is a poor source of iron and inhibits iron absorption.

D. A Consumer's Guide to Formula Advertising versus Breastfeeding Advocacy
1. Formula Advertising Claims and Tactics
   a. Advertisers often strive to create the illusion that formula is identical to human milk.
   b. Formula manufacturers give out coupons and goodie bags to pregnant women or new mothers and may undermine their confidence in breastfeeding.
2. Breastfeeding Advocacy
   a. 60% of infants were breastfeed in 1994; has risen to 74% in 2006
   b. 43% of infants are still breastfeeding at 6 months and 23% are breastfeeding at 1 year.
   c. Table 13-12 lists tips for successful breastfeeding.
3. Where Breastfeeding is Critical
   a. Formula-fed infants in developed nations are healthy and grow normally but they miss out on advantages of breast milk.
   b. Mixing formula with unsanitary water can have tragic consequences for infants in developing countries.
4. Moving Ahead
   a. Breastfeeding is less expensive than formula feeding.
   b. Expectant parents should seek out the facts about each feeding method.

E. An Infant's First Solid Foods – foods can be introduced when the infant is physically ready to handle them
1. When to Introduce Solid Food
   a. Foods may be started gradually beginning sometime between 4 and 6 months of age (see Table 13-13).
   b. Parents should detect and control any possible allergic reactions.
2. Foods to Provide Iron and Vitamin C
   a. Iron ranks highest on the list of nutrients needing attention in infant nutrition.
   b. Infants can receive iron from iron-fortified cereals as well as breast milk or formula.
   c. The best sources of vitamin C are fruits and vegetables.
   d. Fruit juice can provide vitamin C but too much can cause diarrhea and can contribute too many calories to the diet.
3. Physical Readiness for Solid Foods (Table 13-13)
   a. Babies can swallow at 4-6 months and can be fed by spoon
   b. When the baby can sit up, can handle finger foods, and is teething, hard crackers and other finger foods may be introduced under the watchful eye of an adult.
   c. Avoid foods that are choking hazards (see Table 13-14).
4. Preventing Food Allergies – To prevent allergy and to facilitate its prompt identification should it occur, experts recommend introducing single-ingredient foods, one at a time, in small portions, and waiting up to four to five days before introducing the next food.

5. Choice of Infant Foods
    a. Commercial baby foods in the U.S. and Canada are safe, and except for mixed dinners with added starch fillers and heavily sweetened desserts, they have high nutrient density.
    b. Infants should not be fed out of the jar since leftover food can be contaminated.
    c. Families often grind up adult foods without added salts or sugars for the infant to eat.
6. Foods to Omit
    a. Sweets of any kind (including baby food "desserts") have no place in a baby's diet.
    b. Honey and corn syrup should never be fed to infants because of the risk of botulism.
7. Beverages and Foods at One Year
    a. Infants should not drink too much milk since it can interfere with iron absorption from other foods, causing a type of "milk anemia."
    b. Children love to eat what their families eat.

F. Looking Ahead
1. The first year of life is the time to lay the foundation for future health.
2. From the nutrition standpoint, the problems most common in later years are obesity and dental disease.
3. It is important in the first year to encourage eating habits that will support continued normal weight as the child grows.
4. Parents should not provide nutrient-dense foods & allow infants to stop eating when full.
5. Infants should never go to sleep with a bottle of breast milk or formula as it may cause decay of the teeth.

G. Food Feature: Mealtimes with Infants
1. Foster a Sense of Autonomy
2. Some Feeding Guidelines
    a. Discourage unacceptable behavior such as throwing food.
    b. Let the child explore and enjoy food.
    c. Don't force food on children or force the child to finish all of the food.
    d. Provide nutritious foods, and let choose which ones and how much to eat.
    e. Limit sweets strictly.
    f. Don't turn the dining table into a battleground.

VI. Controversy: Childhood Obesity and Early Chronic Diseases

A. Introduction
1. Many children and adolescents in the U.S. are being diagnosed with obesity and type 2 diabetes.
2. $^1/_3$ of children ages 2-19 years are overweight in the U.S. and 17% are obese (Figure C13-1).
3. Childhood obesity rates are increasing all over the world.
4. Characteristics of childhood obesity – While no group has fully escaped this trend, obese children:
    a. Are often male, older, and of non-European descent
    b. Have a low family income
    c. Are sedentary
    d. Have parents who are obese
5. The rates of childhood obesity have stabilized in some parts of the U.S.

B. The Challenge of Childhood Obesity
1. Physical and Emotional Perils
    a. Obese children have higher a risk for atherosclerosis and for CVD in early adulthood; 43% test high for total cholesterol, LDL, and triglycerides.
    b. Obese children often develop hypertension, type 2 diabetes
    c. Asthma is more common amongst obese children and many of these children may also suffer from sleep apnea.
    d. Obese children may also have fatty liver disease.
    e. Obese children often are ridiculed and have low self-esteem.
2. Overweight or Chubby and Healthy: How Can You Tell?
    a. Healthcare providers use BMI measures for children in relation to growth charts.
    b. Above the 85th percentile = overweight; above the 95th percentile = obese
    c. Both genetics and environment play a role in the development of obesity.
3. Darla and Gabby
    a. Darla and Gabby get news that Gabby's BMI is too high.

   b. Darla is concerned due to a history of diabetes in her family.

C. Development of Type 2 Diabetes
   1. 85% of children with type 2 diabetes are obese and are diagnosed around puberty.
   2. Risk of developing type 2 diabetes varies among U.S. ethnic groups and is more prevalent among Indians, African Americans, Asians, Hispanics, and children with a family history of diabetes.
   3. Many children with type 2 diabetes do not experience classic symptoms like glucose in the urine, weight loss, and increased urination.

D. Development of Heart Disease
   1. Atherosclerosis, which only becomes apparent as heart disease in adulthood, begins in youth.
   2. Children with the highest risk of developing heart disease:
      a. Are sedentary and have central obesity
      b. May have diabetes
      c. May have high blood pressure
      d. May have high blood LDL cholesterol
      e. Some teenagers also take up smoking, which increases their risks of CVD even more.
   3. Some obese children may become thinner into adulthood and their risk of developing CVD is not much higher than most people's risk.
   4. High Blood Cholesterol
      a. Cholesterol testing is recommended for overweight children and adolescents with a family history of heart disease or elevated blood cholesterol.
      b. See Table C13-1 for cholesterol guidelines for children and adolescents
      c. Blood cholesterol in children is a good predictor of their future adult cholesterol and like in adults is related to:
         1. High saturated fat intake
         2. Overweight
         3. Sedentary lifestyle
         4. Children with parents with high cholesterol may need to be screened at a younger age.
   5. High Blood Pressure
      a. Hypertension that develops in the first decades of life, especially in overweight children, tends to worsen if untreated.
      b. Children with hypertension can lower their blood pressure by:
         1. Participating in regular activity
         2. Losing weight or maintaining weight as they grow taller
         3. Restricting dietary sodium

E. Early Childhood Influences on Obesity
   1. Young children learn behaviors from their family members
   2. Calories—and Cautions – Figure C13-2 illustrates factors that can influence young children's weight gain.
      a. Gabby loves sweets and eats several high calorie treats throughout the day.
      b. Children can have an occasional treat but should primarily eat healthy foods.
   3. Physical Activity
      a. Children should play outside more and limit their time in front of the TV or computer.
      b. Figure C13-3 shows the prevalence of obesity related to the number of hours of TV per day.
   4. Food Advertising to Children – Children who watch a lot of TV are bombarded by advertising from food companies that sell high-fat and sugary foods as well as soda.
      a. On average, a child sees over 40,000 TV commercials per year.
      b. Internet "advergames" are games built around a manufacturer's food & used to market it.
      c. Some food manufacturers are reducing their advertising to children.

F. Preventing and Reversing Overweight in Children: A Family Affair (see Table C13-2)
   1. Parents Set An Example – children learn food behaviors from their families
   2. Lifestyle Changes First, Medications Later
      a. An initial goal is to slow the obese child's rate of gain—that is, to hold weight steady while the child grows taller.
      b. If high blood cholesterol is not reduced through lifestyle adjustments, then it can be treated with certain drugs.

3. Obesity Surgery – Physically mature adolescents may be candidates for bariatric surgery if their BMI is above 50 or if their BMI is above 40 with at least one other obesity-related health concern.
4. Achievable Goals, Loving Support – Table C13-2
    a. Keeping an upbeat attitude is very important in addition to setting realistic goals.
    b. Educational websites that can help are listed in Table C13-3.

G. Diet Moderation, Not Deprivation – All children should eat an appropriate amount and variety of foods, regardless of their body weight.
1. Fatty Foods – found everywhere and often rich in saturated fat, *trans* fat, sodium, and calories
    a. Better restaurant choices include soups, salads, vegetables, fruits, and grilled or broiled poultry.
    b. Portion sizes are important to help limit intake of fatty foods.
2. Consumption of Added Sugars
    a. Children and adolescents consume about 16% of total caloric intake as added sugars.
    b. Sugar-sweetened punches & sodas have been linked to excess weight in children.

H. Physical Activity – is an important part of any weight loss or weight control effort with children
1. Table C13-4 lists recommendations for diet and activity to prevent obesity in children.
2. Figure C13-4 names age-appropriate physical activities for young and older children.
3. Some video games offer some amount of physical activity.

I. Darla's Efforts and Gabby's Future
1. Gabby is eating breakfast now, which helps her focus in school.
2. Gabby is eating a healthier bag lunch at school.
3. Darla is keeping fruits available for Gabby and herself to eat to satisfy their sweet tooth.
4. Darla and Gabby have started to prepare Friday's meal together, which gives them time to talk about healthy nutrition.
5. Darla is having Gabby try new vegetables.
6. Darla and Gabby are finding time to be active together and Darla is rewarding Gabby for doing physical chores.

Worksheet 13-1: Infant Formula Label Analysis

Instructions: Use the information for the soy infant formula with DHA and ARA below to answer questions 1-4 on a separate sheet of paper.

Nutrients	Unit	Amount per 100 kcal	Amount per 100 g of powder	Amount per 1 liter (prepared)
Calories	kcal	100	501	670
Protein	g	2.5	12.5	16.8
Fat	g	5.1	25.6	34.2
Carbohydrate	g	11.1	55.6	74.4
Water	g	134		
Linoleic Acid	mg	920	4609	6164
Linolenic Acid	mg	90	451	603
Vitamin A	IU	300	1503	2010
Vitamin D	IU	60	301	402
Vitamin E	IU	3	15.0	20.1
Vitamin K	mcg	9	45.1	60.3
Thiamine (Vitamin B_1)	mcg	60	301	402
Riboflavin (Vitamin B_2)	mcg	94	471	630
Vitamin B_6	mcg	60	301	402
Vitamin B_{12}	mcg	0.3	1.5	2.0
Niacin	mcg	1350	6764	9045
Folic Acid (Folacin)	mcg	16	80.2	107
Pantothenic Acid	mcg	500	2505	3350
Biotin	mcg	5	25.1	33.5
Vitamin C (Ascorbic Acid)	mg	12	60.1	80.4
Choline	mg	24	120.2	160.8
Inositol	mg	6	30.1	40.2
Calcium	mg	105	526	704
Phosphorus	mg	63	316	422
Magnesium	mg	11	55.1	73.7
Iron	mg	1.8	9.0	12.1
Zinc	mg	0.9	4.5	6.0
Manganese	mcg	25	125.3	167.5
Copper	mcg	80	401	536
Iodine	mcg	15	75.2	100.5
Selenium	mcg	3	15.0	20.1
Sodium	mg	40	200	268
Potassium	mg	116	581	777
Chloride	mg	71	356	476

Essential amino acids	Unit	Amount per 100 calories	Amount per 100 g of powder	Amount per 1 liter (prepared)
Histidine	mg	60	305	405
Isoleucine	mg	115	580	775
Leucine	mg	205	1020	1365
Lysine	mg	150	755	1010
Methionine	mg	55	280	370
Phenylalanine	mg	130	660	885
Threonine	mg	105	515	690
Tryptophan	mg	35	175	235
Valine	mg	120	595	795

Non-essential amino acids	Unit	Amount per 100 calories	Amount per 100 g of powder	Amount per 1 liter (prepared)
Alanine	mg	105	525	700
Arginine	mg	180	900	1205
Aspartate	mg	295	1465	1960
Cystine	mg	35	165	220
Glutamate	mg	485	2430	3250
Glycine	mg	105	520	695
Proline	mg	130	660	885
Serine	mg	130	645	865
Tyrosine	mg	85	415	555

Powder Ingredients:
Corn Maltodextrin, Vegetable Oils (Palm Olein, Soy, Coconut, and High-Oleic Safflower or High-Oleic Sunflower), Enzymatically Hydrolyzed Soy Protein Isolate, Sucrose, and less than 1.5% of: Calcium Phosphate, Potassium Citrate, Sodium Citrate, Calcium Citrate, M. alpina Oil*, C. cohnii Oil**, Magnesium Chloride, Calcium Chloride, Potassium Chloride, Ferrous Sulfate, Zinc Sulfate, Copper Sulfate, Potassium Iodide, Sodium Selenate, Soy Lecithin, Sodium Ascorbate, Choline Chloride, Inositol, Alpha-Tocopheryl Acetate, Niacinamide, Calcium Pantothenate, Vitamin A Acetate, Riboflavin, Thiamine Mononitrate, Pyridoxine Hydrochloride, Folic Acid, Biotin, Phylloquinone, Vitamin D_3, Vitamin B_{12}, Ascorbyl Palmitate, Mixed Tocopherols, L-Methionine, Taurine, L-Carnitine.

*A source of arachidonic acid (ARA)[1].
**A source of docosahexaenoic acid (DHA)[1].
[1] Naturally found in breastmilk.

1. Why are essential amino acids listed on the label for this formula?
2. a. Do soy isolates provide all of the essential amino acids?
   b. What is the type of protein that is found in soy isolates called?
3. What are the major sources of energy in this formula? Are they the same as those in breast milk?
4. Why are the nutrients listed in 3 different ways:
   a. Per 100 kcalories?
   b. Per 100 grams?
   c. Per 1 liter?

Instructions: Use the information for the hypoallergenic infant formula below to answer questions 5-6 on a separate sheet of paper.

Dietary Information			
Gluten Free	Yes	Fish Free	Yes
Milk Free	No	Vegetarian	Yes
Egg Free	Yes	Vegan	No
Soya Free	Yes	Kosher	No
Wheat Free	Yes	Halaal	No
Nut Free	Yes		

Nutrition Information			
Typical Values	Unit	Per 100ml	Per 100g
Energy	kJ / kcals	300 / 72	2030 / 487
Protein	g	1.98	13.4
Carbohydrate	g	8.7	58.8
Fat	g	3.26	22
Fibre	g	Nil	Nil

Ingredients
Enzymatically Hydrolysed Whey Protein (protein source), Lactose, Potato Starch, Vegetables Oils (Palm, Olein, Low Erucic Rapeseed, Coconut, Sunflower), Sodium Citrate, Calcium Citrate, Calcium Chloride, Sodium Phosphate, Magnesium Chloride, Sodium Chloride, Sodium Ascorbate, Choline Bitatrate, Ferrous Sulphate. Inositol, Niacin (Nicotinamide), Zinc Sulphate, Vitamin E (DL-tocopheryl Acetate), Calcium-d-Pantothenate, Vitamin A (Retinyl Acetate), Copper Sulphate, Vitamin B_6 (Pyridoxine Hydrochloride), Potassium Chloride, Riboflavin, Thiamin, Vitamin D (Cholecalciferol), Folic Acid, Potassium Iodide, Phylloquinone1, D-Biotin, Vitamin B_{12} (Cyanocobalamine).

5. List the "non-vegan" ingredients of this formula.
6. a. Is breast milk a vegan product?
   b. Why or why not?

Worksheet 13-2: Intake Analysis—Pregnancy and Lactation

Eating Plan B (1 Day's Intake)	Eating Plan C (1 Day's Intake)
6 ounces grapefruit juice	6 5"-diameter pancakes
2 scrambled eggs	$^1/_3$ cup pure maple syrup
1 ounce cheddar cheese	¼ pound of bacon
20 ounces coffee	2 scrambled eggs
2 ounces soy milk	6 ounces orange juice
1 cup fresh raspberries	8 ounces 1% fat milk
1 cup cantaloupe	2 slices of unseeded Italian bread
1 honey oat granola bar	3 ounces of thinly sliced pastrami
1 cup vanilla yogurt	2 Tbsp. spicy brown mustard
6 ounces grilled salmon	2 ounces of cheddar cheese
10 cooked asparagus spears	2 cups of Lucky Charms cereal
1 cup broccoli	1 ½ cups 1% fat milk
4 ounces white wine	6 ounces beef tenderloin
4 ounces blueberry juice + seltzer water	1 ½ cups mashed potatoes
20 barbecue flavor soy crisps	1 cup cooked corn
1 cup wasabi peas	1 cup cooked peas
1 3" x 3" spanakopita	10 ounces Seltzer water
1 cup spinach	2 ounces cheddar cheese
$^1/_3$ cup feta cheese	
¼ cup black olives	
5 grape tomatoes	
3 Tbsp. oil & vinegar dressing	
6 ounces white wine	
¼ cup mixed nuts	
1 cup vanilla ice cream	

Look at Eating Plans B and C:

1. a. Which of these eating plans has the highest level of folate?
   b. Why is this nutrient important during pregnancy?
   c. Which of these eating plans has the highest level of vitamin B_{12}?
   d. The highest level of iron?
   e. How do folate, vitamin B_{12}, and iron work together to ensure a healthy outcome in pregnancy for both the newborn and the mother?
2. a. Which intake item in Eating Plan B is of potential concern for a pregnant or lactating woman?
   b. Why?
3. a. Which of these eating plans may alter the breast milk of a lactating woman such that the infant may be irritated by its consumption?
   b. Which foods could be eliminated from this eating plan to reduce the risk of irritating the infant?
4. a. Which of these eating plans supplies enough calcium, iron, magnesium, and zinc?
   b. What changes in these eating plans are needed to provide adequate amounts of each of these nutrients?

Worksheet 13-3: Chapter 13 Review Crossword Puzzle

Across:	Down:
2. Parents should introduce one food at a time into a infant's/toddler's diet to help them detect possible _____ to foods. 4. The _____ website is a valuable resource for reliable nutrition information that parents can use to help their children select healthier foods. 6. The embryonic cluster of cells will embed itself in the uterine wall by the process of _____. 7. A mineral needed by an infant in amounts over seven times those needed by an adult on a per-pound basis 9. A B vitamin that is needed in larger amounts during pregnancy 10. The _____ sac surrounds the developing fetus and provides the cushioning fluid that protects the fetus. 11. An _____ woman should gain about 28-40 pounds during pregnancy for a single child. 12. Human breast milk contains considerably less _____ than cow's milk.	1. A common complaint of pregnancy that can relieved by eating smaller meals and sitting up while eating 3. A form of diabetes that occurs only during pregnancy 5. A pregnancy typically lasts 40 weeks and is divided into thirds known as _____. 8. Vitamin needed by an infant in amounts nearly seven times those needed by an adult on a per-pound basis

Handout 13-1: Effects of Nutrient Deficiencies during Pregnancy

Nutrient	Deficiency Effect
Energy	Low infant birthweight
Protein	Reduced infant head circumference
Essential fatty acids	Disruption of fetal brain development
Folate	Miscarriage and neural tube defects in the fetus Reduced red blood cell production and anemia in the mother
Vitamin B_{12}	Reduced red blood cell production and anemia in the mother
Vitamin D	Low infant birthweight Occasionally, rickets at birth
Calcium	Decreased infant bone density Thinning of the bones of the mother
Iron	Low infant birthweight and premature birth Anemia in the mother Reduced fetal iron stores
Iodide	Cretinism (varying degrees of mental and physical retardation in the infant)
Zinc	Congenital malformations
Magnesium	Sub-optimal fetal bone and tissue development

Note: Any nutrient deficiency can impact the integrity of the placenta such that it may not nourish the infant as well as it could.

Source: Adapted from L. K. DeBruyne and S. R. Rolfes, *Life Cycle Nutrition: Conception Through Adolescence*, ed. E. N. Whitney (St. Paul, Minn.: West, 1989), p. 68.

Handout 13-2: Feeding Infants around the World

- When is it a good idea to introduce solid foods to an infant?
- Is it best to start cereal at 2 months of age or 6 months of age?
- What factors help people decide when it is best to feed an infant solid food?
- Do people in the developed countries start their infants on solid food at the same time as people in developing countries?

There are many studies that look at when women stop exclusively breastfeeding their infants. Exclusive breastfeeding is the practice of giving an infant only breast milk, water, or liquid supplements for the first 6 months of life. After the infant has received breast milk, they may receive solid foods or infant formula in addition to or in place of breast milk.

What factors may cause a woman to stop the practice of exclusively breastfeeding her infant?

In urban areas:
- Access to infant formulas
- Return to work
- Seeing most women bottle feeding their infants

In poor areas:
- Perception that the infant is not growing properly (known as "growth faltering")
- Illness in the mother
- Malnutrition in the mother

What are the current trends seen in terms of exclusive breastfeeding?

- Globally, <40% of infants under 6 months old are exclusively breastfed
- In the United States, as of 2008, 16.3% of infants were exclusively breastfed for the first 6 months
- 36.0% of U.S. infants were exclusively breastfed for 3 months
- 47.2% of U.S. infants were partially breastfed for the first 6 months

References:

World Health Organization. "10 facts on breastfeeding." Available from http://www.who.int/features/factfiles/breastfeeding/en/index.html.

Centers for Disease Control and Prevention. "Breastfeeding Report Card 2012, United States: Outcome Indicators." Available from http://www.cdc.gov/breastfeeding/data/reportcard2.htm.

Handout 13-3: Why Breast Milk Is the Best Food

Why is breast milk the best for a growing infant—besides being a convenient, instantly ready, and inexpensive form of nutrition?

The colostrum is produced right after the baby is born. This is not typical breast milk. It is a yellowish clear fluid containing a lot of antibodies produced by the mother's immune system. It also contains white blood cells that can bind to pathogenic bacteria to protect the infant against infection. Breast milk comes in around 2-3 days after birth. It also contains antibodies as well as other substances listed below.

What is an antibody?

An antibody is a protein that is produced by the immune system. It binds specifically to a bacterium or another foreign substance such as a toxin that can threaten the health of the body. Pathogens coated with antibodies are more easily eliminated by the body's white blood cells.

What type of antibody is found in breast milk?

A special type of antibody called an "IgA or immunoglobulin type alpha" antibody is found in the colostrum and breast milk. This antibody is produced by the mother's immune system and circulates to her breast tissue, where it can enter the milk. This antibody is found along the mucous surfaces of the digestive and respiratory systems in all people. IgA can block the attachment of pathogenic bacteria and viruses to the surfaces of the digestive and respiratory systems.

What does IgA antibody do for the infant?

This antibody can bind to bacteria that get into the infant's digestive system and prevent them from growing and making the infant ill. Breastfed infants often have fewer digestive infections than bottle-fed infants.

These IgA antibodies can also be found in the infant's mucus along their respiratory system. This may lower the risk of respiratory infection in breastfed infants.

White Blood Cells

These are protective blood cells that pass from the mother's immune system into her breast tissue into the breast milk. These cells can kill potentially harmful bacteria that may cause illness in the infant's digestive system.

Immune System Enhancing Substances

The mother's breast milk also contains gamma interferon, which can help the infant's immune system to become stronger so that the infant can avoid or better fight off an infection.

What are the advantages of breastfeeding for the infant?

Breastfeeding is associated with a lower risk of numerous health problems in the infant, including:

- Ear infections
- Stomach viruses
- Diarrhea

- Respiratory infections
- Atopic dermatitis
- Asthma
- Obesity
- Type 1 and type 2 diabetes
- Childhood leukemia
- Sudden infant death syndrome (SIDS)
- Necrotizing enterocolitis (a GI tract disease affecting preterm infants)

What are the advantages of breastfeeding for the mother?

- Breastfeeding uses an additional 500 kilocalories per day, which helps with weight control for the mother.
- Breastfeeding may reduce the risk of type 2 diabetes, breast cancer, ovarian cancer, and postpartum depression.
- Breastfeeding helps the uterus return to its prepregnancy size.
- Breastfeeding strengthens the bond between mother and infant by allowing the mother to sit quietly with and focus on her infant while breastfeeding.

References:

Office on Women's Health, U.S. Department of Health and Human Services. "Benefits of Breastfeeding." Available from: http://www.womenshealth.gov/breastfeeding/benefits/.

FDA Consumer Magazine October 1995 Issue

Morisky, Donald E. et al, Breast Feeding Practices in Pakistan. *Pakistan Journal of Nutrition*, Volume 1 (3), pages 137-142, 2002.

Kramer, Michael S., M.D. and Ritsuko Kakuma, M.Sc. *The Optimal Duration of Exclusive Breastfeeding: A Systematic Review*. World Health Organization, 2001.

Chapter 14 – Child, Teen, and Older Adult

Quick List: IM Resources for Chapter 14

- **Class preparation resources:** learning objectives/key points, suggested activities and projects, lecture outline
- **Assignment materials:** **Related LO**
  - Critical thinking questions (with answer key) 14.1, 14.2, 14.4
  - Discussion questions (with answers) for Controversy 14 .... 14.6
  - Worksheet 14-1: Juice Drink Label Analysis 14.1
  - Worksheet 14-2: Intake Analysis—Children and Older Adults 14.1, 14.4
  - Worksheet 14-3: How to Plan Meals for an Allergic Child 14.1
  - **New!** Worksheet 14-4: Chapter 14 Review Crossword Puzzle
- **Enrichment materials:**
  - Handout 14-1: Supervised Food Activities for Preschoolers[1] 14.1
  - Handout 14-2: Ensuring Adequate Nutrition for the Elderly 14.4

Chapter Learning Objectives and Key Points

14.1 **Discuss the nutritional needs of young children and explain how a food allergy can impact the diet.**
Other than specific recommendations for fluoride, vitamin D, and iron, well-fed children do not need supplements. USDA food patterns provide adequate nourishment for growth without obesity. Healthy eating habits are learned in childhood, and parents teach best by example. Choking can often be avoided by supervision during meals and avoiding hazardous foods. Iron deficiency and toxicity pose a threat to children. Blood lead levels have declined in recent times, but even low lead levels can harm children. Food allergy may be diagnosed by the presence of antibodies. Food aversions can be related to food allergies or to adverse reactions to food. ADHD is not caused by food allergies or additives. Hunger and poverty may cause behavior problems. Carbohydrate-rich foods contribute to dental caries. Breakfast supports school performance. Free or reduced-priced nutritious school meals are available to low-income children. School meals are designed to provide at least a third of certain nutrients that children need daily. Recent changes to the school breakfast and lunch menus include increased availability of fruits, vegetables, whole grains, and low-fat and fat-free fluid milk; reduced sodium in meals; and reduced levels of saturated and *trans* fats. Competitive foods are often high in calories, saturated fat, salt, and sugar but low in key nutrients.

14.2 **Explain ways in which a teenager's choice of soda over milk or soy milk may jeopardize nutritional health.**
The adolescent growth spurt increases the need for energy and nutrients. The normal gain of body fat during adolescence may be mistaken for obesity, particularly in girls. The need for iron increases during adolescence in both boys and girls. Sufficient calcium and vitamin D intakes are also crucial during adolescence. Menstrual cycle hormones affect metabolism, glucose tolerance, and appetite. No single foods have been proved to aggravate acne, but stress can worsen it. The gatekeeper can encourage teens to meet nutrient requirements by providing nutritious snacks.

14.3 **Contrast life expectancy with life span, and name some lifestyle factors associated with successful aging.**
Life expectancy for U.S. adults is increasing, but the human life span is set by genetics. Life choices can greatly affect how long a person lives and the quality of life in the later years.

14.4 **Outline food-related factors that can predict malnutrition in older adults.**
Energy needs decrease with age. Physical activity maintains lean tissue during aging. Protein needs remain about the same through adult life, but physical conditions dictate appropriate protein sources. Including fiber can help older adults to avoid constipation. Arthritis causes pain and immobility, and older people with arthritis often fall for quack cures. Vitamin A absorption increases with aging. Elderly people are vulnerable to deficiencies of vitamin D and vitamin B_{12}. Aging alters vitamin and mineral needs; some rise while others

---

[1] Source: Adapted from A. A. Hertzler, Preschoolers' food handling skills--motor development, *Journal of Nutrition Education* 21 (1989): 100B-100C.

decline. In rats and other species, food energy deprivation lengthens the lives of individuals. Claims for life extension through antioxidants or other supplements are common hoaxes. Alzheimer's disease causes some degree of brain deterioration in many people older than age 65. Nutrition care gains importance as Alzheimer's disease progresses. Food choices of the elderly are affected by aging, altered health status, and changed life circumstances. Federal programs can help to provide nourishment, transportation, and social interactions.

14.5 **Design a healthy meal plan for an elderly widower with a fixed income.**

14.6 **Describe several specific nutrient–drug interactions, and name some herbs that may interfere with the action of medication.**

Critical Thinking Questions

1. a. *Discuss reasons why young children may not be getting enough iron in their diets.*

Many children drink a lot of milk, which contains calcium. A large amount of dietary calcium can interfere with iron absorption and promote iron deficiency. Also, children may not be accustomed to eating foods that contain significant amounts of iron, such as those shown in Table 14-3. Vegetarian children do not consume the more easily absorbed heme iron from animal foods, so they need to get enough iron from non-heme foods as well as ample vitamin C to increase absorption of the non-heme iron.

b. *How can iron deficiency impact the child's health and mental well-being?*

Low levels of iron can interfere with a child's ability to concentrate and learn in school. Some of these children may be labeled as "learning disabled" or "difficult" when all they may be experiencing is an iron deficiency. If a child does have anemia as a result of a more severe iron deficiency, they may be lethargic and may seem less engaged.

2. a. *Distinguish among a food allergy, a food intolerance, and a food aversion.*

A food allergy is caused by the stimulation of the immune system in response to a food. Antibodies can be found in the blood and tissues. These antibodies can trigger a variety of allergic responses from mild itching to severe anaphylaxis. A food allergy can be detected by allergy testing. See Table 14-8 for symptoms of an allergic reaction to food.

A food intolerance is an adverse reaction to a food that does not involve the immune system response but reliably occurs after the ingestion of the food. Lactose intolerance is an example of a food intolerance that can cause unpleasant effects.

Food aversion results from an unpleasant past association with a particular food. A child may avoid a food due to an aversion but it could also be a warning of a more serious food allergy.

b. *How would you manage a food allergy?*

It is very critical for the child to avoid the food that triggers an allergy. Testing would need to be carried out to find out what the child is allergic to. Careful food label reading is required and other people such as cafeteria personnel need to be aware of the child's food allergy. The child should not be in the same room as the food that triggers the allergy. A child should also have access to epinephrine, a drug that can lessen the severity of an anaphylactic reaction.

c. *How would you manage a food aversion?*

Children with food aversions due to lactose intolerance would also want to avoid the food so as not to experience the side effects. Other food aversions may just take time to go away as the person gets older. It is important not to force foods on a child.

3. *Describe how the gatekeeper role of the parent can improve the adolescent's diet to avoid some common diet-related problems often encountered during adolescence.*

Parents can be present and can provide the adolescents with handy, nutritious foods such as whole-wheat crackers, cereals, fresh fruit, milk, yogurt, or cheese sticks for a quick snack that does not supply excess calories. The parent can also discuss with the adolescent the nutritional value of foods. Conditions such as PMS or acne may have a dietary component and may be helped by the addition of nutritious whole foods to the adolescent's diet. Parents are a key influence on an adolescent's beliefs and behaviors.

4. *Discuss two age-related changes that can be prevented or slowed, explaining how lifestyle or diet modifications can impact these age-related changes.*

   Table 14-15 shows age-related changes that can be prevented or slowed by lifestyle measures. High blood cholesterol, for example, could be managed by eating foods that are lower in saturated fats. Also, regular physical activity may help reduce high cholesterol and prevent the slowing of metabolism, buildup of body fat, and loss of joint flexibility associated with aging.

5. *List any 2 essential nutrients that are of special concern to the elderly population and what can be done to ensure that elderly individuals get enough of these nutrients.*

   The elderly don't often get enough water in their diets. Their ability to detect thirst is reduced as they age and they may become confused or disoriented as a result of dehydration. Older adults should drink 9-11 cups of water each day.

   Many elderly do not absorb vitamin B_{12} well as a result of a reduction in stomach acid and intrinsic factor that occurs with age. This can result in anemia and lethargy that could be mistaken for another condition. Some people may need to get injections of vitamin B_{12} or large doses of vitamin B_{12} by mouth to ensure adequate levels in the body. There are other nutrients that could be deficient in the elderly person's diet as well.

6. *Give any 2 reasons why young school-age children today may have lower vitamin D levels than children 30-40 years ago.*

   Many young children do not play outside as much as children did in the past. They tend to watch more TV or play video games indoors. This reduces their exposure to the sun and so their skin makes far less vitamin D precursor.

   Many young children do not drink as much milk. This could due to a variety of factors: (1) Milk is more expensive than in the past, so children may drink more soda or sweetened drinks in place of milk. (2) Many children may be lactose intolerant and do not eat or drink foods that are good sources of vitamin D.

Controversy Discussion Questions

1. *Why are people told not to take certain medications with grapefruit juice?*

   Grapefruit and grapefruit juice contain a compound that can interfere with the metabolism of many drugs, allowing the drugs to build up to undesirable levels in the blood. Most drug labels state, "Take on an empty stomach," which helps reduce the risk of this type of interaction.

2. *List any 3 potential concerns with people taking supplements containing herbal remedies.*

   The safety and effectiveness of herbal remedies have not been rigorously tested by the FDA. An herbal remedy could be less concentrated than the claim states or could be contaminated with toxic substances that are not tested for.

   Some herbal remedies can affect how medicines work in the body. For example, certain herbs can increase the anti-blood clotting effects of pain relievers.

   People who take herbal remedies often do not inform their healthcare providers. Such individuals could be prescribed a drug or have surgery and experience a side-effect from the herbal remedy. This could catch the healthcare team "off guard" since they are not informed about the ingestion of the herbal remedies. See Table C14-3 for other drug-herbal remedy interactions.

3. *How does the use of marijuana affect nutritional status differently than the use of cocaine?*

   Chronic marijuana use often increases the appetite. Many people who use marijuana often eat sugary or fatty foods, and may gain weight as a result.

   Chronic cocaine use results in the decrease of a person's appetite. People who abuse cocaine are usually undernourished and if they have an eating disorder, cocaine use may make this eating disorder worse. In a study, rats given cocaine or food always chose cocaine over the food and would die of starvation.

4. *How does chronic use of laxatives in an attempt to lose weight lead to nutritional deficiencies?*

   Laxatives contain magnesium, which can stimulate the release of water from the cells of the intestines and can speed up the transit of nutrients such that fewer nutrients are absorbed. This can interfere with absorption of glucose, calcium, potassium,vitamin D, and other fat-soluble vitamins. See Table C14-1 for selected drug-nutrient interactions..

Worksheet Answer Key

Worksheet 14-1: Juice Drink Label Analysis

1. a. 200 milliliters.
   b. 200 mL / 236 mL per cup = 0.85 cups which is a bit over ¾ of a cup.
2. 27 grams sugars / 27 grams of total carbohydrate × 100 = 100%
3. a. High-fructose corn syrup
   b. It is a chemically modified form of cornstarch.
4. A container is a box of 10 pouches.
5. a. This would not be a good choice because it is not nutrient dense.
   b. This product is high in added sugars and low in most other nutrients.
   c. A child could have 1% fat milk or 100% fruit juice with more vitamins. He or she could also have water!

Worksheet 14-2: Intake Analysis—Children and Older Adults

1. a. Eating Plan G has healthier choices.
   b. The fruits and vegetables provide ample vitamins and minerals without a lot of fat. The foods are not processed so there are not a lot of artificial ingredients and preservatives.
2. a. Eating Plan D may appeal to more kids since many kids like chocolate milk, crackers, and peanut butter.
   b. Factors such as advertising on TV, convenience of pre-packaged foods, choices of foods of friends, or lack of access to fresh food may influence children's choices.
3. Eating Plan D includes foods containing peanuts and nuts, which are known to cause severe allergies in some children.
4. a. Proteins and monounsaturated fats are at low levels in Eating Plan G.
   b. Whole-grain breads, nuts, or soy products could be added to increase the levels of monounsaturated fats and proteins.
5. a. Eating Plan D may appeal to older people since they may like chocolate milk and peanut butter more than fresh or dried fruits.
   b. Older people may have dental or mouth issues that make it difficult to eat fruits or solid foods.
   c. Older people could eat yogurts, cheese, soft breads, and canned fruits, which are softer in texture but still adequate in most nutrients.

Worksheet 14-4: Chapter 14 Review Crossword Puzzle

1. histamine
2. aversion
3. sarcopenia
4. competitive
5. neophobia
6. Plaque
7. premenstrual
8. potassium
9. vitamin A
10. dehydration
11. Tyramine
12 statins
13. DETERMINE
14. laxatives

Learning Activities & Project Ideas

Activity 14-1: Devise Games for Kids[2] LO 14.1
Have students devise games and game boards for teaching children nutrition facts. These games can be used in dentists' and pediatricians' waiting rooms. For example, students may design a set of cards with a nutrition fact on each one. The object would be for the kids to turn up two matching cards.

Activity 14-2: Assess Nutrition Information Presented on TV Project[3] LO 14.1
Have students view 2 ½ hours of prime time children's television (cartoons). Instruct them to count the total number of ads and categorize them by types (food versus other). Food ads should be further categorized into food groups and miscellaneous. Have students determine the percentage of ads for food items and assess the quality of nutrition information conveyed by the ads.

Activity 14-3: Vending Machine Survey[4] LO 14.2, 14.4
Have students conduct a community-wide survey of foods and beverages in vending machines in public places and comment on the nutritional value of the foods/drinks offered for sale. Students should note any differences in the nutritional value of food items in vending machines at different locations. For example, do school vending machines offer more nutritious food options than vending machines in a public place like a train station?

Chapter Lecture Outline

I. Introduction: 81% of children's diets in the U.S. were ranked as "poor" or "needing improvement."

II. Early and Middle Childhood – Children's nutrient needs reflect their stage of growth.
  A. Feeding a Healthy Young Child
    1. At no time in life does the human diet change faster than during the second year.
      a. From 12 to 24 months, a child's diet changes from infant foods consisting of mostly formula or breast milk to mostly modified adult foods.
      b. Milk remains the central source of calcium, protein, and other nutrients.
    2. Appetite Regulation
      a. An infant's appetite decreases markedly near the first birthday and fluctuates thereafter.
      b. Today's children too often eat foods high in sugars, saturated fat, and calories.
      c. Faced with a tempting array of such foods, children may disregard internal satiety signals and overconsume calories, inviting obesity.
      d. It is best to provide healthy food choices with occasional treats so that children grow and gain weight in an appropriate way.
    3. Energy – See Table 14-1 for energy requirements of children
      a. A child up to a year old needs 800 calories per day; at age 6 years, they need 1600 calories, whereas a 10 year old needs 1,800 calories per day.
      b. Vegan children may not get enough calories from fruits, vegetables, and whole grains so added soy products, legumes, and nut or seed butters may help them meet their energy needs.
    4. Protein – The total amount of protein needed increases as the child gets larger; most American diets provide adequate amounts of protein.
    5. Carbohydrate and Fiber
      a. Carbohydrate recommendations are based on glucose use by the brain.
      b. A one year old's brain is large for the size of the body, so the glucose demanded by the one year old falls in the adult range.
      c. Children's fiber intakes should meet recommendations, but should be adjusted downward for picky eaters who take in too few calories each day (see Table 14-2).
    6. Fat and Fatty Acids
      a. Children need moderate amounts of healthful fats for nutrients and energy.

---

[2] Contributed by Gail Kauwell, University of Florida

[3] Contributed by Kathy Watson, Arizona Western College

[4] Contributed by Louisa Marchionda, Youngstown State University

   b. Saturated fat should be limited to prevent early atherosclerosis.
   c. DRI range for total fat intakes: 30-40% for ages 1-3, 25-35% for ages 4-18
7. The Need for Vitamins and Minerals
   a. As child grows larger, so does the demand for vitamins and minerals.
   b. Well-nourished children do not need supplements, except possibly fluoride, vitamin D, & iron.
8. Vitamin D – Children need 15 micrograms of vitamin D each day; many children do not receive enough vitamin D and so may need to take a supplement.
9. Iron
   a. Iron deficiency is a problem worldwide and occurs in many U.S. toddlers due to:
      1. Switching to whole milk and unfortified milk
      2. Diminished iron stores from birth and more demands for iron as the blood volume increases
      3. Unreliable food consumption
   b. Children's diets should supply about 7-10 milligrams of iron per day.
   c. See Table 14-3 for a list of iron-containing foods that kids like
10. Planning Children's Meals
   a. Figure 14-2 shows the MyPlate resources for children
   b. Table 14-4 shows the USDA eating patterns for children (1000-1800 calories)

B. Mealtimes and Snacking – The childhood years are the last chance to influence the child's food choices.
1. Current U.S. Children's Food Intakes
   a. The Feeding Infants and Toddlers Study found that most infants take in too few fruits and vegetables.
   b. About 25% of children older than 9 years of age eat no fruits and vegetables in a typical day.
   c. Most popular fruit and vegetable are bananas and French fries, neither a rich source of needed vitamins and minerals
   d. Most children consume too little vitamin E, calcium, magnesium, potassium, and fiber.
   e. Most children ate too much saturated fat and sodium.
2. Dealing with Children's Preferences
   a. Children naturally like nutritious foods in all the food groups, with one exception—vegetables.
   b. Presentation and variety may be the key to getting children to like vegetables.
   c. Serve small portions of warm, crunchy, bright vegetables.
   d. Don't bribe or force foods since kids will not develop a preference for these foods anyway.
   e. Most children can have an occasional high-calorie food but these foods should be nutritious.
   f. A steady diet of high-calorie treats leads to nutrient deficiencies and obesity.
3. Fear of New Foods
   a. Children can develop fears of new foods, called food neophobia, for little apparent reason.
   b. Some of these food fears may be a protective mechanism that kept ancestral toddlers from tasting toxic plants.
   c. Children outgrow these fears by adolescence and parental persistence is key.
   d. Table 14-5 gives some good suggestions to help caregivers feed picky eaters.
4. Child Preferences versus Parental Authority – The parent must be responsible for what the child is offered to eat, but the child should be allowed to decide how much and even whether to eat.
5. Snacking
   a. Healthy snacks can be as health promoting as small meals.
   b. Keep snack foods simple and easily available.
6. Restaurant Choices
   a. Selecting healthy foods for children at a restaurant can be challenging to parents.
   b. It may help to split a regular meal or order from the salads and appetizers section of the menu.
   c. Order vegetable toppings or low-fat meats on pizza.
   d. Request water, skim milk, or fruit juice for beverages.
7. Choking – To prevent choking:
   a. Encourage child to sit.
   b. Avoid round foods such as grapes, nuts, hard candies, popcorn, tough meat, peanut butter eaten from the spoon, and pieces of hot dogs.
8. Food Skills
   a. Food skills of children can be employed to involve them in meal preparation.
   b. Table 14-6 describes food skills of preschoolers.

C. How Do Nutrient Deficiencies Affect a Child's Brain?
1. The detrimental effects of nutrient deficiencies in children in developed nations can be subtle.
2. Iron deficiency is the most widespread nutrition problem of children and causes abnormalities in both physical health and behavior.
3. A child's behavior and intellectual performance will be affected by a deficiency of iron before anemia even begins.
4. Iron toxicity, a major form of poisoning in children, is due to accidental ingestion of iron supplements.

D. The Problem of Lead
1. More than 300,000 children in the U.S., most under the age of six, have blood lead concentrations high enough to cause mental, behavior, and other health problems.
2. Sources of Lead
    a. Lead can come from drinking water (from old pipes) or paint or metal that contains lead.
    b. Some chewable vitamins may have lead in them as well.
3. Harm from Lead
    a. Harm from lead results in learning difficulties, hearing problems, & kidney problems that may be very subtle at first.
    b. Adolescents with high lead levels may have reduced IQs and be at risk for violent behavior.
4. Lead and Nutrient Interactions
    a. Children who are deficient in calcium, iron, zinc, vitamin C, or vitamin D may be at increased risk of lead toxicity.
    b. Lead poisoning has declined dramatically due to bans on leaded gasoline and paints.
    c. Lead in older homes with older plumbing or lead-based paints is still a concern.
    d. Table 14-7 describes how to prevent lead poisoning.

E. Food Allergy, Intolerance, and Aversion
1. Introduction
    a. Only about 8% of children have true food allergies.
    b. Children sometimes "grow out" of their food allergies (notably allergy to peanuts may fade with time) until in adulthood food allergies affect only 1 or 2% of the population.
2. Food Allergy
    a. Food allergies always involve the immune system.
        1. A true food allergy occurs when a food protein enters the body and triggers an immune response.
        2 The immune system of an allergic person reacts to the foreign molecule as it does to any antigen: it produces antibodies.
        3. On subsequent exposures, the antibodies react with other body cells, which release histamine, causing the allergic reaction.
        4. In some people, the result is the life-threatening food allergy reaction of anaphylactic shock.
    b. Peanuts, tree nuts, milk, eggs, wheat, soybeans, fish, and shellfish are the foods most likely to trigger this extreme reaction.
    c. Children who experience anaphylaxis should have access to injectable epinephrine.
3. Allergen Ingestion
    a. Foods containing eggs, peanut butter, or soy products can often be found in other foods or on other surfaces.
    b. Parents of allergic children must make sure that the cafeteria does not allow children to swap lunches.
4. Food Labels – Warning labels on foods must clearly identify any potential allergens, as shown in Figure 14-3.
5. Detection of Food Allergy
    a. Elimination diets and skin prick tests can help identify the allergenic food.
    b. Diagnosis is based on the presence of antibodies, and tests are imperative to determine whether allergy exists.
    c. Delayed allergic reactions may be harder to detect.
    d. See Table 14-8 for symptoms of an allergic reaction to food
6. Food Intolerance and Aversion
    a. Food intolerance is characterized by unpleasant symptoms that reliably occur after consumption of certain foods.

b. Food aversion is an intense dislike of food that may be a biological response to a food that once caused trouble.

F. Can Diet Make a Child Hyperactive?
1. Hyperactivity or attention-deficit/ hyperactivity disorder (ADHD) is a learning disability that occurs in 5 to 10% of young, school-aged children.
2. Food Allergies – ADHD is not caused by food allergies or additives, but certain additives (artificial colors & Na benzoate) may worsen hyperactive symptoms
3. Sugar and Behavior – studies have shown that sugar doesn't cause hyperactivity, but may displace healthier food choices
4. Inconsistent Care and Poverty
 a. Temporary "hyper" behavior may reflect excess caffeine consumption or inconsistent care.
 b. Poverty may cause behavior problems, especially if combined with a poor diet and lack of physical activity.
 c. About 12 million U.S. children are hungry at least some of the time; they lack iron, magnesium, zinc, and omega-3 fatty acids.

G. Dental Caries
1. How Caries Develop – Caries are caused by the erosion of tooth enamel by acid produced by bacteria that cling to the teeth (see Figure 14-4).
2. Advanced Dental Disease
 a. The bacteria can work down between the tooth and gum-line to cause gum disease or tooth loss.
 b. The bacteria can get into the bloodstream as well, which could increase the risk of heart disease.
3. Food and Caries
 a. Bacteria produce acid for 20-30 minutes after they exposed to carbohydrates.
 b. Table 14-9 lists foods that are more or less apt to cause dental caries.

H. Is Breakfast Really the Most Important Meal of the Day for Children?
1. A nutritious breakfast is a central feature of a child's diet that supports healthy growth and development.
2. Breakfast is critical to school performance.
3. School breakfast programs help to fill the need.
4. Table 14-10 offers suggestions for preparing breakfast during rushed mornings.

I. How Nourishing Are the Meals Served at School?
1. The National School Lunch and Breakfast Programs – School lunches are designed to provide age-appropriate servings of needed foods each day & to follow the *Dietary Guidelines for Americans.*
 a. About 30 million children receive reduced-cost or free school meals.
 b. For many students, school lunches provide a majority of nutrients consumed each day.
 c. Table 14-11 shows typical school lunch patterns for children of different ages.
2. Competitive Foods at School
 a. There is concern about private vendors in school lunchrooms who offer competitive foods, unregulated meals, or even heavily advertised fast foods that compete with nutritious school lunches.
 b. Children who choose competitive foods eat less fruits and vegetables.
 c. Soda and snack vending machines also tempt students.
 d. Many schools are now reducing or eliminating competitive foods.

III. Nutrition in Adolescence – Teenagers are not fed; they eat.

A. Growth and nutrient needs of teenagers – Need for vitamins, minerals, the energy nutrients, and, in fact, all nutrients is greater during adolescence than at any other time of life except pregnancy and lactation.
1. The Adolescent Growth Spurt – Girls experience a growth spurt at 10-11 years and peak at 12 years while boys start to grow quickly between 12-13 years and peak at 14 years.
2. Energy Needs and Physical Activity
 a. Energy needs for boys and girls vary widely; e.g., a 15-year-old boy may need 3,500 calories whereas a girl of the same age may only need 1,800 calories.
 b. About 15% of U.S. children and adolescents (6-19) are overweight.
3. Weight Standards and Body Fatness
 a. Growth charts are used to monitor gains in height & weight.
 b. Girls develop higher % body fat

B. Nutrient Needs
   1. The Special Case of Iron
      a. The need for iron increases for males and females for different reasons.
      b. Boys need more iron to build more lean body mass.
      c. Iron losses incurred through menstruation increase a woman's need for iron.
      d. Table 14-12 lists iron requirements in adolescence.
   2. Calcium and the Bones
      a. The bones are growing longer at a rapid rate thanks to a special bone structure, the epiphyseal plate, that disappears as a teenager reaches adult height (see Figure 14-5).
      b. Sufficient calcium intake during adolescence is crucial to support normal bone growth & density.
      c. 70% of boys and 85% of girls do not consume the recommended amounts of calcium.
      d. When teens choose soft drinks and abandon milk, they increase their chances of bone disease later on in life.
      e. See Figure 14-7, which shows declining milk consumption of adolescents since 1978
   3. Vitamin D
      a. Needed for calcium absorption and proper bone growth
      b. Youth who do not receive 15 micrograms per day of vitamin D should take a supplement.

C. Common Concerns
   1. Menstruation – can bring hormonal changes that can affect the mood, metabolic rate, glucose tolerance, and food intakes of young women
   2. Acne
      a. No one knows why some people get acne while others do not, but heredity plays a role.
      b. No foods have been shown to worsen acne, but stress can aggravate it.
      c. Supplements are useless against acne, but sunlight, proven medications, & stress relief can help.
   3. A Consumer's Guide to Nutrition for PMS Relief
      a. Who Has It and What It Is
         1. Up to 32%% of women suffer from premenstrual syndrome (PMS) symptoms including: cramps, back pain, aches in the abdomen, acne, swelling of the face and limbs, food cravings, abnormal thirst, pain and lumps in the breast, diarrhea, and mood changes, including depression and nervousness.
         2. The 6 core symptoms of PMS are: anxiety and tension, mood swings, aches and pains, increased appetite and cravings, abdominal cramps, and decreased interest in activities.
      b. Causes
         1. PMS may be due to an altered response to estrogen and progesterone.
         2. This can affect the action of serotonin in the brain, leading to some of the depression-like symptoms.
      c. Energy Metabolism
         1. The basal metabolic rate during sleep speeds up about 2 weeks before menstruation.
         2. Appetite for carbohydrate-containing foods & calorie & possibly alcohol intake increase.
         3. Vitamins and Minerals
            a. Links with calcium and vitamin D are intriguing:
               1. Calcium intakes of 1,000 milligrams per day have significantly improved the symptoms of PMS.
               2. Girls and young women who get plenty of calcium and vitamin D from foods such as milk are reported to have a lower risk of developing PMS.
               3. High doses of vitamin B_6 were thought to alleviate PMS but long-term use of such supplements may affect the function of the nervous system.
         5. Ongoing Research – suggests that taking magnesium supplements, reducing sodium or alcohol intake, or taking diuretics may not help PMS symptoms
      c. Moving Ahead – Simple measures like staying physically active and eating a nutritious diet may help the most with PMS.

D. Eating Patterns and Nutrient Intakes
   1. Roles of Adults
      a. The adult should be the gatekeeper, controlling the type and availability of food in the teenager's environment.
      b. Many adults work outside of the home so the teen becomes the gatekeeper.

2. Snacks
   a. Represent ~ ¼ of energy intake & can provide micronutrients if chosen carefully.
   b. Adolescents who snack more frequently may actually be less likely to be overweight than those who snack less often.
   c. The gatekeeper should set a good example and provide teachable moments about nutrition but ultimately teens make the choices.

IV. The Later Years
  A. As the Twig Is Bent... People who reach old age in good health most often:
    1. Are nonsmokers
    2. Drink alcohol moderately
    3. Are highly physically active
    4. Maintain a healthy body weight
  B. Life Expectancy – How long a person lives depends on several factors.
    1. Since 1950, the population older than age 65 has tripled and the number of people older than 85 has gone up 7-fold.
    2. An estimated 70 to 80% of the average person's life expectancy depends on lifestyle behaviors with genes determining the remaining 20 to 30%.
  C. Human Life Span – No diet or supplement can extend the lifespan, which is thought to be 125 years.

V. Nutrition in the Later Years – see Table 14-14 for nutrient concerns & Table 14-15 for what to expect in aging
  A. Energy and Activity
    1. Body's BMR decreases 3 to 5% per decade as thyroxine diminishes
    2. Energy Recommendations
      a. Decline ~5% per decade after 50
      b. Energy needs decrease with age, but exercise burns off excess fuel, maintains lean tissue, and brings health benefits.
      c. Staying physically active is critical to boosting immunity and metal functioning.
      d. Older people can suffer from a failure to thrive, which includes the following:
        1. Decreased ability to function – inability to shop, cook, or prepare meals
        2. Depression or anxiety
        3. Malnutrition that impairs immune function & wound healing, muscle tissue loss
      e. A BMI of 25-32 is associated with a lower death risk.
    3. Physical Activity – helps reduce loss of lean tissue (muscle & bone)
  B. Protein Needs
    1. Protein needs remain about the same for older people as for young adults.
    2. Proteins from meats may present a problem for people who have dental problems.
    3. Choose low-fat, fiber-rich protein foods to help control other health problems.
  C. Carbohydrates and Fiber
    1. Generous carbohydrate intakes are recommended for older adults.
    2. Few older adults obtain enough dietary fiber, which is important to avoid constipation.
  D. Fats and Arthritis
    1. Osteoarthritis – Nutrition does not seem to play a role in osteoarthritis, a deterioration of the joints, but it is more common in overweight people.
    2. Rheumatoid Arthritis
      a. The omega-3 fatty acid EPA may reduce the affects of one type of arthritis, rheumatoid arthritis.
      b. Rheumatoid arthritis is a malfunction in which the immune system mistakenly attacks the bone coverings as if they were foreign tissue.
    3. Gout – a form of inflammatory arthritis that affects millions of U.S. adults and may be associated with overweight, insulin resistance, higher blood pressure, lead exposure, and intake of meats, alcohol, and sugary drinks
  E. Vitamin Needs
    1. Vitamin A – Vitamin A is the only vitamin whose absorption increases with aging, but older people should still get enough beta-carotene in their diets.
    2. Vitamin D
      a. Older adults should get at least 15-20 micrograms of vitamin D each day.

b. Vitamin D synthesis declines fourfold, setting the stage for deficiency.
c. Older people do not get out into the sun and avoid dairy products.

3. Vitamin B_{12} – absorption also declines due to declining stomach acid production; adults over 51 need 2.4 micrograms/day of vitamin B_{12} from foods
4. Other Vitamins and Phytochemicals – Lifelong high intakes of vegetables correlate with less macular degeneration and cataracts.

F. Water and the Minerals

1. Water
   a. Dehydration is a major risk for older adults.
   b. Total body water decreases with age and so dehydration can occur quickly.
   c. The thirst mechanism is imprecise and the kidneys are less efficient in recapturing water before it is lost as urine.
   d. Older people that are dehydrated can get confused, which is mistaken for a form of senile dementia.
   e. In a bedridden person dehydration can lead to pressure ulcers.
   f. People can keep their drinking cups by the sink to make drinking juice or water a habit.
2. Iron
   a. Iron status generally improves in later life, especially in women after menstruation ceases and in those who take iron supplements, eat red meat regularly, and include vitamin C-rich fruits in their daily diet.
   b. When iron deficiency occurs, it is often due to low food intake or other causes such as from ulcers, hemorrhoids, effects of medication, and poor iron absorption due to reduced stomach acid.
3. Zinc
   a. Zinc deficiencies are also common and can impair the immune system and increase the risk of developing pneumonia.
   b. Zinc deficiency can depress the appetite and blunt the sense of taste, leading to low food intakes and worsening zinc status.
4. Calcium – Calcium absorption declines with age and people fail to consume enough calcium-rich foods due to a increased tendency for lactose intolerance.
5. Multinutrient Supplements – elderly often benefit from balanced low-dose supplement + calcium

G. Can Nutrition Help People to Live Longer?

1. Lifestyle Factors – moderate use of alcohol, regular nutritious meals, weight control, adequate sleep, abstinence from smoking, and regular physical activity can make a difference in aging
2. Energy Restriction
   a. In rats and other species, food energy deprivation may lengthen the lives of individuals (see Table 14-16).
   b. Moderate calorie restriction may help reduce risk of high blood pressure, glucose intolerance, and immune system impairments.

H. Immunity and Inflammation

1. Loss of immune function with aging + over-stimulation by illness = chronic inflammation
2. Conditions such as atherosclerosis, Alzheimer's disease, obesity, and rheumatoid arthritis may involve inflammation.
3. Poor nutrition can compromise immune function & contribute to death by infectious disease.
4. Claims for life extension through antioxidants or other supplements are common hoaxes.

I. Can Foods or Supplements Affect the Course of Alzheimer's Disease?

1. Alzheimer's disease causes some degree of brain deterioration in many people past age 65.
2. The effects of minerals such as aluminum, copper, or zinc on Alzheimer's disease progression are being investigated.
3. The possible protective effects of foods containing DHA are being investigated.

J. Food Choices of Older Adults

1. Introduction
   a. Older people who enjoy a wide variety of foods are better nourished and have a better quality of life than those who eat a monotonous diet.
   b. The quality of life among the 85 and older group has improved.
   c. Evidence supports the idea that a single low-dose multivitamin-mineral tablet a day can improve resistance to disease in older people.

2. Obstacles to Adequacy – The DETERMINE predictors of malnutrition in the elderly (described in Table 14-17):
    a. Disease
    b. Eating poorly
    c. Tooth loss or oral pain
    d. Economic hardship
    e. Reduced social contact
    f. Multiple medications
    g. Involuntary weight loss or gain
    h. Need of assistance with self-care
    i. Elderly person older than 80 years
3. Programs that Help
    a. Assistance programs can help by providing nutritious meals, offering opportunities for social interactions, and easing financial problems.
    b. Examples are Senior Nutrition Program, Meals on Wheels, and Supplemental Nutrition Assistance Program (SNAP)
    c. Approximately 25% of elderly people benefit from these programs.

K. Food Feature: Single Survival and Nutrition on the Run
1. Singles of all ages face problems ranging from selection of restaurant foods to the purchasing, storing, and preparing of food from the grocery store.
2. Is Eating in Restaurants the Answer? – Restaurants can provide convenience and nutrition if you choose correctly.
    a. One can eat an appropriate portion size and have the remainder packaged.
    b. One can get more food from the salad bar and request whole-grain breads and pastas.
3. Dealing with Loneliness – people should try to eat and socialize with others
4. A Word about Food Safety for Elders
    a. Foodborne illnesses in older adults can be more serious.
    b. The *Dietary Guidelines for Americans 2010* suggest the following to ensure food safety:
        1. Do not drink unpasteurized milk or eat raw or undercooked meat and dairy products.
        2. Eat only thoroughly heated deli meats.
    b. Table 14-18 lists ideas for smart shopping and creative cooking.

VI. Controversy – Nutrient-Drug Interactions: Who Should Be Concerned?

A. The Potential for Harm
1. How Drugs and Nutrients Interact
    a. Prescription and over-the-counter medicines can have unintended consequences.
    b. Drugs can interact with nutrients in the following ways, as shown in Figure C14-1:
        1. Food or nutrients can enhance, delay, or prevent drug absorption.
        2. Drugs can enhance, delay, or prevent nutrient absorption.
        3. Nutrients can alter the distribution of a drug or interfere with its metabolism, transport, or elimination.
        4. Drugs can alter the distribution of a nutrient among body tissues or interfere with its metabolism, transport, or excretion.
    c. Drugs also modify taste, appetite, and food intake.
    d. Herbs can also modify drug effects, as described in Table C14-3.
    e. Drugs and nutrients can alter the production of enzymes, transporter proteins, or receptors, which may alter cellular metabolism.
2. Factors that Make Interactions Likely
    a. The average elderly person may take 10 prescription medications at the same time.
    b. Many elderly individuals also take herbal remedies.
    c. People who are overweight or underweight may receive too much or too little medication.

B. Absorption of Drugs and Nutrients – can be reduced given certain combinations
1. Antimicrobial medicines may not be adequately absorbed with calcium-containing foods or with orange juice.
2. Chronic laxative use can also deplete the body of essential nutrients since the intestines are stimulated to move nutrients through too quickly.

C. Metabolic Interactions – can adversely affect the way some drugs work in the body
   1. A component of grapefruit juice blocks an enzyme that is needed for the breakdown of drugs such as Coumadin (blood thinner).
   2. A person who takes Coumadin and drinks grapefruit juice may suffer from prolonged bleeding, which can be life threatening, and this effect can worsened by the ingestion of ginkgo biloba.
   3. People taking monoamine oxidase inhibitors (MAOI) drugs for depression may experience a toxic buildup of tyramine from foods (see Table C14-2).
   4. MAOI drugs reduce the liver's ability to clear tyramine from the system and this can result in potentially fatal interactions.

D. Two Widely Used Drugs: Caffeine and Tobacco
   1. Caffeine is a stimulant that can help some people focus better & is best consumed in moderation.
      a. 200 milligrams (about 2 cups of coffee) of caffeine improves the ability to pay attention but doses above 500 milligrams may worsen mental abilities.
      b. Caffeine may raise blood pressure in some individuals.
   2. Table C14-4 shows the caffeine content of common beverages and foods.
   3. Tobacco smoking tends to lower the user's appetite.
   4. Smokers need more vitamin C than non-smokers.

E. Illicit Drugs
   1. Marijuana users tend to snack on high-calorie sweets.
   2. Users of other illicit drugs tend to be more malnourished.

F. Personal Strategy
   1. When you need to take a medicine, do so wisely.
   2. Ask your healthcare provider or pharmacist for specific instructions about the doses, times, and how to take the medication, for example, with or without meals.
   3. Try to live life in a way that requires less chemical assistance.

Worksheet 14-1: Juice Drink Label Analysis

Instructions: Use the juice drink label below to answer the questions.

1. a. What is the serving size of this product?

   b. How many cups is this?

2. What percentage of the total carbohydrates comes from sugars?

3. a. What is the most prevalent ingredient in this product other than water?

   b. What is this ingredient?

4. What is a container of this product?

5. a. Is this a good drink choice for a school-age child?

   b. Why or why not?

   c. Can you suggest other beverages that a child could drink instead of this product?

Splashdown Juice Drink
Chillin' Fruit Punch
10 pouches (6.75 fl oz ea.)

Nutrition Facts

Serving Size 200ml
Servings Per Container 10

Amount Per Serving	
Calories 100	Calories from Fat 0
	% Daily Value*
Total Fat 0g	**0%**
Saturated Fat 0g	**0%**
Trans Fat 0g	
Cholesterol 0mg	**0%**
Sodium 15mg	**1%**
Total Carbohydrate 27g	**9%**
Dietary Fiber 0g	**0%**
Sugars 27g	
Protein 0g	

Vitamin A 0% • Vitamin C 20%
Calcium 0% • Iron 0%

* Percent Daily Values are based on a 2,000 calorie diet. Your Daily Values may be higher or lower depending on your calorie needs.

	Calories	2,000	2,500
Total Fat	Less than	65g	80g
Sat Fat	Less than	20g	25g
Cholesterol	Less than	300mg	300mg
Sodium	Less than	2400mg	2400mg
Total Carbohydrate		300g	375g
Dietary Fiber		25g	30g

Ingredients: Water, high fructose corn syrup, apple and grape juice concentrates, citric acid, strawberry juice concentrate, ascorbic acid (vitamin C), vitamin E acetate, natural flavor.

Worksheet 14-2: Intake Analysis—Children and Older Adults

Eating Plan D (1 Day's Intake)	**Eating Plan G (1 Day's Intake)**
1 cup of Corn Flakes cereal	1 cup honey dew melon
¾ cup 1% fat milk	1 cup fresh strawberries
6 ounces orange juice	1 large apple
12 ounces coffee	½ avocado
1 honey nut granola bar	½ cup sweet green peppers
6 ounces chocolate milk	½ cup sweet red peppers
2 slices rye bread	¼ cup black olives
2 ounces pastrami	1 medium orange
2 Tbsp. hot mustard	1 medium banana
1 ounce Swiss cheese	1 cup boiled green beans
1 cup 2% fat milk	10 cooked asparagus spears
1 large apple	1 cup sautéed mushrooms
8 Ritz crackers	1 cup kidney beans
2 Tbsp. peanut butter	¼ cup dried apricots
12 ounces Diet Coke	¼ cup dried Craisins
1 cup angel hair pasta	5 dried, pitted dates
¾ cup marinara sauce	
1 cup lettuce & 1 sliced tomato	
⅓ cup shredded cheddar cheese	
5 cucumber slices	
¼ cup Italian dressing	
⅙ of a devil's food cake	
6 ounces red wine	

Look at Eating Plans D and G:

1. a. Which eating plan has healthier snack choices for a school-age child?

   b. Why did you choose this plan?

2. a. Which eating plan's snack choices will appeal more to a typical child?

   b. What factors may influence a school-age child's snack food choices?

3. Which of these eating plans could potentially increase the risk of allergies in a susceptible child?

4. a. What nutrients are lacking in the snacks contained in Eating Plan G?

   b. Suggest alternative snacks that could contribute these needed nutrients without compromising the mission of this eating plan.

5. a. Which of the eating plans have snack choices that would appeal more to an elderly person?

   b. Why might an elderly person prefer the selected snack choices?

   c. Suggest alternative snack choices that will ensure an adequate amount of protein and carbohydrates for an elderly person.

Worksheet 14-3: How to Plan Meals for an Allergic Child

What is a Food Allergy?

The body's immune system can react to a harmless substance such as wheat, nuts, peanuts (type of legume), shellfish, eggs, soy, fish, and walnuts. The symptoms can range from mild itching reactions to a life-threatening anaphylactic reaction where the airways close off or the blood pressure drops to low levels. About 6-8% of all children have this type of food allergy.

How would you plan meals for an allergic child? What types of food substitutes could you find that would help the child avoid the offending foods but would still offer adequate nutrition at home?

1. John is allergic to milk protein. What would a typical day of nutritious foods look like? Design a meal plan that could substitute other nutritious foods for milk products to ensure that John is getting enough protein, calcium, magnesium, and vitamin A in his diet.

2. Sarah is allergic to all types of nuts. Design a meal plan for Sarah that ensures adequate fat, protein, magnesium, and potassium without nuts or nut products.

3. Kevin is allergic to wheat products. Design a meal plan that ensures that Kevin can get enough carbohydrates, B vitamins, and iron in his diet without exposing him to wheat or its products.

You can check whether each of these children is getting enough of the stated nutrients for his/her age by consulting Appendix A in the back of your textbook or by using a diet analysis program such as *Diet Analysis +*.

How can you be sure that these children do not get exposed to the foods that cause allergic reactions when they are not at home?

- Let others know that your child is VERY ALLERGIC to a specific food. You may need to write out the details on a piece of paper so supervising adults do not give your child any suspect foods.
- Check the ingredients lists of foods or ask how a food was prepared to rule out the possibility of the offending food being present.
- Also, ask whether mixing appliances or utensils are cleaned between batches of foods. Small amounts of carryover of nuts or other offending substances from one batch to the next can be enough to cause fatal reactions in an allergic individual!
- Food manufacturers must include a safety warning on food labels if the ingredients in their products have been made on equipment that is used to process nuts, eggs, or wheat.
- Have the child carry a pre-loaded syringe of epinephrine. This drug can reduce the severe reaction until medical help arrives in the event of an exposure to an offending food. These EpiPEN devices are available with a prescription.

References:

Tufts University Health & Nutrition Letter, Volume 19 (7), September 2001, page 8.
Schardt, David, Food Allergies, *Nutrition Action Health Letter*, Voume 28 (3), April 2001, pages 10-12
Myths and Facts About Food Allergies, *University of California, Berkeley Wellness Letter*, Volume 20 (12), September 2004, page 4-5.

Worksheet 14-4: Chapter 14 Review Crossword Puzzle

Across:	Down:
1. A substance produced by immune cells that participates in causing inflammation	2. A food _____ is an intense dislike for a food that has caused problems in the past.
3. Age-related loss of muscle or lean tissue is also known as _____.	4. A type of low-nutrient, energy-dense food that is offered to students at school
7. Women with _____ syndrome experience mood changes or physical pain before the onset of their monthly period.	5. Many children have a fear of new foods. This is known as food _____.
10. A common, treatable cause of unexplained confusion in older adults	6. _____ is the accumulation of bacteria and their deposits on the surface of the teeth.
12. A class of cholesterol-lowering drugs whose effects can be lessened by the intake of grapefruit	8. Increased intake of _____ may help prevent the development or exacerbation of high blood pressure.
13. An acronym for an easy-to-remember list of factors that can lead to malnutrition in the elderly population	9. Absorption of this nutrient increases with age, so the recommended intake levels are lower for older adults
14. Use of these substances/drugs can cause nutrients to pass through the intestines too quickly, which can lead to reduced absorption of vitamins and minerals	11. _____ is produced during the fermentation process used during cheese and wine making. This substance can cause dangerous interactions with antidepressants.

Handout 14-1: Supervised Activities for Preschoolers

Children's muscle development determines their abilities to perform activities involving foods. The ages listed here are average ages; individual children develop on their own schedules.

A two-year-old can use large muscles of the arms to:	• scrub vegetables • tear lettuce • snap beans
A three-year-old can use hand muscles to:	• wrap foods in foil; wrap cheese slices around bread sticks • pour beverages from a small pitcher into a cup • mix cereal snacks in a large bowl with clean hands • shake juices together in a small, sealed container • spread peanut butter, cream cheese, or jelly on bread with a dull butter knife or small spatula
A four-year-old can use the small muscles in the fingers to:	• peel the shells from hard-boiled eggs or the skins from oranges • roll out a ball of ground meat or dough with clean hands • juice citrus fruit by pushing down and turning the fruit on a hand juicer • crack raw eggs by tapping the center of the egg against the side of a bowl • mash a bowl of cooked beans for dip
A five-year-old can use eye-hand coordination to:	• measure ingredients with measuring spoons and cups • cut semi-soft foods such as soft cheese with a dull butter knife and practice keeping fingers away from the blade • grind chunky peanut butter or cooked meats in a hand-turned food grinder, or turn a hand-cranked ice cream maker • grate carrots or cheese on an upright grater with fingers far from the grater to avoid cuts

Source: Adapted from A. A. Hertzler, Preschoolers' food handling skills--motor development, *Journal of Nutrition Education* 21 (1989): 100B-100C.

Handout 14-2: Ensuring Adequate Nutrition for the Elderly

Do you know of an elderly neighbor who does not get out of the house much?

Do they have enough food to eat?

Can they prepare their own food?

Do they have the money to afford good quality food?

Meals on Wheels is a nationwide organization of volunteers who work to bring high-quality, nutritious meals to their neighbors in need. There are millions of elderly and disabled people who receive nutritious meals from neighbors who work together to prepare and deliver meals to homes.

How can you learn more about the Meals on Wheels Program?

Website: http://www.mowaa.org

The **March for Meals program** is a campaign that hopes to expand the reach of the Meals on Wheels Program by:

- Recruiting more volunteers
- Raising money for service to more seniors in need
- Raising awareness of the problem of malnourishment in the elderly and disabled

Any community group such as church groups can contact the Meals on Wheels program to find out how to set up a program in their area. The Meals on Wheels organization can advise a community group on how to identify people in need, how to raise money, and how to recruit volunteers to develop a Meals on Wheels program in their community!

There are many other state-supported programs for food distribution for the elderly. The following links provide information about such programs:

www.fns.usda.gov
www.aoa.gov/AoARoot/AoA_Programs/HCLTC/Nutrition_Services/index.aspx

Chapter 15 – Hunger and the Global Environment

Quick List: IM Resources for Chapter 15

- **Class preparation resources:** learning objectives/key points, suggested activities and projects, lecture outline
- **Assignment materials:** **Related LO**
    - Critical thinking questions (with answer key) 15.1, 15.2, 15.3, 15.4
    - Discussion questions (with answers) for Controversy 15 .... 15.7
    - Worksheet 15-1: "Eco-Friendly" Cereal Label Analysis 15.4, 15.6
    - Worksheet 15-2: Intake Analysis—Hunger and the Environment 15.1, 15.6, 15.7
    - Worksheet 15-3: Feeding America and Other World-Wide Food Security Programs 15.1, 15.6
    - Worksheet 15-4: How Can You Save Food at Home? 15.4, 15.6
    - **New!** Worksheet 15-5: Chapter 15 Review Crossword Puzzle

Chapter Learning Objectives and Key Points

15.1 **Outline the scope and causes of food insecurity in the United States and in the world, and name some U.S. programs aimed at reducing food insecurity.**
As poverty in the United States increases, food insecurity does, too. Children living in food-insecure households often lack the food they need. People with low food security may suffer obesity alongside hunger in the same community or family. Government programs to relieve poverty and hunger are crucial to many people, if not fully successful.

15.2 **Describe the severity of poverty and starvation among the world's poorest peoples.**
Natural causes, along with political and social causes, contribute to hunger and poverty in many developing countries. Women and children are generally the world's poorest poor.

15.3 **Compare and contrast characteristics of acute severe malnutrition with those of chronic malnutrition in children, and describe some basic medical nutrition therapy tools used to restore health.**
Malnutrition in adults most often appears as general thinness and loss of muscle. Individual nutrient deficiencies cause much misery worldwide. Malnutrition in adults is widespread but is often overlooked; severe observable deficiency diseases develop as body systems fail. Many of the world's children suffer from wasting, the deadliest form of malnutrition, called severe acute malnutrition. In many more children, growth is stunted because they chronically lack the nutrients children need to grow normally. Oral rehydration therapy and ready-to-use therapeutic foods, properly applied, can save the life of a starving person. Many health and nutrition professionals work to eradicate childhood malnutrition.

15.4 **Explain how the food supply and environmental conditions are connected, and explain why people in poverty are inclined to have larger families despite food scarcity.**
The world's current food supply is sufficient, but distribution remains a problem. Future food security is threatened by many forces. Environmental degradation caused by people is threatening the world's food and water supplies. Demand for food and water grows with human population growth. Food waste is enormous, and reducing it would increase the food supply without additional production inputs.

15.5 **Identify some steps toward solving the problems that threaten the world's food supply.**
Improvements are slowly taking place in many parts of the world.

15.6 **Discuss several steps that governments, businesses, schools, professionals, and individuals can take to help create sustainability and stem waste in the food supply.**
Government, business, educators, and individuals have opportunities to promote sustainability worldwide and wise resource use at home.

15.7 **Define the term ecological footprint, and list some factors that increase or decrease a person's ecological footprint.**

Critical Thinking Questions

1. *What is the hunger-obesity paradox and why is it of particular concern in this country?*

   People who have limited incomes will buy inexpensive, readily available foods that are often high in fats and sugars but are low in other essential nutrients. People who regularly eat these types of foods are likely exceeding their daily calorie requirements, which could contribute to obesity in the long run. Many urban areas in the U.S. where low-income people live (known as "food deserts") do not have supermarkets with inexpensive, fresh whole foods that would provide the essential nutrients. This further limits people's nutritional options. Figure 15-2 illustrates the link between hunger and obesity.

2. *Describe how the increasing world population contributes to other factors that threaten the world's food supply.*

   People in poorer countries tend to have larger families to ensure that there will be children who live to adulthood to support their families. These individuals will need to compete for a limited food supply. More individuals will drive the need to plant more crops, and if done unsustainably this can contribute to loss of topsoil and water that people will need to survive. More people will need access to fresh water, which is also needed for the production of crops and livestock.

3. a. *Describe any 2 ways that aquaculture can benefit people.*

   Aquaculture makes it possible to provide more fish for more people in spite of dwindling natural fish populations. The fish in these farms can be monitored for safety (from chemical pollutants as well as microbial contaminants) as well.

   b. *Discuss any 3 ways that aquaculture could threaten the environment if not managed carefully.*

   If aquaculture is not managed well, parasites in the farmed fish may be released into the surrounding water and infect the wild fish population. Aquaculture may also result in nutrient and chemical pollution of the surrounding waters, and occupy coastline waters that could otherwise support the more genetically diverse wild fish population.

4. *Describe any 2 ways that water stress can impact the environment and the world's population.*

   Water stress results when the demand for water in an area exceeds availability. The average supply of fresh water per person may decline by one third in the next 20 years. Water stress is accelerated by water pollution. Each day, people dump 2 million tons of waste into the world's freshwater rivers. This leads to aquatic ecosystem destruction, which further degrades the environment and reduces wild food fish populations.

5. a. *Explain how reduced hunger and malnutrition can lead to decreased infant mortality.*

   If women are better nourished before and during their pregnancies, they are less likely to give birth to low-birth weight infants. Also, these infants will have more adequate nutrient stores and better nutrition during critical periods of development such that they will be less likely to be born with a malformation or chronic condition that could endanger their lives or reduce their productivity.

   b. *How can reduced hunger and malnutrition lead to reduced pressure on the environment?*

   Reduced hunger and malnutrition will allow people to be able to grow crops or livestock more sustainably. They will not be desperate for cash and resort to clear-cutting natural lands. This damaging practice leads to loss of land that could be used to grow crops and further ensure people's adequate nutrition. Families may have fewer children if they can be confident that each child has a better chance of surviving into adulthood.

6. *Why do children who suffer from marasmus and kwashiorkor look so different from each other?*

   Children with marasmus look like skin and bone. These children are wasting due to severe malnutrition; their bodies don't have enough protein or other nutrients or calories. Their cells will break down all fats and eventually lean tissue proteins for energy.

Children with kwashiorkor have pronounced swelling, especially in the abdomen. These children are switched from nutritious breast milk to a cereal that is low in protein. Reduction in protein intake may cause a reduction in the levels of albumin in the blood. This causes the fluid to leave the blood and collect in the tissues (edema). The liver develops fatty deposits due to its inability to make lipoproteins. This contributes to the abdominal swelling. Muscle wasting in children with kwashiorkor may be disguised by the edema.

Controversy Discussion Questions

1. *Your friend is very excited about the prospect of using corn as a source of bio-fuels to help lessen the nation's dependency on fossil fuels. You are a little concerned about the use of corn for bio-fuels for a couple of reasons. Explain your concerns to your friend.*

   While it is commendable that crops are being harvested for fuel, corn is also used to feed people, livestock. The additional demand for corn for bio-fuel places a burden on the fields and farmers that produce corn. The lure of higher profits from bio-fuel production may encourage farmers to sell their crops to alternative energy producers instead of distributing their crops to people as a food source.

   Also, vast areas of natural lands may be converted into fields to grow corn for bio-fuel production. This will further reduce the biodiversity that is so important for the health and future of the planet.

2. *In addition to not promoting cruelty to animals, give two other reasons why people may choose to be vegetarians.*

   Vegetarian diets are often lower in cholesterol and saturated fats, especially if a vegan diet is followed. Also, a lot of water, crops, and land are devoted to the growth of livestock for chicken, beef, or pork. Consider that land needs to be used to sustain the animals and more land needs to be used to grow the crops that feed these animals. Animals also produce a lot of methane (a greenhouse gas) and their manure can be harmful to the environment if mishandled. By eating only grain products or living animal products such as milk and eggs, vegetarians are able to better share the food crop with other people in the world.

3. a. *Describe 1 unsustainable practice that farmers use for each of the following: to reduce infections in animals and to reduce the level of weeds in the fields.*

   When livestock are held in feedlots, they are often crowded together and may even be exposed to each others' wastes. The close proximity promotes rapid spread of infections, so many owners indiscriminately administer antibiotics to their livestock to prevent infections. This encourages the development of antibiotic-resistant microbes that can make both animals and humans sick with infections that are difficult to treat.

   Another unsustainable practice is to apply chemical herbicides to the plants and surrounding soil to prevent the growth of weeds within the crops. These herbicides can leave toxic residues on the crops as well as cause damage to the insects and animals that may feed on the crops or surrounding soils.

   b. *Describe one sustainable practice that farmers can use for each of the following: to reduce infections in animals and to reduce the level of weeds in the field.*

   A sustainable practice would be to better maintain the animals' health to promote their natural immunity and allow them to have more room in the fields so they are not as crowded together. This would reduce the incidence of infections and their transmission to other animals.

   A sustainable practice would be to spot weeds by sight and remove them. Using a special type of hoe can also remove weeds in the soil around the crops. While this practice may be more labor intensive, it is far better for the health of the environment and the consumer in the long run.

4. *How can livestock farming be conducted so as to lessen the burden on the environment?*

   Livestock can be housed more humanely such that they do not produce a large amount of wastes that collect in a given area. The manure can harm the environment by unleashing pathogenic microbes, greenhouse gases, or nutrients that upset the surrounding ecosystem. Livestock can be allowed to graze on natural pasturelands.

Worksheet Answer Key

Worksheet 15-1: "Eco-Friendly" Cereal Label Analysis

1. a. "USDA organic" suggests that the ingredients that go into this product were grown without the use of synthetic pesticides or fertilizers and hormones, and produced without genetic engineering.

   b. Using fewer pesticides kills fewer of the insects, which are part of the food chain for birds and other animals. There is also less release of toxic chemicals into the environment.

2. One could look at government information or information from environment or food safety advocacy groups.
3. The products will state the term "organic" and there will be a USDA seal of certification. One can also write to the manufacturer of the product to request more information about this product.
4. The claims are:
   Enriched drought-resistant soil, which allows producers to use less precious water.
   Less soil erosion, which allows more fertile soil to remain for future crop growth.
   Less groundwater pollution, which helps maintain the ecosystems of the bodies of water.
   Improved farm biodiversity, which allows for the most natural and robust crops to be grown at a farm without the need for pesticides or fertilizers.

Worksheet 15-2: Intake Analysis—Hunger and the Environment

1. Eating Plan J will appeal to people with limited means because it is inexpensive and pre-made.
2. a. Lack of money, cooking facilities, a refrigerator, time, or knowledge could encourage a person to choose the fast food in Plan J over the home-cooked foods in Plan K.

   b. Strategies include choosing milk instead of root beer, requesting a salad instead of French fries, and ordering vegetables on the burger instead of cheese.

3. a. Eating Plan A has more of a negative impact on the environment because it includes more animal products.

   b. Eating Plan A includes more animal products. In order to produce beef, a lot of fertilizer, corn, and water must be used. A lot of wastes are produced and released into the environment.

4. People could set up community gardens for growing fresh vegetables. People should visit local farmers' markets and buy products in bulk if possible.
5. At first, just add a piece of fruit each day. Next, replace some of the cheese with nuts or another piece of fruit. Finally, reduce the amount of beef eaten or replace it with chicken or fish, which are lower-fat alternatives.
6. a. Eating Plan A provides protein and calcium to the diet, which helps with tissue repair and bone health.

   b. There are not a lot of benefits other than the fact that the diet is not entirely based on meat and dairy products.

Worksheet 15-5: Chapter 15 Review Crossword Puzzle

1. marasmus
2. stunting
3. hierarchy
4. rotating
5. food bank
6. kwashiorkor
7. wasting
8. methane
9. composter
10. integrated
11. Switchgrass
12. agroecology
13. aquaculture
14. poverty
15. food secure

Learning Activities & Project Ideas

Activity 15-1: Caring for the Homeless and Hungry Project[1] LO 15.1

Ask students how familiar they are with hunger problems in their own community. Nutrition students often lack experience working with low-income groups, including those who are homeless, the homebound elderly, and those needing emergency food assistance. To address this need, more universities are incorporating community service projects into their curriculums.

---

[1] Contributed by Lori W. Turner, Ph.D., R.D., University of Alabama

To give students in an introductory nutrition course an idea of how hunger affects people, have them volunteer to participate in a local food recovery program that provides meals to the hungry. Have them write a report about the experience and discuss what they learned with the class.

Activity 15-2: Attending Local Council Meetings Project[1] LO 15.4

To help students gain awareness of local environmental issues, encourage them to attend local city council meetings about issues pertaining to the environment. For example, they could attend a meeting on industry's impact on local water quality. Extra credit can be given for oral or written reports about the meetings.

Activity 15-3: Explore Impact of Food Purchasing Habits[1] LO 15.6

To increase students' awareness of their impact on the environment, discuss ways in which those who purchase and prepare their own food can pay attention to packaging, how often they shop, and how much fuel they use to shop for food. Students who live in dorms may want to discuss the ways in which they could encourage the foodservices to make changes that would benefit the environment.

To illustrate the savings in gas that a family could achieve by shopping nearby and only once a week: A family that shops every day for 30 years at a store 5 miles away in a 25 mile-per-gallon car will drive over 1,000,000 miles just for groceries. In contrast, another family that shops once a week at a store 1 mile away in a 50-mile-per-gallon car for 30 years will drive only some 3,000 miles. Each gallon of gas burned in a car releases some 20 pounds of carbon dioxide, so the second family will generate about 40 tons less carbon dioxide than the first family, just by making fewer and shorter trips to the grocery store.

Activity 15-4: Explore Opportunities to Recycle, Reuse, and Reduce[1] LO 15.6

The instructor could begin a discussion about what opportunities students presently have to recycle, reuse, and reduce and what opportunities they take advantage of. What other opportunities might they be able to take advantage of in the future?

Chapter Lecture Outline

I. Introduction
   A. In spite of the country's prosperity, almost 6.4 million U.S. households live with very low food security.
   B. Another 10.8 million households experienced low or marginal food security.
   C. Around a 1 billion people worldwide experience chronic food insufficiency (Table 15-1).
   D. Young people are getting involved in their communities working in soup kitchens, repairing homes, and educating children to help alleviate hunger and suffering.

II. U.S. Food Insecurity – Table 15-2 explains how to identify food insecurity in a U.S. household.
   A. Food Poverty in the United States
      1. The chronically hungry typically suffer from undernutrition.
      2. In the U.S., the primary cause of hunger is food poverty, the lack of enough money to pay for nutritious food and for other essentials.
      3. More than 12% of the U.S. lives in a general state of poverty.
      4. Limited Nutritious Food Intakes
         a. To stretch meager food supplies, adults may skip meals or cut their portions.
         b. They may beg from strangers, steal from markets, eat pet foods, or even harvest road kill or look through garbage cans.
         c. Many people eat inexpensive foods such as white bread, fats, sugary punches, and other foods that do not provide essential nutrients.
         d. Children from such families have physical, social, and behavioral problems.
      5. Rising Food Costs
         a. Reduced crop supplies are pushing up the global prices of cereals, sugars, and meats.
         b. In the U.S., food prices have not risen as much and are tied to labor, packaging, and transportation costs.
      6. The Poverty-Obesity Paradox (Figure 15-2)
         a. In the U.S. and elsewhere, obesity rates are highest among the lowest income groups.

   b. They often eat foods that provide too many calories with too few nutrients such as refined grains, sweets, inexpensive meats, oils, and fast foods.
   c. People in poor urban areas live in food deserts and only have access to convenience stores or fast-food restaurants that sell foods high in fat and sugar and low in nutrients.

B. What U.S. Food Programs Address Low Food Security?
   1. Nationwide Efforts
      a. Government programs (e.g., SNAP) to relieve poverty and hunger are tremendously helpful but are not completely successful at eliminating hunger amongst those who receive benefits.
      b. The USDA is studying the spending habits of SNAP recipients to determine if they are obtaining nutritious foods with their debit cards.
   2. Community Efforts
      a. The largest food recovery program, Feeding America, coordinates the efforts of more than 250 food banks, food pantries, emergency kitchens, and homeless shelters in providing food to local agencies that feed over 25 million people a year.
      b. Table 15-4 describes goals for addressing community hunger.

III. World Poverty and Hunger
   A. The Staggering Statistics
      1. The primary form of hunger is still food poverty, but the poverty is more extreme.
      2. One-fifth of the world's 7 billion people have no land and no possessions at all.
      3. The "poorest poor" survive on less than one dollar each day, they lack water that is safe to drink, and they cannot read or write.
      4. Food prices rose substantially from 2006 to 2011 due to grain production for biofuels and droughts.
   B. Women and Children – are usually the poorest of the poor
      1. Malnourished girls become malnourished mothers who give birth to low-birth weight babies.
      2. Poor people tend to have more children to increase the odds of some of the children surviving into adulthood.
   C. Famine
      1. Famine is a true food shortage in an area that causes multitudes of people to starve and die.
      2. Natural causes of famine—drought, flood, and pests—have, in recent years, taken second place behind political and social causes.
      3. Figure 15-3 shows the hunger hotspots in the world.

IV. The Malnutrition of Extreme Poverty – Many people suffer from malnutrition but are not properly diagnosed because their symptoms, such as lack of energy and motivation, are vague.
   A. "Hidden Hunger"—Micronutrient Deficiencies
      1. Almost 2 billion people have food to provide energy but lack iron, vitamin A, and other nutrients.
      2. 30% or more of the world's population have iron-deficiency anemia that can lead to maternal death, preterm birth, low birth weight, infections, and premature death.
      3. 40 million infants per year suffer from reversible mental retardation due to iodine deficiency.
      4. Vitamin A deficiency causes blindness in over 5 million young children and robs 180 million of them of the ability to fight infections.
      5. 20% of the world's population suffers from zinc deficiency.
      6. Tens of thousands die of malnutrition every day.
   B. Two Faces of Childhood Malnutrition
      1. Severe Acute Malnutrition – Wasting
         a. SAM occurs when the food supply suddenly dwindles due to drought or war
         b. In children with SAM, wasting due to a profound energy deficit leaves virtually no subcutaneous fat and little lean tissue.
         c. Starving children exert as little energy as possible and their GI tract lining deteriorates such that they become unable to absorb any nutrients ingested.
         d. 7.6 million pre-school children die from SAM each year as a result of the diarrhea and dehydration that go along with infections.
      2. Chronic Malnutrition – Stunting
         a. 25% of the children in the world subsist on diluted cereal drinks that supply energy but little protein or other nutrients.

   b. These children have stunted growth and suffer from infections and diarrhea.
3. Kwashiorkor & Marasmus – 2 manifestations of overall malnutrition (lack of food) that can appear individually or together
   a. In some societies, each baby is weaned from breast milk as soon as the next comes along. The older baby, who no longer receives breast milk and is given a watery cereal with scant protein of low quality, develops kwashiorkor.
   b. The edema and enlarged liver characteristic of kwashiorkor are apparent in a child's swollen belly.
   c. In marasmus, lack of food causes wasting, disruption of brain development, and weakening of the heart and the immune system.
   d. A marasmic child lacks subcutaneous fat and loses a substantial amount of muscle mass.

C. Rehabilitation
1. Oral rehydration therapy (ORT) has saved millions of people by slowly reintroducing safe water and electrolytes into their bodies.
2. Children can then receive therapeutic foods (RUTF) such as ground peanuts, powdered milk, and protein sources in pouches that can be easily distributed and consumed and resist contamination.

V. The Future Food Supply and the Environment

A. Introduction
1. Today's total world food supply can abundantly feed the entire current population.
2. Distribution of food to those in need remains a problem.

B. Threats to the Food Supply – Many forces compound to threaten world food production and distribution in the next decades:
1. Hunger, poverty, and population growth:
   a. 105 people die each minute but 254 people are born to replace them.
   b. There are over 78 million new people to feed each year (see Figure 15-4).
2. Loss of food-producing land by 24 billion fewer tons of topsoil each year
3. Accelerating fossil fuel use, which results in pollution and global climate changes
4. Atmosphere and global climate changes, droughts, and floods – Carbon dioxide levels are 26% higher than 200 years ago, causing extreme weather conditions that can threaten the food supply.
5. Ozone loss from the outer atmosphere, which causes melting of polar ice caps and additional UV light that may damage plants
6. Water shortages – 1 billion people lack access to clean water now, & over the next 20 years, the fresh water supply will decline by one third per person
7. Ocean pollution and overfishing are depleting the ocean's fish populations.

C. Environmental Degradation and Hunger
1. Introduction
   a. Hunger and poverty interact with a third force—environmental degradation.
   b. Poor people often destroy the very resources they need for survival.
   c. They cut all available trees for firewood or timber to sell, then lose the soil to erosion.
   d. Environmental degradation caused by people is threatening the world's soils, grazing lands, fisheries, climate, air, and water.
2. Soil Erosion and Grazing Lands
   a. Soil erosion affects agriculture in every nation.
   b. Deforestation of the world's rain forests dramatically adds to land loss.
   c. Without the forest covering to hold the soil in place, it washes off the rocks beneath, drastically reducing the land's productivity.
   d. Irrigation and fertilizer cannot compensate for the loss of topsoil.
   e. Much land in its natural state is being used to feed animals to meet the increasing demand for beef, pork, and poultry.
3. Diminishing of Wild Fisheries and Expansion of Aquaculture
   a. 80% of fish food stocks are exploited or overexploited.
   b. Many countries lack the political will to stop overfishing.
   c. Pollution is reducing the wild fish population as well.
   d. As ocean temperatures rise, the phytoplankton begin to die off.
   e. Aquaculture (fish farming) provides about ½ of the world's fish for consumption.
   f. Fish are confined in cages in lakes or ocean water.

g. The nutrients from the fish farms can contaminate the surrounding water.
h. Farmed fish are fed chow such as sardines from the wild and this can cause shortages for people and other fish, like cod, that depend on sardines.

4. Limited Fresh Water
   a. The demand for fresh water is increasing and many parts of the world are water stressed.
   b. Due to people dumping 2 million tons of waste into the water each day
   c. By 2025, 2 of 3 people will live in water-stressed conditions if the current trends continue.
5. Overpopulation
   a. The human population will exceed the earth's estimated carrying capacity by 2033.
   b. Overpopulation may well be the most serious threat that humankind faces today.
6. Food Waste – one third of all food produced each year goes to waste
   a. 25% of all the fresh water used each year is spent producing food that is wasted.
   b. 300 million barrels of oil were used in the production of that wasted food.
   c. Figure 15-5 shows the scope of U.S. food waste.
   d. Figure 15-6 shows some strategies for recovering food and reducing food waste.
   e. Table 15-6 shows how to stretch dollars spent on food and how to reduce food waste.

VI. A World Moving toward Solutions
   A. Improvements are slowly taking place in many parts of the world.
   B. More children are going to school than in the past, which is encouraging.
   C. The current use of the earth's resources is unsustainable.
   D. Wealthy countries need to stop using so many of the earth's resources and developing countries need to devise a plan to adhere to a sustainable way of growth.

VII. How Can People Help? – Every segment of our society can play a role in the fight against poverty, hunger, and environmental degradation.
   A. Government Action – such as investment in solar, wind, and biofuel development to reduce dependence on fossil fuels
   B. Private and community enterprises – are supporters of antihunger programs; e.g., restaurants are giving food to shelters or food banks
   C. Educators and Students – can teach family, friends, and community members about the relationships among adequate nutrition, effective political action, and sustainability
   D. Food and Nutrition Professionals – can show good stewardship and leadership through recycling, energy conservation, and sustainability efforts in their personal lives and through their businesses
   E. Individuals – can make small decisions that can add up to large impacts on the environment

VIII. A Consumer's Guide to Making "Green" Choices
   A. Less Buying, More Doing – do more for yourself, save money
   B. New Daily Habits
      1. Ride a bike to work or classes.
      2. Shop "carless" and plan to make fewer shopping trips.
      3. Reduce food waste as described in Table 15-6.
      4. Carry reusable grocery sacks to the store.
      5. Use fewer electric gadgets.
      6. Choose foods low on the food chain.
   C. Choosing Wisely
      1. Choose small fish more often.
      2. Avoid overly packaged items; buy bulk with minimal packaging or reusable or recyclable packaging
      3. Use reusable pans and dishes.
      4. Use reusable towels.
      5. Choose Fair Trade coffee and other items.
      6. Plant a garden or join a community garden.
   D. Venturing Out – Shop at farmers' markets and roadside stands for local foods.
   E. Bigger Ideas
      1. Join and support organizations that lobby for changes & help the poor.
      2. Purchase the most efficient appliances—look for the Energy Star logo in Figure 15-7.

3. Insulate the home.
4. Consider solar power, especially to heat water.
5. Remember: reduce, reuse, and recycle

F. Moving Ahead – teach others & volunteer for "green" activities

IX. Controversy: Can We Feed Ourselves Sustainably?

A. Introduction
1. If fuel need predictions hold true, the world's food producers will soon face increased pressure not only to feed a growing world population but also to provide the raw materials to meet world demand for biofuels.
2. Will new technologies be able to integrate food production and energy production in sustainable ways?

B. Costs of Current Food Production Methods – Producing food has always cost the earth dearly.
1. Introduction
   a. The environmental and social costs of agriculture and the food industry take many forms.
   b. Among them are resource waste and pollution, energy overuse, and tolls on human workers in farm communities.
2. Impacts on Land and Water
   a. Native ecosystems are cleared away for crop-producing lands.
   b. Nutrients that crops remove from soil are replaced with fertilizers that can add to greenhouse gases.
   c. The fertilizers run off into waterways and cause algal blooms in the oceans.
   d. Algal blooms deplete the water of oxygen, creating dead zones.
   e. The pesticides and herbicides used can pollute rivers, lakes, and groundwater.
   f. Irrigation adds salts to the soil in many areas, which leads to further drying of soil and need for more irrigation.
3. Soil Depletion – The soil can be depleted by farming, deforestation, and overgrazing by cattle.
4. Loss of Species – As people eat more of the same type of crop, the demand and desire to preserve other naturally occurring and diverse crops will decrease.
   a. By 2050, approximately 40,000 species of plants will become extinct.
   b. Global eating habits are becoming more uniform, which contributes to species loss.
   c. Some of these plants may be able to adapt to harsher conditions brought on by climate change.
5. Fuel Use and Energy Sources
   a. Massive fossil fuel use is threatening our planet by causing ozone depletion, water pollution, ocean pollution, and other ills and by making global warming likely.
   b. An increase in the use of biofuels may help to reduce carbon dioxide emissions from agricultural activities, but these fuels require production of crops with all of their associated costs and problems.
   c. Large areas of land are being cleared of natural plant species and are being used to grow corn and soybeans for food and for biofuels.
   d. Wild grasses, a type of cane, and algae may provide better alternative sources of biofuels.
6. Fossil Energy In Food Production
   a. For example, it takes over 6000 calories of fuel to produce a can of corn that yields 300 calories
   b. Transportation of foods also consumes a lot of energy.
   c. Food production represents 25% of U.S. fossil energy consumption in addition to the use of fertilizers, pesticides, and irrigation.

C. The Problems of Livestock
1. U.S. Meat Production – Raising livestock takes a toll on the land:
   a. Losses of native plants and animals as land is cleared for livestock
   b. Huge masses of animal waste leach into water supplies.
   c. Farmers can work with the USDA to have their farms monitored.
   d. The crops that are used to feed livestock also take a toll on the environment.
   e. In the U.S., more land is used to produce grain for animals than people.
2. World Trends in Meat Consumption
   a. Many people in other countries are starting to eat more beef and dairy products, which puts more stress on the earth's ecosystems.

b. In 1989, less than 40% of Chinese people got most of their calories from meat but in 2006, that percent had increased to 67%.

D. A Sustainable Future Starts Now
 1. Low-Input and Precision Agriculture
  a. Alternative or low-input agriculture emphasizes careful use of natural processes wherever possible, rather than chemically intensive methods.
  b. One form is integrated pest management (IPM).
  c. Uses crop rotation and natural predators rather than pesticides alone
  d. Low-input agriculture is compared to conventional agriculture in Table C15-2.
  e. Precision agriculture allows farmers to adjust soil and crop management to meet the precise needs of various areas of the farm.
  f. Irrigation, fertilizers, and pesticides can be customized for each area.
  g. The global positioning satellite (GPS) system is at the heart of precision farming.
 2. Soil Conservation
  a. The U.S. Conservation Reserve Program provides federal assistance to farmers and ranchers who wish to improve their conservation of soil, water, and related natural resources on environmentally sensitive lands.
  b. The goal of this program is to: reduce soil erosion, prevent runoff of chemicals or nutrients into waterways, preserve wetlands, and improve the habitat for wildlife.
 3. The Potential of Genetic Engineering – Many farmers report both financial and conservation benefits from planting genetically engineered crops.
  a. Herbicide-resistant crops require less pesticides to control weeds.
  b. Pesticide-resistant crops require less application of toxic pesticides.
  c. Salt-resistant crops can grow in soil with high salt content.
 4. Preserving Genetic Diversity of Food
  a. The Svalbard seed vault in Norway stores over 1.1 million genetic variations of 64 of the world's most important food crops.
  b. Such seeds could be available if a blight or climate disaster were to destroy many of the existing plants.
 5. Energy Conservation (see Table C 15-3)
  a. Many farmers are devising ways to reduce their energy usage during food production.
  b. Switchgrass, which can grow in nutrient-poor soil, is being harvested and used as a biofuel.
  c. Light-emitting algae is being harvested because it can produce oils for fuel.
  d. Wind, sun, and heat from the ground are being harvested and put to use.
 6. Energy Recycling – Farmers are taking part in energy recycling by using byproducts of food production to power the production of foods.
  a. Farmers in Vermont and Wisconsin are harvesting methane gas from cows for use as fuel.
  b. Some farmers bury plant wastes underground and turn them into charcoal, which can also produce fertilizer while trapping excess carbon.
  c. Some utility companies provide home composters to citizens so that they can produce fertilizer for their home gardens.
  d. Other communities are using methane gas to power vehicles.

E. Roles of Consumers
 1. Keeping Local Profits Local – buy from roadside produce stands or join a farm share
 2. Eating Lower on the Food Chain – vegetarian diets require only $^{1}/_{3}$ the energy to produce that omnivorous diets require

F. Conclusion
 1. Although many problems are global in scope, the actions of individual people lie at the heart of their solutions.
 2. Table C15-4 helps one determine how big one's ecological footprint really is.

Worksheet 15-1: "Eco-Friendly" Cereal Label Analysis

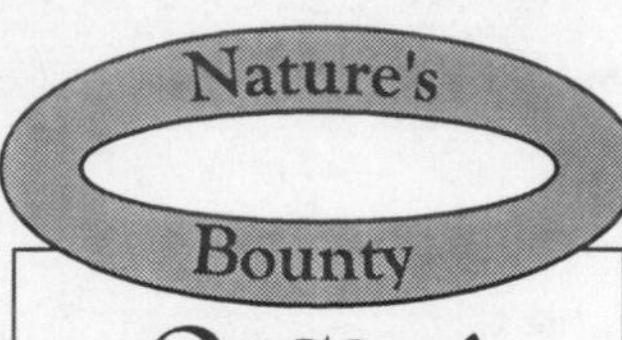

Organic Raisin & Pumpkin Seed with Flax Meal

What does organic mean for you?

No synthetic pesticides
No synthetic herbicides
No additives
No preservatives
No irradiation
No genetically engineered ingredients or seeds

Good Ecology

Enriched, drought-resistant soil
Less soil erosion
Less groundwater pollution
Improved farm biodiversity

650mg OMEGA-3s

WHOLE GRAIN

HIGH FIBER

Nutrition Facts

Serving Size $^{3}/_{4}$ cup (55g)
Servings Per Container about 7

Amount Per Serving	Cereal	+ 125 ml fortified skim milk
Calories	200	240
Calories from Fat	40	40
	% Daily Value**	
Total Fat 4g*	**6%**	**9%**
Saturated Fat 0.5g	**3%**	**3%**
Trans Fat 0g		
Polyunsaturated Fat 2.5g		
Monounsaturated Fat 1g		
Cholesterol 0mg	**0%**	**0%**
Sodium 150mg	**6%**	**9%**
Potassium 340mg	**10%**	**16%**
Total Carbohydrate 41g	**14%**	**16%**
Dietary Fiber 9g	**36%**	**36%**
Sugars 12g		
Protein 6g		
Vitamin A	0%	4%
Vitamin C	0%	0%
Calcium	4%	20%
Iron	20%	20%

* Amount in cereal. One half cup of skim milk contributes an additional 40 calories, 65mg sodium, 6g total carbohydrates (6g sugars) and 4g protein.
**Percent Daily Values are based on a 2,000 calorie diet. Your Daily Values may be higher or lower depending on your calorie needs.

Ingredients: Organic whole wheat meal, organic wheat bran, organic raisins (coated with organic sunflower oil), organic rolled oats, organic evaporated cane juice, organic flax meal, organic soy oil, organic brown rice flour, organic oat bran, organic pumpkin seeds, organic barley malt extract, organic flaxseeds, sea salt, organic oat syrup solids, tocopherols (natural vitamin E), organic molasses, organic rice bran extract, organic cinnamon.
Produced in a facility that contains peanuts, tree nuts, soy & wheat.

Instructions: Use the cereal label to answer the following questions.

1. a. What is meant by the term "USDA organic"?

   b. How does organic farming impact food production and safety on a local or global scale?

2. How could you find out if other countries have standards for organic food?

3. How can you tell that the ingredients in this product are organic?

4. List any two "good ecology" claims that are listed on the label and discuss why these practices are important to ensure the adequacy of the food supply for all.

Worksheet 15-2: Intake Analysis—Hunger and the Environment

<table>
<tr>
<td><u>Eating Plan A (1 Day's Intake)</u>
1 cup of Corn Flakes cereal
1 cup of 1% fat milk
2 cups of coffee
2 slices of whole-wheat bread
2 ounces thinly sliced baked ham
2 ounces cheddar jalapeño cheese
8 ounces chocolate milk
3 12-ounce beers
2 beef and cheese enchiladas</td>
<td rowspan="2"><u>Eating Plan E (1 Day's Intake)</u>
¾ cup Nature's Path flax cereal
½ cup soy milk
½ cup acai juice + seltzer water
1 medium banana
12 ounces coffee
6 ounces 6-grain yogurt
½ cup blueberries
¾ cup raspberries
2 Mushroom Lover's Veggie Burgers
1 cup roasted carrot soup
½ cup sweet green peppers
6 carrot sticks
2 whole-wheat wasa crackers
8 ounces Vruit juice
8 ounces soy milk
1 peanut butter Fiber One Bar
6 ounces grilled salmon
10 cooked asparagus spears
6 ounces white wine
½ cup olives
½ cup sun-dried tomatoes
½ cup whole-wheat angel hair pasta
¼ cup mixed nuts</td>
<td><u>Eating Plan H (1 Meal)</u>
1 cup New England clam chowder
1 2-ounce cheesy biscuit
4 ounces broiled lobster tail
4 ounces broiled scallops
3 Tbsp. drawn, melted butter
1 cup rice pilaf
1 cup boiled carrot and green beans
12 ounces sweetened ice tea
1 cup vanilla ice cream</td>
</tr>
<tr>
<td><u>Eating Plan J (1 Meal)</u>
1 medium French fries
1 Quarter Pounder with cheese
20 ounces root beer</td>
<td><u>Eating Plan K (1 Meal)</u>
6 ounces meat loaf
1 cup mashed potatoes
1 cup cooked peas
12 ounces 1% fat milk
$^1/_6$ (slice) apple pie</td>
</tr>
</table>

Look at Eating Plans H, J, and K:

1. Which of these meals is most likely to be selected by a person with limited means?
2. a. What are some of the obstacles present in a person's life that could influence a person to choose Eating Plan J over Eating Plan K?
   b. How could Eating Plan J be modified to become more adequate and varied?

Look at Eating Plans A and E:

3. a. Which of these eating plans has more of a negative impact on the health of the environment?
   b. Describe why the selected eating plan has more of an negative impact on the environment.
4. Suggest some strategies to make foods found in Eating Plan E more available to everyone.
5. Describe small steps to modify Eating Plan A so that it has more variety, adequacy, and moderation in calories.
6. a. What are the strengths of Eating Plan A in terms of impact on health of the body?
   b. Health of the environment?

Worksheet 15-3: Feeding America and Other World-Wide Food Security Programs

Does it bother you to see old produce in the store that will end up in a landfill?

Do you know if your community has a food pantry to help neighbors in need?

Do you want to learn how to distribute food more fairly for everyone in all countries?

Feeding America is a national organization of volunteers who work together to distribute food to needy people all over the country. They work to distribute food through local food pantries. They also have food rescue operations that distribute perishable foods to needy people in a timely fashion. This helps people in need obtain healthy, prepared foods as well. The Feeding America program relies on volunteers, financial donors, and other service organizations to make it possible to distribute food to people who need it.

How can you learn more about the Feeding America program?

Website: http://feedingamerica.org

How can you help? You can help by donating food to your local food pantry. There is a food pantry locator feature on the Feeding America Website.

You can donate money to the program directly.

You can shop where you can donate a small amount of money (around $1.50) to a local hunger relief agency. You can also check for a local food relief agency on the Feeding America Website.

You can tell your friends about Feeding America and the work that they do.

There are other food security and distribution agencies that work on a worldwide scale as well, such as Freedom from Hunger at www.freedomfromhunger.org/what-we-do or the Food and Agriculture Organization of the United Nations at www.fao.org/index_en.htm.

Instructions: Address the following questions on a separate sheet of paper after checking out the www.freedomfromhunger.org/what-we-do and www.fao.org websites:

1. What populations are served by each of these organizations?
2. Who administers the programs for each of these organizations?
   a. Does a government, corporation, or a private group run these organizations?
   b. Do these organizations have volunteers from more than one country?
   c. Can you get involved in furthering the mission of either of these organizations?
3. What are the shortcomings of each of these organizations?
4. What other organizations can you find who have a similar mission?
5. Do these organization have efforts related to environmental conservation?
6. Do these organizations suggest strategies to minimize the wasting of foods?
7. What types of farming practices are endorsed by these organizations?
8. Do these organizations provide means for people to become self-sufficient?

Worksheet 15-4: How Can You Save Food at Home?

- Does your fruit or bread get moldy before you even get around to eating it?
- Does your meat or butter pick up an "off" taste that causes you to toss it into the trash?
- Does your bread or cereal get stale before you get to enjoy it?
- Do you get tired of throwing away your money?

Think of several strategies for saving food so that you do not have to throw away so much.

- How can you store your food to keep it fresh longer?
- How can you shop so that you use the food that you buy more quickly?

Consult the United States Department of Agriculture's Website at http://www.fsis.usda.gov/fact_sheets/Safe_Food_Handling_Fact_Sheets/index.asp for information on safe storage times and conditions for various types of food.

Conduct a survey in your home to determine the amount of food that is wasted in a given week.

Food Survey Tracking Table				
Food Type	**Date Purchased**	**Ideal Storage Condition/Time**	**Preparation and Intended Use**	**Amount Consumed**

1. Obtain a receipt to know when the food was purchased from the store.

2. Consult the label on a meat/egg/dairy/grain product to determine when the product should be sold by or used by.

   For produce, use the USDA Fact Sheets to determine the optimum amount of storage time at room temperature or in the refrigerator.

3. Note when a particular food is processed, cooked, and consumed.

4. Is all of the food consumed within a reasonable amount of time?

5. a. Do certain foods get discarded more than others do owing to insufficient consumption?

   b. If so, make a note of this and see if it is possible to buy a smaller portion or number of food items.

6. Do you buy larger portions of a food (that is, buy bulk goods) to save money?

7. Which foods acquire a bad taste that makes them less appetizing?

8. Which foods get moldy from being exposed to the air for too long?

9. Based on your answers to the questions above, can you identify any trends in your food purchasing, storing, cooking, or consumption rate behaviors that may cause you to waste food needlessly?

You can think of some strategies that may help you counteract some of these wasteful behaviors. Note both the behaviors/trends and the strategies in the table below.

Wasteful Behavior and/or Trend	Strategy for Minimizing Waste

Once you have identified some of your behaviors that cause you to waste food, you may find ways to minimize such waste, which will save you money and possibly help ensure adequate food for others!

Worksheet 15-5: Chapter 15 Review Crossword Puzzle

(clues provided on following page)

Across:	Down:
1. A form of severe childhood malnutrition that is characterized by dramatic weight loss, a "skin and bones" appearance, and inability to absorb nutrients 3. The EPA's food recovery _____ is a visual tool to help people or organizations find ways to reduce food waste. 5. A facility that collects and distributes food donations to authorized organizations feeding the hungry 6. A form of severe childhood malnutrition that is characterized by swelling and fatty liver 11. _____ is a native plant that can grow without fertilizer and intensive energy input and is a source of energy. 12. A scientific discipline that helps people find ways to produce food sustainably 13. Fish farming, also known as _____, can provide more fish to people but can have negative effects on the environment. 14. People who are hungry because they lack money, are being deprived for political reasons, live in a country at war, lack transportation, etc. experience food _____. 15. 85.1% of U.S. households report no issues with access to food. These households are considered to be _____.	2. Chronic malnutrition's effect on children is known as _____. 4. Farmers can increase the nutrients in the soil by _____ crops every year. 7. Severe acute malnutrition is also referred to as _____. 8. Farmers are using _____ gas produced from cow manure to produce electricity. 9. A home _____ can turn yard and kitchen waste into fertilizer to grow new crops. 10. Scientists and farmers have developed methods to control insects using biological and natural methods. This _____ pest management method reduces the need for chemicals.

CPSIA information can be obtained
at www.ICGtesting.com
Printed in the USA
FFOW04n1033020813
1509FF

9 781133 6